THE CAUSES OF THE AMERICAN CIVIL WAR

Problems in American Civilization

UNDER THE EDITORIAL DIRECTION OF *George Rogers Taylor*

THE CAUSES OF
THE AMERICAN CIVIL WAR

EDITED WITH AN INTRODUCTION BY

Edwin C. Rozwenc

AMHERST COLLEGE

D. C. HEATH AND COMPANY: Boston

ENGLEWOOD · CHICAGO · DALLAS · SAN FRANCISCO · ATLANTA

INTRODUCTION

ALTHOUGH a full century has elapsed since the Civil War, the story of that traumatic experience in our history still has an overpowering fascination. Indeed, the never-ending stream of books about the Civil War suggests that Americans have a compulsive need to talk about this bloody moment of fratricide in our historical memory.

American poets and novelists have searched for poetic truths in the stories and legends of this fateful period. When we reflect about the Civil War in relation to our literary tradition, we think not only of Stephen Crane, or Carl Sandburg, or Stephen Vincent Benét, who have written directly of the conflict; we think also of Walt Whitman, Mark Twain, or William Faulkner as writers whose perceptions of the American character have been strongly affected by their musings about the meaning of the conflict.

But the real keepers of the story of the Civil War are the historians. Theirs is the function to relate what has happened and, for so great and complex a happening as the Civil War, a hundred years is scarcely enough time to assemble all of the facts of the story.

This is not to say that the historian's function is as limited as Aristotle makes it appear when he asserts that the historian simply describes the thing that has been, whereas the poet describes what is possible — in the sense of being probable and necessary. To Aristotle, the historian, like a Herodotus, is a kind of garrulous gossip about the past, whereas the poet's work is something more philosophic and of graver import because he creates a more rigorous connection of events in order to demonstrate "the law of probability or necessity" in human affairs.

Aristotle's distinction between poetry and history started to break down when Thucydides began his great history of the Peloponnesian War with an explanation of the cause of the war and an account of the reasons for making war that were openly expressed by the Spartans and the Athenians. By and large, the example of Thucydides has become the model of the main body of historical writing in Western civilization. Historical explanation, or "the interpretation of history," has, therefore, become the imputation of causal connections in human affairs. The historian does not merely tell a story — "what has happened" — he interprets the story also by attempting to explain why it happened.

And so it is with American historians who write of the Civil War. They are not only the keepers of the story; they also write something of serious import when they try to tell us the causes of this crisis in our historical experience.

The imputation of causal connections in human affairs may have delighted the minds of men since the days of the Greeks, but we must recognize that it is a very risky intellectual enterprise. When we explain the cause of an event, we are asserting that some aspect or factor of a social situation has changed enough to produce the described result. And since all social situations include a complex of conditions, we try to demonstrate that changes in a particular condition or set of conditions are what made the difference between what occurred and what would probably have occurred in their absence. If we remember, also, the enormous complexity of so great an event as the Civil War and the fragmentary nature of much of our evidence, we can begin to understand why the explanation of the causes of the Civil War by historians breeds so much uncertainty and controversy.

The selections in this volume have been made with the conviction that the problem of explaining the causes of the American Civil War can best be understood by examining the efforts of historical interpreters to offer reasonable explanations of the causes of the sectional conflict. In the last analysis it is the historian who makes the connections among occurrences and conditions; it is to his statements that we must look for the proper analysis of causal explanations, and not to a scissors-and-paste collection of contemporary documents.

It should also be noted that the selections in this volume include causal explanations made in every generation since the 1850's. The reader may, therefore, gain some understanding of the way in which this particular historical tradition has been shaped and reshaped since the guns first boomed at Fort Sumter.

The first group of selections represents attempts by leading Americans to explain the developing crisis before the coming of the Civil War. The speeches of Calhoun, Seward, Douglas, and Lincoln exhibit a sense of crisis, and represent in diverse ways their efforts to explain the nature of the sectional crisis by reference to disturbances in the social equilibrium which had occurred in the antecedent historical experience of the United States. It is interesting to discover that these premonitory speeches anticipate many of the varying emphases — political, economic, social, and psychological — of the historical interpretations developed by historians long after the war had ended.

The second group of selections contains the official explanations concerning the responsibility for starting the armed conflict made by President Jefferson Davis to the Confederate Congress and by Abraham Lincoln to the Congress of the Union. Both are important because they summarize the events which precipitated the conflict and try to relate them to the broader sweep and meaning of American history.

The third group of selections represents what might be called "primitive" historical writings concerning the causes of the Civil War. All of these writers — James Buchanan, Alexander Stephens, Henry Wilson, Edward A. Pollard, John W. Draper — had experienced the war and the emotions of wartime at first hand. All of them wrote their histories immediately after the guns had ceased firing, and to a large extent they sought to place the primary guilt for the bloodshed upon their opponents while stoutly justifying their own actions. Although the partisan emotions of many of these writings have reappeared in later interpretations, it is also interesting to see that some of these writings exhibit an attempt to understand the more complex causes of the conflict arising from climate and geography and from the contrasting cultures of the two sections. In this regard, the chapters taken from Edward A. Pollard's *The Lost Cause* and John W. Draper's *History of the American Civil War* are particularly noteworthy.

The fourth group of writings represents the efforts of historians in the years of our own century to search for more complex causes and to emphasize the inevitability of the conflict by reference to basic institutional and ideological differences. James Ford Rhodes saw the difference in the political and moral conflict over the institution of slavery; Charles A. Beard emphasized the economic conflict of the diverging sections; Frank Lawrence Owsley also emphasized the conflict of an agrarian with an industrial society, each exhibiting a set of dominant ideas and values; while Rollin G. Osterweis seeks to analyze the idea of Southern nationalism using concepts developed by modern historians. Moreover, Rhodes, Beard, and Osterweis are able to achieve a high degree of objective detachment — only Owsley still finds it necessary to write his interpretation in a highly partisan and emotional manner.

The fifth group of historians represents the most important controversy among interpreters of the Civil War in recent years. The "revisionist" historians of the Civil War tend to reject the notion that there were irreconcilable institutional and ideological differences between the North and the South. Instead, they are prone to blame the coming of the Civil War on irresponsible agitators and blundering statesmen, operating in an atmosphere of whipped-up emotions and false propaganda. The first three selections develop many of the ideas of the revisionist historians. Charles W. Ramsdell argues that slavery had reached its natural limits and suggests that an intelligent leadership was lacking to construct the right national policies which would be in accord with this basic social reality. James G. Randall develops the core of the revisionist arguments in his article on "The Blundering Generation," and Avery Craven examines the way in which

the emphasis on slogans and symbols helped bring about the breakdown of the democratic process. The concluding essays in this group, by Arthur M. Schlesinger, Jr., and Pieter Geyl, are the two best-known attacks upon the revisionist thesis.

The final group of readings begins with some selections from Allan Nevins' monumental effort to make a new interpretive synthesis of the vast body of data and hypotheses about the Civil War which has appeared in our time. The selection by Thomas J. Pressly raises some cogent questions about Allan Nevins' *Ordeal of the Union,* and my own essay closes the volume with further questions about present attempts to make a historical explanation of the causes of the Civil War.

After reading all the selections in this volume, anyone might well ask: Can we ever hope to reconcile the differences among the historians in explaining the causes of the Civil War? Can we ever hope to really know the causes of the Civil War? Anyone might be tempted to look upon the effort to explain the causes of so great and complex an event as something akin to being led into a labyrinth, not with a golden thread to guide us but with many threads to confuse us. But if the causal explanation of the Civil War is a puzzle, it is a puzzle which historians have helped to create and, as creators, their logic and tests of evidence can give us some points of control and some sense of order.

At any rate, the game is worth the candle. Anyone who enjoys detective stories can appreciate the fun and excitement that lie in the task of historical explanation. Moreover, in the explanation of causes in human affairs, the historian is performing an activity of a most serious philosophic import in the Aristotelian sense. In the search for causes in human affairs, we come to understand more clearly the springs of human thought and action, we learn to know ourselves, and we discover the destinies which our historical experience will allow us to choose.

EDWIN C. ROZWENC

CONTENTS

HIGHLIGHTS OF THE HISTORICAL CONTROVERSY

And of the American Civil War it may safely be asserted there was a single cause, slavery.

— JAMES FORD RHODES

Complex though the factors were which finally caused the war, they all grew out of two fundamental differences which existed between the two sections: the North was commercial and industrial, and the South was agrarian. The fundamental and passionate ideal for which the South stood and fell was the ideal of an agrarian society.

— FRANK L. OWSLEY

If one word or phrase were selected to account for the war, that word would not be slavery, or economic grievance, or states rights, or diverse civilizations. It would have to be such a word as fanaticism.

— JAMES G. RANDALL

The main root of the conflict (and there were minor roots) was the problem of slavery *with its complementary problem of race-adjustment;* the main source of the tragedy was the refusal of either section to face these conjoined problems squarely and pay the heavy costs of a peaceful settlement.

— ALLAN NEVINS

A society closed in the defense of evil institutions thus creates moral differences far too profound to be solved by compromise. . . . To reject the moral actuality of the Civil War is to foreclose the possibility of an adequate account of its causes.

— ARTHUR M. SCHLESINGER, JR.

I. PREMONITORY EXPLANATIONS OF THE SECTIONAL CRISIS

John C. Calhoun: THE CAUSES BY WHICH THE UNION IS
ENDANGERED

*John C. Calhoun was probably the best spokesman for the aspira-
tions of the South as a self-conscious minority. "Whatever road one
travels," V. L. Parrington writes, "one comes at last upon the austere
figure of Calhoun, commanding every highway of the southern mind."
His last speech to the Senate, presented on March 4, 1850, was an attack
upon the Compromise of 1850. Too ill to speak, he sat silent and
spectral-looking while a colleague read his speech. His speech is a
brilliant analysis of the causes of sectional controversy from a Southern
point of view as well as a warning of even greater dangers to come.
The selection is taken from* The Works of John C. Calhoun.

I HAVE, Senators, believed from the first that the agitation of the subject of slavery would, if not prevented by some timely and effective measure, end in disunion. Entertaining this opinion, I have, on all proper occasions, endeavored to call the attention of both the two great parties which divide the country to adopt some measure to prevent so great a disaster, but without success. The agitation has been permitted to proceed, with almost no attempt to resist it, until it has reached a point when it can no longer be disguised or denied that the Union is in danger. You have thus had forced upon you the greatest and the gravest question that can ever come under your consideration — How can the Union be preserved?

To give a satisfactory answer to this mighty question, it is indispensable to have an accurate and thorough knowledge of the nature and the character of the cause by which the Union is endangered. Without such knowledge it is impossible to pronounce, with any certainty, by what measure it can be saved; just as it would be impossible for a physician to pronounce, in the case of some dangerous disease, with any certainty, by what remedy the patient could be saved, without similar knowledge of the nature and character of the cause which produced it. The first question, then, presented for consideration, in the investigation I propose to make, in order to obtain such knowledge, is — What is it that has endangered the Union?

To this question there can be but one answer, — that the immediate cause is the almost universal discontent which pervades all the States composing the Southern section of the Union. This widely-extended discontent is not of recent origin. It commenced with the agitation of the slavery question, and has been increasing ever since. The next question, going one step further back, is — What has caused this widely diffused and almost universal discontent?

It is a great mistake to suppose, as it is

From Richard C. Crallé, ed., *The Works of John C. Calhoun* (New York, 1854), Vol. IV, pp. 542–559.

by some, that it originated with demagogues, who excited the discontent with
the intention of aiding their personal
advancement, or with the disappointed
ambition of certain politicians, who resorted to it as the means of retrieving
their fortunes. On the contrary, all the
great political influences of the section
were arrayed against excitement, and exerted to the utmost to keep the people
quiet. The great mass of the people of
the South were divided, as in the other
section, into Whigs and Democrats. The
leaders and the presses of both parties
in the South were very solicitous to prevent excitement and to preserve quiet;
because it was seen that the effects of
the former would necessarily tend to
weaken, if not destroy, the political ties
which united them with their respective
parties in the other section. Those who
know the strength of party ties will
readily appreciate the immense force
which this cause exerted against agitation, and in favor of preserving quiet.
But, great as it was, it was not sufficient
to prevent the wide-spread discontent
which now pervades the section. No;
some cause, far deeper and more powerful than the one supposed, must exist, to
account for discontent so wide and deep.
The question then recurs — What is the
cause of this discontent? It will be found
in the belief of the people of the Southern States, as prevalent as the discontent
itself, that they cannot remain, as things
now are, consistently with honor and
safety, in the Union. The next question
to be considered is — What has caused
this belief?

One of the causes is, undoubtedly, to
be traced to the long-continued agitation
of the slave question on the part of the
North, and the many aggressions which
they have made on the rights of the South
during the time. I will not enumerate
them at present, as it will be done hereafter in its proper place.

There is another lying back of it — with
which this is intimately connected — that
may be regarded as the great and primary cause. This is to be found in the
fact that the equilibrium between the
two sections, in the Government as it
stood when the constitution was ratified
and the Government put in action, has
been destroyed. At that time there was
nearly a perfect equilibrium between the
two, which afforded ample means to each
to protect itself against the aggression of
the other; but, as it now stands, one
section has the exclusive power of controlling the Government, which leaves
the other without any adequate means of
protecting itself against its encroachment
and oppression. To place this subject
distinctly before you, I have, Senators,
prepared a brief statistical statement,
showing the relative weight of the two
sections in the Government under the
first census of 1790 and the last census
of 1840.

According to the former, the population of the United States, including Vermont, Kentucky, and Tennessee, which
then were in their incipient condition of
becoming States, but were not actually
admitted, amounted to 3,929,827. Of
this number the Northern States had
1,997,899, and the Southern 1,952,072,
making a difference of only 45,827 in
favor of the former States. The number
of States, including Vermont, Kentucky,
and Tennessee, were sixteen; of which
eight, including Vermont, belonged to
the Northern section, and eight, including Kentucky and Tennessee, to the
Southern, — making an equal division of
the States between the two sections under the first census. There was a small
preponderance in the House of Representatives, and in the electoral college,

in favor of the Northern, owing to the fact that, according to the provisions of the constitution, in estimating federal numbers five slaves count but three; but it was too small to affect sensibly the perfect equilibrium which, with that exception, existed at the time. Such was the equality of the two sections when the States composing them agreed to enter into a Federal Union. Since then the equilibrium between them has been greatly disturbed.

According to the last census the aggregate population of the United States amounted to 17,063,357, of which the Northern section contained 9,728,920, and the Southern 7,334,437, making a difference, in round numbers, of 2,400,000. The number of States had increased from sixteen to twenty-six, making an addition of ten States. In the meantime the position of Delaware had become doubtful as to which section she properly belonged. Considering her as neutral, the Northern States will have thirteen and the Southern States twelve, making a difference in the Senate of two Senators in favor of the former. According to the apportionment under the census of 1840, there were two hundred and twenty-three members of the House of Representatives, of which the Northern States had one hundred and thirty-five, and the Southern States (considering Delaware as neutral) eighty-seven, making a difference in favor of the former in the House of Representatives of forty-eight. The difference in the Senate of two members, added to this, gives to the North, in the electoral college, a majority of fifty. Since the census of 1840, four States have been added to the Union — Iowa, Wisconsin, Florida, and Texas. They leave the difference in the Senate as it stood when the census was taken; but add two to the side of the North in

the House, making the present majority in the House in its favor fifty, and in the electoral college fifty-two.

The result of the whole is to give the Northern section a predominance in every department of the Government, and thereby concentrate in it the two elements which constitute the Federal Government, — majority of States, and a majority of their population, estimated in federal numbers. Whatever section concentrates the two in itself possesses the control of the entire Government.

But we are just at the close of the sixth decade, and the commencement of the seventh. The census is to be taken this year, which must add greatly to the decided preponderance of the North in the House of Representatives and in the electoral college. The prospect is, also, that a great increase will be added to its present preponderance in the Senate, during the period of the decade, by the addition of new States. Two territories, Oregon and Minnesota, are already in progress, and strenuous efforts are making to bring in three additional States from the territory recently conquered from Mexico; which, if successful, will add three other States in a short time to the Northern section, making five States; and increasing the present number of its States from fifteen to twenty, and of its Senators from thirty to forty. On the contrary, there is not a single territory in progress in the Southern section, and no certainty that any additional State will be added to it during the decade. The prospect then is, that the two sections in the Senate, should the efforts now made to exclude the South from the newly acquired territories succeed, will stand, before the end of the decade, twenty Northern States to fourteen Southern (considering Delaware as neutral), and forty Northern Senators to twenty-eight Southern. This great increase of Senators, added to the great increase of members of the House of Representatives and the electoral college on the part of the North, which must take place under the next decade, will effectually and irretrievably destroy the equilibrium which existed when the Government commenced.

Had this destruction been the operation of time, without the interference of Government, the South would have had no reason to complain; but such was not the fact. It was caused by the legislation of this Government, which was appointed, as the common agent of all, and charged with the protection of the interests and security of all. The legislation by which it has been effected, may be classed under three heads. The first is, that series of acts by which the South has been excluded from the common territory belonging to all the States as members of the Federal Union — which have had the effect of extending vastly the portion allotted to the Northern section, and restricting within narrow limits the portion left the South. The next consists in adopting a system of revenue and disbursements, by which an undue proportion of the burden of taxation has been imposed upon the South, and an undue proportion of its proceeds appropriated to the North; and the last is a system of political measures, by which the original character of the Government has been radically changed. I propose to bestow upon each of these, in the order they stand, a few remarks, with the view of showing that it is owing to the action of this Government, that the equilibrium between the two sections has been destroyed, and the whole powers of the system centered in a sectional majority.

The first of the series of acts by which the South was deprived of its due share of the territories, originated with the con-

federacy which preceded the existence of this Government. It is to be found in the provision of the ordinance of 1787. Its effect was to exclude the South entirely from that vast and fertile region which lies between the Ohio and the Mississippi rivers, now embracing five States and one territory. The next of the series is the Missouri compromise, which excluded the South from that large portion of Louisiana which lies north of 36° 30', excepting what is included in the State of Missouri. The last of the series excluded the South from the whole of the Oregon Territory. All these, in the slang of the day, were what are called slave territories, and not free soil; that is, territories belonging to slaveholding powers and open to the emigration of masters with their slaves. By these several acts, the South was excluded from 1,238,025 square miles — an extent of country considerably exceeding the entire valley of the Mississippi. To the South was left the portion of the Territory of Louisiana lying south of 36° 30', and the portion north of it included in the State of Missouri, with the portion lying south of 36° 30', including the States of Louisiana and Arkansas, and the territory lying west of the latter, and south of 36° 30', called the Indian country. These, with the Territory of Florida, now the State, make, in the whole, 283,503 square miles. To this must be added the territory acquired with Texas. If the whole should be added to the Southern section, it would make an increase of 325,520, which would make the whole left to the South, 609,023. But a large part of Texas is still in contest between the two sections, which leaves it uncertain what will be the real extent of the portion of territory that may be left to the South.

I have not included the territory recently acquired by the treaty with Mexico. The North is making the most strenuous efforts to appropriate the whole to herself, by excluding the South from every foot of it. If she should succeed, it will add to that from which the South has already been excluded, 526,078 square miles, and would increase the whole which the North has appropriated to herself, to 1,764,023, not including the portion that she may succeed in excluding us from in Texas. To sum up the whole, the United States, since they declared their independence, have acquired 2,373,046 square miles of territory, from which the North will have excluded the South, if she should succeed in monopolizing the newly acquired territories, about three-fourths of the whole, leaving to the South but about one-fourth.

Such is the first and great cause that has destroyed the equilibrium between the two sections in the Government.

The next is the system of revenue and disbursements which has been adopted by the Government. It is well known that the Government has derived its revenue mainly from duties on imports. I shall not undertake to show that such duties must necessarily fall mainly on the exporting States, and that the South, as the great exporting portion of the Union, has in reality paid vastly more than her due portion of the revenue; because I deem it unnecessary, as the subject has on so many occasions been fully discussed. Nor shall I, for the same reason, undertake to show that a far greater portion of the revenue has been disbursed at the North, than its due share; and that the joint effect of these causes has been, to transfer a vast amount from South to North, which, under an equal system of revenue and disbursements, would not have been lost to her. If to this be added, that many of the duties were imposed, not for revenue,

but for protection, — that is, intended to put money, not in the treasury, but directly into the pocket of the manufacturers, — some conception may be formed of the immense amount which, in the long course of sixty years, has been transferred from South to North. There are no data by which it can be estimated with any certainty; but it is safe to say, that it amounts to hundreds of millions of dollars. Under the most moderate estimate, it would be sufficient to add greatly to the wealth of the North, and thus greatly increase her population by attracting emigration from all quarters to that section.

This, combined with the great primary cause, amply explains why the North has acquired a preponderance in every department of the Government by its disproportionate increase of population and States. The former, as has been shown, has increased, in fifty years, 2,400,000 over that of the South. This increase of population, during so long a period, is satisfactorily accounted for, by the number of emigrants, and the increase of their descendants, which have been attracted to the Northern section from Europe and the South, in consequence of the advantages derived from the causes assigned. If they had not existed — if the South had retained all the capital which has been extracted from her by the fiscal action of the Government; and, if it had not been excluded by the ordinance of 1787 and the Missouri compromise, from the region lying between the Ohio and the Mississipi rivers, and between the Mississippi and the Rocky Mountains north of 36° 30′ — it scarcely admits of a doubt, that it would have divided the emigration with the North, and by retaining her own people, would have at least equalled the North in population under the census of 1840, and probably under that about to be taken. She would also, if she had retained her equal rights in those territories, have maintained an equality in the number of States with the North, and have preserved the equilibrium between the two sections that existed at the commencement of the Government. The loss, then, of the equilibrium is to be attributed to the action of this Government.

But while these measures were destroying the equilibrium between the two sections, the action of the Government was leading to a radical change in its character, by concentrating all the power of the system in itself. The occasion will not permit me to trace the measures by which this great change has been consummated. If it did, it would not be difficult to show that the process commenced at an early period of the Government; and that it proceeded, almost without interruption, step by step, until it absorbed virtually its entire powers; but without going through the whole process to establish the fact, it may be done satisfactorily by a very short statement.

That the Government claims, and practically maintains the right to decide in the last resort, as to the extent of its powers, will scarcely be denied by any one conversant with the political history of the country. That it also claims the right to resort to force to maintain whatever power it claims, against all opposition, is equally certain. Indeed it is apparent, from what we daily hear, that this has become the prevailing and fixed opinion of a great majority of the community. Now, I ask, what limitation can possibly be placed upon the powers of a government claiming and exercising such rights? And, if none can be, how can the separate governments of the States maintain and protect the powers reserved to

them by the constitution — or the people of the several States maintain those which are reserved to them, and among others, the sovereign powers by which they ordained and established, not only their separate State Constitutions and Governments, but also the Constitution and Government of the United States? But, if they have no constitutional means of maintaining them against the right claimed by this Government, it necessarily follows, that they hold them at its pleasure and discretion, and that all the powers of the system are in reality concentrated in it. It also follows, that the character of the Government has been changed in consequence, from a federal republic, as it originally came from the hands of its framers, into a great national consolidated democracy. It has indeed, at present, all the characteristics of the latter, and not one of the former, although it still retains its outward form.

The result of the whole of these causes combined is — that the North has acquired a decided ascendency over every department of this Government, and through it a control over all the powers of the system. A single section governed by the will of the numerical majority, has now, in fact, the control of the Government and the entire powers of the system. What was once a constitutional federal republic, is now converted, in reality, into one as absolute as that of the Autocrat of Russia, and as despotic in its tendency as any absolute government that ever existed.

As, then, the North has the absolute control over the Government, it is manifest, that on all questions between it and the South, where there is a diversity of interests, the interest of the latter will be sacrificed to the former, however oppressive the effects may be; as the South possesses no means by which it can resist, through the action of the Government. But if there was no question of vital importance to the South, in reference to which there was a diversity of views between the two sections, this state of things might be endured, without the hoard of destruction to the South. But such is not the fact. There is a question of vital importance to the Southern section, in reference to which the views and feelings of the two sections are as opposite and hostile as they can possibly be.

I refer to the relation between the two races in the Southern section, which constitutes a vital portion of her social organization. Every portion of the North entertains views and feelings more or less hostile to it. Those most opposed and hostile, regard it as a sin, and consider themselves under the most sacred obligation to use every effort to destroy it. Indeed, to the extent that they conceive they have power, they regard themselves as implicated in the sin, and responsible for not suppressing it by the use of all and every means. Those less opposed and hostile, regard it as a crime — an offence against humanity, as they call it; and, although not so fanatical, feel themselves bound to use all efforts to effect the same object; while those who are least opposed and hostile, regard it as a blot and a stain on the character of what they call the Nation, and feel themselves accordingly bound to give it no countenance or support. On the contrary, the Southern section regards the relation as one which cannot be destroyed without subjecting the two races to the greatest calamity, and the section to poverty, desolation, and wretchedness; and accordingly they feel bound, by every consideration of interest and safety, to defend it.

This hostile feeling on the part of the North towards the social organization of the South long lay dormant, but it only required some cause to act on those who felt most intensely that they were responsible for its continuance, to call it into action. The increasing power of this Government, and of the control of the Northern section over all its departments, furnished the cause. It was this which made an impression on the minds of many, that there was little or no restraint to prevent the Government from doing whatever it might choose to do. This was sufficient of itself to put the most fanatical portion of the North in action, for the purpose of destroying the existing relation between the two races in the South.

The first organized movement towards it commenced in 1835. Then, for the first time, societies were organized, presses established, lecturers sent forth to excite the people of the North, and incendiary publications scattered over the whole South, through the mail. The South was thoroughly aroused. Meetings were held everywhere, and resolutions adopted, calling upon the North to apply a remedy to arrest the threatened evil, and pledging themselves to adopt measures for their own protection, if it was not arrested. At the meeting of Congress, petitions poured in from the North, calling upon Congress to abolish slavery in the District of Columbia, and to prohibit, what they called, the internal slave trade between the States — announcing at the same time, that their ultimate object was to abolish slavery, not only in the District, but in the States and throughout the Union. At this period, the number engaged in the agitation was small, and possessed little or no personal influence.

Neither party in Congress had, at that time, any sympathy with them or their cause. The members of each party presented their petitions with great reluctance. Nevertheless, small and contemptible as the party then was, both of the great parties of the North dreaded them. They felt, that though small, they were organized in reference to a subject which had a great and a commanding influence over the Northern mind. Each party, on that account, feared to oppose their petitions, lest the opposite party should take advantage of the one who might do so, by favoring them. The effect was, that both united in insisting that the petitions should be received, and that Congress should take jurisdiction over the subject. To justify their course, they took the extraordinary ground, that Congress was bound to receive petitions on every subject, however objectionable they might be, and whether they had, or had not, jurisdiction over the subject. These views prevailed in the House of Representatives, and partially in the Senate; and thus the party succeeded in their first movements, in gaining what they proposed — a position in Congress, from which agitation could be extended over the whole Union. This was the commencement of the agitation, which has ever since continued, and which, as is now acknowledged, has endangered the Union itself.

As for myself, I believed at that early period, if the party who got up the petitions should succeed in getting Congress to take jurisdiction, that agitation would follow, and that it would in the end, if not arrested, destroy the Union. I then so expressed myself in debate, and called upon both parties to take grounds against assuming jurisdiction; but in vain. Had my voice been heeded, and had Congress refused to take jurisdiction, by the united votes of all parties, the agitation which followed would have been prevented, and the fanatical zeal that gives impulse to the agitation, and which has brought us to our present perilous condition, would have become extinguished, from the want of fuel to feed the flame. *That* was the time for the North to have shown her devotion to the Union; but, unfortunately, both of the great parties of that section were so intent on obtaining or retaining party ascendency, that all other considerations were overlooked or forgotten.

What has since followed are but natural consequences. With the success of their first movement, this small fanatical party began to acquire strength; and with that, to become an object of courtship to both the great parties. The necessary consequence was, a further increase of power, and a gradual tainting of the opinions of both of the other parties with their doctrines, until the infection has extended over both; and the great mass of the population of the North, who, whatever may be their opinion of the original abolition party, which still preserves its distinctive organization, hardly ever fail, when it comes to acting, to co-operate in carrying out their measures. With the increase of their influence, they extended the sphere of their action. In a short time after the commencement of their first movement, they had acquired sufficient influence to induce the legislatures of most of the Northern States to pass acts, which in effect abrogated the clause of the constitution that provides for the delivery up of fugitive slaves. Not long after, petitions followed to abolish slavery in forts, magazines, and dockyards, and all other places where Congress had exclusive power of legislation. This was followed by petitions and resolutions of legislatures of the Northern States, and popular meetings, to exclude the Southern States from all territories acquired, or to be acquired, and to prevent the admission of any State hereafter into the Union, which, by its constitution, does not prohibit slavery. And Congress is invoked to do all this, expressly with the view to the final abolition of slavery in the States. That has been avowed to be the ultimate object from the beginning of the agitation until the present time; and yet the great body of both parties of the North, with the full knowledge of the fact, although disavowing the abolitionists, have co-operated with them in almost all their measures.

Such is a brief history of the agitation, as far as it has yet advanced. Now I ask, Senators, what is there to prevent its further progress, until it fulfils the ultimate end proposed, unless some decisive measure should be adopted to prevent it? Has any one of the causes, which has added to its increase from its original small and contemptible beginning until it has attained its present magnitude, diminished in force? Is the original cause of the movement — that slavery is a sin, and ought to be suppressed — weaker now than at the commencement? Or is the abolition party less numerous or influential, or have they less influence with, or control over the two great parties of the North in elections? Or has the South greater means of influencing or controlling the movements of this Government now, than it had when the agitation commenced? To all these questions but one answer can be given: No — no — no. The very reverse is true. Instead of being weaker, all the elements in favor of agitation are stronger now than they were in 1835, when it first commenced, while all the elements of influence on the part of the South are weaker. Unless something decisive is done, I again ask, what is to stop this agitation, before the great and final object at which it aims — the abolition of slavery in the States — is consummated? Is it, then, not certain, that if something is not done to arrest it, the South will be forced to choose be-

tween abolition and secession? Indeed, as events are now moving, it will not require the South to secede, in order to dissolve the Union. Agitation will of itself effect it, of which its past history furnishes abundant proof — as I shall next proceed to show.

It is a great mistake to suppose that disunion can be effected by a single blow. The cords which bound these States together in one common Union, are far too numerous and powerful for that. Disunion must be the work of time. It is only through a long process, and successively, that the cords can be snapped, until the whole fabric falls asunder. Already the agitation of the slavery question has snapped some of the most important, and has greatly weakened all the others, as I shall proceed to show.

The cords that bind the States together are not only many, but various in character. Some are spiritual or ecclesiastical; some political; others social. Some appertain to the benefit conferred by the Union, and others to the feeling of duty and obligation.

The strongest of those of a spiritual and ecclesiastical nature, consisted in the unity of the great religious denominations, all of which originally embraced the whole Union. All these denominations, with the exception, perhaps, of the Catholics, were organized very much upon the principle of our political institutions. Beginning with smaller meetings, corresponding with the political divisions of the country, their organization terminated in one great central assemblage, corresponding very much with the character of Congress. At these meetings the principal clergymen and lay members of the respective denominations, from all parts of the Union, met to transact business relating to their common concerns. It was not confined to what appertained to the doctrines and discipline of the respective denominations, but extended to plans for disseminating the Bible — establishing missions, distributing tracts — and of establishing presses for the publication of tracts, newspapers, and periodicals, with a view of diffusing religious information — and for the support of their respective doctrines and creeds. All this combined contributed greatly to strengthen the bonds of the Union. The ties which held each denomination together formed a strong cord to hold the whole Union together; but, powerful as they were, they have not been able to resist the explosive effect of slavery agitation.

The first of these cords which snapped, under its explosive force, was that of the powerful Methodist Episcopal Church. The numerous and strong ties which held it together, are all broken, and its unity gone. They now form separate churches; and, instead of that feeling of attachment and devotion to the interests of the whole church which was formerly felt, they are now arrayed into two hostile bodies, engaged in litigation about what was formerly their common property.

The next cord that snapped was that of the Baptists — one of the largest and most respectable of the denominations. That of the Presbyterian is not entirely snapped, but some of its strands have given way. That of the Episcopal Church is the only one of the four great Protestant denominations which remains unbroken and entire.

The strongest cord, of a political character, consists of the many and powerful ties that have held together the two great parties which have, with some modifications, existed from the beginning of the Government. They both extended to every portion of the Union, and strongly contributed to hold all its parts together. But this powerful cord has fared no better than the spiritual. It resisted, for a long time, the explosive tendency of the agitation, but has finally snapped under its force — if not entirely, in a great measure. Nor is there one of the remaining cords which has not been greatly weakened. To this extent the Union has already been destroyed by agitation, in the only way it can be, by sundering and weakening the cords which bind it together.

If the agitation goes on, the same force, acting with increased intensity, as has been shown, will finally snap every cord, when nothing will be left to hold the States together except force. But, surely, that can, with no propriety of language, be called a Union, when the only means by which the weaker is held connected with the stronger portion is *force*. It may, indeed, keep them connected; but the connection will partake much more of the character of subjugation, on the part of the weaker to the stronger, than the union of free, independent, and sovereign States, in one confederation, as they stood in the early stages of the Government, and which only is worthy of the sacred name of Union. . . .

William H. Seward: THE IRREPRESSIBLE CONFLICT

William Henry Seward, as Senator for New York, was a spokes-man in the 1850's for the antislavery North; for the free-soilers and the quasi-abolitionists who were determined that slavery should be con-tained within its existing limits. A leader of the antislavery Whigs at the start of the decade, he ambitiously sought after the Republican nomination to the presidency in 1860. More than any other political leader, Seward was responsible for developing the popular concept of an "irrepressible conflict" between the slave system of the South and the free labor system of the North. The following speech with that title was delivered in Rochester, New York, October 25, 1858, and is taken from The Works of William Seward.

THE unmistakable outbreaks of zeal which occur all around me, show that you are earnest men — and such a man am I. Let us therefore, at least for a time, pass by all secondary and collateral questions, whether of a personal or of a general nature, and consider the main subject of the present canvass. The dem-ocratic party — or, to speak more accu-rately, the party which wears that attrac-tive name — is in possession of the federal government. The republicans propose to dislodge that party, and dismiss it from its high trust.

The main subject, then, is, whether the democratic party deserves to retain the confidence of the American people. In attempting to prove it unworthy, I think that I am not actuated by prejudices against that party, or by prepossessions in favor of its adversary; for I have learned, by some experience, that virtue and patriotism, vice and selfishness, are found in all parties, and that they differ less in their motives than in the policies they pursue.

Our country is a theatre, which ex-hibits, in full operation, two radically different political systems; the one rest-ing on the basis of servile or slave labor, the other on the basis of voluntary labor of freemen.

The laborers who are enslaved are all negroes, or persons more or less purely of African derivation. But this is only acci-dental. The principle of the system is, that labor in every society, by whomso-ever performed, is necessarily unintel-lectual, groveling and base; and that the laborer, equally for his own good and for the welfare of the state, ought to be en-slaved. The white laboring man, whether native or foreigner, is not enslaved, only because he cannot, as yet, be reduced to bondage.

You need not be told now that the slave system is the older of the two, and that once it was universal.

The emancipation of our own ances-tors, Caucasians and Europeans as they were, hardly dates beyond a period of five hundred years. The great meliora-tion of human society which modern times exhibit, is mainly due to the in-complete substitution of the system of voluntary labor for the old one of servile labor, which has already taken place. This African slave system is one which, in its origin and in its growth, has been altogether foreign from the habits of the

From George E. Baker, ed., *The Works of William Seward* (Boston, 1884), Vol. IV, pp. 289–302.

races which colonized these states, and established civilization here. It was introduced on this new continent as an engine of conquest, and for the establishment of monarchial power, by the Portuguese and the Spaniards, and was rapidly extended by them all over South America, Central America, Louisiana and Mexico. Its legitimate fruits are seen in the poverty, imbecility, and anarchy, which now pervade all Portuguese and Spanish America. The free-labor system is of German extraction, and it was established in our country by emigrants from Sweden, Holland, Germany, Great Britain, and Ireland.

We justly ascribe to its influences the strength, wealth, greatness, intelligence, and freedom, which the whole American people now enjoy. One of the chief elements of the value of human life is freedom in the pursuit of happiness. The slave system is not only intolerable, unjust, and inhuman, towards the laborer, whom, only because he is a laborer, it loads down with chains and converts into merchandise, but is scarcely less severe upon the freeman, to whom, only because he is a laborer from necessity, it denies facilities for employment, and whom it expels from the community because it cannot enslave and convert him into merchandise also. It is necessarily improvident and ruinous, because, as a general truth, communities prosper and flourish or droop and decline in just the degree that they practise or neglect to practise the primary duties of justice and humanity. The free-labor system conforms to the divine law of equality, which is written in the hearts and consciences of man, and therefore is always and everywhere beneficent.

The slave system is one of constant danger, distrust, suspicion, and watchfulness. It debases those whose toil alone can produce wealth and resources for defense, to the lowest degree of which human nature is capable, to guard against mutiny and insurrection, and thus wastes energies which otherwise might be employed in national development and aggrandizement.

The free-labor system educates all alike, and by opening all the fields of industrial employment, and all the departments of authority, to the unchecked and equal rivalry of all classes of men, at once secures universal contentment, and brings into the highest possible activity all the physical, moral and social energies of the whole state. In states where the slave system prevails, the masters, directly or indirectly, secure all political power, and constitute a ruling aristocracy. In states where the free-labor system prevails, universal suffrage necessarily obtains, and the state inevitably becomes, sooner or later, a republic or democracy.

Russia yet maintains slavery, and is a despotism. Most of the other European states have abolished slavery, and adopted the system of free labor. It was the antagonistic political tendencies of the two systems which the first Napoleon was contemplating when he predicted that Europe would ultimately be either all Cossack or all republican. Never did human sagacity utter a more pregnant truth. The two systems are at once perceived to be incongruous. But they are more than incongruous — they are incompatible. They never have permanently existed together in one country, and they never can. It would be easy to demonstrate this impossibility, from the irreconcilable contrast between their great principles and characteristics. But the experience of mankind has conclusively established it. Slavery, as I have already intimated, existed in every state in Europe.

Free labor has supplanted it everywhere except in Russia and Turkey. State necessities developed in modern times, are now obliging even those two nations to encourage and employ free labor; and already, despotic as they are, we find them engaged in abolishing slavery. In the United States, slavery came into collision with free labor at the close of the last century, and fell before it in New England, New York, New Jersey and Pennsylvania, but triumphed over it effectually, and excluded it for a period yet undetermined, from Virginia, the Carolinas and Georgia. Indeed, so incompatible are the two systems, that every new state which is organized within our ever extending domain makes its first political act a choice of the one and the exclusion of the other, even at the cost of civil war, if necessary. The slave states, without law, at the last national election, successfully forbade, within their own limits, even the casting of votes for a candidate for president of the United States supposed to be favorable to the establishment of the free-labor system in new states.

Hitherto, the two systems have existed in different states, but side by side within the American Union. This has happened because the Union is a confederation of states. But in another aspect the United States constitute only one nation. Increase of population, which is filling the states out to their very borders, together with a new and extended net-work of railroads and other avenues, and an internal commerce which daily becomes more intimate, is rapidly bringing the states into a higher and more perfect social unity or consolidation. Thus, these antagonistic systems are continually coming into closer contact, and collision results. Shall I tell you what this collision means? They who think that it is acci-dental, unnecessary, the work of interested or fanatical agitators, and therefore ephemeral, mistake the case altogether. It is an irrepressible conflict between opposing and enduring forces, and it means that the United States must and will, sooner or later, become either entirely a slaveholding nation, or entirely a free-labor nation. Either the cotton and rice-fields of South Carolina and the sugar plantations of Louisiana will ultimately be tilled by free labor, and Charleston and New Orleans become marts for legitimate merchandise alone, or else the rye-fields and wheat-fields of Massachusetts and New York must again be surrendered by their farmers to slave culture and to the production of slaves, and Boston and New York become once more markets for trade in the bodies and souls of men. It is the failure to apprehend this great truth that induces so many unsuccessful attempts at final compromise between the slave and free states, and it is the existence of this great fact that renders all such pretended compromises, when made, vain and ephemeral. Startling as this saying may appear to you, fellow citizens, it is by no means an original or even a moderate one. Our forefathers knew it to be true, and unanimously acted upon it when they framed the constitution of the United States. They regarded the existence of the servile system in so many of the states with sorrow and shame, which they openly confessed, and they looked upon the collision between them, which was then just revealing itself, and which we are now accustomed to deplore, with favor and hope. They knew that either the one or the other system must exclusively prevail.

Unlike too many of those who in modern time invoke their authority, they had a choice between the two. They preferred the system of free labor, and they determined to organize the government, and so to direct its activity, that that system should surely and certainly prevail. For this purpose, and no other, they based the whole structure of government broadly on the principle that all men are created equal, and therefore free — little dreaming that, within the short period of one hundred years, their descendants would bear to be told by any orator, however popular, that the utterance of that principle was merely a rhetorical rhapsody; or by any judge, however venerated, that it was attended by mental reservations, which rendered it hypocritical and false. By the ordinance of 1787, they dedicated all of the national domain not yet polluted by slavery to free labor immediately, thenceforth and forever; while by the new constitution and laws they invited foreign free labor from all lands under the sun, and interdicted the importation of African slave labor, at all times, in all places, and under all circumstances whatsoever. It is true that they necessarily and wisely modified this policy of freedom, by leaving it to the several states, affected as they were by differing circumstances, to abolish slavery in their own way and at their own pleasure, instead of confiding that duty to congress; and that they secured to the slave states, while yet retaining the system of slavery, a three-fifths representation of slaves in the federal government, until they should find themselves able to relinquish it with safety. But the very nature of these modifications fortifies my position that the fathers knew that the two systems could not endure within the Union, and expected that within a short period slavery would disappear forever. Moreover, in order that these modifications might not altogether defeat their grand design

of a republic maintaining universal equality, they provided that two-thirds of the states might amend the constitution.

It remains to say on this point only one word, to guard against misapprehension. If these states are to again become universally slaveholding, I do not pretend to say with what violations of the constitution that end shall be accomplished. On the other hand, while I do confidently believe and hope that my country will yet become a land of universal freedom, I do not expect that it will be made so otherwise than through the action of the several states coöperating with the federal government, and all acting in strict conformity with their respective constitutions.

The strife and contentions concerning slavery, which gently-disposed persons so habitually deprecate, are nothing more than the ripening of the conflict which the fathers themselves not only thus regarded with favor, but which they may be said to have instituted.

It is not to be denied, however, that thus far the course of that contest has not been according to their humane anticipations and wishes. In the field of federal politics, slavery, deriving unlooked-for advantages from commercial changes, and energies unforeseen from the facilities of combination between members of the slaveholding class and between that class and other property classes, early rallied, and has at length made a stand, not merely to retain its original defensive position, but to extend its sway throughout the whole Union. It is certain that the slaveholding class of American citizens indulge this high ambition, and that they derive encouragement for it from the rapid and effective political successes which they have already obtained. The plan of operation is this: By continued appliances of patronage and threats of disunion, they will keep a majority favorable to these designs in the senate, where each state has an equal representation. Through that majority they will defeat, as they best can, the admission of free states and secure the admission of slave states. Under the protection of the judiciary, they will, on the principle of the Dred Scott case, carry slavery into all the territories of the United States now existing and hereafter to be organized. By the action of the president and the senate, using the treaty-making power, they will annex foreign slaveholding states. In a favorable conjuncture they will induce congress to repeal the act of 1808, which prohibits the foreign slave trade, and so they will import from Africa, at the cost of only twenty dollars a head, slaves enough to fill up the interior of the continent. Thus relatively increasing the number of slave states, they will allow no amendment to the constitution prejudicial to their interest; and so, having permanently established their power, they expect the federal judiciary to nullify all state laws which shall interfere with internal or foreign commerce in slaves. When the free states shall be sufficiently demoralized to tolerate these designs, they reasonably conclude that slavery will be accepted by those states themselves. I shall not stop to show how speedy or how complete would be the ruin which the accomplishment of these slaveholding schemes would bring upon the country. For one, I should not remain in the country to test the sad experiment. Having spent my manhood, though not my whole life, in a free state, no aristocracy of any kind, much less an aristocracy of slaveholders, shall ever make the laws of the land in which I shall be content to live. Having seen the society around me universally engaged in agriculture, manufactures and trade, which were innocent and beneficent, I shall never be a denizen of a state where men and women are reared as cattle, and bought and sold as merchandise. When that evil day shall come, and all further effort at resistance shall be impossible, then, if there shall be no better hope for redemption than I can now foresee, I shall say with Franklin, while looking abroad over the whole earth for a new and more congenial home, "Where liberty dwells, there is my country."

You will tell me that these fears are extravagant and chimerical. I answer, they are so; but they are so only because the designs of the slaveholders must and can be defeated. But it is only the possibility of defeat that renders them so. They cannot be defeated by inactivity. There is no escape from them, compatible with non-resistance. How, then, and in what way, shall the necessary resistance be made? There is only one way. The democratic party must be permanently dislodged from the government. The reason is, that the democratic party is inextricably committed to the designs of the slaveholders, which I have described. Let me be well understood. I do not charge that the democratic candidates for public office now before the people are pledged to — much less that the democratic masses who support them really adopt — those atrocious and dangerous designs. Candidates may, and generally do, mean to act justly, wisely and patriotically, when they shall be elected; but they become the ministers and servants, not the dictators, of the power which elects them. The policy which a party shall pursue at a future period is only gradually developed, depending on the occurrence of events never fully foreknown. The motives of men, whether acting as electors or in any other capacity, are generally pure. Nevertheless, it is not more true that "hell is paved with good intentions," than it is that earth is covered with wrecks resulting from innocent and amiable motives.

The very constitution of the democratic party commits it to execute all the designs of the slaveholders, whatever they may be. It is not a party of the whole Union, of all the free states and of all the slave states; nor yet is it a party of the free states in the north and in the northwest; but it is a sectional and local party, having practically its seat within the slave states, and counting its constituency chiefly and almost exclusively there. Of all its representatives in congress and in the electoral colleges, two-thirds uniformly come from these states. Its great element of strength lies in the vote of the slaveholders, augmented by the representation of three-fifths of the slaves. Deprive the democratic party of this strength, and it would be a helpless and hopeless minority, incapable of continued organization. The democratic party, being thus local and sectional, acquires new strength from the admission of every new slave state, and loses relatively by the admission of every new free state into the Union.

A party is in one sense a joint stock association, in which those who contribute most direct the action and management of the concern. The slaveholders contributing in an overwhelming proportion to the capital strength of the democratic party, they necessarily dictate and prescribe its policy. The inevitable caucus system enables them to do so with a show of fairness and justice. If it were possible to conceive for a moment that the democratic party should disobey the behests of the slaveholders, we should then see a withdrawal of the slaveholders, which would leave the party to perish. The portion of the party which is found in the free states is a mere appendage, convenient to modify its sectional character, without impairing its sectional constitution, and is less effective in regulating its movement than the nebulous tail of the comet is in determining the appointed though apparently eccentric course of the fiery sphere from which it emanates.

To expect the democratic party to resist slavery and favor freedom, is as unreasonable as to look for protestant missionaries to the catholic propaganda of Rome. The history of the democratic party commits it to the policy of slavery. It has been the democratic party, and no other agency, which has carried that policy up to its present alarming culmination. Without stopping to ascertain, critically, the origin of the present democratic party, we may concede its claim to date from the era of good feeling which occurred under the administration of President Monroe. At that time, in this state, and about that time in many others of the free states, the democratic party deliberately disfranchised the free colored or African citizen, and it has pertinaciously continued this disfranchisement ever since. This was an effective aid to slavery; for, while the slaveholder votes for his slaves against freedom, the freed slave in the free states is prohibited from voting against slavery.

In 1824, the democracy resisted the election of John Quincy Adams — himself before that time an acceptable democrat — and in 1828 it expelled him from the presidency and put a slaveholder in his place, although the office had been filled by slaveholders thirty-two out of forty years.

In 1836, Martin Van Buren — the first non-slaveholding citizen of a free state to whose election the democratic party ever consented — signalized his inauguration into the presidency by a gratuitous announcement, that under no circumstances would he ever approve a bill for the abolition of slavery in the District of Columbia. From 1838 to 1844, the subject of abolishing slavery in the District of Columbia and in the national dockyards and arsenals, was brought before congress by repeated popular appeals. The democratic party thereupon promptly denied the right of petition, and effectually suppressed the freedom of speech in congress, so far as the institution of slavery was concerned.

From 1840 to 1843, good and wise men counseled that Texas should remain outside the Union until she should consent to relinquish her self instituted slavery; but the democratic party precipitated her admission into the Union, not only without that condition, but even with a covenant that the state might be divided and reörganized so as to constitute four slave states instead of one.

In 1846, when the United States became involved in a war with Mexico, and it was apparent that the struggle would end in the dismemberment of that republic, which was a non-slaveholding power, the democratic party rejected a declaration that slavery should not be established within the territory to be acquired. When, in 1850, governments were to be instituted in the territories of California and New Mexico, the fruits of that war, the democratic party refused to admit New Mexico as a free state, and only consented to admit California as a free state on the condition, as it has since explained the transaction, of leaving all of New Mexico and Utah open to slavery, to which was also added the concession of perpetual slavery in the District of Columbia, and the passage of an uncon-

stitutional, cruel and humiliating law, for the recapture of fugitive slaves, with a further stipulation that the subject of slavery should never again be agitated in either chamber of congress. When, in 1854, the slaveholders were contentedly reposing on these great advantages, then so recently won, the democratic party unnecessarily, officiously and with superserviceable liberality, awakened them from their slumber, to offer and force on their acceptance the abrogation of the law which declared that neither slavery nor involuntary servitude should ever exist within that part of the ancient territory of Louisiana which lay outside of the state of Missouri, and north of the parallel of 36° 30′ of north latitude — a law which, with the exception of one other, was the only statute of freedom then remaining in the federal code.

In 1856, when the people of Kansas had organized a new state within the region thus abandoned to slavery, and applied to be admitted as a free state into the Union, the democratic party contemptuously rejected their petition, and drove them with menaces and intimidations from the halls of congress, and armed the president with military power to enforce their submission to a slave code, established over them by fraud and usurpation. At every subsequent stage of the long contest which has since raged in Kansas, the democratic party has lent its sympathies, its aid, and all the powers of the government which it controlled, to enforce slavery upon that unwilling and injured people. And now, even at this day, while it mocks us with the assurance that Kansas is free, the democratic party keeps the state excluded from her just and proper place in the Union, under the hope that she may be dragooned into the acceptance of slavery.

The democratic party, finally, has procured from a supreme judiciary, fixed in its interest, a decree that slavery exists by force of the constitution in every territory of the United States, paramount to all legislative authority, either within the territory, or residing in congress.

Such is the democratic party. It has no policy, state or federal, for finance, or trade, or manufacture, or commerce, or education, or internal improvements, or for the protection or even the security of civil or religious liberty. It is positive and uncompromising in the interest of slavery — negative, compromising, and vacillating in regard to everything else. It boasts its love of equality, and wastes its strength, and even its life, in fortifying the only aristocracy known in the land. It professes fraternity, and, so often as slavery requires, allies itself with proscription. It magnifies itself for conquests in foreign lands, but it sends the national eagle forth always with chains, and not the olive branch, in his fangs.

This dark record shows you, fellow citizens, what I was unwilling to announce at an earlier stage of this argument, that of the whole nefarious schedule of slaveholding designs which I have submitted to you, the democratic party has left only one yet to be consummated — the abrogation of the law which forbids the African slave trade.

Now, I know very well that the democratic party has, at every stage of these proceedings, disavowed the motive and the policy of fortifying and extending slavery, and has excused them on entirely different and more plausible grounds. But the inconsistency and frivolity of these pleas prove still more conclusively the guilt I charge upon that party. It must, indeed, try to excuse such guilt before mankind, and even to the consciences of its own adherents. There is an instinctive abhorrence of slavery, and an inborn and inhering love of freedom in the human heart, which render palliation of such gross misconduct indispensable. It disfranchised the free African on the ground of a fear that, if left to enjoy the right of suffrage, he might seduce the free white citizens into amalgamation with his wronged and despised race. The democratic party condemned and deposed John Quincy Adams, because he expended twelve millions a year, while it justifies his favored successor in spending seventy, eighty and even one hundred millions, a year. It denies emancipation in the District of Columbia, even with compensation to masters and the consent of the people, on the ground of an implied constitutional inhibition, although the constitution expressly confers upon congress sovereign legislative power in that district, and although the democratic party is tenacious of the principle of strict construction. It violated the express provisions of the constitution in suppressing petition and debate on the subject of slavery, through fear of disturbance of the public harmony, although it claims that the electors have a right to instruct their representatives, and even demand their resignation in cases of contumacy. It extended slavery over Texas, and connived at the attempt to spread it across the Mexican territories, even to the shores of the Pacific ocean, under a plea of enlarging the area of freedom. It abrogated the Mexican slave law and the Missouri compromise prohibition of slavery in Kansas, not to open the new territories to slavery, but to try therein the new and fascinating theories of non-intervention and popular sovereignty; and, finally, it overthrew both these new and elegant systems by the English Lecompton bill and the Dred Scott decision, on the ground that the free states ought not to enter the Union without a population equal to the representative basis of one member of congress, although slave states might come in without inspection as to their numbers.

Will any member of the democratic party now here claim that the authorities chosen by the suffrages of the party transcended their partisan platforms, and so misrepresented the party in the various transactions, I have recited? Then I ask him to name one democratic statesman or legislator, from Van Buren to Walker, who, either timidly or cautiously like them, or boldly and defiantly like Douglas, ever refused to execute a behest of the slaveholders and was not therefor, and for no other cause, immediately denounced, and deposed from his trust, and repudiated by the democratic party for that contumacy.

I think, fellow citizens, that I have shown you that it is high time for the friends of freedom to rush to the rescue of the constitution, and that their very first duty is to dismiss the democratic party from the administration of the government.

Why shall it not be done? All agree that it ought to be done. What, then, shall prevent its being done? Nothing but timidity or division of the opponents of the democratic party.

Some of these opponents start one objection, and some another. Let us notice these objections briefly. One class say that they cannot trust the republican party; that it has not avowed its hostility to slavery boldly enough, or its affection for freedom earnestly enough.

I ask, in reply, is there any other party which can be more safely trusted? Every one knows that it is the republican party, or none, that shall displace the democratic party. But I answer, further, that the character and fidelity of any party are determined, necessarily, not by its pledges, programmes, and platforms, but by the public exigencies, and the temper of the people when they call it into ac-

tivity. Subserviency to slavery is a law written not only on the forehead of the democratic party, but also in its very soul — so resistance to slavery, and devotion to freedom, the popular elements now actively working for the republican party among the people, must and will be the resources for its ever-renewing strength and constant invigoration.

Others cannot support the republican party, because it has not sufficiently exposed its platform, and determined what it will do, and what it will not do, when triumphant. It may prove too progressive for some, and too conservative for others. As if any party ever foresaw so clearly the course of future events as to plan a universal scheme of future action, adapted to all possible emergencies. Who would ever have joined even the whig party of the revolution, if it had been obliged to answer, in 1775, whether it would declare for independence in 1776, and for this noble federal constitution of ours in 1787, and not a year earlier or later? The people will be as wise next year, and even ten years hence, as we are now. They will oblige the republican party to act as the public welfare and the interests of justice and humanity shall require, through all the stages of its career, whether of trial or triumph.

Others will not venture an effort, because they fear that the Union would not endure the change. Will such objectors tell me how long a constitution can bear a strain directly along the fibres of which it is composed? This is a constitution of freedom. It is being converted into a constitution of slavery. It is a republican constitution. It is being made an aristocratic one. Others wish to wait until some collateral questions concerning temperance, or the exercise of the elective franchise are properly settled. Let me ask all such persons, whether time enough has not been wasted on these points already, without gaining any other than this single advantage, namely, the discovery that only one thing can be effectually done at one time, and that the one thing which must and will be done at any one time is just that thing which is most urgent, and will no longer admit of postponement or delay. Finally, we are told by faint-hearted men that they despond; the democratic party, they say is unconquerable, and the dominion of slavery is consequently inevitable. I reply that the complete and universal dominion of slavery would be intolerable enough, when it should have come, after the last possible effort to escape should have been made. There would then be left to us the consoling reflection of fidelity to duty.

But I reply further, that I know — few, I think, know better than I — the resources and energies of the democratic party, which is identical with the slave power. I do ample prestige to its traditional popularity. I know, further — few, I think, know better than I — the difficulties and disadvantages of organizing a new political force, like the republican party, and the obstacles it must encounter in laboring without prestige and without patronage. But, understanding all this, I know that the democratic party must go down, and that the republican party must rise into its place. The democratic party derived its strength, originally, from its adoption of the principles of equal and exact justice to all men. So long as it practised this principle faithfully, it was invulnerable. It became vulnerable when it renounced the principle, and since that time it has maintained itself, not by virtue of its own strength, or even of its traditional merits, but because there as yet had appeared in the political field no other party that had the conscience and the courage to take up, and avow, and practice the life-inspiring principle

which the democratic party had surrendered. At last, the republican party has appeared. It avows, now, as the republican party of 1800 did, in one word, its faith and its works, "Equal and exact justice to all men." Even when it first entered the field, only half organized, it struck a blow which only just failed to secure complete and triumphant victory. In this, its second campaign, it has already won advantages which render that triumph now both easy and certain.

The secret of its assured success lies in that very characteristic which, in the mouth of scoffers, constitutes its great and lasting imbecility and reproach. It lies in the fact that it is a party of one idea; but that idea is a noble one — an idea that fills and expands all generous souls; the idea of equality — the equality of all men before human tribunals and human laws, as they all are equal before the Divine tribunal and Divine laws.

I know, and you know, that a revolution has begun. I know, and all the world knows, that revolutions never go backward. Twenty senators and a hundred representatives proclaim boldly in congress to-day sentiments and opinions and principles of freedom which hardly so many men, even in this free state, dared to utter in their own homes twenty years ago. While the government of the United States, under the conduct of the democratic party, has been all that time surrendering one plain and castle after another to slavery, the people of the United States have been no less steadily and perseveringly gathering together the forces with which to recover back again all the fields and all the castles which have been lost, and to confound and overthrow, by one decisive blow, the betrayers of the constitution and freedom forever.

Stephen A. Douglas: THE IRRESPONSIBLE AGITATORS

Stephen A. Douglas, the most prominent Northern Democrat by the mid-fifties, was the champion of "popular sovereignty" as a means of preventing conflicts between the North and the South over the settlement and organization of the territories of the United States. As chief sponsor of the Kansas-Nebraska Act, Douglas was convinced that Republicans and Northern antislavery men were irresponsible agitators who were whipping up a war of sections. The selection below is a speech in the Lincoln-Douglas debates made in Bloomington, Illinois, July 16, 1858.

AND this brings me to the consideration of the two points at issue between Mr. Lincoln and myself. The Republican Convention, when it assembled at Springfield, did me and the country the honor of indicating the man who was to be their standard-bearer, and the embodiment of their principles, in this State. I owe them my gratitude for thus making up a direct issue between Mr. Lincoln and myself. I shall have no controversies of a personal character with Mr. Lincoln. I have known him well for a quarter of a century. I have known him, as you all know him, a kind-hearted, amiable gentleman, a right good fellow, a worthy citizen, of eminent ability as a lawyer, and, I have no doubt, sufficient ability to make a good Senator. The question, then, for you to decide is, whether his principles are more in accordance with the genius of our free institutions, the peace and harmony of the Republic, than those which I advocate. He tells you, in his speech made at Springfield, before the Convention which gave him his unanimous nomination, that, —

"A house divided against itself cannot stand."

"I believe this government cannot endure permanently, half slave and half free."

"I do not expect the Union to be dissolved, I don't expect the house to fall; but I do expect it will cease to be divided."

"It will become all one thing or all the other."

That is the fundamental principle upon which he sets out in this campaign. Well, I do not suppose you will believe one word of it when you come to examine it carefully, and see its consequences. Although the Republic has existed from 1789 to this day, divided into Free States and Slave States, yet we are told that in the future it cannot endure unless they shall become all free or all slave. For that reason, he says, as the gentleman in the crowd says, that they must be all free. He wishes to go to the Senate of the United States in order to carry out that line of public policy, which will compel all the States in the South to become free. How is he going to do it? Has Congress any power over the subject of slavery in Kentucky, or Virginia, or any other State of this Union? How, then, is Mr. Lincoln going to carry out that principle which he says is essential to the existence of this Union, to-wit: That slavery must be abolished in all the States of the Union, or must be established in them all? You convince the South that they must either

From *Political Debates Between Abraham Lincoln and Stephen A. Douglas* (Cleveland, 1902), pp. 43–47.

establish slavery in Illinois, and in every other Free State, or submit to its abolition in every Southern State, and you invite them to make a warfare upon the Northern States in order to establish slavery, for the sake of perpetuating it at home. Thus, Mr. Lincoln invites, by his proposition, a war of sections, a war between Illinois and Kentucky, a war between the Free States and the Slave States, a war between the North and the South, for the purpose of either exterminating slavery in every Southern State, or planting it in every Northern State. He tells you that the safety of this Republic, that the existence of this Union, depends upon that warfare being carried on until one section or the other shall be entirely subdued. The States must all be free or slave, for a house divided against itself cannot stand. That is Mr. Lincoln's argument upon that question. My friends, is it possible to preserve peace between the North and the South if such a doctrine shall prevail in either section of the Union? Will you ever submit to a warfare waged by the Southern States to establish slavery in Illinois? What man in Illinois would not lose the last drop of his heart's blood before he would submit to the institution of slavery being forced upon us by the other States, against our will? And if that be true of us, what Southern man would not shed the last drop of his heart's blood to prevent Illinois, or any other Northern State, from interfering to abolish slavery in his State? Each of these States is sovereign under the Constitution; and if we wish to preserve our liberties, the reserved rights and sovereignty of each and every State must be maintained. I have said on a former occasion, and I here repeat, that it is neither desirable nor possible to establish uniformity in the local and domestic institutions of all the States of

this Confederacy. And why? Because the Constitution of the United States rests upon the right of every State to decide all its local and domestic institutions for itself. It is not possible, therefore, to make them conform to each other, unless we subvert the Constitution of the United States. No, sir, that cannot be done. God forbid that any man should ever make the attempt. Let that Constitution ever be trodden under foot and destroyed, and there will not be wisdom and patriotism enough left to make another that will work half so well. Our safety, our liberty, depends upon preserving the Constitution of the United States as our fathers made it, inviolate, at the same time maintaining the reserved rights and the sovereignty of each State over its local and domestic institutions, against Federal authority, or any outside interference.

The difference between Mr. Lincoln and myself upon this point is, that he goes for a combination of the Northern States, or the organization of a sectional political party in the Free States, to make war on the domestic institutions of the Southern States, and to prosecute that war until they shall all be subdued, and made to conform to such rules as the North shall dictate to them. I am aware that Mr. Lincoln, on Saturday night last, made a speech at Chicago, for the purpose, as he said, of explaining his position on this question. I have read that speech with great care, and will do him the justice to say that it is marked by eminent ability, and great success in concealing what he did mean to say in his Springfield speech. His answer to this point, which I have been arguing, is, that he never did mean, and that I ought to know that he never intended to convey the idea, that he wished the "people of the Free States to *enter into* the Southern

States, and interfere with slavery." Well, I never did suppose that he ever dreamed of entering into Kentucky to make war upon her institutions; nor will any Abolitionist ever enter into Kentucky to wage such war. Their mode of making war is not to enter into those States where slavery exists, and there interfere, and render themselves responsible for the consequences. Oh, no! They stand on this side of the Ohio River and shoot across. They stand in Bloomington, and shake their fists at the people of Lexington; they threaten South Carolina from Chicago. And they call that bravery! But they are very particular, as Mr. Lincoln says, not to enter into those States for the purpose of interfering with the institution of slavery there. I am not only opposed to entering into the Slave States, for the purpose of interfering with their institutions, but I am opposed to a sectional agitation to control the institutions of other States. I am opposed to organizing a sectional party, which appeals to Northern pride, and Northern passion and prejudice, against Southern institutions, thus stirring up ill-feeling and hot blood between brethren of the same Republic. I am opposed to that whole system of sectional agitation, which can produce nothing but strife, but discord, but hostility, and, finally disunion. And yet Mr. Lincoln asks you to send him to the Senate of the United States, in order that he may carry out that great principle of his, that all the States must be slave, or all must be free. I repeat, how is he to carry it out when he gets to the Senate? Does he intend to introduce a bill to abolish slavery in Kentucky? Does he intend to introduce a bill to interfere with slavery in Virginia? How is he to accomplish what he professes must be done in order to save the Union? Mr. Lincoln is a lawyer, sagacious and able

enough to tell you how he proposes to do it. I ask Mr. Lincoln how it is that he proposes ultimately to bring about this uniformity in each and all the States of the Union. There is but one possible mode which I can see, and perhaps Mr. Lincoln intends to pursue it; that is, to introduce a proposition into the Senate to change the Constitution of the United States, in order that all the State Legislatures may be abolished, State sovereignty blotted out, and the power conferred upon Congress to make local laws and establish the domestic institutions and police regulations uniformly throughout the United States. Are you prepared for such a change in the institutions of your country? Whenever you shall have blotted out the State sovereignties, abolished the State Legislatures, and consolidated all the power in the Federal Government, you will have established a consolidated Empire as destructive to the liberties of the people and the rights of the citizen as that of Austria, or Russia, or any other despotism that rests upon the necks of the people. How is it possible for Mr. Lincoln to carry out his cherished principle of abolishing slavery everywhere or establishing it everywhere, except by the mode which I have pointed out, — by an amendment to the Constitution to the effect that I have suggested? There is no other possible mode. Mr. Lincoln intends resorting to that, or else he means nothing by the great principle upon which he desires to be elected. My friends, I trust that we will be able to get him to define what he does mean by this scriptural quotation that "A house divided against itself cannot stand;" that the government cannot endure permanently, half slave and half free; that it must be all one thing, or all the other. Who among you expects to live, or have his children live, until slavery shall be established in Illinois or abolished in South Carolina? Who expects to see that occur during the life-time of ourselves or our children?

There is but one possible way in which slavery can be abolished, and that is by leaving a State, according to the principle of the Kansas-Nebraska bill, perfectly free to form and regulate its institutions in its own way. That was the principle upon which this Republic was founded, and it is under the operation of that principle that we have been able to preserve the Union thus far. Under its operations, slavery disappeared from New Hampshire, from Rhode Island, from Connecticut, from New York, from New Jersey, from Pennsylvania, from six of the twelve original slaveholding States; and this gradual system of emancipation went on quietly, peacefully, and steadily, so long as we in the Free States minded our own business and left our neighbors alone. But the moment the abolition societies were organized throughout the North, preaching a violent crusade against slavery in the Southern States, this combination necessarily caused a counter-combination in the South, and a sectional line was drawn which was a barrier to any further emancipation . Bear in mind that emancipation has not taken place in any one State since the Free-soil party was organized as a political party in this country. Emancipation went on gradually in State after State so long as the Free States were content with managing their own affairs and leaving the South perfectly free to do as they pleased; but the moment the North said, We are powerful enough to control you of the South, the moment the North proclaimed itself the determined master of the South, that moment the South combined to resist the attack, and thus sectional parties were formed, and gradual emancipation ceased in all the Northern slaveholding States. And yet Mr. Lincoln, in view of these historical facts, proposes to keep up this sectional agitation, band all the Northern States together in one political party, elect a President by Northern votes alone, and then, of course, make a cabinet composed of Northern men, and administer the government by Northern men only, denying all the Southern States of this Union any participation in the administration of affairs whatsoever. I submit to you, my fellow-citizens, whether such a line of policy is consistent with the peace and harmony of the country? Can the Union endure under such a system of policy? He has taken his position in favor of sectional agitation and sectional warfare. I have taken mine in favor of securing peace, harmony, and good-will among all the States, by permitting each to mind its own business, and discountenancing any attempt at interference on the part of one State with the domestic concerns of the others. . . .

Abraham Lincoln: THE HOUSE DIVIDED

Abraham Lincoln, an astute Whig lawyer and politician, became the spokesman for the moderate central core of the Republican party. His debates with Douglas reveal clearly the difference between his moderate and pragmatic views on slavery and the more extreme position of the radical free-soilers and abolitionists. Cautious on questions concerning the social equality of the races, he was adamant in his opposition to slavery on moral and political grounds and looked for ways to limit the institution of slavery within Constitutional bounds. The following selection is a reply made in Chicago, July 10, 1858, to Senator Douglas' repeated attacks on the "house-divided" doctrine.

JUDGE DOUGLAS made two points upon my recent speech at Springfield. He says they are to be the issues of this campaign. The first one of these points he bases upon the language in a speech which I delivered at Springfield, which I believe I can quote correctly from memory. I said there that "we are now far into the fifth year since a policy was instituted for the avowed object, and with the confident promise, of putting an end to slavery agitation; under the operation of that policy, that agitation had not only not ceased, but had constantly augmented." "I believe it will not cease until a crisis shall have been reached and passed. 'A house divided against itself cannot stand.' I believe this Government cannot endure permanently, half slave and half free." "I do not expect the Union to be dissolved," — I am quoting from my speech, — "I do not expect the house to fall, but I do expect it will cease to be divided. It will become all one thing or the other. Either the opponents of slavery will arrest the spread of it and place it where the public mind shall rest, in the belief that it is in the course of ultimate extinction, or its advocates will push it forward until it shall become alike lawful in all the States, North as well as South."

What is the paragraph? In this paragraph, which I have quoted in your hearing, and to which I ask the attention of all, Judge Douglas thinks he discovers great political heresy. I want your attention particularly to what he has inferred from it. He says I am in favor of making all the States of this Union uniform in all their internal regulations; that in all their domestic concerns I am in favor of making them entirely uniform. He draws this inference from the language I have quoted to you. He says that I am in favor of making war by the North upon the South for the extinction of slavery; that I am also in favor of inviting (as he expresses it) the South to a war upon the North for the purpose of nationalizing slavery. Now, it is singular enough, if you will carefully read that passage over, that I did not say that I was in favor of anything in it. I only said what I expected would take place. I made prediction only, — it may have been a foolish one, perhaps. I did not even say that I desired that slavery should be put in course of ultimate extinction. I do say so now, however, so there need be no longer

From *Political Debates Between Abraham Lincoln and Stephen A. Douglas* (Cleveland, 1902), pp. 26–29.

any difficulty about that. It may be written down in the great speech.

Gentlemen, Judge Douglas informed you that this speech of mine was probably carefully prepared. I admit that it was. I am not master of language; I have not a fine education; I am not capable of entering into a disquisition upon dialectics, as I believe you call it; but I do not believe the language I employed bears any such construction as Judge Douglas puts upon it. But I don't care about a quibble in regard to words. I know what I meant, and I will not leave this crowd in doubt, if I can explain it to them, what I really meant in the use of that paragraph.

I am not, in the first place, unaware that this Government has endured eighty-two years half slave and half free. I know that. I am tolerably well acquainted with the history of the country, and I know that it has endured eighty-two years half slave and half free. I *believe* — and that is what I meant to allude to there — I *believe* it has endured, because during all that time, until the introduction of the Nebraska bill, the public mind did rest all the time in the belief that slavery was in course of ultimate extinction. That was what gave us the rest that we had through that period of eighty-two years, — at least, so I believe. I have always hated slavery, I think, as much as any Abolitionist, — I have been an Old Line Whig, — I have always hated it; but I have always been quiet about it until this new era of the introduction of the Nebraska bill began. I always believed that everybody was against it, and that it was in course of ultimate extinction. [Pointing to Mr. Browning, who stood near by.] Browning thought so; the great mass of the nation have rested in the belief that slavery was in course of ultimate extinction. They had reason so to believe.

The adoption of the Constitution and its attendant history led the people to believe so; and that such was the belief of the framers of the Constitution itself, why did those old men, about the time of the adoption of the Constitution, decree that slavery should not go into the new Territory, where it had not already gone? Why declare that within twenty years the African Slave Trade, by which slaves are supplied, might be cut off by Congress? Why were all these acts? I might enumerate more of these acts; but enough. What were they but a clear indication that the framers of the Constitution intended and expected the ultimate extinction of that institution? And now, when I say, as I said in my speech, that Judge Douglas has quoted from, when I say that I think the opponents of slavery will resist the farther spread of it, and place it where the public mind shall rest with the belief that it is in course of ultimate extinction, I only mean to say that they will place it where the founders of this Government originally placed it.

I have said a hundred times, and I have now no inclination to take it back, that I believe there is no right, and ought to be no inclination, in the people of the Free States to enter into the Slave States, and interfere with the question of slavery at all. I have said that always; Judge Douglas has heard me say it, if not quite a hundred times, at least as good as a hundred times; and when it is said that I am in favor of interfering with slavery where it exists, I know it is unwarranted by anything I have ever *intended*, and, as I believe, by anything I have ever *said*. If, by any means, I have ever used language which could fairly be so construed (as, however, I believe I never have), I now correct it.

So much, then, for the inference that Judge Douglas draws, that I am in favor of setting the sections at war with one another. I know that I never meant any such thing, and I believe that no fair mind can infer any such thing from anything I have ever said.

Now, in relation to his inference that I am in favor of a general consolidation of all the local institutions of the various States. I will attend to that for a little while, and try to inquire, if I can, how on earth it could be that any man could draw such an inference from anything I said. I have said, very many times, in Judge Douglas's hearing, that no man believed more than I in the principle of self-government; that it lies at the bottom of all my ideas of just government, from beginning to end. I have denied that his use of that term applies properly. But for the thing itself, I deny that any man has ever gone ahead of me in his devotion to the principle, whatever he may have done in efficiency in advocating it. I think that I have said it in your hearing, that I believe each individual is naturally entitled to do as he pleases with himself and the fruit of his labor, so far as it in no wise interferes with any other man's rights; that each community, as a State, has a right to do exactly as it pleases with all the concerns within that State that interferes with the right of no other State; and that the General Government, upon principle, has no right to interfere with anything other than that general class of things that does concern the whole. I have said that at all times. I have said, as illustrations, that I do not believe in the right of Illinois to interfere with the cranberry laws of Indiana, the oyster laws of Virginia, or the liquor laws of Maine. I have said these things over and over again, and I repeat them here as my sentiments.

How is it, then, that Judge Douglas infers, because I hope to see slavery put where the public mind shall rest in the belief that it is in the course of ultimate extinction, that I am in favor of Illinois going over and interfering with the cranberry laws of Indiana? What can authorize him to draw any such inference? I suppose there might be one thing that at least enabled *him* to draw such an inference that would not be true with me or many others, that is, because he looks upon all this matter of slavery as an exceedingly little thing, — this matter of keeping one-sixth of the population of the whole nation in a state of oppression and tyranny unequaled in the world. He looks upon it as being an exceedingly little thing, — only equal to the question of the cranberry laws of Indiana; as something having no moral question in it; as something on a par with the question of whether a man shall pasture his land with cattle, or plant it with tobacco; so little and so small a thing that he concludes, if I could desire that if anything should be done to bring about the ultimate extinction of that little thing, I must be in favor of bringing about an amalgamation of all the other little things in the Union. Now, it so happens — and there, I presume, is the foundation of this mistake — that the Judge thinks thus; and it so happens that there is a vast portion of the American people that do *not* look upon that matter as being this very little thing. They look upon it as a vast moral evil; they can prove it as such by the writings of those who gave us the blessings of liberty which we enjoy, and that they so looked upon it, and not as an evil merely confining itself to the States where it is situated; and . . . we agree that, by the Constitution we assented to, in the States where it exists, we have no right to interfere with it, because it is in the Constitution; and we are by both duty and inclination to stick by that Constitution, in all its letter and spirit, from beginning to end.

II. OFFICIAL EXPLANATIONS OF THE CAUSES OF THE CIVIL WAR

Jefferson Davis: TO THE CONFEDERATE CONGRESS, APRIL 29, 1861

> *As President of the new Southern Confederacy, Jefferson Davis, on April 29, 1861, two weeks after Lincoln's call for troops, presented before a special session of the Confederate Congress his official account of the causes of the war. By combining a review of Northern "aggressions" against the property rights of slaveowners in the South with a careful statement of the constitutional doctrine of states rights, President Davis' message represents a skillful synthesis of the views of Southern radicals and of Southern moderates as they had developed in the preceding decades.*

Gentlemen of Congress: — It is my pleasing duty to announce to you that the Constitution framed for the establishment of a permanent government of the Confederate States of America has been ratified by the several conventions of each of those States which were referred to to inaugurate the said Government in its full proportions and upon its own substantial basis of the popular will.

It only remains that elections should be held for the designation of the officers to administer it.

There is every reason to believe that at no distant day other States, identical in political principles and community of interests with those which you represent, will join this Confederacy, giving to its typical constellation increased splendor — to its government of free, equal and sovereign States, a wider sphere of usefulness, and to the friends of constitutional liberty a greater security for its harmonious and perpetual existence.

It was not, however, for the purpose of making this announcement that I have deemed it my duty to convoke you at an earlier day than that fixed by yourselves for your meeting.

The declaration of war made against this Confederacy, by Abraham Lincoln, President of the United States, in his proclamation, issued on the 15th day of the present month, renders it necessary, in my judgment, that you should convene at the earliest practicable moment to devise the measures necessary for the defence of the country.

The occasion is, indeed, an extraordinary one. It justifies me in giving a brief review of the relations heretofore existing between us and the States which now unite in warfare against us, and a succinct statement of the events which have resulted to the end, that mankind may pass intelligent and impartial judgment on our motives and objects.

During the war waged against Great Britain by her colonies on this continent, a common danger impelled them to a close alliance, and to the formation of a Confederation by the terms of which

From Frank Moore, ed., *The Rebellion Record* (New York, 1861), Vol. I, pp. 166–172.

the colonies, styling themselves States, entered severally into a firm league of friendship with each other for their common defence, the security of their liberties, and their mutual and general welfare, binding themselves to assist each other against all force offered to, or attacks made upon them, or any of them, on account of religion, sovereignty, trade, or any other pretence whatever.

In order to guard against any misconstruction of their compact, the several States made an explicit declaration in a distinct article — that each State retain its sovereignty, freedom and independence, and every power of jurisdiction and right which is not by this said confederation expressly delegated to the United States in Congress assembled under this contract of alliance.

The war of the Revolution was successfully waged, and resulted in the treaty of peace with Great Britain in 1783, by the terms of which the several States were each by name recognized to be independent.

The articles of confederation contained a clause whereby all alterations were prohibited, unless confirmed by the Legislatures of every State after being agreed to by the Congress; and in obedience to this provision, under the resolution of Congress of the 21st of February, 1787, the several States appointed delegates for the purpose of revising the articles of confederation, and reporting to Congress and the several Legislatures such alterations and provisions therein as shall, when agreed to in Congress, and confirmed by the States, render the Federal Constitution adequate to the exigencies of the Government, and the preservation of the Union.

It was by the delegates chosen by the several States under the resolution just quoted, that the Constitution of the United States was formed in 1787, and submitted to the several States for ratification, as shown by the seventh article, which is in these words: "The ratification of the conventions of nine States shall be sufficient for the establishment of this Constitution between the States so ratifying the same."

I have italicised certain words in the resolutions just made for the purpose of attracting attention to the singular and marked caution with which the States endeavored in every possible form to exclude the idea that the separate and independent sovereignty of each State was merged into one common government or nation; and the earnest desire they evinced to impress on the Constitution its true character — that of a compact between independent States — the Constitution of 1787, however, admitting the clause already recited from the articles of confederation, which provided in explicit terms that each State reclaimed its sovereignty and independence.

Some alarm was felt in the States, when invited to ratify the Constitution, lest this omission should be construed into an abandonment of their cherished principles, and they refused to be satisfied until amendments were added to the Constitution, placing beyond any pretence of doubt the reservation by the States of their sovereign rights and powers not expressly delegated to the United States by the Constitution.

Strange, indeed, must it appear to the impartial observer, that it is none the less true that all these carefully worded clauses proved unavailing to prevent the rise and growth in the Northern States of a political school which has persistently claimed that the Government set above and over the States, an organization created by the States, to secure the blessings of liberty and independence against foreign aggression, has been gradually perverted into a machine for their control in their domestic affairs.

The creature has been exalted above its Creator — the principals have been made subordinate to the agent appointed by themselves.

The people of the Southern States, whose almost exclusive occupation was agriculture, early perceived a tendency in the Northern States to render a common government subservient to their own purposes by imposing burthens on commerce as protection to their manufacturing and shipping interests.

Long and angry controversies grew out of these attempts, often successful, to benefit one section of the country at the expense of the other, and the danger of disruption arising from this cause was enhanced by the fact that the Northern population was increasing, by emigration and other causes, more than the population of the South.

By degrees, as the Northern States gained preponderance in the National Congress, self-interest taught their people to yield ready assent to any plausible advocacy of their right as majority to govern the minority. Without control, they learn to listen with impatience to the suggestion of any constitutional impediment to the exercise of their will, and so utterly have the principles of the Constitution been corrupted in the Northern mind that, in the inaugural address delivered by President Lincoln in March last, he asserts a maxim which he plainly deems to be undeniable, that the theory of the Constitution requires, in all cases, that the majority shall govern. And in another memorable instance the same Chief Magistrate did not hesitate to liken the relations between States and the United States to those which exist between the county and the State in which it is situated, and by which it was created.

This is the lamentable and fundamental error in which rests the policy that has culminated in his declaration of war against these Confederate States.

In addition to the long-continued and deep-seated resentment felt by the Southern States at the persistent abuse of the powers they had delegated to the Congress for the purpose of enriching the manufacturing and shipping classes of the North at the expense of the South, there has existed for nearly half a century another subject of discord, involving interests of such transcendent magnitude as at all times to create the apprehension in the minds of many devoted lovers of the Union that its permanence was impossible.

When the several States delegated certain powers to the United States Congress, a large portion of the laboring population were imported into the colonies by the mother country. In twelve out of the fifteen States, negro slavery existed, and the right of property existing in slaves was protected by law; this property was recognized in the Constitution, and provision was made against its loss by the escape of the slave.

The increase in the number of slaves by foreign importation from Africa was also secured by a clause forbidding Congress to prohibit the slave trade anterior to a certain date, and in no clause can there be found any delegation of power to the Congress to authorize it in any manner to legislate to the prejudice, detriment or discouragement of the owners of that species of property, or excluding it from the protection of the Government.

The climate and soil of the Northern States soon proved unpropitious to the continuance of slave labor, while the reverse being the case at the South, made unrestricted free intercourse between the two sections unfriendly.

The Northern States consulted their own interests by selling their slaves to the South and prohibiting slavery between their limits. The South were willing purchasers of property suitable to their wants, and paid the price of the acquisition, without harboring a suspicion that their quiet possession was to be disturbed by those who were not only in want of constitutional authority, but by good faith as vendors, from disquieting a title emanating from themselves.

As soon, however, as the Northern States, that prohibited African slavery within their limits, had reached a number sufficient to give their representation a controlling vote in the Congress, a persistent and organized system of hostile measures against the rights of the owners of slaves in the Southern States was inaugurated and gradually extended. A series of measures was devised and prosecuted for the purpose of rendering insecure the tenure of property in slaves.

Fanatical organizations, supplied with money by voluntary subscriptions, were assiduously engaged in exciting amongst the slaves a spirit of discontent and revolt. Means were furnished for their escape from their owners, and agents secretly employed to entice them to abscond.

The constitutional provision for their rendition to their owners was first evaded, then openly denounced as a violation of conscientious obligation and religious duty. Men were taught that it was a merit to elude, disobey, and violently oppose the execution of the laws enacted to secure the performance of the promise contained in the constitutional compact.

Often owners of slaves were mobbed and even murdered in open day solely for applying to a magistrate for the arrest of a fugitive slave.

The dogmas of the voluntary organization soon obtained control of the Legislatures of many of the Northern States, and laws were passed for the punishment, by ruinous fines, and long-continued imprisonment in gaols and penitentiaries, of citizens of the Southern States who should dare ask of the officers of the law for the recovery of their property. Emboldened by success, on the theatre of agitation and aggression, against the clearly expressed constitutional rights of the Congress, Senators and Representatives were sent to the common councils of the nation, whose chief title to this distinction consisted in the display of a spirit of ultra fanaticism, and whose business was not to promote the general welfare, or ensure domestic tranquillity — but to awaken the bitterest hatred against the citizens of sister States by violent denunciations of their institutions.

The transactions of public affairs was impeded by repeated efforts to usurp powers not delegated by the Constitution, for the purpose of impairing the security of property in slaves, and reducing those States which held slaves to a condition of inferiority.

Finally, a great party was organized for the purpose of obtaining the administration of the Government, with the avowed object of using its power for the total exclusion of the slave States from all participation in the benefits of the public domain acquired by all the States in common, whether by conquest or purchase, surrounded them entirely by States in which slavery should be prohibited, thus rendering the property in slaves so insecure as to be comparatively worthless, and thereby annihilating in effect property worth thousands of millions of dollars.

This party, thus organized, succeeded in the month of November last in the election of its candidate for the Presidency of the United States.

In the meantime, under the mild and genial climate of the Southern States, and the increasing care for the well-being and comfort of the laboring classes, dictated alike by interest and humanity, the African slaves had augmented in number from about six hundred thousand, at the date of the adoption of the constitutional compact, to upwards of four millions.

In a moral and social condition they had been elevated from brutal savages into docile, intelligent, and civilized agricultural laborers, and supplied not only with bodily comforts, but with careful religious instruction, under the supervision of a superior race. Their labor had been so directed as not only to allow a gradual and marked amelioration of their own condition, but to convert hundreds of thousands of square miles of the wilderness into cultivated lands covered with a prosperous people. Towns and cities had sprung into existence, and it rapidly increased in wealth and population under the social system of the South.

The white population of the Southern slaveholding States had augmented from about 1,250,000, at the date of the adoption of the Constitution, to more than 8,500,000 in 1860, and the productions of the South in cotton, rice, sugar and tobacco, for the full development and continuance of which the labor of African slaves was and is indispensable, had swollen to an amount which formed nearly three-fourths of the export of the whole United States, and had become absolutely necessary to the wants of civilized man.

With interests of such overwhelming magnitude imperiled, the people of the Southern States were driven by the conduct of the North to the adoption of some course of action to avoid the dangers with which they were openly menaced. With this view, the Legislatures of the several States invited the people to select delegates to conventions to be held for the purpose of determining for themselves what measures were best to be adopted to meet so alarming a crisis in their history.

Here it may be proper to observe that, from a period as early as 1798, there had existed in all of the States of the Union a party almost uninterruptedly in the majority, based upon the creed that each State was, in the last resort, the sole judge as well of its wrongs as of the mode and measures of redress. Indeed, it is obvious that under the law of nations this principle is an axiom as applied to the relations of independent sovereign States, such as those which had united themselves under the constitutional compact.

The Democratic party of the United States repeated, in its successful canvass in 1836, the deduction made in numerous previous political contests, that it would faithfully abide by, and uphold the principles laid down in the Kentucky and Virginia Legislatures of 1799, and that it adopts those principles as constituting one of the main foundations of its political creed.

The principles thus emphatically announced embrace that to which I have already adverted — the right of each State to judge of and redress the wrongs of which it complains. Their principles were maintained by overwhelming majorities of the people of all the States of the Union at different elections, especially in the election of Mr. Jefferson in 1805, Mr. Madison in 1809, and Mr. Pierce in

1852. In the exercise of a right so ancient, so well established, and so necessary for self-preservation, the people of the Confederate States in their conventions determined that the wrongs which they had suffered, and the evils with which they were menaced, required that they should revoke the delegation of powers to the Federal Government which they had ratified in their several conventions. They consequently passed ordinances resuming all their rights as sovereign and independent States, and dissolved their connection with the other States of the Union. Having done this, they proceeded to form a new compact among themselves by new articles of confederation, which have been also ratified by conventions of the several States, with an approach to unanimity far exceeding that of the conventions which adopted the Constitutions of 1787. They have organized their new government in all its departments. The functions of the executive, legislative and judicial magistrates are performed in accordance with the will of the people, as displayed not merely in a cheerful acquiescence, but in the enthusiastic support of the government thus established by themselves; and but for the interference of the Government of the United States, this legitimate exercise of a people to self-government has been manifested in every possible form.

Scarce had you assembled in February last, when, prior even to the inauguration of the chief-magistrate you had elected, you expressed your desire for the appointment of commissioners, and for the settlement of all questions of disagreement between the two governments upon principles of right, justice, equity and good faith.

It was my pleasure as well as my duty to coöperate with you in this work of peace. Indeed, in my address to you on taking the oath of office, and before receiving from you the communication of this resolution, I had said that "as a necessity, not as a choice, we have resorted to the remedy of separating, and henceforth our energies must be directed to the conduct of our own affairs, and the perpetuity of the Confederacy which we have formed. If a just perception of mutual interest shall permit us to peaceably pursue our separate political career, my most earnest desire will then have been fulfilled."

It was in furtherance of these accordant views of the congress and the executive, that I made choice of three discreet, able and distinguished citizens, who repaired to Washington. Aided by their cordial coöperation and that of the Secretary of State, every effort compatible with self-respect and the dignity of the Confederacy was exhausted before I allowed myself to yield to the conviction that the Government of the United States was determined to attempt the conquest of this people, and that our cherished hopes of peace were unobtainable.

On the arrival of our commissioners in Washington on the 5th of March, they postponed, at the suggestion of a friendly intermediator, doing more than giving informal notice of their arrival. This was done with a view to afford time to the President of the United States, who had just been inaugurated, for the discharge of other pressing official duties in the organization of his administration, before engaging his attention in the object of their mission.

It was not until the 12th of the month that they officially addressed the Secretary of State, informing him of the purpose of their arrival, and stating in the language of their instructions their wish to make to the Government of the United

States overtures for the opening of negotiations, assuring the Government of the
United States that the president, congress, and people of the Confederate
States desired a peaceful solution of these
great questions — that it was neither their
interest nor their wish to make any demand which is not founded on the strict-
est principles of justice, nor to do any
act to injure their late confederates.

To this communication no formal reply
was received until the 8th of April. During the interval, the commissioners had
consented to waive all questions of form,
with the firm resolve to avoid war if possible. They went so far even as to hold,
during that long period, unofficial intercourse through an intermediary, whose
high position and character inspired the
hope of success, and through whom constant assurances were received from the
Government of the United States of its
peaceful intentions — of its determination to evacuate Fort Sumter; and further,
that no measure would be introduced
changing the existing status prejudicial
to the Confederate States; that in the
event of any change in regard to Fort
Pickens, notice would be given to the
commissioners.

The crooked path of diplomacy can
scarcely furnish an example so wanting
in courtesy, in candor and directness, as
was the course of the United States Government toward our commissioners in
Washington. For proof of this I refer to
the annexed documents marked, taken in
connection with further facts which I
now proceed to relate.

Early in April the attention of the
whole country was attracted to extraordinary preparations for an extensive military and naval expedition in New York
and other Northern ports. These preparations commenced in secrecy, for an
expedition whose destination was concealed, and only became known when
nearly completed, and on the 5th, 6th,
and 7th of April, transports and vessels
of war with troops, munitions and military supplies, sailed from Northern ports
bound southward.

Alarmed by so extraordinary a demonstration, the commissioners requested the
delivery of an answer to their official
communication of the 12th of March,
and the reply dated on the 15th of the
previous month, from which it appears
that during the whole interval, whilst the
commissioners were receiving assurances
calculated to inspire hope of the success
of their mission, the Secretary of State
and the President of the United States
had already determined to hold no intercourse with them whatever — to refuse
even to listen to any proposals they had
to make, and had profited by the delay
created by their own assurances, in order
to prepare secretly the means for effective hostile operations.

That these assurances were given, has
been virtually confessed by the Government of the United States, by its act of
sending a messenger to Charleston to
give notice of its purpose to use force if
opposed in its intention of supplying Fort
Sumter.

No more striking proof of the absence
of good faith in the confidence of the
Government of the United States toward
the Confederacy can be required, than is
contained in the circumstances which
accompanied this notice.

According to the usual course of navigation, the vessels composing the expedition, and designed for the relief of Fort
Sumter, might be looked for in Charleston harbor on the 9th of April. Yet
our commissioners in Washington were
detained under assurances that notice

should be given of any military movement. The notice was not addressed to
them, but a messenger was sent to
Charleston to give notice to the Governor
of South Carolina, and the notice was so
given at a late hour on the 8th of April,
the eve of the very day on which the fleet
might be expected to arrive.

That this manœuvre failed in its purpose was not the fault of those who controlled it. A heavy tempest delayed the
arrival of the expedition, and gave time
to the commander of our forces at
Charleston to ask and receive instructions of the government. Even then,
under all the provocation incident to the
contemptuous refusal to listen to our
commissioners, and the treacherous
course of the Government of the United
States, I was sincerely anxious to avoid
the effusion of blood, and directed a proposal to be made to the commander of
Fort Sumter, who had avowed himself
to be nearly out of provisions, that we
would abstain from directing our fire on
Fort Sumter if he would promise to not
open fire on our forces unless first attacked. This proposal was refused. The
conclusion was, that the design of the
United States was to place the besieging
force at Charleston between the simul-
taneous fire of the fleet. The fort should,
of course, be at once reduced. This order
was executed by Gen. Beauregard with
skill and success, which were naturally to
be expected from the well-known character of that gallant officer; and, although
the bombardment lasted some thirty-
three hours, our flag did not wave over
the battered walls until after the appearance of the hostile fleet off Charleston.

Fortunately not a life was lost on our
side, and we were gratified in being prepared. The necessity of an useless effusion of blood by the prudent caution of
the officers who commanded the fleet, in
abstaining from the evidently futile effort
to enter the harbor for the relief of Major
Anderson, was spared.

I refer to the report of the Secretary of
War, and the papers accompanying it, for
further particulars of this brilliant affair.

In this connection I cannot refrain from
a well-deserved tribute to the noble State,
the eminently soldierly qualities of whose
people were conspicuously displayed.
The people of Charleston for months had
been irritated by the spectacle of a fort-
ress held within their principal harbor as
a standing menace against their peace
and independence — built in part with
their own money — its custody confided
with their long consent to an agent who
held no power over them other than such
as they had themselves delegated for
their own benefit, intended to be used
by that agent for their own protection
against foreign attack. How it was held
out with persistent tenacity as a means
of offence against them by the very Government which they had established for
their own protection, is well known.
They had beleaguered it for months,
and felt entire confidence in their power
to capture it, yet yielded to the requirements of discipline, curbed their impatience, submitted without complaint to
the unaccustomed hardships, labors and
privations of a protracted siege, and
when at length their patience was relieved by the signal for attack, and success had crowned their steady and gallant conduct, even in the very moment of
triumph they evinced a chivalrous regard
for the feelings of the brave but unfortunate officer who had been compelled to
lower his flag.

All manifestations or exultations were
checked in his presence. Their commanding general, with their cordial

approval and the consent of his government, refrained from imposing any terms that would wound the sensibility of the commander of the fort. He was permitted to retire with the honors of war, to salute his flag, to depart freely with all his command, and was escorted to the vessel on which he embarked with the highest marks of respect from those against whom his guns had so recently been directed.

Not only does every event connected with the siege reflect the highest honor on South Carolina, but the forbearance of her people and of this government from making any harangue of a victory obtained under circumstances of such peculiar provocation, attest to the fullest extent the absence of any purpose beyond securing their own tranquillity, and the sincere desire to avoid the calamities of war.

Scarcely had the President of the United States received intelligence of the failure of the scheme which he had devised for the reinforcement of Fort Sumter, when he issued the declaration of war against this Confederacy, which has prompted me to convoke you. In this extraordinary production, that high functionary affects total ignorance of the existence of an independent government, which, possessing the entire and enthusiastic devotion of its people, is exercising its functions without question over seven sovereign States — over more than five millions of people — and over a territory whose area exceeds five hundred thousand square miles.

He terms sovereign States "combinations too powerful to be suppressed in the ordinary course of judicial proceedings, or by the powers vested in the marshals by law."

He calls for an army of seventy-five thousand men to act as the posse comitatus in aid of the process of the courts of justice in States where no courts exist, whose mandates and decrees are not cheerfully obeyed and respected by a willing people.

He avows that the first service to be assigned to the forces which have been called out will not be to execute the processes of courts, but to capture forts and strongholds situated within the admitted limits of this Confederacy, and garrisoned by its troops, and declares that this effort is intended to maintain the perpetuity of popular government.

He concludes by commanding the persons composing the "combinations" aforesaid, to wit: the five millions of inhabitants of these States, to retire peaceably to their respective abodes within twenty days.

Apparently contradictory as are the terms of this singular document, one point was unmistakably evident. The President of the United States calls for an army of 75,000 men, whose first service was to be to capture our forts. It was a plain declaration of war which I was not at liberty to disregard, because of my knowledge that under the Constitution of the United States the President was usurping a power granted exclusively to the congress.

He is the sole organ of communication between that country and foreign powers. The law of nations did not permit me to question the authority of the Executive of a foreign nation to declare war against this Confederacy. Although I might have refrained from taking active measures for our defence, if the States of the Union had all imitated the action of Virginia, North Carolina, Arkansas, Kentucky, Tennessee and Missouri, by denouncing it as an unconstitutional usurpation of power to which they refuse to respond, I was not at liberty to disregard the fact that many of the States seemed quite content to submit to the exercise of the powers assumed by the President of the United States, and were actively engaged in levying troops for the purpose indicated in the proclamation. Deprived of the aid of congress, at the moment I was under the necessity of confining my action to a call on the States for volunteers for the common defence, in accordance with the authority you had confided to me before your adjournment.

I deemed it proper further to issue a proclamation, inviting applications from persons disposed to aid in our defence in private armed vessels on the high seas, to the end that preparations might be made for the immediate issue of letters of marque and reprisal, which you alone, under the constitution, have the power to grant.

I entertain no doubt that you will concur with me in the opinion, that in the absence of an organized navy, it will be eminently expedient to supply their place with private armed vessels, so happily styled by the publicists of the United States the militia of the sea, and so often and justly relied on by them as an efficient and admirable instrument of defensive warfare.

I earnestly recommend the immediate passage of a law authorizing me to accept the numerous proposals already received.

I cannot close this review of the acts of the Government of the United States without referring to a proclamation issued by their President under date of the 19th inst., in which, after declaring that an insurrection has broken out in this Confederacy against the Government of the United States, he announces a blockade of all the ports of these States, and threatens to punish as pirates all persons who shall molest any vessel of the United States under letters of marque issued by this government. Notwithstanding the authenticity of this proclamation, you will concur with me that it is hard to believe that it could have emanated from a President of the United States.

Its announcement of a mere paper blockade is so manifestly a violation of the law of nations, that it would seem incredible that it could have been issued by authority; but by conceding this to be the case, so far as the Executive is concerned, it will be difficult to satisfy the people of these States that their late confederates will sanction its declarations — will determine to ignore the usages of civilized nations, and will inaugurate a war of extermination on both sides, by treating as pirates open enemies acting under the authority of commissions issued by an organized government.

If such proclamation was issued, it could only have been published under the sudden influence of passion, and we may rest assured that mankind will be spared the horrors of the conflict it seems to invite. . . .

Abraham Lincoln: MESSAGE TO CONGRESS IN SPECIAL SESSION, JULY 4, 1861

In his carefully prepared address to the special session of Congress which assembled on July 4, 1861, Abraham Lincoln set forth his interpretation of the events leading to war. He not only blamed the Confederates for beginning the war but also attempted to define the nature of the "rebellion" which was taking place and the larger meaning of the war in America's historical experience.

Fellow-citizens of the Senate and House of Representatives: Having been convened on an extraordinary occasion, as authorized by the Constitution, your attention is not called to any ordinary subject of legislation.

At the beginning of the present presidential term, four months ago, the functions of the Federal Government were found to be generally suspended within the several States of South Carolina, Georgia, Alabama, Mississippi, Louisiana, and Florida, excepting only those of the Post-office Department.

Within these States all the forts, arsenals, dockyards, customhouses, and the like, including the movable and stationary property in and about them, had been seized, and were held in open hostility to this government, excepting only Forts Pickens, Taylor, and Jefferson, on and near the Florida coast, and Fort Sumter, in Charleston Harbor, South Carolina. The forts thus seized had been put in improved condition, new ones had been built, and armed forces had been organized and were organizing, all avowedly with the same hostile purpose.

The forts remaining in the possession of the Federal Government in and near these States were either besieged or menaced by warlike preparations, and especially Fort Sumter was nearly surrounded by well-protected hostile batteries, with guns equal in quality to the best of its own, and outnumbering the latter as perhaps ten to one. A disproportionate share of the Federal muskets and rifles had somehow found their way into these States, and had been seized to be used against the government. Accumulations of the public revenue lying within them had been seized for the same object. The navy was scattered in distant seas, leaving but a very small part of it within the immediate reach of the government. Officers of the Federal army and navy had resigned in great numbers; and of those resigning a large proportion had taken up arms against the government. Simultaneously, and in connection with all this, the purpose to sever the Federal Union was openly avowed. In accordance with this purpose, an ordinance had been adopted in each of these States, declaring the States respectively to be separated from the National Union. A formula for instituting a combined government of these States had been promulgated; and this illegal organization, in the character of confederate States, was already invoking recognition, aid, and intervention from foreign powers.

Finding this condition of things, and believing it to be an imperative duty upon the incoming executive to prevent, if possible, the consummation of such attempt to destroy the Federal Union, a

From John G. Nicolay and John Hay, *Abraham Lincoln, Complete Works* (New York, 1894), Vol. II, pp. 55–65.

choice of means to that end became indispensable. This choice was made and was declared in the inaugural address. The policy chosen looked to the exhaustion of all peaceful measures before a resort to any stronger ones. It sought only to hold the public places and property not already wrested from the government, and to collect the revenue, relying for the rest on time, discussion, and the ballot-box. It promised a continuance of the mails, at government expense, to the very people who were resisting the government; and it gave repeated pledges against any disturbance to any of the people, or any of their rights. Of all that which a President might constitutionally and justifiably do in such a case, everything was forborne without which it was believed possible to keep the government on foot.

On the 5th of March (the present incumbent's first full day in office), a letter of Major Anderson, commanding at Fort Sumter, written on the 28th of February and received at the War Department on the 4th of March, was by that department placed in his hands. This letter expressed the professional opinion of the writer that reinforcements could not be thrown into that fort within the time for his relief, rendered necessary by the limited supply of provisions, and with a view of holding possession of the same, with a force of less than twenty thousand good and well-disciplined men. This opinion was concurred in by all the officers of his command, and their memoranda on the subject were made inclosures of Major Anderson's letter. The whole was immediately laid before Lieutenant-General Scott, who at once concurred with Major Anderson in opinion. On reflection, however, he took full time, consulting with other officers, both of the army and the navy, and at the end of four days came reluctantly but decidedly to the same conclusion as before. He also stated at the same time that no such sufficient force was then at the control of the government, or could be raised and brought to the ground within the time when the provisions in the fort would be exhausted. In a purely military point of view, this reduced the duty of the administration in the case to the mere matter of getting the garrison safely out of the fort.

It was believed, however, that to so abandon that position, under the circumstances, would be utterly ruinous; that the necessity under which it was to be done would not be fully understood; that by many it would be construed as a part of a voluntary policy; that at home it would discourage the friends of the Union, embolden its adversaries, and go far to insure to the latter a recognition abroad; that, in fact, it would be our national destruction consummated. This could not be allowed. Starvation was not yet upon the garrison, and ere it would be reached Fort Pickens might be reinforced. This last would be a clear indication of policy, and would better enable the country to accept the evacuation of Fort Sumter as a military necessity. An order was at once directed to be sent for the landing of the troops from the steamship *Brooklyn* into Fort Pickens. This order could not go by land, but must take the longer and slower route by sea. The first return news from the order was received just one week before the fall of Fort Sumter. The news itself was that the officer commanding the *Sabine*, to which vessel the troops had been transferred from the *Brooklyn*, acting upon some *quasi* armistice of the late administration (and of the existence of which the present administration, up to the time the order was despatched, had only too vague and uncertain rumors to fix attention), had refused to land the troops. To now reinforce Fort Pickens before a crisis would be reached at Fort Sumter was impossible — rendered so by the near exhaustion of provisions in the latter-named fort. In precaution against such a conjuncture, the government had, a few days before, commenced preparing an expedition as well adapted as might be to relieve Fort Sumter, which expedition was intended to be ultimately used, or not, according to circumstances. The strongest anticipated case for using it was now presented, and it was resolved to send it forward. As had been intended in this contingency, it was also resolved to notify the governor of South Carolina that he might expect an attempt would be made to provision the fort; and that, if the attempt should not be resisted, there would be no effort to throw in men, arms, or ammunition, without further notice, or in case of an attack upon the fort. This notice was accordingly given; whereupon the fort was attacked and bombarded to its fall, without even awaiting the arrival of the provisioning expedition.

It is thus seen that the assault upon and reduction of Fort Sumter was in no sense a matter of self-defense on the part of the assailants. They well knew that the garrison in the fort could by no possibility commit aggression upon them. They knew — they were expressly notified — that the giving of bread to the few brave and hungry men of the garrison was all which would on that occasion be attempted, unless themselves, by resisting so much, should provoke more. They knew that this government desired to keep the garrison in the fort, not to assail them, but merely to maintain visible possession, and thus to preserve the Union from actual and immediate dissolution —

trusting, as hereinbefore stated, to time, discussion, and the ballot-box for final adjustment; and they assailed and reduced the fort for precisely the reverse object — to drive out the visible authority of the Federal Union, and thus force it to immediate dissolution. That this was their object the executive well understood; and having said to them in the inaugural address, "You can have no conflict without being yourselves the aggressors," he took pains not only to keep this declaration good, but also to keep the case so free from the power of ingenious sophistry that the world should not be able to misunderstand it. By the affair at Fort Sumter, with its surrounding circumstances, that point was reached. Then and thereby the assailants of the government began the conflict of arms, without a gun in sight or in expectancy to return their fire, save only the few in the fort sent to that harbor years before for their own protection, and still ready to give that protection in whatever was lawful. In this act, discarding all else, they have forced upon the country the distinct issue, "immediate dissolution or blood."

And this issue embraces more than the fate of these United States. It presents to the whole family of man the question whether a constitutional republic or democracy — a government of the people by the same people — can or cannot maintain its territorial integrity against its own domestic foes. It presents the question whether discontented individuals, too few in numbers to control administration according to organic law in any case, can always, upon the pretenses made in this case, or on any other pretenses, or arbitrarily without any pretense, break up their government, and thus practically put an end to free government upon the earth. It forces us to ask: "Is there, in all republics, this inherent and fatal weakness?" "Must a government, of necessity, be too strong for the liberties of its own people, or too weak to maintain its own existence?"

So viewing the issue, no choice was left but to call out the war power of the government; and so to resist force employed for its destruction, by force for its preservation.

The call was made, and the response of the country was most gratifying, surpassing in unanimity and spirit the most sanguine expectation. Yet none of the States commonly called slave States, except Delaware, gave a regiment through regular State organization. A few regiments have been organized within some others of those States by individual enterprise, and received into the government service. Of course the seceded States, so called (and to which Texas had been joined about the time of the inauguration), gave no troops to the cause of the Union. The border States, so called, were not uniform in their action, some of them being almost for the Union, while in others — as Virginia, North Carolina, Tennessee, and Arkansas — the Union sentiment was nearly repressed and silenced. The course taken in Virginia was the most remarkable — perhaps the most important. A convention elected by the people of that State to consider this very question of disrupting the Federal Union was in session at the capital of Virginia when Fort Sumter fell. To this body the people had chosen a large majority of professed Union men. Almost immediately after the fall of Sumter, many members of that majority went over to the original disunion minority, and with them adopted an ordinance for withdrawing the State from the Union. Whether this change was wrought by their great approval of the assault upon

Sumter, or their great resentment at the government's resistance to that assault, is not definitely known. Although they submitted the ordinance for ratification to a vote of the people, to be taken on a day then somewhat more than a month distant, the convention and the legislature (which was also in session at the same time and place), with leading men of the State not members of either, immediately commenced acting as if the State were already out of the Union. They pushed military preparations vigorously forward all over the State. They seized the United States armory at Harper's Ferry, and the navy-yard at Gosport, near Norfolk. They received — perhaps invited — into their State large bodies of troops, with their warlike appointments, from the so-called seceded States. They formally entered into a treaty of temporary alliance and coöperation with the so-called "Confederate States," and sent members to their congress at Montgomery. And, finally, they permitted the insurrectionary government to be transferred to their capital at Richmond.

The people of Virginia have thus allowed this giant insurrection to make its nest within her borders; and this government has no choice left but to deal with it where it finds it. And it has the less regret as the loyal citizens have, in due form, claimed its protection. Those loyal citizens this government is bound to recognize and protect, as being Virginia.

In the border States, so called, — in fact, the Middle States, — there are those who favor a policy which they call "armed neutrality"; that is, an arming of those States to prevent the Union forces passing one way, or the disunion the other, over their soil. This would be disunion completed. Figuratively speaking, it would be the building of an impassable wall along the line of separation — and yet not quite an impassable one, for under the guise of neutrality it would tie the hands of Union men and freely pass supplies from among them to the insurrectionists, which it could not do as an open enemy. At a stroke it would take all the trouble off the hands of secession, except only what proceeds from the external blockade. It would do for the disunionists, that which, of all things, they most desire — feed them well, and give them disunion without a struggle of their own. It recognizes no fidelity to the Constitution, no obligation to maintain the Union; and while very many who have favored it are doubtless loyal citizens, it is, nevertheless, very injurious in effect.

Recurring to the action of the government, it may be stated that at first a call was made for 75,000 militia; and, rapidly following this, a proclamation was issued for closing the ports of the insurrectionary districts by proceedings in the nature of blockade. So far all was believed to be strictly legal. At this point the insurrectionists announced their purpose to enter upon the practice of privateering.

Other calls were made for volunteers to serve for three years, unless sooner discharged, and also for large additions to the regular army and navy. These measures, whether strictly legal or not, were ventured upon, under what appeared to be a popular demand and a public necessity; trusting then, as now, that Congress would readily ratify them. It is believed that nothing has been done beyond the constitutional competency of Congress.

Soon after the first call for militia, it was considered a duty to authorize the commanding general in proper cases, according to his discretion, to suspend the privilege of the writ of *habeas corpus*, or, in other words, to arrest and detain, without resort to the ordinary processes and forms of law, such individuals as he might deem dangerous to the public safety. This authority has purposely been exercised but very sparingly. Nevertheless, the legality and propriety of what has been done under it are questioned, and the attention of the country has been called to the proposition that one who has sworn to "take care that the laws be faithfully executed" should not himself violate them. Of course some consideration was given to the questions of power and propriety before this matter was acted upon. The whole of the laws which were required to be faithfully executed were being resisted and failing of execution in nearly one third of the States. Must they be allowed to finally fail of execution, even had it been perfectly clear that by the use of the means necessary to their execution some single law, made in such extreme tenderness of the citizen's liberty that, practically, it relieves more of the guilty than of the innocent, should to a very limited extent be violated? To state the question more directly, are all the laws but one to go unexecuted, and the government itself go to pieces lest that one be violated? Even in such a case, would not the official oath be broken if the government should be overthrown, when it was believed that disregarding the single law would tend to preserve it? But it was not believed that this question was presented. It was not believed that any law was violated. The provision of the Constitution that "the privilege of the writ of *habeas corpus* shall not be suspended, unless when, in cases of rebellion or invasion, the public safety may require it," is equivalent to a provision — is a provision — that such privilege may be suspended when, in case of rebellion or invasion, the public safety does require it. It was decided that we have a case of rebellion, and that the public safety does require the qualified suspension of the privilege of the writ which was authorized to be made. Now it is insisted that Congress, and not the executive, is vested with this power. But the Constitution itself is silent as to which or who is to exercise the power; and as the provision was plainly made for a dangerous emergency, it cannot be believed the framers of the instrument intended that in every case the danger should run its course until Congress could be called together, the very assembling of which might be prevented, as was intended in this case, by the rebellion.

No more extended argument is now offered, as an opinion at some length will probably be presented by the attorney-general. Whether there shall be any legislation upon the subject, and if any, what, is submitted entirely to the better judgment of Congress.

The forbearance of this government had been so extraordinary and so long continued as to lead some foreign nations to shape their action as if they supposed the early destruction of our National Union was probable. While this, on discovery, gave the executive some concern, he is now happy to say that the sovereignty and rights of the United States are now everywhere practically respected by foreign powers; and a general sympathy with the country is manifested throughout the world.

The reports of the Secretaries of the Treasury, War, and the Navy will give the information in detail deemed necessary and convenient for your deliberation and action; while the executive and all the departments will stand ready to supply omissions, or to communicate new facts considered important for you to know.

It is now recommended that you give the legal means for making this contest a short and decisive one: that you place at the control of the government for the work at least four hundred thousand men and $400,000,000. That number of men is about one tenth of those of proper ages within the regions where, apparently, all are willing to engage; and the sum is less than a twenty-third part of the money value owned by the men who seem ready to devote the whole. A debt of $600,-000,000 now is a less sum per head than was the debt of our Revolution when we came out of that struggle; and the money value in the country now bears even a greater proportion to what it was then than does the population. Surely each man has as strong a motive now to preserve our liberties as each had then to establish them.

A right result at this time will be worth more to the world than ten times the men and ten times the money. The evidence reaching us from the country leaves no doubt that the material for the work is abundant, and that it needs only the hand of legislation to give it legal sanction, and the hand of the executive to give it practical shape and efficiency. One of the greatest perplexities of the government is to avoid receiving troops faster than it can provide for them. In a word, the people will save their government if the government itself will do its part only indifferently well.

It might seem, at first thought, to be of little difference whether the present movement at the South be called "secession" or "rebellion." The movers, however, well understand the difference. At the beginning they knew they could never raise their treason to any respectable magnitude by any name which implies violation of law. They knew their people possessed as much of moral sense, as much of devotion to law and order, and as much pride in and reverence for the history and government of their common country as any other civilized and patriotic people. They knew they could make no advancement directly in the teeth of these strong and noble sentiments. Accordingly, they commenced by an insidious debauching of the public mind. They invented an ingenious sophism which, if conceded, was followed by perfectly logical steps, through all the incidents, to the complete destruction of the Union. The sophism itself is that any State of the Union may consistently with the National Constitution, and therefore lawfully and peacefully, withdraw from the Union without the consent of the Union or of any other State. The little disguise that the supposed right is to be exercised only for just cause, themselves to be the sole judges of its justice, is too thin to merit any notice.

With rebellion thus sugar-coated they have been drugging the public mind of their section for more than thirty years, and until at length they have brought many good men to a willingness to take up arms against the government the day after some assemblage of men have enacted the farcical pretense of taking their State out of the Union, who could have been brought to no such thing the day before.

This sophism derives much, perhaps the whole, of its currency from the assumption that there is some omnipotent and sacred supremacy pertaining to a State — to each State of our Federal Union. Our States have neither more nor less power than that reserved to them in the Union by the Constitution — no one of them ever having been a State out of the Union. The original ones passed into the Union even before they cast off their British colonial dependence; and the new ones each came into the Union directly from a condition of dependence, excepting Texas. And even Texas, in its temporary independence, was never designated a State. The new ones only took the designation of States on coming into the Union, while that name was first adopted for the old ones in and by the Declaration of Independence. Therein the "United Colonies" were declared to be "free and independent States"; but even then the object plainly was not to declare their independence of one another or of the Union, but directly the contrary, as their mutual pledge and their mutual action before, at the time, and afterward, abundantly show. The express plighting of faith by each and all of the original thirteen in the Articles of Confederation, two years later, that the Union shall be perpetual, is most conclusive. Having never been States either in substance or in name outside of the Union, whence this magical omnipotence of "State Rights," asserting a claim of power to lawfully destroy the Union itself? Much is said about the "sovereignty" of the States; but the word even is not in the National Constitution, nor, as is believed, in any of the State constitutions. What is "sovereignty" in the political sense of the term? Would it be far wrong to define it "a political community without a political superior"? Tested by this, no one of our States except Texas ever was a sovereignty. And even Texas gave up the character on coming into the Union; by which act she acknowledged the Constitution of the United States, and the laws and treaties of the United States made in pursuance of the Constitution, to be for her the supreme law of the land. The States have their status in the Union, and they have no other legal status. If they break from this, they can only do so against law and by revolution. The Union, and not themselves separately, procured their independence and their liberty. By conquest or purchase the Union gave each of them whatever of independence or liberty it has. The Union is older than any of the States, and, in fact, it created them as States. Originally some dependent colonies made the Union, and, in turn, the Union threw off their old dependence for them, and made them States, such as they are. Not one of them ever had a State constitution independent of the Union. Of course, it is not forgotten that all the new States framed their constitutions before they entered the Union — nevertheless, dependent upon and preparatory to coming into the Union.

Unquestionably the States have the powers and rights reserved to them in and by the National Constitution; but among these surely are not included all conceivable powers, however mischievous or destructive, but, at most, such only as were known in the world at the time as governmental powers; and certainly a power to destroy the government itself had never been known as a governmental, as a merely administrative power. This relative matter of national power and State rights, as a principle, is no other than the principle of generality and locality. Whatever concerns the whole should be confided to the whole — to the General Government; while whatever concerns only the State should be left exclusively to the State. This is all there is of original principle about it. Whether the National Constitution in defining boundaries between the two has applied the principle with exact accuracy, is not to be questioned. We are all bound by that defining, without question.

What is now combated is the position that secession is consistent with the Constitution — is lawful and peaceful. It is not contended that there is any express

law for it; and nothing should ever be implied as law which leads to unjust or absurd consequences. The nation purchased with money the countries out of which several of these States were formed. Is it just that they shall go off without leave and without refunding? The nation paid very large sums (in the aggregate, I believe, nearly a hundred millions) to relieve Florida of the aboriginal tribes. Is it just that she shall now be off without consent or without making any return? The nation is now in debt for money applied to the benefit of these so-called seceding States in common with the rest. Is it just either that creditors shall go unpaid or the remaining States pay the whole? A part of the present national debt was contracted to pay the old debts of Texas. Is it just that she shall leave and pay no part of this herself?

Again, if one State may secede, so may another; and when all shall have seceded, none is left to pay the debts. Is this quite just to creditors? Did we notify them of this sage view of ours when we borrowed their money? If we now recognize this doctrine by allowing the seceders to go in peace, it is difficult to see what we can do if others choose to go or to extort terms upon which they will promise to remain.

The seceders insist that our Constitution admits of secession. They have assumed to make a national constitution of their own, in which of necessity they have either discarded or retained the right of secession as they insist it exists in ours. If they have discarded it, they thereby admit that on principle it ought not to be in ours. If they have retained it by their own construction of ours, they show that to be consistent they must secede from one another whenever they shall find it the easiest way of settling their debts, or effecting any other selfish or unjust object. The principle itself is one of disintegration, and upon which no government can possibly endure.

If all the States save one should assert the power to drive that one out of the Union, it is presumed the whole class of seceder politicians would at once deny the power and denounce the act as the greatest outrage upon State rights. But suppose that precisely the same act, instead of being called "driving the one out," should be called "the seceding of the others from that one," it would be exactly what the seceders claim to do, unless, indeed, they make the point that the one, because it is a minority, may rightfully do what the others, because they are a majority, may not rightfully do. These politicians are subtle and profound on the rights of minorities. They are not partial to that power which made the Constitution and speaks from the preamble calling itself "We, the People."

It may well be questioned whether there is to-day a majority of the legally qualified voters of any State, except perhaps South Carolina, in favor of disunion. There is much reason to believe that the Union men are the majority in many, if not in every other one, of the so-called seceded States. The contrary has not been demonstrated in any one of them. It is ventured to affirm this even of Virginia and Tennessee; for the result of an election held in military camps, where the bayonets are all on one side of the question voted upon, can scarcely be considered as demonstrating popular sentiment. At such an election, all that large class who are at once for the Union and against coercion would be coerced to vote against the Union.

It may be affirmed without extravagance that the free institutions we enjoy have developed the powers and improved the condition of our whole people beyond any example in the world. Of this we now have a striking and an impressive illustration. So large an army as the government has now on foot was never before known, without a soldier in it but who has taken his place there of his own free choice. But more than this, there are many single regiments whose members, one and another, possess full practical knowledge of all the arts, sciences, professions, and whatever else, whether useful or elegant, is known in the world; and there is scarcely one from which there could not be selected a President, a cabinet, a congress, and perhaps a court, abundantly competent to administer the government itself. Nor do I say this is not true also in the army of our late friends, now adversaries in this contest; but if it is, so much better the reason why the government which has conferred such benefits on both them and us should not be broken up. Whoever in any section proposes to abandon such a government would do well to consider in deference to what principle it is that he does it — what better he is likely to get in its stead — whether the substitute will give, or be intended to give, so much of good to the people? There are some foreshadowings on this subject. Our adversaries have adopted some declarations of independence in which, unlike the good old one, penned by Jefferson, they omit the words "all men are created equal." Why? They have adopted a temporary national constitution, in the preamble of which, unlike our good old one, signed by Washington, they omit "We, the People," and substitute, "We, the deputies of the sovereign and independent States." Why? Why this deliberate pressing out of view the rights of men and the authority of the people?

This is essentially a people's contest. On the side of the Union it is a struggle for maintaining in the world that form and substance of government whose leading object is to elevate the condition of men — to lift artificial weights from all shoulders; to clear the paths of laudable pursuit for all; to afford all an unfettered start, and a fair chance in the race of life. Yielding to partial and temporary departures, from necessity, this is the leading object of the government for whose existence we contend.

I am most happy to believe that the plain people understand and appreciate this. It is worthy of note that while in this, the government's hour of trial, large numbers of those in the army and navy who have been favored with the offices have resigned and proved false to the hand which had pampered them, not one common soldier or common sailor is known to have deserted his flag.

Great honor is due to those officers who remained true, despite the example of their treacherous associates; but the greatest honor, and most important fact of all, is the unanimous firmness of the common soldiers and common sailors. To the last man, so far as known, they have successfully resisted the traitorous efforts of those whose commands, but an hour before, they obeyed as absolute law. This is the patriotic instinct of the plain people. They understand, without an argument, that the destroying of the government which was made by Washington means no good to them.

Our popular government has often been called an experiment. Two points in it our people have already settled — the successful establishing and the successful administering of it. One still remains — its successful maintenance against a formidable internal attempt to overthrow it. It is now for them to demonstrate to the world that those who can fairly carry an election can also suppress a rebellion; that ballots are the rightful and peaceful successors of bullets; and that when ballots have fairly and constitutionally decided, there can be no successful appeal back to bullets; that there can be no successful appeal, except to ballots themselves, at succeeding elections. Such will be a great lesson of peace: teaching men that what they cannot take by an election, neither can they take it by a war; teaching all the folly of being the beginners of a war.

III. PRIMITIVE HISTORICAL WRITINGS CONCERNING THE CAUSES OF THE AMERICAN CIVIL WAR

Edward A. Pollard: A PECULIAR AND NOBLE TYPE OF CIVILIZATION

Edward A. Pollard, a Richmond journalist, was the most popular and prolific historical writer in the Confederate states during the Civil War decade. His numerous histories were colorful and dramatic, reflecting the partisan emotions of wartime. While he venerated the "sublime" principle of states rights, he also saw the war as a conflict between two civilizations: the "coarse and materialistic" civilization of the North and the "peculiar and noble type of civilization" established in the South. The selection is taken from Edward A. Pollard, The Lost Cause.

ALTHOUGH the American Union, as involving the Federal principle, contained in itself an element ultimately fatal to its form of government, it is not to be denied that by careful and attentive statesmanship a rupture might have been long postponed. We have already briefly seen that, at a most remarkable period in American history, it was proposed by the great political scholar of his times — John C. Calhoun — to modify the Federal principle of the Union and to introduce an ingenious check upon its tendencies to controversy — a measure that might long have extended the term of the Union, and certainly would have realized a very beautiful idea of political association.

But we must notice here another cause of disunion that supervened upon that of Federal incoherence, and rapidly divided the country. It was that Sectional Animosity, far more imposing than any mere discord of States, inasmuch as it put in opposition, as it were, two distinct nations on a geographical line, that by a single stroke divided the country, and thus summarily effected what smaller differences would have taken long to accomplish.

We have elsewhere briefly referred to the divisions of population between the Northern and Southern States, marked as they were by strong contrasts between the characters of the people of each. Had these divisions existed only in a contracted space of country, they might have resulted in nothing more than the production of parties or the formation of classes. But extending as they did over the space of a continent, these divisions ceased to be political parties or classes of one community, and really existed in the condition of distinct communities or nations. A recent English writer has properly and acutely observed: "In order to master the difficulties of American politics, it will be very important to realize the fact that we have to consider, not the action of rival parties or opposing inter-

From Edward A. Pollard, *The Lost Cause* (New York, 1866), pp. 45–62.

ests within the limits of one body politic, but practically that of two distinct communities or peoples, speaking indeed a common language, and united by a federal bond, but opposed in principles and interests, alienated in feeling, and jealous rivals in the pursuit of political power."

No one can read aright the history of America, unless in the light of a North and a South: two political aliens existing in a Union imperfectly defined as a confederation of States. If insensible or forgetful of this theory, he is at once involved in an otherwise inexplicable mass of facts, and will in vain attempt an analysis of controversies, apparently the most various and confused.

The Sectional Animosity, which forms the most striking and persistent feature in the history of the American States, may be dated certainly as far back as 1787. In the Convention which formed the Constitution, Mr. Madison discovered beneath the controversy between the large and small States another clashing of interests. He declared that the States were divided into different interests by other circumstances as well as by their difference of size; the most material of which resulted partly from climate, but principally from the effects of their having or not having slaves. "These two causes," he said, "concurred in forming the great division of interests in the United States;" and "if any defensive power were necessary it ought to be mutually given to these two sections." In the South Carolina Convention which ratified the Constitution, Gen. Pinckney spoke of the difference between the inhabitants of the Northern and Southern States. He explained: "When I say Southern, I mean Maryland and the States southward of her. There, we may truly observe that nature has drawn as strong marks of distinction in the habits and manners of the people, as she has in her climates and productions."

There was thus early recognized in American history a political North and a political South; the division being coincident with the line that separated the slave-holding from the non-slave-holding States. Indeed, the existence of these two parties and the line on which it was founded was recognized in the very frame-work of the Constitution. That provision of this instrument which admitted slaves into the rule of representation (in the proportion of three-fifths), is significant of a conflict between North and South; and as a compact between the slave-holding and non-slave-holding interests, it may be taken as a compromise between sections, or even, in a broader and more philosophical view, as a treaty between two nations of opposite civilizations. For we shall see that the distinction of North and South, apparently founded on slavery and traced by lines of climate, really went deeper to the very elements of the civilization of each; and that the Union, instead of being the bond of diverse States, is rather to be described, at a certain period of its history, as the forced alliance and rough companionship of two very different peoples.

When Gen. Sullivan complained to Washington that there was a party in New England opposed to his nomination as minister of war, because they considered he had "apostatized from the true New England faith, by sometimes voting with the Southern States," he declared thus early the true designs of the North to get sectional control of the government.

The slavery question is not to be taken as an independent controversy in American politics. It was not a moral dispute. It was the mere incident of a sectional animosity, the causes of which lay far beyond the domain of morals. Slavery furnished a convenient line of battle between the disputants; it was the most prominent ground of distinction between the two sections; it was, therefore, naturally seized upon as a subject of controversy, became the dominant theatre of hostilities, and was at last so conspicuous and violent, that occasion was mistaken for cause, and what was merely an incident came to be regarded as the main subject of controversy.

The institution of slavery, as the most prominent cause of distinction between the civilizations or social autonomies of North and South, was naturally bound up in the Sectional Animosity. As that animosity progressed, the slavery question developed. This explains, indeed, what is most curious in the political history of slavery — namely that the early part of that history is scarcely more than an enumeration of dates and measures, which were taken as matters of course, and passed without dispute. The Fugitive Slave Law of 1793 was passed without a division in the Senate, and by a vote of forty-eight to seven in the House. Louisiana and Florida, slave-holding territories, were organized without agitation. Kentucky, Tennessee, Mississippi and Alabama were admitted into the Union without any question as to their domestic institutions. The action of Congress, with respect to the north-west territory, was based upon a *pre-existing* anti-slavery ordinance, and had no significance. There was nothing or but little in the early days of the Union, to betoken the wild and violent controversy on slavery, that was to sweep the country like a storm and strew it with scenes of horrour.

With the jealousy of Southern domination came the slavery agitation; proving clearly enough its subordination to the main question, and that what was asserted as a matter of conscience, and attempted to be raised to the position of an independent controversy, was but part of or an attachment to an animosity that went far below the surface of local institutions. The Hartford Convention, in 1814, which originated in jealousy of the political power of the South, proposed to strike down the slave representation in Congress, and to have the representation conformed to the number of free persons in the Union. A few years later, the country was more distinctly arrayed into two sectional parties, struggling for supremacy with regard to the slavery question. The legislation on the admission of Missouri in 1820, by which the institution of slavery was bounded by a line of latitude, indicated the true nature of the slavery controversy, and simply revealed what had all along existed: a political North and a political South. It was here that we find the initial point of that war of sections which raged in America for forty years, and at last culminated in an appeal to arms. The Missouri legislation was the preliminary trace of disunion. "A geographical line," wrote Mr. Jefferson, "coinciding with a marked principle, moral and political, once conceived and held up to the angry passions of men will not be obliterated; and every new irritation will make it deeper and deeper."

The North naturally found or imagined in slavery the leading cause of the distinctive civilization of the South, its higher sentimentalism, and its superior refinements of scholarship and manners. It revenged itself on the cause, diverted its envy in an attack upon slavery, and defamed the institution as the relic of barbarism and the sum of all villainies. But, whatever may have been the defamation of the institution of slavery, no man can write its history without recognizing contributions and naming prominent results beyond the domain of controversy. It bestowed on the world's commerce in a half-century a single product whose annual value was two hundred millions of dollars. It founded a system of industry by which labour and capital were identified in interest, and capital therefore protected labour. It exhibited the picture of a land crowned with abundance, where starvation was unknown, where order was preserved by an unpaid police; and where many fertile regions accessible only to the labour of the African were brought into usefulness, and blessed the world with their productions.

We shall not enter upon the discussion of the moral question of slavery. But we may suggest a doubt here whether that odious term "slavery," which has been so long imposed, by the exaggeration of Northern writers, upon the judgment and sympathies of the world, is properly applied to that system of servitude in the South which was really the mildest in the world; which did not rest on acts of debasement and disenfranchisement, but elevated the African, and was in the interest of human improvement; and which, by the law of the land, protected the negro in life and limb, and in many personal rights, and, by the practice of the system, bestowed upon him a sum of individual indulgences, which made him altogether the most striking type in the world of cheerfulness and contentment. But it is not necessary to prolong this consideration. For, we repeat, the slavery question was not a moral one in the North, unless, perhaps, with a few thousand persons of disordered conscience. It was significant only of a contest for political power, and afforded nothing more than a convenient ground of dispute between two parties, who represented not two moral theories, but hostile sections and opposite civilizations.

In the ante-revolutionary period, the differences between the populations of the Northern and Southern colonies had already been strongly developed. The early colonists did not bear with them from the mother-country to the shores of the New World any greater degree of congeniality than existed among them at home. They had come not only from different stocks of population, but from different feuds in religion and politics. There could be no congeniality between the Puritan exiles who established themselves upon the cold and rugged and cheerless soil of New England, and the Cavaliers who sought the brighter climate of the South, and drank in their baronial halls in Virginia confusion to roundheads and regicides.

In the early history of the Northern colonists we find no slight traces of the modern *Yankee;* although it remained for those subsequent influences which educate nations as well as individuals to complete that character, to add new vices to it, and to give it its full development. But the intolerance of the Puritan, the painful thrift of the Northern colonists, their external forms of piety, their jaundiced legislation, their convenient morals, their lack of the sentimentalism which makes up the half of modern civilization, and their unremitting hunt after selfish aggrandizement are traits of character which are yet visible in their descendants. On the other hand, the colonists of Virginia and the Carolinas were from the first distinguished for their polite manners, their fine sentiments, their attachment to a sort of feudal life, their landed gentry, their love of field-sports and dangerous adventure, and the prodigal and improvident aristocracy that dispensed its stores in constant rounds of hospitality and gaiety.

Slavery established in the South a peculiar and noble type of civilization. It was not without attendant vices; but the virtues which followed in its train were numerous and peculiar, and asserted the general good effect of the institution on the ideas and manners of the South. If habits of command sometimes degenerated into cruelty and insolence; yet, in the greater number of instances, they inculcated notions of chivalry, polished the manners and produced many noble and generous virtues. If the relief of a large class of whites from the demands of physical labour gave occasion in some instances for idle and dissolute lives, yet at the same time it afforded opportunity for extraordinary culture, elevated the standards of scholarship in the South, enlarged and emancipated social intercourse, and established schools of individual refinement. The South had an element in its society — a landed gentry — which the North envied, and for which its substitute was a coarse ostentatious aristocracy that smelt of the trade, and that, however it cleansed itself and aped the elegance of the South, and packed its houses with fine furniture, could never entirely subdue a sneaking sense of its inferiority. There is a singularly bitter hate which is inseparable from a sense of inferiority; and every close observer of Northern society has discovered how there lurked in every form of hostility to the South the conviction that the Northern man, however disguised with ostentation, was coarse and inferiour in comparison with the aristocracy and chivalry of the South.

The civilization of the North was coarse and materialistic. That of the South was scant of shows, but highly refined and sentimental. The South was a vast agricultural country; waste lands, forest and swamps often gave to the eye a dreary picture; there were no thick and intricate nets of internal improvements to astonish and bewilder the traveller, no country picturesque with towns and villages to please his vision. Northern men ridiculed this apparent scantiness of the South, and took it as an evidence of inferiority. But this was the coarse judgment of the surface of things. The agricultural pursuits of the South fixed its features; and however it might decline in the scale of gross prosperity, its people were trained in the highest civilization, were models of manners for the whole country, rivalled the sentimentalism of the oldest countries of Europe, established the only schools of honour in America, and presented a striking contrast in their well-balanced character to the conceit and giddiness of the Northern people.

Foreigners have made a curious and unpleasant observation of a certain exaggeration of the American mind, an absurd conceit that was never done asserting the unapproachable excellence of its country in all things. The Washington affair was the paragon of governments; the demagogical institutions of America were the best under the sun; the slipshod literature of the country, the smattered education of the people were the *foci* of the world's enlightenment; and, in short, Americans were the lords of creation. De Tocqueville observed: "the Americans are not very remote from believing themselves to belong to a distinct race of mankind."

But it is to be remarked that this boastful disposition of mind, this exaggerated conceit was peculiarly *Yankee*. It belonged to the garish civilization of the North. It was Daniel Webster who wrote, in a diplomatic paper, that America was "the only great republican power." It was Yankee orators who established the

Fourth-of-July school of rhetoric, exalted the American eagle, and spoke of the Union as the last, best gift to man. This *afflatus* had but little place among the people of the South. Their civilization was a quiet one; and their characteristic as a people has always been that sober estimate of the value of men and things, which, as in England, appears to be the best evidence of a substantial civilization and a real enlightenment. Sensations, excitements on slight causes, fits of fickle admiration, manias in society and fashion, a regard for magnitude, display and exaggeration, all these indications of a superficial and restless civilization abounded in the North and were peculiar to its people. The sobriety of the South was in striking contrast to these exhibitions, and was interpreted by the vanity of the North as insensibility and ignorance, when it was, in fact, the mark of the superiour civilization.

This contrast between the Northern and Southern minds is vividly illustrated in the different ideas and styles of their worship of that great American idol — the Union. In the North there never was any lack of rhetorical fervour for the Union; its praises were sounded in every note of tumid literature, and it was familiarly entitled "the glorious." But the North worshipped the Union in a very low, commercial sense; it was a source of boundless profit; it was productive of tariffs and bounties; and it had been used for years as the means of sectional aggrandizement.

The South regarded the Union in a very different light. It estimated it at its real value, and although quiet and precise in its appreciation, and not given to transports, there is this remarkable assertion to be made: that the *moral* veneration of the Union was peculiarly a sentiment of the South and entirely foreign

to the Northern mind. It could not be otherwise, looking to the different political schools of the two sections. In the North, the doctrine of State Rights was generally rejected for the prevalent notion that America was a single democracy. To the people of the North the Union was therefore a mere geographical name, a political designation which had no peculiar claims upon their affection. In the South the Union was differently regarded. State Rights was the most marked peculiarity of the politics of the Southern people; and it was this doctrine that gave the Union its moral dignity, and was the only really possible source of sentimental attachment to it. The South bowed before neither an idol of gain, nor the shadow of a name. She worshipped that picture of the Union drawn by John C. Calhoun: a peculiar association in which sovereign States were held by high considerations of good faith; by the exchanges of equity and comity; by the noble attractions of social order; by the enthused sympathies of a common destiny of power, honour and renown. But, alas! this picture existed only in the imagination; the idea of Mr. Calhoun was never realized; and the South, torn from its moral and sentimental attachment to the Union, found that it had no other claims upon its affection.

To understand how the Union became a benefit to the North and resulted in the oppression of the South, it is only necessary to compare the two sections in the elements of prosperity, and to explore the sources of those elements as far as they can be traced within the domain of the Union.

*　　*　　*

It is not unusual in countries of large extent for the tides of population and enterprise to change their directions and establish new seats of power and prosperity. But the change which in little more than a generation after the American Revolution shifted the numbers and enterprise of the country from the Southern to the Northern States was so distinctly from one side of a line to the other, that we must account such the result of certain special and well-defined causes. To discover these causes, and to explain that most remarkable phenomenon — the sharply-defined transfer of population, enterprise, and commercial empire from the South to the North — we shall pass rapidly in review a number of years in the history of the American States.

About the revolutionary period Virginia held the front rank of the States. Patrick Henry designated her as "the most mighty State in the Union." "Does not Virginia," exclaimed this orator, "surpass every State in the Union in the number of inhabitants, extent of territory, felicity of position, in affluence and wealth?" Her arms had been singularly illustrious in the seven years' war; and no State had contributed to this great contest a larger measure of brilliant and patriotic service. James Monroe, himself a soldier of the Revolution, declared: "Virginia braved all dangers. From Quebec to Boston, from Boston to Savannah she shed the blood of her sons."

The close of the Revolution was followed by a distress of trade that involved all of the American States. Indeed, they found that their independence, commercially, had been very dearly purchased: that the British Government was disposed to revenge itself for the ill-success of its arms by the most severe restrictions on the trade of the States, and to affect all Europe against any commercial negotiations with them. The tobacco of Virginia and Maryland was loaded down with duties and prohibitions; the rice and

indigo of the Carolinas suffered similarly; but in New England the distress was out of all proportion to what was experienced in the more fortunate regions of the South, where the fertility of the soil was always a ready and considerable compensation for the oppression of taxes and commercial imposts. Before the Revolution, Great Britain had furnished markets for more than three-fourths of the exports of the eight Northern States. These were now almost actually closed to them. Massachusetts complained of the boon of independence, when she could no longer find a market for her fish and oil of fish, which at this time constituted almost wholly the exports of that region, which has since reached to such insolence of prosperity, and now abounds with the seats of opulence. The most important branch of New England industry — the whale fisheries — had almost perished; and driven out of employment, and distressed by an unkind soil, there were large masses of the descendants of the Puritans ready to move wherever better fortune invited them, and the charity of equal laws would tolerate them.

In these circumstances it is not surprising that, in the early stages of the Federal Republic, the South should have been reckoned the seat of future empire.

There was a steady flow of population from the sterile regions of the North to the rich but uncultivated plains of the South. In the Convention that formed the Constitution Mr. Butler, a delegate from New England, had declared, with pain, that "the people and strength of America were evidently bearing southwardly and southwestwardly." As the sectional line was then supposed to run, there were only five States on the southern side of it: eight on the northern. In the House of Representatives the North had thirty-six votes; the South only twenty-nine. But the most persistent statement made in favour of the Constitution in Virginia and other Southern States, was, that though the North, at the date of this instrument, might have a majority in the representation, the increase of population in the South would, in the course of a few years, change it in their favour. So general and imposing was the belief that the Southern States were destined to hold the larger share of the numbers and wealth of America. And not without reason was such a prospect indulged at this time. The people of New England were then emigrating to Kentucky, and even farther to the South and Southwest. In vain the public men of the North strove to drive back the flow of population upon the unoccupied lands of Maine, then a province of Massachusetts. Land was offered there for a dollar an acre. But the inducement of even such a price was insufficient to draw the emigrant to the inhospitable regions of the Penobscot. There was the prosperous agriculture to tempt him that had made Virginia the foremost of the British colonies. There were the fertile and undulating prairie lands of Kentucky to invite and reward his labours. There were the fruitful vales of Frankland — a name then given to the western district of North Carolina — to delight his vision with the romances of picturesque prosperity. To these regions the Northern emigration flowed with steady progress, if not with the rapidity and spirit of a new adventure.

Virginia did not need the contributions of numbers or of capital moving from the North after the Revolution, to make her the foremost State of the Union. She was already so. In 1788, her population was estimated at more than half a million, and her military force at fifty thousand militiamen. Her early land system, in which the soil was cultivated by tenants, and thus most effectively divided for labour, had put her agricultural interest far above that of the other States, and during the colonial period had drawn to her borders the best class of population in America — that of the yeomanry of England. The Chesapeake was the chosen resort of the trader. Alexandria, then the principal commercial city of Virginia, was thought to hold the keys to the trade of a continent. The election of George Washington to the Presidency of the United States interrupted him in a project, by which he hoped to unite the Bay of Chesapeake, by her two great arms, the James and Potomac rivers, with the Ohio, and eventually to drain the commerce of the Lakes into the same great basin, and, extending yet further the vision of this enterprise, to make Alexandria the eastern depot of the fur trade. Everywhere was blazoned the prosperity of Virginia; and, indeed, in coming into the Union, many of her public men had said that she sacrificed an empire in itself for a common concern.

Of the decline of the South, after the early periods of the government, in population and industry, Virginia affords the most striking example. To show the general fact and to illustrate especially the decline of that State, we may take two pictures of Virginia, placing an interval between them of scarcely more than one generation of men.

At the time of the adoption of the Constitution, Virginia was in the heyday of prosperity. Her system of tenant farms spread before the eye a picture of thrifty and affluent agriculture. In 1800 she had a great West Indian and a flourishing European trade. She imported for herself and for a good part of North Carolina and, perhaps, of Tennessee. She presented a picture in which every element of prosperity combined with lively effect.

In 1829 it was estimated in her State Convention that her lands were worth only half what they were in 1817. Her slave property had proportionately declined, and negro men could be bought for one hundred and fifty dollars each. Her landed system had become extinct. Regions adapted to the growth of the grasses were converted into pasture lands. The busy farms disappeared; they were consolidated to make cattle-ranges and sheep-walks. Where once the eye was entertained with the lively and cheerful scenes of an abundant prosperity it looked over wasted fields, stunted forests of secondary growth of pine and cedar, and mansions standing partly in ruins or gloomily closed in tenantless silence.

The contrast between such prosperity and such decay, witnessed in every part of the South, though not perhaps to the extent displayed in Virginia, and taking place within a short and well-defined period of time, demands explanations and strongly invites the curiosity of the historical inquirer. And yet the explanation is easy when we regard obvious facts, instead of betaking ourselves to remote and refined speculations after the usual fashion of the curious, with respect to striking and remarkable phenomena.

It has been a persistent theory with Northern writers that the singular decline of the South in population and industry, while their own section was constantly ascending the scale of prosperity, is to be ascribed to the peculiar institution of negro slavery. But this is the most manifest nonsense that was ever spread on the pages of history. Negro slavery had no point of coincidence with the decline referred to; it had existed in the South from the beginning; it had been compatible with her early prosperity extending over the period of the Constitution; it had existed in Virginia when Virginia was most flourishing. But the fallacy of the anti-slavery argument is not only apparent in the light of the early history of America: examples in other parts of the world emphasize it, and add to the illustration. Cuba and Brazil are standing examples of the contribution of negro slavery to agricultural wealth and material prosperity; while on the other hand Jamaica affords the example of decline in these respects from the very abolition of this institution of labour.

The true causes of that sectional lapse, in which the South became by far the inferiour part of the American Union in every respect of material prosperity, will naturally be looked for in the peculiar history of that Union. We shall make this discovery of adequate causes in not more than two prominent considerations, having reference to the geographical and political history of the American States.

1. The Louisiana Purchase, although opposed by the North, on the ground that it was an acquisition to the territorial and political power of the South, was mainly instrumental in turning the scale of population as between the two sections. It opened the Mississippi River; turned the tide of emigration to its upper branches; opened a new empire — the Northwest, soon to become known as "the Great West;" and drew to these distant fields much of the numbers and wealth that had before tended to the South and Southwest for the rewards of enterprise.

2. But by far the more important cause of that decline we have marked in the South was the unequal legislation of Congress and the constant discrimination of the benefits of the Union as between the two sections of the country.

And here in this consideration it is not too much to say that we find the key to the whole political history of America. The great defect of the American Constitution was that it rested too much power upon the fluctuating basis of *population*. In the Convention that formed this instrument there were Southern members who made light of the Northern majority in representation. They thought the next census would set all right. But the Northern party understood the advantage of getting the control of the government in the outset; they strained every nerve to gain it; and they have never since relinquished it.

Population, where the soil is not too densely peopled, and yields a good average of production, is the obvious source of national wealth, which, in turn, increases population. This great productive power was thrown into the Northern scale. By the two measures, of the exclusion of slavery from the Territories and the interdiction of the slave trade, Congress turned the tides of population in favour of the North, and confirmed in the Northern majority the means of a sectional domination.

What effect this turn in the population had upon the political power of the South in the Union is at once seen in the startling changes of her representation in the lower house of Congress. The population of the South had, of course, largely increased, since the date of the Revolution; but it had not been able to keep up with the changes in the ratio of representation. This had been at first 33,000; in the census of 1860, it was raised to 127,-381. In the first House of Representatives, Virginia had ten members to six from New York; the proportion under the last census was, Virginia eleven to New York thirty. South Carolina, which originally had one-thirteenth of the popular

representation in Congress, would only return, under the census of 1860, four members in a house of two hundred and thirty-three. The representative power in the North had become enormously in excess, and whenever it chose to act unanimously, was capable of any amount of oppression upon the rival section.

Under this sectional domination grew up a system of protections and bounties to the North without parallel in the history of class legislation and of unequal laws in a common country. Virginia had accepted the Constitution in the hope that the General Government, having "power to regulate commerce," would lift the restrictions from her trade. This consideration was held out as a bribe for votes in the Convention. She was bitterly disappointed. In the Virginia Convention of 1822, Mr. Watkins Leigh declared: "Every commercial operation of the Federal Government, since I attained manhood, has been detrimental to the Southern Atlantic slaveholding, planting States."

The South had no protection for her agriculture. At the time of the adoption of the Constitution, the manufacturing interest was a very unimportant one in the country. But manufactures soon became a prominent and special branch of industry in the North; and a course of sectional legislation was commenced to exact from the South a large portion of the proceeds of her industry, and bestow it upon the North in the shape of bounties to manufacturers and appropriations in a thousand forms. "Protection" was the cry which came up from every part of the North. Massachusetts, although unwilling to be taxed on the importation of molasses, wanted protection for the rum she made from it, and contended that it should be fenced in by high duties from a competition with the rum of

Jamaica. Pennsylvania sought protection for her manufactures of steel and her paper mills. Connecticut had manufactures of woollens and manufactures of cordage, which she declared would perish without protection. New York demanded that every article should be protected that her people were able to produce. And to such clamours and demands the South had for a long time to submit, so helpless indeed that she was scarcely treated as a party to common measures of legislation. The foundation of the *protective* tariff of 1828 — "the bill of abominations," as it was styled by Mr. Calhoun — was laid in a Convention of Northern men at Harrisburg, Pennsylvania; and from this Convention were excluded all sections of the country intended to be made tributary under the act of Congress.

Of the tariff of 1828 Senator Benton remarked: "The South believed itself impoverished to enrich the North by this system; and certainly an unexpected result had been seen in these two sections. In the colonial state the Southern were the richer part of the colonies, and they expected to do well in a state of independence. But in the first half century after independence this expectation was reversed. The wealth of the North was enormously aggrandized; that of the South had declined. Northern towns had become great cities, Southern cities had decayed or become stationary; and Charleston, the principal port of the South, was less considerable than before the Revolution. The North became a money-lender to the South, and Southern citizens made pilgrimages to Northern cities to raise money upon their patrimonial estates. The Southern States attributed this result to the action of the Federal Government — its double action of levying revenue upon the industry of

one section of the Union and expending it in another — and especially to its protective tariffs."

Again, contrasting the condition of the South then with what it had been at the Revolutionary period, the same Senator remarked: "It is a tradition of the colonies that the South had been the seat of wealth and happiness, of power and opulence; that a rich population covered the land, dispensing a baronial hospitality, and diffusing the felicity which themselves enjoyed; that all was life, and joy, and affluence then. And this tradition was not without similitude to the reality, as this writer can testify; for he was old enough to have seen (after the Revolution) the still surviving state of Southern colonial manners, when no traveller was allowed to go to a tavern, but was handed over from family to family through entire States; when holidays were days of festivity and expectation long prepared for, and celebrated by master and slave with music and feasting, and great concourse of friends and relations; when gold was kept in chests, after the downfall of Continental paper, and weighed in scales, and lent to neighbours for short terms without note, interest, witness, or security; and when petty litigation was at so low an ebb that it required a fine of forty pounds of tobacco to make a man serve as constable. The reverse of all this was now seen and felt — not to the whole extent which fancy or policy painted, but to extent enough to constitute a reverse, and to make a contrast, and to excite the regrets which the memory of past joys never fails to awaken."

The early history of the tariff makes a plain exhibition of the stark outrage perpetrated by it upon the Southern States. The measure of 1816 had originated in the necessities of a public revenue — for the war commenced against England four years before had imposed a debt upon the United States of one hundred and thirty millions of dollars. It was proposed to introduce into this tariff the *incidental* feature of "protection;" and it was argued that certain home manufactures had sprung up during the exigencies of the war, which were useful and deserving, and that they were likely to lapse under the sudden return of peace and to sink under foreign competition. A demand so moderate and ingenious the South was not disposed to resist. Indeed, it was recommended by John C. Calhoun himself, who voted for the bill of 1816. But the danger was in the precedent. The principle of protection once admitted maintained its hold and enlarged its demands; it was successively carried farther in the tariffs of 1820, '24, and '28. And in 1831, when it was shown by figures in Congress that the financial exigencies that had first called the tariff into existence had completely passed away, and that the government was, in fact, collecting about twice as much revenue as its usual expenditures required, the North still held to its demands for protection, and strenuously resisted any repeal or reduction of the existing tariff.

The demand of the South at this time, so ably enforced by Calhoun, for the repeal of the tariff, was recommended by the most obvious justice and the plainest prudence. It was shown that the public debt had been so far diminished as to render it certain that, at the existing rate of revenue, in three years the last dollar would be paid, and after three years there would be an annual surplus in the treasury of twelve or thirteen millions. But the North was insensible to these arguments, and brazen in its demands. The result of this celebrated controversy, which shook the Union to its foundations, was a compromise or a modification of

the tariff, in which however enough was saved of the protective principle to satisfy for a time the rapacity of the North, and that through the demagogical exertions of Henry Clay of Kentucky, who courted Northern popularity, and enjoyed in Northern cities indecent feasts and triumphs for his infidelity to his section.

But the tariff of 1833 was a deceitful compromise, and its terms were never intended by the North to be a final settlement of the question. In 1842 the settlement was repudiated, and the duties on manufactures again advanced. From that time until the period of Disunion the fiscal system of the United States was persistently protective; the South continued to decline; she had no large manufactures, no great cities, no shipping interests; and although the agricultural productions of the South were the basis of the foreign commerce of the United States, yet Southern cities did not carry it on.

Nor was the tariff the only measure of Northern aggrandizement in the Union. Besides manufactures, the North had another great interest in navigation. A system of high differential duties gave protection to it; and this, of course, bore with peculiar hardship on the Southern States, whose commodities were thus burdened by a new weight put upon them by the hand of the General Government. In tariffs, in pensions, in fishing bounties, in tonnage duties, in every measure that the ingenuity of avarice could devise, the North exacted from the South a tribute, which it could only pay at the expense and in the character of an inferiour in the Union.

But in opposition to this view of the helplessness of the South and her inability to resist the exactions of the North, it may be said that the South had an important political alliance in the North, that she was aided there by the Democratic party, and that she thus held the reins of government during the greater portion of the time the tariffs alleged to be so injurious to her interests existed. And here we touch a remarkable fact in American politics. It is true that a large portion of the Democratic party resided in the North, and that many of the active politicians there pretended to give in their adhesion to the States Rights school of politics. But this Democratic alliance with the South was one only for party purposes. It was extravagant of professions, but it carefully avoided trials of its fidelity; it was selfish, cunning, and educated in perfidy. It was a deceitful combination for party purposes, and never withstood the test of a practical question. The Northern Democrat was always ready to contend against the Whig, but never against his own pocket, and the peculiar interests of his section. The moment economical questions arose in Congress, the Northern Democrat was on the side of Northern interests, and the Southern ranks, very imposing on party questions, broke into a scene of mutiny and desertion. It was indeed the weak confidence which the South reposed in the Democratic party of the North that more than once betrayed it on the very brink of the greatest issues in the country, and did more perhaps to put it at disadvantage in the Union than the party of open opposition.

It was through such a train of legislation as we have briefly described that the South rapidly declined in the Union. By the force of a numerical majority — a thing opposed to the American system, properly understood — a Union, intended to be one of mutual benefits, was made a conduit of wealth and power to the North, while it drained the South of nearly every element of material prosperity.

It is true that the numerical majority of the North the South held long in check by superior and consummate political skill. Party complications were thrown around the Sectional Animosity. But it was easy to see that some time or other that animosity would break the web of party; and that whenever on sectional questions the North chose to act in a mass, its power would be irresistible, and that no resource would be left for the South than to remain helpless and at mercy in the Union or to essay a new political destiny. We shall see that in the year 1860 the North did choose to *act in a mass*, and that the South was thus and then irresistibly impelled to the experiment of Disunion.

James Buchanan: REPUBLICAN FANATICISM AS A CAUSE OF THE CIVIL WAR

After leaving Washington in March of 1861, James Buchanan retired to his home, "Wheatland," in Pennsylvania. During the war years he spent much of his time preparing a defense of his actions as President. James Buchanan regarded the war as a "needless war" caused primarily by the work of fanatical antislavery agitators in the North whose reckless acts enabled the disunion agitators of the South to prepare "the Southern mind" for the "final catastrophe." The selection is taken from James Buchanan, Mr. Buchanan's Administration on the Eve of Rebellion.

SENATOR SEWARD, of New York, was at this period the acknowledged head and leader of the Republican party. Indeed, his utterances had become its oracles. He was much more of a politician than a statesman. Without strong convictions, he understood the art of preparing in his closet, and uttering before the public, antithetical sentences well calculated both to inflame the ardor of his anti-slavery friends and to exasperate his pro-slavery opponents. If he was not the author of the "irrepressible conflict," he appropriated it to himself and converted it into a party oracle. He thus aroused passions, probably without so intending, which it was beyond his power afterwards to control. He raised a storm which, like others of whom we read in history, he wanted both the courage and the power to quell.

We quote the following extract from his famous speech at Rochester on the 25th of October, 1858: "Free labor and slave labor, these antagonistic systems, are continually coming into close contact, and collision results. Shall I tell you what this collision means? They who think it is accidental, unnecessary, the work of interested or fanatical agitators, and therefore ephemeral, mistake the case altogether. It is an *irrepressible conflict* between opposing and enduring forces, and it means that the United States must and will, sooner or later, become either entirely a slaveholding nation or entirely a free-labor nation. Either the cotton and rice fields of South Carolina and the sugar plantations of Louisiana will ultimately be tilled by free labor, and Charleston and New Orleans become marts for legitimate merchandise alone, or else the rye fields and wheat fields of Massachusetts and New York must again be surrendered by their farmers to slave culture and to the production of slaves, and Boston and New York become once more markets for trade in the bodies and souls of men."

However impossible that Massachusetts and New York should ever again become slaveholding States, and again engage in the African slave trade, yet such was the temper of the times that this absurd idea produced serious apprehensions in the North. It gave rise to still more serious apprehensions in the South. There they believed or affected to believe that the people of the North, in order to avoid the dreaded alternative of having slavery restored among themselves, and having their rye fields and wheat

From James Buchanan, *Mr. Buchanan's Administration on the Eve of Rebellion* (New York, 1866), pp. 57–66, 84–85.

fields cultivated by slave labor, would put forth all their efforts to cut up slavery by the roots in the Southern States. These reckless fancies of Senator Seward made the deeper impression upon the public mind, both North and South, because it was then generally believed that he would be the candidate of the Republican party at the next Presidential election. In accordance with the views expressed by Senator Seward, Hinton Helper's "Impending Crisis" soon afterwards appeared, a book well calculated to alarm the southern people. This was ushered into the world by the following warm commendation from Mr. Seward himself: "I have read the 'Impending Crisis of the South' with great attention. It seems to me a work of great merit, rich yet accurate in statistical information, and logical in analysis."

On the 9th of March, 1859, a Republican committee in New York, consisting of Horace Greeley, Thurlow Weed, and others, issued a circular warmly commending the book, and proposing to publish one hundred thousand copies of a compendium of it at a cheap rate for gratuitous circulation. In order to raise subscriptions for the purpose, they obtained the recommendation of this plan by sixty-eight Republican members of Congress, with Schuyler Colfax at their head. It is in the following terms: "We the undersigned, members of the House of Representatives of the National Congress, do cordially indorse the opinion and approve the enterprise set forth in the foregoing circular."

The author of the book is by birth a North Carolinian, though of doubtful personal character, but his labors have since been recognized and rewarded by his appointment as Consul of the United States at Buenos Ayres.

Published under such auspices, the "Impending Crisis" became at once an authoritative exposition of the principles of the Republican party. The original, as well as a compendium, were circulated by hundreds of thousands, North, South, East, and West. No book could be better calculated for the purpose of intensifying the mutual hatred between the North and the South. This book, in the first place, proposes to abolish slavery in the slaveholding States by exciting a revolution among those called "the poor whites," against their rich slaveholding neighbors. To accomplish this purpose, every appeal which perverse ingenuity and passionate malignity could suggest, was employed to excite jealousy and hatred between these two classes. The cry of the poor against the rich, the resort of demagogues in all ages, was echoed and reëchoed. The plan urged upon the non-slaveholding citizens of the South was —

1st. "Thorough organization and independent political action on the part of the non-slaveholding whites of the South."

2d. "Ineligibility of pro-slavery slaveholders. Never another vote to any one who advocates the retention and perpetuation of human slavery."

3d. "No coöperation with pro-slavery politicians — no fellowship with them in religion — no affiliation with them in society."

4th. "No patronage to pro-slavery merchants — no guestship in slave-waiting hotels — no fees to pro-slavery lawyers — no employment of pro-slavery physicians — no audience to pro-slavery parsons."

5th. "No more hiring of slaves by non-slaveholders."

6th. "Abrupt discontinuance of subscription to pro-slavery newspapers."

7th. "The greatest possible encouragement to free white labor."

"This, then," says Mr. Helper, "is the outline of our scheme for the abolition of slavery in the Southern States. Let it be acted upon with due promptitude, and as certain as truth is mightier than error, fifteen years will not elapse before every foot of territory, from the mouth of the Delaware to the emboguing of the Rio Grande, will glitter with the jewels of freedom. Some time during this year, next, or the year following, let there be a general convention of non-slaveholders from every slave State in the Union, to deliberate on the momentous issues now pending." Not confining himself even within these limits, Mr. Helper proceeds to still greater extremities, and exclaims: "But, sirs, slaveholders, chevaliers, and lords of the lash, we are unwilling to allow you to cheat the negroes out of all the rights and claims to which, as human beings, they are most sacredly entitled. Not alone for ourself as an individual, but for others also, particularly for five or six millions of southern non-slaveholding whites, whom your iniquitous Statism has debarred from almost all the mental and material comforts of life, do we speak, when we say, you must sooner or later emancipate your slaves, and pay each and every one of them at least sixty dollars cash in hand. By doing this you will be restoring to them their natural rights, and remunerating them at the rate of less than twenty-six cents per annum for the long and cheerless period of their servitude from the 20th of August, 1620, when, on James River, in Virginia, they became the unhappy slaves of heartless tyrants. Moreover, by doing this you will

be performing but a simple act of justice to the non-slaveholding whites, upon whom the system of slavery has weighed scarcely less heavily than upon the negroes themselves. You will, also, be applying a saving balm to your own outraged hearts and consciences, and your children — yourselves   in   fact — freed from the accursed stain of slavery, will become respectable, useful, and honorable members of society."

He then taunts and defies the slaveholders in this manner: "And now, sirs, we have thus laid down our ultimatum. What are you going to do about it? Something dreadful of course! Perhaps you will dissolve the Union again. Do it, if you dare! Our motto, and we would have you to understand it, is, *'The abolition of slavery and the perpetuation of the American Union.'* If, by any means, you do succeed in your treasonable attempts to take the South out of the Union to-day, we will bring her back to-morrow; if she goes away with you, she will return without you.

"Do not mistake the meaning of the last clause of the last sentence. We could elucidate it so thoroughly that no intelligent person could fail to comprehend it; but, for reasons which may hereafter appear, we forego the task.

"Henceforth there are other interests to be consulted in the South, aside from the interests of negroes and slaveholders. A profound sense of duty incites us to make the greatest possible efforts for the abolition of slavery; an equally profound sense of duty calls for a continuation of those efforts until the very last foe to freedom shall have been utterly vanquished. To the summons of the righteous monitor within, we shall endeavor to prove faithful; no opportunity for inflicting a mortal wound in the side of slavery shall be permitted to pass us unimproved.

"Thus, terror engenderers of the South, have we fully and frankly defined our position; we have no modifications to propose, no compromises to offer, nothing to retract. Frown, sirs, fret, foam, prepare your weapons, threat, strike, shoot, stab, bring on civil war, dissolve the Union, nay, annihilate the solar system if you will — do all this, more, less, better, worse, any thing — do what you will, sirs, you can neither foil nor intimidate us; our purpose is as firmly fixed as the eternal pillars of heaven; we have determined to abolish slavery, and so help us God, abolish it we will! Take this to bed with you to-night, sirs, and think about it, dream over it, and let us know how you feel to-morrow morning."

Such are specimens from the book indorsed and commended by the acknowledged leader of the Republican party, after having read it "with great attention," and by sixty-eight prominent Republican members of Congress! In the midst of the excitement produced by this book, both North and South, occurred the raid of John Brown into Virginia. This was undertaken for the avowed purpose of producing a servile insurrection among the slaves, and aiding them by military force in rising against their masters.

John Brown was a man violent, lawless, and fanatical. Amid the troubles in Kansas he had distinguished himself, both by word and by deed, for boldness and cruelty. His ruling passion was to become the instrument of abolishing slavery, by the strong hand, throughout the slaveholding States. With him, this amounted almost to insanity. Notwithstanding all this, he was so secret in his purposes that he had scarcely any confidants. This appears in a striking manner from the testimony taken before the Senate Committee. Several abolitionists had contributed money to him in aid of the anti-slavery cause generally, but he had not communicated to them for what particular purpose this was to be employed. He had long meditated an irruption into Virginia, to excite and to aid a rising of the slaves against their masters, and for this he had prepared. He had purchased two hundred Sharp's carbines, two hundred revolver pistols, and about one thousand pikes, with which to arm the slaves. These arms he had collected and deposited in the vicinity of Harper's Ferry. When the plot was ripe for execution, a little before midnight on Sunday evening, the 16th of October, 1859, he, with sixteen white and five negro confederates, rushed across the Potomac to Harper's Ferry, and there seized the armory, arsenal, and rifle factory belonging to the United States. When the inhabitants awoke in the morning they found, greatly to their terror and surprise, that these places, with the town itself, were all in possession of John Brown's force. It would be a waste of time to detail the history of this raid. Suffice it to say that on Tuesday morning, 18th, the whole band, with the exception of two who had escaped, were either killed or captured. Among the latter was John Brown himself, badly wounded. In the mean time, however, his party had murdered five individuals, four of them unarmed citizens, and had wounded nine others. It is proper to observe that John Brown, after all his efforts, received no support from the slaves in the neighborhood. The news of this attack on Harper's Ferry spread rapidly over the country. All were at first ignorant of the strength of the force, and public rumor had greatly exaggerated it. The President immediately sent a detachment of marines to the spot, by which John

Brown and his party were captured in the engine house, where they had fled for shelter and defence. Large numbers of volunteers from Virginia and Maryland had also hastened to the scene of action. John Brown and several of his party were afterwards tried before the appropriate judicial authorities of Virginia, and were convicted and executed.

In the already excited condition of public feeling throughout the South, this raid of John Brown made a deeper impression on the southern mind against the Union than all former events. Considered merely as the isolated act of a desperate fanatic, it would have had no lasting effect. It was the enthusiastic and permanent approbation of the object of his expedition by the abolitionists of the North, which spread alarm and apprehension throughout the South. We are told by Fowler in his "Sectional Controversy," that on the day of Brown's execution bells were tolled in many places, cannon fired, and prayers offered up for him as if he were a martyr; he was placed in the same category with Paul and Silas, for whom prayers were made by the Church, and churches were draped in mourning. Nor were these honors to his memory a mere transient burst of feeling. The Republican party have ever since honored him as a saint or a martyr in a cause which they deemed so holy. According to them, "whilst his body moulders in the dust his spirit is still marching on" in the van to accomplish his bloody purposes. Even blasphemy, which it would be improper to repeat, has been employed to consecrate his memory.

Fanaticism never stops to reason. Driven by honest impulse, it rushes on to its object without regard to interposing obstacles. Acting on the principle avowed in the Declaration of Independence, "that all men are created equal," and believing slavery to be sinful, it would not hesitate to pass from its own State into other States, and to emancipate their slaves by force of arms. We do not stop to inquire whether slavery is sinful. We may observe, however, that under the old and new dispensations, slaves were held both by Jews and Christians, and rules were prescribed for their humane treatment. In the present state of civilization, we are free to admit that slavery is a great political and social evil. If left to the wise ordinances of a superintending Providence, which never acts rashly, it would have been gradually extinguished in our country, peacefully and without bloodshed, as has already been done throughout nearly the whole of Christendom. It is true that other countries enjoyed facilities for emancipation which we do not possess. In them the slaves were of the same color and race with the rest of the community, and in becoming freemen they soon mingled with the general mass on equal terms with their former masters.

But even admitting slavery to be a sin, have the adherents of John Brown never reflected that the attempt by one people to pass beyond their own jurisdiction, and to extirpate by force of arms whatever they may deem sinful among another people, would involve the nations of the earth in perpetual hostilities? We Christians are thoroughly convinced that Mahomet was a false prophet; shall we, therefore, make war upon the Turkish empire to destroy Islamism? If we would preserve the peace of the world and avoid much greater evils than we desire to destroy, we must act upon the wise principles of international law, and leave each people to decide domestic questions for themselves. Their sins are not our sins. We must intrust their punishment and reformation to their own authorities, and to the Supreme Governor of nations. This spirit of interference with what we may choose to consider the domestic evils of other nations, has in former periods covered the earth with blood. Even since the advent of Christianity, until a comparatively late period, Catholics and Protestants, acting on this false principle, have, with equal sincerity, made war against each other, to put down dogmas of faith which they mutually believed to be sinful and dangerous to the soul's salvation, and this in the name of Him who descended from heaven to establish a kingdom of peace and charity on earth. Spain waged a reckless war against the poor Indians of Mexico, to root out the sin of idolatry from their midst and compel them to embrace the Christian faith; and whoever shall read the life of Cortes must admit that he acted with perfect sincerity, and was intent on their souls' salvation. Mahometans, believing Christianity to be sinful, have, in a similar spirit, made war on Christian nations to propagate their own faith.

We might fill volumes with like examples from history. These days of darkness and delusion, of doing evil that good might come, have, it is to be hoped, passed away for ever under the pure light of the Gospel. If all these acts were great wrongs in the intercourse between independent nations, if they violated the benign principles of Christianity, how much greater would the wrong have been had one portion of the sovereign States of a confederate union made war against the remainder to extirpate from them the sin of slavery! And this more especially when their common constitution, in its very terms, recognizes slavery, restores the runaway slave to his master, and even makes the institution a basis for the exercise of the elective franchise. With like reason might the State of Maine, whilst the delusion of the Maine liquor law prevailed, have made war on her sister States to enforce its observance upon their people, because drunkenness is a grievous sin in the belief of all Christians. In justification of this, she might have alleged that the intemperance tolerated among her neighbors, and not her own spirit to intermeddle with their concerns, was the cause of the war, just as it has been asserted that slavery in the Southern States was the cause of the late war. We may believe and indeed know that the people of the North, however much they may have extolled the conduct of John Brown, would never in practice have carried out his teachings and his example; but justice requires that we should make a fair allowance for the apprehensions of the Southern people, who necessarily viewed the whole scene from an opposite standpoint. Under these circumstances it is no wonder that the South should have entertained fearful apprehensions for their peace and safety, in the event that the Abolition party should succeed in obtaining the reins of the government, an event soon thereafter rendered morally certain by the breaking up of the Charleston Democratic Convention. . . .

An entire new generation had now come upon the stage in the South, in the midst of the anti-slavery agitation. The former generation, which had enjoyed the blessings of peace and security under the Constitution and the Union, had passed away. That now existing had grown up and been educated amid assaults upon their rights, and attacks from the North upon the domestic institution inherited from their fathers. Their post-offices had been perverted for the circulation of incendiary pictures and publications intended to excite the slaves to servile insurrection. In the North, the press, State Legislatures, anti-slavery societies, abolition lecturers, and above all the Christian pulpit, had been persistently employed in denouncing slavery as a sin, and rendering slaveholders odious. Numerous abolition petitions had been presented to Congress, from session to session, portraying slavery as a grievous sin against God and man. The Fugitive Slave Law enacted by the first Congress, as well as that of 1850, for the security of their property, had been nullified by the Personal Liberty Acts of Northern Legislatures, and by the organized assistance afforded by abolitionists for the escape of their slaves. Wilmot provisos had been interposed to defeat their constitutional rights in the common Territories, and even after these rights had been affirmed by the Supreme Court, its decision had been set at naught not only by the Republican but by the Douglas party. "The irrepressible conflict" of Senator Seward, and the Helper book, both portending the abolition of slavery in the States, had been circulated broadcast among the people. And finally the desperate fanatic, John Brown, inflamed by these teachings, had invaded Virginia, and murdered a number of her peaceful citizens, for the avowed purpose of exciting a servile insurrection; and although he had expiated his crimes on the gallows, his memory was consecrated by the abolitionists, as though he had been a saintly martyr.

In the midst of these perils the South had looked with hope to the action of the Democratic National Convention at Charleston, but in this they had been sadly disappointed. This series of events had inflamed the Southern mind with intense hostility against the North, and enabled the disunion agitators to prepare it for the final catastrophe. . . .

Alexander H. *Stephens*: THE WAR FOR STATES RIGHTS

Alexander H. Stephens, vice-president of the Confederate States, had been a reluctant secessionist in Georgia in the critical winter of 1860–61. During the Civil War, he was often bitterly critical of the centralization of power in the Davis administration and openly sympathized with Georgia's defiance of Confederate authorities. As one who had been a vigorous decentralist in his career in the Union and in the Confederacy, Stephens saw the war primarily as a struggle between decentralizing and centralizing principles of government. The selection is taken from Alexander H. Stephens, A Constitutional View of the War Between the States.

IT IS a postulate, with many writers of this day, that the late War was the result of two opposing ideas, or principles, upon the subject of African Slavery. Between these, according to their theory, sprung the "irrepressible conflict," in principle, which ended in the terrible conflict of arms. Those who assume this postulate, and so theorize upon it, are but superficial observers.

From Alexander H. Stephens, *A Constitutional View of the War Between the States* (Philadelphia, 1868), Vol. I, pp. 9–12.

That the War had its origin in *opposing principles,* which, in their action upon the *conduct of men,* produced the ultimate collision of arms, may be assumed as an unquestionable fact. But the opposing principles which produced these results in physical action were of a very different character from those assumed in the postulate. They lay in the organic Structure of the Government of the States. The conflict in principle arose from different and opposing ideas as to the nature of what is known as the General Government. The contest was between those who held it to be strictly Federal in its character, and those who maintained that it was thoroughly National. It was a strife between the principles of Federation, on the one side, and Centralism, or Consolidation, on the other.

Slavery, so called, was but *the question* on which these antagonistic principles, which had been in conflict, from the beginning, on divers *other questions,* were finally brought into actual and active collision with each other on the field of battle.

Some of the strongest Anti-slavery men who ever lived were on the side of those who opposed the Centralizing principles which led to the War. Mr. Jefferson was a striking illustration of this, and a prominent example of a very large class of both sections of the country, who were, most unfortunately, brought into hostile array against each other. No more earnest or ardent devotee to the emancipation of the Black race, upon humane, rational and Constitutional principles, ever lived than he was. Not even Wilberforce himself was more devoted to that cause than Mr. Jefferson was. And yet Mr. Jefferson, though in private life at the time, is well known to have been utterly opposed to the Centralizing principle, when *first* presented, on *this question,* in the attempt to impose conditions and restrictions on the State of Missouri, when she applied for admission into the Union, under the Constitution. He looked upon the movement as a political manœuvre to bring this delicate subject (and one that lay so near his heart) into the Federal Councils, with a view, by its agitation in a forum where it did not properly belong, to strengthen the Centralists in their efforts to revive their doctrines, which had been so signally defeated on so many other questions. The first sound of their movements on this question fell upon his ear as a "fire bell at night." The same is true of many others. Several of the ablest opponents of that State Restriction, in Congress, were equally well known to be as decidedly in favor of emancipation as Mr. Jefferson was. Amongst these, may be named Mr. Pinckney and Mr. Clay, from the South, to say nothing of those men from the North, who opposed that measure with equal firmness and integrity.

It is the fashion of many writers of the day to class all who opposed the Consolidationists in *this,* their *first* step, as well as all who opposed them in all their subsequent steps, on *this question,* with what they style the Pro-Slavery Party. No greater injustice could be done any public men, and no greater violence be done to the truth of History, than such a classification. Their opposition to that measure, or kindred subsequent ones, sprung from no attachment to Slavery; but, as Jefferson's, Pinckney's and Clay's, from their strong convictions that the Federal Government had no rightful or Constitutional control or jurisdiction over such questions; and that no such action, as that proposed upon them, could be taken by Congress without destroying the elementary and vital principles upon which the Government was founded.

By their acts, they did not identify themselves with the Pro-Slavery Party (for, in truth, no such Party had, at that time, or at any time in the History of the Country, any organized existence). They only identified themselves, or took position, with those who maintained the Federative character of the General Government.

In 1850, for instance, what greater injustice could be done any one, or what greater violence could be done the truth of History, than to charge Cass, Douglas, Clay, Webster and Fillmore, to say nothing of others, with being advocates of Slavery, or following in the lead of the Pro-Slavery Party, because of their support of what were called the adjustment measures of that year?

Or later still, out of the million and a half, and more, of the votes cast, in the Northern States, in 1860, against Mr. Lincoln, how many, could it, with truth, be said, were in favor of Slavery, or even that legal subordination of the Black race to the White, which existed in the Southern States?

Perhaps, not one in ten thousand! It was a subject, with which, they were thoroughly convinced, they had nothing to do, and could have nothing to do, under the terms of the Union, by which the States were Confederated, except to carry out, and faithfully perform, all the obligations of the Constitutional Compact, in regard to it.

They simply arrayed themselves against that Party which had virtually hoisted the banner of Consolidation. The contest, so commenced, which ended in the War, was, indeed, a contest between opposing principles; but not such as bore upon the policy or impolicy of African Subordination. They were principles deeply underlying all considerations of that sort. They involved the very nature and organic Structure of the Government itself. The conflict, on *this question* of Slavery, in the Federal Councils, from the beginning, was not a contest between the advocates or opponents of that peculiar Institution, but a contest, as stated before, between the supporters of a strictly Federative Government, on the one side, and a thoroughly National one, on the other.

It is the object of this work to treat of these opposing principles, not only in their bearings upon the *minor question* of Slavery, as it existed in the Southern States, and on which they were brought into active collision with each other, but upon others (now that this element of discord is removed) of far more transcendant importance, looking to the great future, and the preservation of that Constitutional Liberty which is the birthright of every American, as well as the solemnly-guaranteed right of all who may here, in this new world, seek an asylum from the oppressions of the old. . . .

Henry Wilson: THE SLAVE POWER CONSPIRACY

Henry Wilson, like the typical hero in the nineteenth-century American success story, had risen from farm laborer to Vice-President. Active in politics in the 1840's, he had won a reputation as a champion of New England workingmen and an opponent of slavery. During the war he was chairman of the Senate committee on military affairs and repeatedly pressed President Lincoln to emancipate the slaves as a war measure. Like most radical Republicans, Henry Wilson believed that the bloody tragedy had been caused primarily by a conspiracy of Southern slaveholders who had dragooned the South into secession. The selection is taken from Henry Wilson, The History of the Rise and Fall of Slavepower in America.

NO intelligent and adequate estimate of the Rebellion and its causes, immediate and remote, can be formed without special note of the small proportion of the people of the South who were at the outset in favor of that extreme measure. Even in the six States which first seceded, South Carolina possibly excepted, there was far from a majority who originally gave it their approval. In the remaining five the proportion was much smaller; though this large preponderance was overcome by able, adroit, and audacious management. By means illegitimate and indefensible, reckless of principle and of consequences, a comparatively few men succeeded in dragooning whole States into the support of a policy the majority condemned, to following leaders the majority distrusted and most cordially disliked. As no sadder and more suggestive commentary was ever afforded of the utter demoralization of slaveholding society, and of the helpless condition of a community that accepted slavery, and accommodated itself to the only conditions on which it could be maintained, it seems needful, to an intelligent apprehension of the subject, though it will be necessary to anticipate

events somewhat, that notice should be taken here of the process by which this was done.

How, then, could such an object be accomplished? How could such a result be secured? How came it to pass that this comparatively small number could persuade whole States to support a policy that not only was, but was seen to be, suicidal? How could a class of men who despised the colored man because he was colored, and the poor whites because they were poor, inspire the latter with a willingness, an enthusiasm even, to take up arms, subject themselves to all the hardships and hazards of war, for the express purpose of perpetuating and making more despotic a system that had already despoiled them of so much, and was designed to make still more abject their degradation? A summary and substantial answer might be that it was by the adoption of the same principles and of the same policy by which the Slave Power had dominated and so completely controlled the nation for the preceding two generations; only aggravated and made more intolerant in the immediate communities where slavery was domiciled and had become the controlling

From Henry Wilson, *The History of the Rise and Fall of Slavepower in America* (Boston, 1877), pp. 127–138.

social as well as political element. But there was an individuality and a specific character about this last and dying effort of slaveholding control that may justify and call for a more detailed account, even though it require the reproduction of some facts and features thereof of which mention has been already made. Nor does it seem amiss, in this connection, to introduce the words of another, — a foreigner, who thus records the impressions of one who made his observations uninfluenced at least by Northern prejudices and prepossessions.

The first item or element in the answer now sought must be looked for in the mental and moral condition of Southern society. Alluding to this point in his recent History of the Civil War in America, the Comte de Paris, says: "Notwithstanding all that has been said on the subject [slavery], our people, who fortunately have not had to wrestle with it, are not aware how much this subtle poison instils itself into the sore" which "the enlightenment and patriotism of their successors" would "heal" to the opinion that regarded "the social system founded upon slavery as the highest state of perfection that modern civilization had reached," he thus sets forth his estimate of Southern society as it existed at the opening of the Rebellion: "In proportion as slavery thus increased in prosperity and power, its influence became more and more preponderant in the community which had adopted it. Like a parasitical plant, which, drawing to itself all the sap of the most vigorous tree, covers it gradually with a foreign verdure and poisonous fruits, so slavery was impairing the morals of the South, and the spirit of her institutions. The form of liberty existed, the press seemed to be free, the deliberations of legislative bodies were tumultuous, and every man boasted of his independence. But the spirit of true liberty, tolerance towards the minority and respect for individual opinion, had departed, and those deceitful appearances concealed the despotism of an inexorable master, slavery, — a master before whom the most powerful of slaveholders was himself but a slave, as abject as the meanest of his laborers.

"No one had a right to question its legitimacy, and like the *Eumenides*, which the ancients feared to offend by naming them, so wherever the Slave Power was in the ascendant, people did not even dare to mention its name, for fear of touching upon too dangerous a subject. It was on this condition only that such an institution could maintain itself in a prosperous and intelligent community. It would have perished on the very day when the people should be at liberty to discuss it.

"Therefore, notwithstanding their boasted love of freedom, the people of the South did not hesitate to commit any violence in order to crush out, in its incipiency, any attempt to discuss the subject. Any one who had ventured to cast the slightest reflection upon the slavery system could not have continued to live in the South; it was sufficient to point the finger at any stranger and call him an Abolitionist, to consign him at once to the fury of the populace."

Dwelling at some length upon the plantation system and "the inconveniences felt in a region of country yet half wild," with a mention of some of the incidents and contingencies attending the working of "their large domains" by servile labor, he noted the division of Southern society into three classes, "at the foot of the ladder the negro bowed down upon the soil he had to cultivate; . . . . at the top the masters, in the midst of an entirely servile population, more intelligent than educated, brave but irascible, proud but overbearing, eloquent but intolerant, devoting themselves to public affairs — the exclusive direction of which belonged to them — with all the ardor of their temperament.

"The third class — that of common whites, the most important on account of its numbers — occupied a position below the second, and far above the first, without, however, forming an intermediate link between them, for it was deeply imbued with all the prejudices of color. This was the *plebs romana*, the crowds of clients who parade with ostentation the title of citizen, and only exercise its privileges in blind subserviency to the great slaveholders, who were the real masters of the country. If slavery had not existed in their midst, they would have been workers and tillers of the soil, and might have become farmers and small proprietors. But the more their poverty draws them nearer to the inferior class of slaves, the more anxious are they to keep apart from them, and they spurn work in order to set off more ostentatiously their quality of freemen. This unclassified population, wretched and restless, supplied Southern policy with the fighting vanguard which preceded the planter's invasion of the West with his slaves. At the beginning of the war the North believed that this class would join her in condemnation of the servile institution, whose ruinous competition it ought to have detested. But the North was mistaken in thinking that reason would overcome its prejudices. It showed, on the contrary, that it was ardently devoted to the maintenance of slavery. Its pride was even more at stake than that of the great slaveholders; for while the latter were always sure of remaining in a position far above the freed negroes, the former feared lest their

emancipation should disgrace the middle white classes by raising the blacks to their level."

Without the adduction of other particulars, or the recognition of other elements, these make the improbability of the results now under consideration seem less than they would otherwise appear. For certainly it is sufficiently obvious that a society made up of such materials could not but present an inviting field for the machinations of the shrewd, unscrupulous, and designing. With ignorance so profound, with prejudices so unreasoning, and with passions so inflammable, it was not difficult to hoodwink and commit such people to purposes and plans not only dangerous to others but destructive to themselves. But there were other causes. There were auxiliaries that gave greatly increased potency to those elements of mischief. There were combination and careful and long-considered preparation. Indeed, division of labor and assignment of parts have seldom been more carefully attended to. "Each man," says the Comte, "had his part laid out. Some, delegated by their own States, constantly visited the neighboring States in order to secure that unanimity to the movement which was to constitute its strength; others were endeavoring to win over the powerful border States, such as Virginia, Kentucky, Missouri, as well as North Carolina and Tennessee, which stood aghast, terrified at the approach of the crisis brought on by their associates; some, again, were even pleading their cause in the North, in the hope of recruiting partisans among those Democrats whom they had forsaken at the last election; while others kept their seats in Congress in order to be able to paralyze its action; forming, at the same time, a centre whence they issued directions to their friends in the South to complete the dismemberment of the Republic. Jefferson Davis himself continued to take part in the deliberations of the Senate."

Corroborative of the above, and at the same time indicative of the actual method adopted by the conspirators, is the following letter which appeared in the "National Intelligencer," at Washington on the morning of January 11, 1861. It is introduced by the editor, with the remark that it was from "a distinguished citizen of the South who formerly represented his State with great distinction in the popular branch of Congress." It has since transpired that the writer was the Hon. L. D. Evans of Texas, formerly a member of the XXXIVth Congress, and subsequently a judge of the Supreme Court of his adopted State. A native of Tennessee and long resident in Texas, he ever remained true to the Union, and not only advised but encouraged and supported Governor Houston to resist the clamors of the revolutionists in their demands for an extra session of the legislature. Though overborne in this and compelled to leave the State, he rendered essential service to the Union cause and the administration of Mr. Lincoln. He writes: —

"I charge that on last Saturday night a caucus was held in this city by the Southern secession Senators from Florida, Georgia, Alabama, Mississippi, Louisiana, Arkansas, and Texas. It was then and there resolved in effect to assume to themselves the political power of the South and the control of all political and military operations for the present. They telegraphed to complete the plan of seizing forts, arsenals, and customhouses, and advised the conventions now in session, and soon to assemble, to pass ordinances for immediate secession; but, in order to thwart any operations of the government here, the conventions of

the seceding States are to retain their representatives in the Senate and the House.

"They also advised, ordered, or directed the assembling of a convention of delegates from the seceding States at Montgomery on the 4th of February. This can of course only be done by the revolutionary conventions usurping the powers of the people, and sending delegates over whom they will lose all control in the establishment of a provisional government, which is the plan of the dictators.

"This caucus also resolved to take the most effectual means to dragoon the legislatures of Tennessee, Kentucky, Mississippi, Arkansas, Texas, and Virginia into following the seceding States.

"Maryland is also to be influenced by such appeals to popular passion as have led to the revolutionary steps which promise a conflict with the State and Federal governments in Texas. They have possessed themselves of all the avenues of information in the South, — the telegraph, the press, and the general control of the postmasters. They also confidently rely upon defections in the army and navy.

"The spectacle here presented is startling to contemplate. Senators intrusted with the representative sovereignty of the States, and sworn to support the Constitution of the United States, while yet acting as the privy counsellors of the President, and anxiously looked to by their constituents to effect some practical plan of adjustment, deliberately conceive a conspiracy for the overthrow of the government through the military organizations, the dangerous secret order, the Knights of the Golden Circle, 'Committees of Safety,' Southern leagues, and other agencies at their command; they have instituted as thorough a military and civil despotism as ever cursed a maddened country.

"It is not difficult to foresee the form of government which a convention thus hurriedly thrown together at Montgomery will irrevocably fasten upon a deluded and unsuspecting people. It must essentially be 'a monarchy founded upon military principles' or it cannot endure. Those who usurp power never fail to forge strong chains. It may be too late to sound the alarm. Nothing may be able to arrest the action of revolutionary tribunals whose decrees are principally in 'secret sessions.' But I call upon the people to pause and reflect before they are forced to surrender every principle of liberty, or to fight those who are becoming their masters rather than their servants."

Abundant corroboration of these statements has since been found, revealing the fact of such a meeting and its action. Among the proofs is a letter, written by Senator Yulee, one of the conspirators, and found in Florida after the capture of Fernandina, giving an account of the meeting and its purposes, among which, as he expresses it, was the thought, that by retaining their seats in Congress, "we can keep the hands of Mr. Buchanan tied, and disable the Republicans from effecting any legislation which will strengthen the hands of the incoming administration."

The next morning Mr. Wilson met Mr. Evans, and, surmising him to have been the writer of the communication, inquired whether or not his surmise was correct. Receiving an affirmative answer, with the remark that the members of that secret conclave should be arrested, Mr. Wilson replied that they deserved expulsion and punishment for their treason, but he felt constrained to add,

"There are too many of them, and to expel them will be to precipitate the revolution"; so perilous did he deem the situation, so really weak was the government, and so illy prepared to cope with its traitorous foes, and repel the dangers that threatened and surrounded it. Even such high-handed treason could be enacted with impunity, and that within the sacred precincts of the capitol.

Subsidiary to and a most important part of this preparation was the enrolment of volunteers. The chronic fear of slave-insurrections had always invested with importance the local militia of the South, which similar organizations at the North had never possessed. Under the guise, therefore, of being prepared to maintain Southern rights and protect Southern interests against all possible contingencies, agents, who were in the secret and who were carrying out purposes of the conspirators, were active in inviting and securing such volunteer enlistments. The Comte de Paris thus refers to this branch of the work of preparation that had been quietly going forward. "The volunteers," he said, "repaired to the recruiting-offices which had been opened by the initiative action of the most zealous and ambitious persons in every district. The formation of regiments which were thus spontaneously called into existence throughout the Southern States was generally the private work of a few individuals, associated together for that purpose in their respective villages or quarters. Consequently, while the North was sincerely trying to effect some kind of political compromise, companies of volunteers were seen assembling and arming in haste throughout the whole of the slave States. Their minds were bent upon war, and they went to work with the greatest energy.

The zeal of the women stimulated that of the men, and in that population, essentially indolent, whoever hesitated to don the uniform was set down as a coward."

But more effective than any other agency, and more successful in crushing out the Unionism of the slaveholding States were the violence and a system of terrorism which filled that whole land with the tortures of soul as well as those of the body, crushed out everything like freedom of action, of speech, or of thought, and made the words "the sunny South" but the mockery of a name.

This is the testimony of the Comte: "A few exceptions and a considerable number of forced enlistments sufficed to crush out every expression of Union sentiments. Vigilance committees were formed in all the Southern States; and if they did not everywhere proceed to the extremes of violence, they everywhere trampled under foot all public and individual liberties, by resorting to search-warrants and other vexatious proceedings, which, by intimidating the weak and stimulating the irresolute, contributed to fill up the *cadres* of the volunteer regiments rapidly.

"In each of the growing centres of civilization, where farmers came from afar across the forests to attend to their political and commercial affairs, vigilance committees were formed, composed of men who had been conspicuous for their excesses during the electoral struggles. Assuming unlimited power without authority, they united in themselves the attributes of a committee of public safety with the functions of a revolutionary tribunal. The bar-room was generally the place of their meetings, and a revolting parody of the august forms of justice was mingled with their noisy orgies. Around the counter on which gin and whiskey

circulated freely, a few frantic individuals pronounced judgment upon their fellow-citizens, whether present or absent; the accused saw the fatal rope being made ready even before he had been interrogated; the person in contumacy was only informed of his sentence when he fell by the bullet of the executioner, stationed behind a bush for that purpose." Nor was this kind of preparation confined to these classes. Judge Paschal of Texas, visiting the military school at Lexington, Virginia, about the middle of January, 1861, wrote to a friend in Washington that, from conversation with the young men gathered there from the several Southern States, he had become convinced that "the South was virtually in arms and in motion northward," their objective point being the seizure of the national capital, and that General McCulloch was relied on to lead them in the threatened onset. A week later than the date of his letter to the "National Intelligencer," Judge Evans addressed another to Secretary Stanton. From "reliable information" he informed him that there were in process of formation "military associations" throughout the South; that "within the last two weeks they have reached the magnitude and solidity of an army ready and willing to move at any moment and to any point"; that "wild enthusiasm which now animates them supplies the place of a regular organization, and facilitates the greatest rapidity of communication"; that "the movement comprises almost the entire youth of the South, all the restless and ambitious spirits, and all the ever floating population." After describing the general expectation that the government was on the verge of overthrow, that Congress would be broken up before the 15th of February, and that Lincoln would not be inaugurated, he added: "How far this idea has taken form I cannot say, but certain it is that among the members of the associations the belief is universal that such an expedition is intended."

Such substantially was the state of Southern society, and such were the conditions of success, when the secession leaders resolved to make their appeal to the people to come to their support in their great and guilty treason. Though they hoped that every slaveholding State would respond to that appeal and flock to their standard, they knew that some might fail. Accordingly they resolved that such failure should be the result of no hesitation on their part to appeal to any motives or resort to any measures, however desperate or indefensible. That they did fail in some and succeed in others was due to circumstances and contingencies, agents and agencies, beyond all human prescience and control, as also to that higher agency of Him who was without doubt no less active in preventing some States from joining the Rebellion than He was, as the nation with few exceptions gratefully admitted, in preventing those that did join from accomplishing their fell purposes of dismemberment and destruction. Enough yielded to effect the great purposes of the war, but not enough to destroy the nation. . . .

John W. Draper: THE CONFLICT ARISES FROM NATURAL CAUSES

John W. Draper was a well-known Northern writer on scientific topics and a trained scientist who had conducted investigations in the fields of chemistry, photography, and telegraphy. His scientific interests had a strong philosophical orientation which led him to study the history of the intellectual development of Western civilization. Although Draper shared many Northern prejudices about the superiority of Northern society and the existence of a conspiracy against the Republic by Southern leaders, his history of the Civil War demonstrates that it was possible, even in a period of highly charged emotions, for a historian to search for more objective causal explanations. Draper explained the war ultimately in terms of natural forces of climate and geography which differentiated the American people into two "distinct national types." The selection is taken from John William Draper, History of the American Civil War.

I PURPOSE in these volumes to treat of the Origin and History of the Civil War which has so lately distracted and desolated the American nation; to seek out the causes that occasioned it, and consider in what manner they acted; to show how division and antagonism have arisen among a people once thought to be homogeneous; and to present a narrative of enthusiastic exertion and defeat on one side, of invincible perseverance and victory on the other. I shall have to describe military operations eclipsing in magnitude and splendor those of the French empire; a revolution in the art of war through the introduction of the

From John William Draper, *History of the American Civil War*, Vol. I, pp. 17–30.

steam-engine, the locomotive, the electric telegraph, rifled ordnance, iron-clad ships, and other inventions of this scientific age, sustained by the development and use of financial resources on a scale that has no parallel in the history of the world. I shall have to relate how from the midst of a free people armies emerged, which, in spite of appalling disasters and losses, were maintained for years at a million of men, how sanitary commissions and private benevolence supported and, indeed, excelled the providence of the government, depriving the battle-field and hospital of half their terrors. Inadequately as I may relate the story, no imperfection of mine can ever conceal the great result, recognized with transport by true men all over the world, that a republic, resting on free institutions and universal education can maintain itself undismayed in the shock of war, and calm in the hour of triumph. Not without the conscious pride of patriotism I shall have to tell, that the conquering soldiers of Gettysburg and Richmond, recalling the example of their ancestors the conquerors of Yorktown, went back when their work was done to the farm, the workshop, or to trade; that an assaulted but victorious government disdained the cruel retributions of the scaffold, and acted with security on the principle that the causes of political crimes must be remedied, but the crimes themselves not avenged. The narrative of this great civil war abounds in lessons that will be of use to the descendants of those who participated in its sufferings and glory.

Of us it may be said, as Pericles said of his Athenian countrymen, that we are the only people of our times who have been found to be greater by experience than by report. If we have suddenly become a portent in the eyes of foreign nations, and have risen to a height of glory and of power, let us not forget that it is through those who have fallen on our battle-fields — those who have made this continent a sepulchre of illustrious men.

Perhaps, however, it may be thought that the time has not yet come to deal with these events impartially — that we are too near their occurrence. In this respect the truth of history depends on two conditions, fullness of information as to the facts, and freedom from bias as to persons. But there never was a war in the course of which publicity was so freely permitted, and the interior causes of movements so completely understood. As to bias, it is a mistake to suppose that time is any remedy for it. The life of Cæsar might have been written in the reign of Augustus not less impartially than nineteen centuries subsequently.

Even if the historian of contemporary events does labor under these disadvantages to the extent commonly supposed, he is not altogether without compensating benefits. The appreciation of an eyewitness must necessarily be more vivid than that of a remote inquirer. The motives of men are better interpreted by those who have known them personally than by those who must trust to tradition. It is for these reasons that there is so much significance in the remark of Niebuhr, that of all the great acts of Grecian antiquity the Peloponnesian War was the most immortal, because it was described by Thucydides, who served in it, and kept a journal of its events.

Such reflections have led me to suppose that, if it be not intrinsically impossible to relate with truth and impartiality the momentous events that have taken place in the nation and age in which I live, I might devote my declining years to this work of useful labor. Appreciating the difficulty of the task, in view of the mass of material to be considered, the interests that have been disturbed, the passions that have been excited, the hopes that remain unsatisfied, I submit these pages to the generosity of the reader rather than to his critical judgment.

There are three acts in the drama of American national life.

1st. The development of a sentiment of Unionism, which in time gathered strength sufficient to convert a train of feeble colonies scattered along the Atlantic coast into a great and powerful nation.

2d. The separation or differentiation of that nation, chiefly through the agency of climate, into two sections, conveniently known as the North and the South, or the free and the slave powers.

3d. The conflict of those powers for supremacy.

The outline of these acts is as follows:

From a nearly homogeneous English stock, the Atlantic coast of North America received two immigrations. That which settled in the South was of persons devoted to material objects, and appreciating ease and pleasure. That which found a home in the North was more austere: its moving influence was moral and religious ideas.

In one sense these two colonial bodies were not dissimilar, since they had come from a common ancestral home. In another they showed diversity, for they were of different social grades that had been sorted and parted from each other by antecedent English civil wars.

These immigrating bodies were affected by the climate to which they had come. It happened — or perhaps it was the result of prior and purposed selection — that there was a congeniality in each

case between the temperament of the colonist and the place of his abode. The man of enjoyment found an acceptable home in the winterless fertile South; the man of reflection amid the austerities of the North.

Climate thus augmented and perpetuated the initial differences of character. It converted what had been merely different classes in England into distinct national types in America.

For a long time the colonists experienced similar exterior pressures. At first they had to maintain themselves against the Indians; then they had a common enemy in the French; still later, both felt the tyranny of the mother country. A sentiment that it would be well for such feeble communities as they were to unite for mutual protection gradually gained strength. It appeared first more than two hundred years ago (1643), among the New England colonies.

The establishment of THE UNION was the final embodiment of that sentiment.

Unionism implied a single NATION.

Though there was thus an initial race-difference between the North and the South, since they were respectively offshoots from different grades of English society, we must not give too much importance to that difference. In the scientific treatment of American history it can not be overlooked, but the antagonism arising from it was very feeble; so feeble, indeed, as scarcely to retard the progress of Unionism.

The differentiation or separation of the American people, though it had its beginning in English life and in pre-colonial times, may, without much error, be considered as having been substantially produced by the climate of this continent. The Teutonic characteristics of the Northern people were rendered more intense; the Southern people assumed those qualities which pertain to the nations of the southern border of the Mediterranean Sea.

A self-conscious democracy, animated by ideas of individualism, was the climate issue in the North; an aristocracy, produced by sentiments of personal independence and based upon human slavery, was the climate issue in the South — an aristocracy sub-tropical in its attributes, the counterpart to that which is found in the latitudes extending from the Pillars of Hercules to the banks of the Indus, imperious to its friends, ferocious to its enemies, and rapidly losing the capacity of vividly comprehending European political ideas.

Let us now observe each of these components of the Union as a power.

In a hot climate men work no more than necessity compels; they instinctively look with favor on slave labor. There had always been that disposition in the Southern states. Accidental circumstances gave it strength.

At the time of the Declaration of Independence, Virginia was the most powerful of the colonies; she occupied a central position, and had in Norfolk one of the best harbors on the Atlantic. She had a vast western territory, an imposing commerce, and in the production and export of tobacco not only a source of wealth, but, from the mercantile connections it gave her in Europe, a means of refinement. It was through this circumstance that so many of her young men were educated abroad. When the epoch of separation from the mother country had come, and the question of confederation arose, she might have asserted her colonial supremacy; she might have been the central power. Many of her ablest men subsequently thought that, in her voluntary equalization with the feeblest colonies, the spontaneous surrender of her vast domain, the self-abnegation with which she laid all her privileges on the altar of the Union, she had made a fatal mistake. In her action there was something very noble.

Tobacco, which was the source of the wealth of Virginia, was altogether produced by slaves.

The progress of the physical sciences in Europe, and many admirable inventions of industrial art, created in the course of time a demand for another product, cotton, which experience proved could be more advantageously produced in the Southern states than any where else, but produced in them only by slaves.

Hence, very soon, the whole economy of the South centred on slavery. That system gave to the master wealth, and, what was of equal importance, it gave to him personal leisure. His thoughts naturally reverted to the management of public affairs; his material prosperity and ease of circumstances led him to the pursuit of political power. In a few years the South had possession of all the departments of the Union government. It dominated in the nation.

In maintaining this supremacy, doubtless the intrinsic political power of Virginia, and the moral force arising from the acknowledged sacrifices she had made, contributed in no small degree. The first President of the United States was a Virginian, and he was re-elected. The second was from the North, perhaps a fraternal concession due to revolutionary recollections; but he was not re-elected. The third President was a Virginian, and he was re-elected. The fourth was a Virginian, and he was re-elected. The fifth was a Virginian, and he was re-elected. No small proportion of the profits of place and power poured into the South. Was there ever to be an end of this?

It will be seen on subsequent pages

that, from the first attempt at confederation, the smaller states were in mortal terror of being overwhelmed by the greater. Maryland, Rhode Island, Delaware were full of apprehension as to what Virginia might do. Their protection consisted in asserting and upholding their rights as original and equal elements in the association — sovereigns, as they designated themselves. It was plain from the beginning that this doctrine of state-rights would always be upheld by the smaller states against the greater, by the weaker against the stronger, by the stationary against the progressive, and therefore, eventually, by the South against the North.

Now from the South let us turn to the North, and observe what was transpiring there.

In a cold climate man maintains an individual combat with nature and with competing men; he is every moment forced to make good his own ground. Hence he becomes self-reliant, and is perpetually occupied in carrying out his own intentions. With his own hand he makes his own fortune. The self-working North feels itself in irrevocable antagonism to vicarious labor; it detests negro slavery.

The idealistic North — the materialistic South — there they stand in presence of one another. The former asks herself what it is that has given her companion paramount control in their common association — their Union. She sees that it is the very institution of which her conscience disapproves.

I shall relate in this volume how, during the administration of Mr. Monroe, the North, then become rich, prosperous, intelligent, and determined to end this unfair exclusion, struck a blow at the vital part — the labor system of the South: it was the Missouri struggle. I shall relate how that was in due time retaliated by a counterblow, nullification, struck by the South at the industry of the North.

Meantime climate kept up its dissevering influence. Alienation was passing into antagonism. It became evident that there would be a struggle for the mastery.

I shall relate the stages of that struggle, and the various fortunes it exhibited. A history of the civil war has all the grand features of an epic poem. It is the story of contending powers for empire — the free and the slave; it is a record of the victory of an idea.

There is a political force in ideas which silently renders protestations, promises and guarantees, no matter in what good faith they may have been given, of no avail, and which makes constitutions obsolete. Against the uncontrollable growth of the anti-slavery idea the South was forced to contend.

It is interesting to observe the history of that idea in America. The early colonists were all on an equality. Their language, their occupations, their hardships were all the same. They had the same relations with the mother country; they had endured at her hands the same wrongs; they rejoiced in the same victories, and were saddened by the same defeats; their hopes of future prosperity were in common. In their festivities they sang the same songs; in their devotions they knelt before the same God.

When, therefore, the Declaration of Independence asserted the equality of all men, it met with a willing assent. In the thin strand of country that lay along the Atlantic, the differentiation of society into orders had hardly yet begun. Among the whites there was a general equality. No castes or grades existed.

The African population at that time gave no concern. It was thought that, from uncongeniality of climate and other causes, it would die out of itself.

But when the Revolutionary War was fairly commenced, and the negro, both in the North and the South, was seen fighting by the side of his master, thoughtful men began to perceive that they were committing a wrong. In Massachusetts the Africans respectfully represented to the Honorable Council and House that they had "cheerfully entered the field of battle in defense of the common cause," and asked as a reward that their children might be free at the age of twenty-one years. The moderation with which these persons bore themselves in the matter made them many friends, and eventually and imperceptibly slavery died out in that state.

In this manner, the abstract idea of human rights, which had been promulgated and upheld by the great French writers of those times, found its practical exemplification in America.

At the formation of the Constitution it was also believed that African slavery would in like manner die in the South as it was dying in the North. Without serious opposition from any quarter, three very important points were introduced into that instrument.

The first of these was equality of state representation in the United States Senate: this, in the subsequent course of events, led to the doctrine of the balance of power between the North and the South, its inevitable result being a rivalry in territorial expansion. The second was the three-fifths slave computation in the apportionment of federal numbers, which at once tended to enhance the political value of the negro, and to exclude all other forms of labor and the use of machinery. The third was the contingent stoppage of the African trade, the emigrant supply for the North being un-

checked. The South would never have consented to this had its operation been foreseen. It was this that eventually overwhelmed her.

While things were in this position at the close of the last century, and good men all over the republic were expecting that an institution which, perhaps not altogether correctly, they affirmed had been forced upon them by the mother country, would presently pass away, a new influence destined to disappoint their hopes was coming into operation.

The physical sciences and industrial arts had been rapidly advancing in England. The steam-engine had been invented, and machinery for spinning and weaving greatly improved. An increasing demand for cotton had arisen. It was discovered that the Gulf States could supply it more advantageously than any other part of the world, but, under the circumstances of the times, it could only be secured in them by the labor of African slaves. The slave therefore brought his master gold from abroad, and gave him political power in Congress at home.

It was not wonderful, then, that the slave system struck its roots through Southern society. From the beginning it had not been unacceptable to the climate-changed people, who, little disposed to work themselves, looked upon labor as discreditable.

Warmth and cold had decomposed the American people, and ranged them in climate sections north and south. Unforeseen circumstances that were happening in Europe had given to each its special interests, and those interests were hourly becoming more and more antagonistic. In the competition that ensued there was an unlimited foreign labor supply for the one — that for the other was cut off. When the competition rose to a struggle, and the struggle became an exasperated conflict, it was not difficult to see what must be the inevitable result of this disparity.

In the contest for territory, which politically meant a contest for the balance of power in the United States Senate, the North could solidly make good her ground; as her expansion went on, she could put her voting emigrants on every acre; but the South, though she might claim territory, had not the means of filling it. Her policy spontaneously defeated itself.

In two particulars, therefore, the South was placed at a disadvantage. She was contending with a moral idea which was momentarily increasing in force — the wrongfulness of slavery. She was also contending with a momentarily increasing material force arising from the physical growth of the North.

The first clear view of the position of affairs in the republic was had, as I have already remarked, during the presidency of Mr. Monroe, by the ruined Federalists. In their meditations during an exclusion from place and power, forced upon them for twenty years by the allied Democratic and slavery influences, they had detected the weak point of their adversaries. The movement they initiated in the Missouri struggle was sure in the end, though party names might change, to be crowned with success.

The blow thus aimed against the industry of the South was retaliated by Nullification, a blow aimed against the industry of the North, and from 1833 to 1860 attacks and compromises were made. But, at the time of the election of Mr. Lincoln, it was not possible to compose the differences any more. To the slaveholders the vote that had been given in 1856 to Mr. Fremont was the sound of a death-knell. It was plain that power was slipping forever away from the hands that had hitherto held it. In their judgment, the choice lay between the destruction of slavery and the destruction of the Union.

From being the chiefs of a political party, the leaders of the South had become, by insensible degrees, conspirators against the republic. They resolved to attempt the perpetuation of slavery by separating from the North. History shows how much easier it is to deceive than to undeceive mankind; yet not without difficulty did they persuade their people to take that fatal step, assuring them that the Democracy of the North would, as heretofore, be their ally, and that secession, so far from occasioning war, would be peaceably accomplished. They knew that if that step were once taken, a military enthusiasm would arise which would justify any thing, and accordingly so it proved. The South was brought to the belief that she was right in her revolt, the conspiracy became an armed insurrection, warlike preparations of all kinds were openly carried on, forts, custom-houses, post-offices, navy yards were seized, mints were plundered, the Mississippi was blockaded, and the few who had misgivings as to what was taking place were awed into muteness.

For us who are contemporaries of this struggle, and who have witnessed the carnage, it becomes a solemn duty to raise up a voice to posterity. The conditions that brought on this conflict exist in other directions, and will in due time exert their deleterious power. Though in one sense slavery was an ephemeral incident, and abolition an ephemeral instinct of our national life, they will have future equivalents under other forms. Varied climate and opposing interests will tend to renew these contests hereafter. If this has been the issue between the North Atlantic and the Gulf States, what may not be expected from the rivalries of the dwellers in the Great Basin, those of the Pacific slope, those of the Columbian Northwest — the Germany of America? The imperial republic shortly to be made manifest has a Persia, an India, a Palestine, a Tartary of its own. To bind together so many diverse people; to co-ordinate their conflicting rights; to concentrate into one nation men who, though all of American birth, are in one place representatives of the fair European, in another of the turbaned Asiatic, in another of the dusky African, will demand a statesmanship that recognizes as its animating principle JUSTICE TO ALL. On that alone can the vast structure of the future republic solidly stand.

Contemplating such various and colossal interests, each of which must be satisfied, we can not fail to remark how transitory all constitutional forms are liable to be, except in so far as they are pervaded by that immortal principle. While we view with veneration the political work of our forefathers, it is well for us to profit by their example. Their first attempt — the Confederation — was, in their own estimation, an acknowledged failure; their second attempt — the Constitution — we have outgrown. Wherever it compromised justice for the sake of expediency, it has proved to be an insufficient guide. A great nation must recognize principle, and not form, as its rule of life; as it gathers knowledge, it must not hesitate to modify its written Constitution according to its improving light. . . .

IV. THE SEARCH FOR INSTITUTIONAL AND IDEOLOGICAL DIFFERENCES

James Ford Rhodes: SLAVERY AS A SINGLE CAUSE

James Ford Rhodes represents a new group of historians at the turn of the century whose personal experience with the Civil War consisted largely of childhood memories and who belonged to a generation which was concerned with new issues of national policy no longer so directly affected by wartime emotions. Rhodes was a successful Cleveland businessman who quit business in 1885 to devote his entire time to the study and writing of history. He brought to his historical writing many of the attitudes of upper-middle class America, including confidence in a business society, faith in progress, and moderation in judgment. Although he continued to reflect the traditional belief of his section that slavery had been the primary cause of the Civil War, he did not seek to place sectional and personal guilt exclusively upon Southerners because of slavery. He recognized that slavery was a complex institution whose growth had been influenced by powerful social and economic forces. The selection is taken from James Ford Rhodes, Lectures on the American Civil War.

GARDINER'S title "History of Our Great Civil War" has always struck me as apt. A historian so careful in his use of adjectives could not have adopted one so expressive without reflection. The English Civil War was great in itself and its consequences, and, though it may not convey as important lessons to the whole civilized world as did that one of which Thucydides was the historian, yet for its influence on American colonial life and on the development of our history to the formation of our Constitution, it is for us a more "pregnant" study. Moreover Gardiner's history of it is a model for the historian of our Civil War.

There is risk in referring any historic event to a single cause. Lecky entitled his celebrated chapter, "Causes of the French Revolution." Social and political, as well as religious, reasons, according to Gardiner, brought on the Great Civil War. Thucydides, on the other hand, though he did indeed set forth the "grounds of quarrel," stated his own belief that "the real though unavowed cause" of the war was "the growth of the Athenian power." And of the American Civil War it may safely be asserted that there was a single cause, slavery. In 1862 John Stuart Mill in *Fraser's Magazine*, and Professor Cairnes in a pamphlet on the Slave Power, presented this view to the English public with force, but it is always difficult to get to the bottom of a foreign dispute, and it is not surprising that many failed to comprehend the real nature of the conflict. When in July, 1862, William E. Forster said in the House of Commons that he believed it

James Ford Rhodes, *Lectures on the American Civil War* (New York: The Macmillan Co., 1913), pp. 1–6, 10–29, 41–66. Reprinted by permission.

was generally acknowledged that slavery was the cause of the war, he was answered with cries, "No, no!" and "The tariff!" Because the South was for free trade and the North for a protective tariff this was a natural retort, though proceeding from a misconception, as a reference to the most acute tariff crisis in our history will show.

In 1832, South Carolina, by act of her Convention legally called, declared that the tariff acts passed by Congress in 1828 and 1832 were "null, void, no law," and that no duties enjoined by those acts should be paid or permitted to be paid in the State of South Carolina. It is a significant fact that she failed to induce any of her sister Southern States to act with her. By the firmness of President Jackson and a conciliatory disposition on the part of the high tariff party the act of nullification was never put in force; but the whole course of the incident and the yielding of South Carolina demonstrated that the American Union could not be broken up by a tariff dispute. Natural causes since 1832 have modified the geographical character of the controversy. The production of sugar in Louisiana, the mining of coal and the manufacture of iron in a number of Southern States have caused their senators and representatives to listen kindly to pleas for a protective tariff.

Here is a further illustration of the unique character of the divisional or, as we should say, sectional dispute concerning slavery. Sixteen years ago, the money question, the demand for the free coinage of silver, took on a sectional character in arraying the West and the South against the East, but the advocates of the gold standard always had a hearing and a party in the States devoted to silver. But after 1850, there was no antislavery party in the South and men advocating even the gradual abolition of slavery would not have been suffered to speak. Again, in 1896, natural causes had play; they took from the dispute about the money standard its sectional character. The disappearance of the grasshoppers that ate the wheat and maize, the breaking of the severe drought of the preceding years, the extension further west of the rain belt, good crops of cotton, maize and wheat with a good demand, brought prosperity to the farmers and with it a belief that the gold standard best served their interests.

Some of our younger writers, impressed with the principle of nationality that prevailed in Europe during the last half of the nineteenth century, have read into our conflict European conditions and asserted that the South stood for disunion in her doctrine of States' rights and that the war came because the North took up the gage of battle to make of the United States a nation. I shall have occasion to show the potency of the Union sentiment as an aid to the destruction of slavery, but when events are reduced to their last elements, it plainly appears that the doctrine of States' rights and secession was invoked by the South to save slavery, and by a natural antagonism, the North upheld the Union because the fight for its preservation was the first step toward the abolition of negro servitude. The question may be isolated by the incontrovertible statement that if the negro had never been brought to America, our Civil War could not have occurred.

✳   ✳   ✳

As slavery was out of tune with the nineteenth century, the States that held fast to it played a losing game. This was evident from the greater increase of population at the North. When Washington became President (1789), the population of the two sections was nearly equal, but thirty-one years later, in a total of less than ten millions there was a difference of 667,000 in favor of the North, and when, twelve years later still, the immigration from Europe began, the preponderance of the North continued to increase. The South repelled immigrants for the reason that freemen would not work with slaves. In the House of Representatives, chosen on the basis of numerical population, the North, at each decennial census and apportionment, gained largely on the South, whose stronghold was the Senate. Each State, irrespective of population, had two senators, and since the formation of the Constitution, States had been admitted in pairs by a tacit agreement, each free State being counterbalanced by a slave State. The admission of California which would disturb this equilibrium was resisted by the South with a spirit of determination made bitter by disappointment over California's spontaneous act. The Mexican War had been for the most part a Southern war; the South, as Lowell made Hosea Biglow say, was "after bigger pens to cram with slaves," and now she saw this magnificent domain of California escaping her clutches. She had other grievances which, from the point of view of a man of 1850 reverencing the letter of the Constitution, were undoubtedly well founded, but the whole dispute really hinged on the belief of the South that slavery was right and the belief of the majority of Northerners that it was wrong.

At the time of the formation of the Constitution the two sections were not greatly at variance. A large number of Southern men, among them their ablest and best leaders, thought slavery was a moral and political evil to be got rid of gradually. In due time, the foreign slave trade was prohibited, but the Yankee invention of the cotton-gin made slavery apparently profitable in the culture of cotton on the virgin soil of the new States in the South; and Southern opinion changed. From being regarded as an evil, slavery began to be looked upon as the only possible condition of the existence of the two races side by side and by 1850 the feeling had grown to be that slavery was "no evil, no scourge, but a great religious, social and moral blessing." As modern society required hewers of wood and drawers of water, the slave system of the South, so the argument ran, was superior to the industrial system of England, France and the North.

In 1831, William Lloyd Garrison began his crusade against slavery. In a weekly journal, the *Liberator*, published in Boston, he preached with fearless emphasis that slavery was wrong and, though his immediate followers were never many, he set people to thinking about the question, so that six years later Daniel Webster, one of our greatest statesmen with a remarkable power of expression, said, the subject of slavery "has not only attracted attention as a question of politics, but it has struck a far deeper-toned chord. It has arrested the religious feeling of the country; it has taken strong hold on the consciences of men." In the nineteen years before 1850 the opinion constantly gained ground at the North that slavery was an evil and that its existence at the South was a blot on the national honor.

In 1850, there were at the South 347,000 slaveholders out of a white population of six millions, but the head and centre of the oligarchy was to be found amongst the large planters, possessors of fifty or more slaves, whose elegance, luxury and hospitality are recited in tales of travellers, over whose estates and lives the light of romance and poetry has been profusely shed; of these, there were less than eight thousand. Around them clustered the fashionable circles of the cities, composed of merchants, doctors and lawyers, a society seen to the best advantage in New Orleans, Charleston and Richmond. The men composing this oligarchy were high-spirited gentlemen, with a keen sense of honor showing itself in hatred of political corruption, resentment of personal attack by speech or by pen, to the length of the fatal duel and a reverence for and readiness to protect female virtue. Most of them were well educated and had a taste for reading; but they avoided American literature as emanating mostly from New England, the hotbed of abolitionism, and preferred the earlier English literature to that of the nineteenth century. But their ability manifested itself not at all in letters or in art but ran entirely to law and politics, in which they were really eminent. English travellers before the Civil War liked the Southerners for their aristocratic bearing and enjoyed their conversation, which was not redolent of trade and the dollar, like much that they heard at the North. It is obvious that men of this stamp could not be otherwise than irritated when Northern speeches, books and newspapers were full of the charge that they were living in the daily practice of evil, that negro chattel slavery was cruel, unjust and barbaric. This irritation expressed itself in recrimination and insolent demands at the same time that it helped to bring them to the belief that property in negroes was as right and sacred as the ownership of horses and mules.

In 1850, the South repeatedly asserted that she must have her rights or she would secede from the Union; and her action eleven years later proved that this was not an idle threat. She would submit to the admission of California provided she received certain guarantees. There resulted the Compromise of 1850, proposed by Henry Clay and supported by Daniel Webster and finally enacted by Congress. Under it California came in free. Slavery was not prohibited in New Mexico. Webster argued that such prohibition was unnecessary as the territory was not adapted to slavery. "I would not," he said, "take pains uselessly to reaffirm an ordinance of nature, nor to reënact the will of God." The South obtained a more stringent Fugitive Slave Law. Most of the negroes yearned for freedom, and, while their notions of geography were vague, they knew that freedom lay in the direction of the north star, and with that guidance a thousand escaped yearly into the free States. The rendition of fugitive slaves was a right under the Constitution, and as the South maintained that the law of 1793 was inadequate, she demanded one more stringent. In the end, a bill based on the draft of James Mason (the Mason of Mason-Slidell fame) was enacted. It ran counter to the Roman maxim that, if a question arose about the civil status of a person, he was presumed to be free until proved to be a slave, thus laying the burden of proof on the master and giving the benefit of the doubt to the weaker party. Under this Act of ours the negro had no chance: the meshes of the law were artfully contrived to aid the master and entrap the alleged slave. By an extraordinary provision, the commissioner who determined the matter received a fee of ten dollars if he adjudged the negro to slavery and one half of that amount if he held the fugitive to be a freeman. The real purpose of the law was not so much to recover the runaway negroes as it was to irritate the

North (or, in the current figure of speech, to crack the whip over the heads of Northern men) by its rigorous enforcement. To this end being admirably designed, it became one of the minor influences that brought the North to her final resolute stand against the extension of slavery.

Mason was the sort of man to think that he had done a clever thing when, in drawing an act to enforce the constitutional right of the South, he made its enforcement needlessly irritating to the North. But it proved a menace and a plague to the section it was intended to benefit. For the Fugitive Slave Law inspired Harriet Beecher Stowe to write Uncle Tom's Cabin, the greatest of American novels which, in the interest that it aroused and the influence that it exerted, has not unfitly been compared to La nouvelle Héloïse. Though the author possessed none of Rousseau's force and grace of style, her novel, and the play founded on it, could not have secured the attention of England and France unless its human element had been powerfully presented. Macaulay wrote that "on the whole, it is the most valuable addition that America has made to English literature." England and her colonies bought a million and a half copies. Two London theatres produced the play. Three daily newspapers in Paris published it as a serial and the Parisians filled two theatres nightly to laugh at Topsy and weep at the hard fate of Uncle Tom. Many other stories were written to exhibit the wrongs of the negro under chattel slavery, but they are all forgotten. Slavery, in the destruction of which Uncle Tom's Cabin had a potent influence, is gone, but the novel, published in 1852, is still read and the drama acted, telling the present generation of the great political and social

revolution wrought in their father's time.

From 1852 to 1860, the year in which Lincoln was elected President, the influence of this story on Northern thought was immense. The author had made no effort to suppress the good side of slavery, but had shown an intelligent sympathy for the well-meaning masters, who had been reared under the system; at the same time she had laid bare the injustice, cruelty and horror of the white man's ownership of the negro with a fidelity to nature that affected every reader. The election of Lincoln is a great fact in the destruction of slavery and, in gaining voters for him, Uncle Tom's Cabin was one of the effective influences. It made a strong appeal to women, and the mothers' opinion was a potent educator during these eight years; boys who had read Uncle Tom's Cabin in their early teens reached the voting age at a time when they could give slavery a hard knock.

The Compromise of 1850 was an adroit device, as compromises go, and, with the exception of the indefensible portions of the Fugitive Slave Law, was fair to both sections. It abated the antislavery agitation at the North and the threats of disunion at the South and would probably have maintained quiet between the two sections for a considerable period had not an able Democratic senator opened the question afresh in 1854.

Slavery, as a sectional issue, had first claimed the attention of Congress in 1820 in the form of a proposition to admit Missouri as a slave State. "This momentous question," wrote Jefferson from his retirement, "like a fire-bell in the night awakened and filled me with terror. I considered it at once as the knell of the Union." The result of the agitation was the Missouri Compromise. Missouri was admitted as a slave State, but her Southern boundary of 36° 30′ was henceforward taken as the line between slavery and freedom in the rest of the great territory of the Louisiana Purchase. North of that line slavery was forever prohibited.

In 1854, Stephen A. Douglas, a senator from Illinois, filled the public eye. Though he had never received any systematic education, he was a man of natural parts and had achieved a considerable success at the bar; then, finding politics more to his liking than the law, he had been able so to commend himself to his community that his political advancement was rapid and, up to a point, practically continuous. He had become one of the leaders of the Democratic party and craved the presidency; being no believer in the maxim that everything comes to him who waits, he naturally adopted the boldest methods for gratifying his restless ambition. As chairman of the Committee on Territories and leader of the Democrats in the Senate, he introduced a bill for the organization of the territories of Nebraska and Kansas, one clause in which provided for the repeal of the Missouri Compromise of 1820. Here was an open bid for Southern support in his contest for the presidency. His bill became a law and the slavery question was opened anew. For instead of being closed to slavery by formal Congressional act, these territories were now open to settlers from both North and South, the one bringing their horses and mules, and the others having the privilege of bringing their slaves as well.

The North was indignant at this violation of a solemn compact by a movement initiated by one of her own sons. As I look back upon this episode, with every disposition to be fair to Douglas and not unmindful of apologies for his conduct that conscientious historical students have made, I believe that he merits strong condemnation from history. By his act was revived a perilous dispute that was thought to have been settled. Douglas loved his country and reverenced the Constitution, but he could not see the evil of slavery; he did not appreciate that it was out of tune with his century. Not intending, at first, to go the full length of repealing the Missouri Compromise, he found that, upon opening the question, he had invoked a sentiment at the South that demanded full measure. To retreat would be cowardly, even ridiculous. He must go forward or give up his position as a leader. Therefore he demanded, in the end without evasion, the repeal of the Missouri Compromise and supported his measure by adroit but specious reasoning. He stood for the doctrine which went by the high-sounding name of popular sovereignty and meant that the people of the territories themselves should determine whether slavery should be protected or prohibited within their borders, and he accordingly carried the notion of local government to an unworkable and dangerous extreme, considering that the question involved was slavery. Give the people a chance to decide, he argued continually. "If they wish slavery, they have a right to it." "I care not whether slavery is voted down or voted up."

Of parliamentarians, in the English sense of the word, Douglas is one of the cleverest in our annals. The conduct of his measure through the Senate, where he was opposed by men of remarkable ability and where the closure does not obtain, was a master stroke of parliamentary management. With the help of the President and the zeal of Southern representatives, who were quick to see their advantage, the House adopted Douglas's measure despite the rise of indignant sentiment in the North at the betrayal of a sacred pledge. This outburst of public opinion was predicted on the day that the Senate passed the bill. On that sombre March morning of 1854, when the cannon from the navy-yard was booming out the legislative victory, Senator Chase, an earnest opponent of the bill, said to his intimate and sympathizing friend, Senator Sumner, as they walked away from the Capitol together, "They celebrate a present victory but the echoes they awake will never rest until slavery itself shall die."

Chase was right. The antislavery men, a powerful majority of the North, deemed the bill an outrage. From the press and the public platform, from the "stump," as we say, in grove or park, came emphatic condemnation of the conduct of Douglas and of the act of Congress. Douglas's unpopularity in the North was intense and widespread. It was then a common practice to burn in effigy the public man whose course was disapproved. "I could travel," said Douglas, "from Boston to Chicago by the light of my own effigies." Arriving in Chicago, his home, he gave notice that he would address his constituents, but his opponents went to the meeting and, by cries of execration, denied him a hearing.

Like Mason's Fugitive Slave Bill, Douglas's repeal of the Missouri Compromise reacted to the detriment of its author. It destroyed his chance for the presidency. It brought about the formation of the Republican party. On the 1st of January, 1854, the two chief parties in the country were the Democratic and Whig, the Democratic having the presidency and a good majority in both the Senate and the House. There was a third party, the Free-Soil, which, holding as its cardinal doctrine, opposition to slavery, sometimes held the balance of power

in closely contested Northern States, but which had only a small representation in Congress. The repeal of the Missouri Compromise roused the dormant antislavery feeling in the country and brought home to many the conviction that a new party should be formed to unite Whigs, antislavery Democrats and Free-Soilers in their resistance to the aggression of the slave power. Seward's ability and political experience seemed to mark him out for leadership, but he was a devoted Whig and, as the Northern Whigs had, to a man, opposed the repeal of the Missouri Compromise and would form the predominant element in the new partnership, he thought that all antislavery men should enlist under their banner. Westerners thought differently and, being less trammelled by political organizations than their Eastern cousins, proceeded to inaugurate the movement that was really demanded by the posture of affairs. Five weeks after the repeal of the Missouri Compromise, a large body of earnest, intelligent and reputable men, the leading citizens of the State of Michigan, came together at Jackson and, as the largest hall was inadequate for their accommodation, they met in a grove of famous oaks in the outskirts of the village. Here they resolved to suspend all differences regarding economic or administrative policy, to act cordially and faithfully in unison with all opposed to the extension of slavery and to be known as Republicans until the end of the contest. Other States followed this example.

*   *   *

For three years the national legislature and executive had endeavored to solve the slavery problem with conspicuous failure. Now the Supreme Court was to try its hand. Its Chief Justice has great power in directing the consideration of the Court to constitutional questions which may arise in any case before it. The present Chief, Taney, had been on the Bench for twenty-two years and had gained a solid reputation for accurate knowledge of law and clearness of statement. Being of broadly patriotic temper, he made up his mind that his Court could settle the slavery question, and, in a case where it was necessary only to determine whether a certain negro named Dred Scott was slave or freeman, he delivered a carefully prepared opinion in which he asserted that "the right of property in a slave is distinctly and expressly affirmed in the Constitution"; that Congress had no more power over slave property than over property of any other kind; consequently the Missouri Compromise Act "is not warranted by the Constitution and is therefore void." Five judges agreed with Taney and these made two-thirds of the Court. This decision which neutralized the Republican doctrine that Congress had the power to prohibit slavery in the territories, was a blow to those Republican leaders who were good lawyers and who reverenced the Supreme Court. It was met in the common-sense way by Abraham Lincoln, who declared that the Republicans offered no resistance to the decision, but, believing it to be erroneous, would do their best to get the Court to overrule it as it had previously overruled other decisions.

This so-called Dred Scott opinion was delivered two days after the inauguration of Buchanan, and though it did not dispose of the Kansas question, it gave a theoretical basis to slavery in the territories and furnished a strong support for the next move of the slave power.

The effort to make Kansas an actual slave territory had failed, as it had now within its borders only 200 or 300 slaves; but, as there were sixteen free to fifteen slave States, the proslavery party eagerly desired the political power of another State — its two senators and one or more representatives — to restore the equilibrium existing before 1850. A plan to this end was promptly devised. Originating probably with Southerners of high position in Washington, it found ready instruments in Kansas. A sham election resulted in a constitutional convention, which framed a Constitution establishing slavery in the most unequivocal terms and which, as it could not avoid the time-honored precedent of submitting the Constitution to a popular vote, provided for a submission of it that, in the words of the Democratic governor of the territory, was "a vile fraud, a base counterfeit and a wretched device" to prevent the people from deciding whether or not they would have slavery. For the Convention did not dare to provide for a fair election, as the proslavery advocates would have been outvoted three to one. President Buchanan, though from a Northern State, had a great admiration for Southern politicians whose persuasion and threats induced him to support his plan, which was known as the Lecompton scheme.

The proceeding was a travesty of the doctrine of popular sovereignty, and when the Senate met in December, 1857, Douglas boldly denounced it. His manner was haughty and defiant as he set himself in opposition to his party, the Democratic, which was strongly entrenched in all three branches of the government, and he did not hesitate to characterize the scheme "as a trick, a fraud upon the rights of the people." Despite Douglas's opposition, the Democratic Senate voted to admit Kansas as a State under her proslavery constitution, but to this the House, in closer contact with the people, would not agree. The excitement in Washington was intense, and, during a heated all-night session of the House, an altercation between a Southern and Northern representative resulted in a fisticuff, in which thirty men were engaged, but no weapons drawn. In the end, a compromise was agreed upon between the Senate and the House, the effect of which was to offer to Kansas a large amount of public lands if she would accept the Lecompton constitution. By a vote of 11,300 to 1800 she rejected the bribe and thus determined that slavery should not exist in Kansas. But the affair left an irreconcilable breach in the Democratic party.

We are now in the year 1858, in the spring of which year Douglas was the best-known and most popular man in the North, so effectively had he won back public esteem by his resistance to the Lecompton project. The relations between him and the Republicans in Congress were cordial and the possibility that their party should nominate him as their candidate for the presidency two years hence was considered by no means out of the question. Seward was coquetting with him but had no idea of stepping aside in his favor if the conditions were propitious for Republican success. Douglas must stand this year for reëlection as senator from Illinois and the leading Eastern Republicans, nearly every Republican senator and many representatives desired that their party should make no opposition to him. Greeley in his powerful journal warmly favored his return to the Senate; but the Republicans in Illinois, under the lead of Abraham Lincoln, protested against it.

The son of a shiftless poor white of the slave State of Kentucky, Lincoln was brought up in that State and the southern part of Indiana, moving to Illinois when he was twenty-one. The southern Indiana of that day might have suggested the Eden of Martin Chuzzlewit. Its farms and villages were rude and ill-kept; fever and ague were unrepressed; the most ordinary refinements of human existence were lacking even to what would be considered there today the actual necessaries of civilization. Lincoln said that the story of his early life was told in a single sentence of Gray's Elegy, —

"The short and simple annals of the poor."

His schooling was necessarily meagre, but he had an active mind and an extraordinary power of application. He was a thorough student of the Bible and Shakespeare and mastered the first six books of Euclid. Reading few books, he thought long and carefully on what he read, and his opinions on all subjects were generally the result of severe study and profound reflection. He studied law and at the age of twenty-eight began practice; but his interest in politics was so deep as to brook no enduring rival. He loved and believed in the common people; he amused them and interested them in himself. His early associates were American born, dwellers in village and lonely farm and the stories he told them were of the order that there prevails; if they were amusing, he cared little if they were coarse as well. A frequenter of the tavern he used neither spirits nor tobacco; his personal morals were good. He served one term in the Illinois legislature, another in the United States House of Representatives, but not belonging to the dominant party in his State, he failed to remain continuously in the public service. He reached a high rank in his profession, being esteemed the strongest jury lawyer in Illinois; but he was a bad advocate in an unjust cause. The repeal of the Missouri Compromise diverted his attention from law to politics, and a speech, in which he demolished Douglas's political and historical sophistry, made him the leader of the Republicans in his State. Lincoln was then nearly elected United States senator, but although deeply disappointed, he, with rare magnanimity and judgment, withdrew in favor of another candidate, to prevent the defeat of the cause. Intensely ambitious, he nevertheless loved truth and justice better than political place and power. At twenty-four he had been dubbed "honest Abe." At no time in his eventful life did he do anything to cast a shadow of discredit on this epithet sprung from the rude soil of Illinois.

At the age of forty-nine, Lincoln was hardly known beyond the confines of his own State or, wherever known in the East, was regarded as a "backwoods lawyer"; yet he stood forth to contest the senatorship with the most formidable debater in the country. He gave the keynote of the campaign in the most carefully prepared speech that he had ever made, addressed to the Republican State Convention, which had unanimously nominated him as the candidate of their party for senator. "A house divided against itself cannot stand," he said. "I believe this government cannot endure permanently half slave and half free. . . . Either the opponents of slavery will arrest the further spread of it and place it where the public mind shall rest in the belief that it is in the course of ultimate extinction; or its advocates will push it forward till it shall become alike lawful in all the States, old as well as new, North as well as South."

When Douglas went to Chicago to open the campaign, his town gave him an enthusiastic reception, which contrasted strikingly with his home-coming four years earlier. In his first speech he attacked with great force Lincoln's "House-divided-against-itself" doctrine, which doctrine, though soon to be demonstrated in hard and cruel fact, had in 1858 not many adherents. When submitted to a dozen of Lincoln's political friends before public pronouncement, it had received the approval of only one, and after it was uttered, there was no doubt whatever that, inasmuch as it was in advance of his party's thought, it counted against him in his contest with Douglas. Douglas's progress through his State amounted to a continuous ovation. Travelling in special trains — an unusual proceeding at the time — the trains being drawn by decorated locomotives, he was met at each city by committees of escort, and, to the thunder of cannon and the music of brass bands, was driven under triumphal arches, on which was emblazoned the legend, "Popular Sovereignty." The blare and flare of the campaign were entirely to his liking, but they were merely the theatrical accessories of a truly remarkable actor.

His short and massive frame was surmounted by an enormous head, from which shone forth eyes of a penetrating keenness; his appearance alone justified the title of "little giant" long since given him. A melodious voice and a clear incisive enunciation combined with apt and forcible gestures to point the ingenious arguments that kindled a genuine enthusiasm in the sons of Illinois, whose admiration and love he had gained.

As a boy, I saw Douglas often at the house of my father, who was his warm personal and political friend. His great head seemed out of proportion to his short body, giving one the idea of a preponderance of the intellect. But he was not a reader and I do not remember ever seeing a book in his hand. Knowing little of Europe, he had absorbed the history of his own country and used this knowledge with ready skill. His winning manner was decisive with boys and he gained a hold on young voters, which he retained until Lincoln came to appeal to their moral sense.

Lincoln realized that the current was setting against him, but he felt no regret for his action in setting forth the positive doctrine of his opening speech. Believing that his adroit and plausible opponent could be better answered from a platform shared in common, he challenged him to a series of joint debates. He showed a profound confidence in his cause when he pitted himself against the man who in senatorial debate had got the better of Seward and Sumner and more recently had discomfited the champions of the Lecompton scheme. Lincoln was tall, gaunt, awkward; his face was dark, yellow, wrinkled and dry, voice shrill and unpleasant, movements shy and odd. In oratorical power and personal magnetism he was inferior to Douglas, but when he was warmed to his subject, his face glowed with the earnestness of conviction and he spoke with excellent result.

The joint debates, in different portions of the State, were seven; they are the most celebrated in our history. Illinois, though by no means fully aware of the crucial character of this contest, was nevertheless sufficiently aroused to turn out audiences of from five to twenty thousand at these day meetings, held in groves or on the prairie. Here Lincoln by his remorseless logic brought Douglas to bay. He showed that the slavery question was at rest when Douglas disturbed it by the Repeal of the Missouri Compromise. *Why could you not leave it alone?* he asked with emphasis. The doctrine of Popular Sovereignty was "*a living creeping lie.*" Douglas, he asserted, has undertaken to "build up a system of policy upon the basis of caring nothing about *the very thing that everybody does care the most about.*" The real issue, Lincoln truly declared, is whether slavery is right or wrong.

Each partisan who went to these meetings thought that his candidate got the better of the other. Douglas won the senatorship and for the moment the general opinion of the country that he had overpowered his antagonist in debate; but when the debates were published in book form, in 1860, opinion changed. Careful reading showed that in the dialectic contest Lincoln prevailed over Douglas; but he had an immense advantage in the just cause and the one to which public sentiment was tending.

The country now had four leaders, Lincoln, Douglas, Seward and Jefferson Davis. In October, 1858, Seward declared that there existed "an irrepressible conflict" between slavery and freedom. During the ensuing session of the Senate, Davis took the position that Congress was bound to protect slavery in the territories. This was a startling advance on the doctrine of Calhoun and the Supreme Court, who had simply maintained that Congress had no right or power to prohibit it. In truth the apparent necessity of fostering slavery had driven the Southerners to extreme ground. Having failed to secure Kansas or any other Western territory, they now made an effort to acquire Cuba, where the slave system already prevailed. Further acquisitions were hoped for in Mexico and Central America, where it was believed that slavery could be easily introduced. Moreover, as there were not negroes enough to cultivate the cotton, sugar and rice in the existing slave States, a large, possibly a predominant, party began to advocate the revival of the African slave trade. Indeed, during 1859, a large number of negroes were smuggled into the Southern States.

Towards the end of 1859, John Brown made his memorable attack on slavery. The method of the Republicans did not suit him; they respected slavery in the States where already established. The Abolitionists had "milk-and-water principles," issuing merely in talk. His own belief was that action was needed. Gathering eighteen followers, five of whom were negroes, he succeeded, on the cold, dark Sunday night of October 16, in capturing the United States armory, arsenal and rifle works at Harper's Ferry, Virginia, which were under civil, not military, guard. He expected the slaves of Virginia and the free negroes of the North to flock to his standard. These he would arm with pikes. Fortified against attack and subsisting on the enemy, he would make his name a terror throughout the South, so that property in man would become insecure and eventually slavery might thus be destroyed. When his friends urged the folly of attacking the State of Virginia, the United States government and the slave power with so small a band, he said, "If God be for us, who can be against us?" Imbued as he was with the lessons of the Old Testament, he undoubtedly imagined God would work for him the wonders that He had wrought for Joshua and Gideon.

The attempt, of course, failed quickly. During the Monday fighting was carried on with the people of Harper's Ferry; early next morning Colonel Robert E. Lee, at the head of a company of United States Marines, took Brown and four of his followers prisoners. Ten of them had been killed. Of the inhabitants and attacking parties five were killed and nine wounded.

Virginia was in an uproar. While the rabble would have liked to lynch Brown, men of education and position could not but admire his courage. He had a fair trial, was of course found guilty and, forty-five days later, hanged.

The Southerners believed that he had "whetted knives of butchery for their mothers, sisters, daughters, and babes." To Northern statesmen, it was clear that he could have achieved success only by stirring up a servile war and unchaining passions such as had made the memory of San Domingo horrible. If this were the whole of his strange story, History could visit on Brown only the severest condemnation. But his words and behavior between arrest and execution, his composure on the scaffold under circumstances peculiarly distressing must give the ingenuous student pause. Though the contemporary raptures of Emerson and Victor Hugo now look preposterous, it must nevertheless be admitted that Brown suffered martyrdom for the anti-slavery cause. Nor is it possible to forget how Northern soldiers, as they marched to the front to fight for the freedom of the negro, were inspired by the stirring music and words, —

"John Brown's body lies a-mouldering in
   the grave,
 But his soul goes marching on."

Three days after the execution of Brown the Thirty-sixth Congress assembled. In the intense excitement that prevailed the House attempted organization in the usual manner by election of a Speaker, but this was soon found to be difficult, as no one of the four parties who met in the chamber had a majority, although the Republican was the most numerous. The contest began on December 5 and did not end until February 1, when a conservative Republican was elected. At times some of the Southern members became excited and made extravagant statements. They accused the Republicans of complicity in John Brown's raid; they censured Seward for his "irrepressible conflict" speech; and they threatened to dissolve the Union in the event of the election of a Republican President. On one day an altercation between two Illinois members, on another a hot personal dispute between a Southerner and Northerner, ending in a challenge to personal combat, helped to keep the excitement up to fever heat. A few days later an anti-Lecompton Democrat from New York was making bitter personal remarks about another member when a pistol accidentally fell to the floor from the breast pocket of his coat. Some members thinking that he had intentionally drawn the weapon rushed towards him ready for a fight if one should ensue. A senator from South Carolina wrote in a private letter, "I believe every man in both Houses is armed with a revolver — some with two — and a bowie knife." Jefferson Davis, feeling the responsibility of leadership, was generally guarded in the expression of his views, but he gave the Senate to understand that the Union would be dissolved if Seward was elected President.

We are now in the year 1860, a year for the election of a President. As arranged four years previously, the Democratic Convention met in Charleston, South Carolina, the hotbed of disunion. The Douglas delegates were in a majority and adopted their platform, whereupon the delegates from the cotton States seceded from the Convention. As under the Democratic rule, it required two-thirds to nominate a President, and as Douglas could not secure that number, the Convention adjourned to meet in Baltimore forty-six days later. There

Douglas was finally nominated, but as soon as this nomination seemed inevitable, another secession took place and these seceding delegates, joined by most of those from the Charleston Convention, adopted the Southern platform and nominated a Southern Democrat.

In the meantime the most interesting of our Conventions, and the first one to resemble a huge mass-meeting, was held in Chicago. The 466 Republican delegates met in a wigwam, a temporary frame structure, which, it was said, would hold ten thousand people, although three times that number of strangers, mostly from the Northwest, clamored for admittance. The conditions for serious deliberation were unfavorable, yet the delegates acted as wisely as if they had assembled in a hall fit for conference with ample leisure and a suitable environment. In their platform they asserted that the rights of the States should be maintained inviolate; denounced the John Brown invasion "as among the gravest of crimes"; inveighed against the new dogma that the Constitution of its own force carries slavery into the territories; denied "the authority of Congress, of a territorial legislature or of any individual to give legal existence to slavery in any territory"; and branded "the recent reopening of the African slave-trade as a burning shame to our country and age." There were only two possible nominees for President, Seward and Lincoln. Seward had wrought in the vineyard longer, was considered the more radical of the two and partly for this reason the weaker candidate in four of the so-called doubtful States. Lincoln had attracted much attention by his debates with Douglas and by a noble speech made in February in New York City. He received the nomination on the third ballot.

Our presidential election is made by States, each State choosing the same number of electors as she has senators and representatives in Congress. Lincoln carried all of the free States except New Jersey, whose electoral vote was divided between him and Douglas; having thus a majority of the electoral votes, he was regularly chosen for the presidency and would enter into office on the following 4th of March.

In the election of Lincoln the North had spoken. In every man's mind rose unbidden the question, What would be the answer of the South?

✻   ✻   ✻

Through the election of Lincoln the majority of the Northern people declared that slavery was wrong and should not be extended. The sectional character of the contest is clearly manifest, inasmuch as in ten out of the eleven States that afterwards seceded and made up the Southern Confederacy Lincoln did not receive a single vote. As soon as the result was known, South Carolina led off with a prompt reply. Since 1850, disunion sentiment within her borders had been strong, but a considerable opposition had always existed. Now, the day after Lincoln's election, the majority suddenly expanded to unanimity. The crowd that thronged the streets of Charleston felt that they had an undoubted grievance and that their sole remedy was secession. The legislature immediately called a convention, an act that was received with enthusiasm. Speeches, newspaper leaders, sermons from the pulpit were alike in their absolute sincerity. The North has made an attack on slavery, our cherished institution — so ran the unanimous contention — it has encroached upon our rights. We can preserve our liberty and our property only by separation. "The tea has been thrown overboard, the revolution of 1860 has been initiated."

Charles A. Beard: THE APPROACH OF THE SECOND AMERICAN REVOLUTION

Charles A. Beard was born a decade after the Civil War and to him the Civil War was "history" rather than remembered personal experience. Educated at De Pauw, Oxford, and Columbia, Beard became an enthusiastic pioneer in the "new history" movement which sought to apply the analytic methods of the emerging social sciences to the interpretation of history. While Beard's historical writing displays an interest in a wide range of social institutions, he tended to focus particular attention on economic institutions, on economic causes and economic results in his most significant efforts at historical explanation. The selection is taken from Charles A. Beard, The Rise of American Civilization.

HAD the economic systems of the North and the South remained static or changed slowly without effecting immense dislocations in the social structure, the balance of power might have been maintained indefinitely by repeating the compensatory tactics of 1787, 1820, 1833, and 1850; keeping in this manner the inherent antagonisms within the bounds of diplomacy. But nothing was stable in the economy of the United States or in the moral sentiments associated with its diversities.

Within each section of the country, the necessities of the productive system were generating portentous results. The periphery of the industrial vortex of the Northeast was daily enlarging, agriculture in the Northwest was being steadily supplemented by manufacturing, and the area of virgin soil open to exploitation by planters was diminishing with rhythmic regularity—shifting with mechanical precision the weights which statesmen had to adjust in their efforts to maintain the equilibrium of peace. Within each of the three sections also occurred an increasing intensity of social concentration as railways, the telegraph, and the press made travel and communication cheap and almost instantaneous, facilitating the centripetal process that was drawing people of similar economic status and parallel opinions into coöperative activities. Finally the intellectual energies released by accumulating wealth and growing leisure — stimulated by the expansion of the reading public and the literary market — developed with deepened accuracy the word-patterns of the current social persuasions, contributing with galvanic effect to the consolidation of identical groupings.

§

As the years passed, the planting leaders of Jefferson's agricultural party insisted with mounting fervor that the opposition, first of the Whigs and then of the Republicans, was at bottom an association of interests formed for the purpose of plundering productive management and labor on the land. And with steadfast insistence they declared that in the insatiable greed of their political foes lay the source of the dissensions which were tearing the country asunder.

Charles A. Beard, *The Rise of American Civilization* (New York: The Macmillan Co., 1927), Vol. II, pp. 3–13, 19–21, 28–54. Reprinted by permission.

"There is not a pursuit in which man is engaged (agriculture excepted)," exclaimed Reuben Davis of Mississippi in 1860, "which is not demanding legislative aid to enable it to enlarge its profits and all at the expense of the primary pursuit of man — agriculture. . . . Those interests, having a common purpose of plunder, have united and combined to use the government as the instrument of their operation and have thus virtually converted it into a consolidated empire. Now this combined host of interests stands arrayed against the agricultural states; and this is the reason of the conflict which like an earthquake is shaking our political fabric to its foundation." The furor over slavery is a mere subterfuge to cover other purposes. "Relentless avarice stands firm with its iron heel upon the Constitution." This creature, "incorporated avarice," has chained "the agricultural states to the northern rock" and lives like a vulture upon their prosperity. It is the effort of Prometheus to burst his manacles that provokes the assault on slavery. "These states struggle like a giant," continued Davis, "and alarm these incorporated interests, lest they may break the chain that binds them to usurpation; and therefore they are making this fierce onslaught upon the slave property of the southern states."

The fact that free-soil advocates waged war only on slavery in the territories was to Jefferson Davis conclusive proof of an underlying conspiracy against agriculture. He professed more respect for the abolitionist than for the free-soiler. The former, he said, is dominated by an honest conviction that slavery is wrong everywhere and that all men ought to be free; the latter does not assail slavery in the states — he merely wishes to abolish it in the territories that are in due course to be admitted to the Union.

With challenging directness, Davis turned upon his opponents in the Senate and charged them with using slavery as a blind to delude the unwary: "What do you propose, gentlemen of the Free-Soil party? Do you propose to better the condition of the slave? Not at all. What then do you propose? You say you are opposed to the expansion of slavery. . . . Is the slave to be benefited by it? Not at all. It is not humanity that influences you in the position which you now occupy before the country. . . . It is that you may have an opportunity of cheating us that you want to limit slave territory within circumscribed bounds. It is that you may have a majority in the Congress of the United States and convert the Government into an engine of northern aggrandizement. It is that your section may grow in power and prosperity upon treasures unjustly taken from the South, like the vampire bloated and gorged with the blood which it has secretly sucked from its victim. . . . You desire to weaken the political power of the southern states; and why? Because you want, by an unjust system of legislation, to promote the industry of the New England states, at the expense of the people of the South and their industry."

Such in the mind of Jefferson Davis, fated to be president of the Confederacy, was the real purpose of the party which sought to prohibit slavery in the territories; that party did not declare slavery to be a moral disease calling for the severe remedy of the surgeon; it merely sought to keep bondage out of the new states as they came into the Union — with one fundamental aim in view, namely, to gain political ascendancy in the government of the United States and fasten upon the country an economic policy that meant the exploitation of the South for the benefit of northern capitalism.

But the planters were after all fighting against the census returns, as the phrase of the day ran current. The amazing growth of northern industries, the rapid extension of railways, the swift expansion of foreign trade to the ends of the earth, the attachment of the farming regions of the West to the centers of manufacture and finance through transportation and credit, the destruction of state consciousness by migration, the alien invasion, the erection of new commonwealths in the Valley of Democracy, the nationalistic drive of interstate commerce, the increase of population in the North, and the southward pressure of the capitalistic glacier all conspired to assure the ultimate triumph of what the orators were fond of calling "the free labor system." This was a dynamic thrust far too powerful for planters operating in limited territory with incompetent labor on soil of diminished fertility. Those who swept forward with it, exulting in the approaching triumph of machine industry, warned the planters of their ultimate subjection.

To statesmen of the invincible forces recorded in the census returns, the planting opposition was a huge, compact, and self-conscious economic association bent upon political objects — the possession of the government of the United States, the protection of its interests against adverse legislation, dominion over the territories, and enforcement of the national fugitive slave law throughout the length and breadth of the land. No phrase was more often on the lips of northern statesmen than "the slave power." The pages of the Congressional Globe bristled with references to " the slave system" and its influence over the government of the country. But it was left for William H. Seward of New York to describe it with a fullness of familiar knowledge that made his characterization a classic.

Seward knew from experience that a political party was no mere platonic society engaged in discussing abstractions. "A party," he said, "is in one sense a joint stock association, in which those who contribute most direct the action and management of the concern. The slaveholders contributing in an overwhelming proportion to the capital strength of the Democratic party, they necessarily dictate and prescribe its policy. The inevitable caucus system enables them to do this with a show of fairness and justice." This class of slaveholders, consisting of only three hundred and forty-seven thousand persons, Seward went on to say, was spread from the banks of the Delaware to the banks of the Rio Grande; it possessed nearly all the real estate in that section, owned more than three million other "persons" who were denied all civil and political rights, and inhibited "freedom of speech, freedom of press, freedom of the ballot box, freedom of education, freedom of literature, and freedom of popular assemblies. . . . The slaveholding class has become the governing power in each of the slaveholding states and it practically chooses thirty of the sixty-two members of the Senate, ninety of the two hundred and thirty-three members of the House of Representatives, and one hundred and five of the two hundred and ninety-five electors of the President and Vice-President of the United States."

Becoming still more concrete, Seward accused the President of being "a confessed apologist of the slave-property class." Examining the composition of the Senate, he found the slave-owning group in possession of all the important committees. Peering into the House of Representatives he discovered no impregnable bulwark of freedom there. Nor did respect for judicial ermine compel him to spare the Supreme Court. With irony he exclaimed, "How fitting does the proclamation of its opening close with the invocation: 'God save the United States and this honorable court. . . .' The court consists of a chief justice and eight associate justices. Of these five were called from slave states and four from free states. The opinions and bias of each of them were carefully considered by the President and Senate when he was appointed. Not one of them was found wanting in soundness of politics, according to the slaveholder's exposition of the Constitution, and those who were called from the free states were even more distinguished in that respect than their brethren from the slaveholding states."

Seward then analyzed the civil service of the national government and could descry not a single person among the thousands employed in the post office, the treasury, and other great departments who was "false to the slaveholding interest." Under the spoils system, the dominion of the slavocracy extended into all branches of the federal administration. "The customs-houses and the public lands pour forth two golden streams — one into the elections to procure votes for the slaveholding class; and the other into the treasury to be enjoyed by those whom it shall see fit to reward with places in the public service." Even in the North, religion, learning, and the press were under the spell of this masterful class, frightened lest they incur its wrath.

Having described the gigantic operating structure of the slavocracy, Seward drew with equal power a picture of the opposing system founded on "free labor." He surveyed the course of economy in the North — the growth of industry, the spread of railways, the swelling tide of European immigration, and the westward roll of free farmers — rounding out

the country, knitting it together, bringing "these antagonistic systems" continually into closer contact. Then he uttered those fateful words which startled conservative citizens from Maine to California — words of prophecy which proved to be brutally true — "the irrepressible conflict."

This inexorable clash, he said, was not "accidental, unnecessary, the work of interested or fanatical agitators and therefore ephemeral." No. "It is an irrepressible conflict between opposing and enduring forces." The hopes of those who sought peace by appealing to slave owners to reform themselves were as chaff in a storm. "How long and with what success have you waited already for that reformation? Did any property class ever so reform itself? Did the patricians in old Rome, the noblesse or clergy in France? The landholders in Ireland? The landed aristocracy in England? Does the slaveholding class even seek to beguile you with such a hope? Has it not become rapacious, arrogant, defiant?" All attempts at compromise were "vain and ephemeral." There was accordingly but one supreme task before the people of the United States — the task of confounding and overthrowing "by one decisive blow the betrayers of the Constitution and freedom forever." In uttering this indictment, this prophecy soon to be fulfilled with such appalling accuracy, Seward stepped beyond the bounds of cautious politics and read himself out of the little group of men who were eligible for the Republican nomination in 1860. Frantic efforts to soften his words by explanations and additions could not appease his critics.

§

Given an irrepressible conflict which could be symbolized in such unmistakable patterns by competent interpreters of opposing factions, a transfer of the issues from the forum to the field, from the conciliation of diplomacy to the decision of arms was bound to come. Each side obdurately bent upon its designs and convinced of its rectitude, by the fulfillment of its wishes precipitated events and effected distributions of power that culminated finally in the tragedy foretold by Seward. Those Democrats who operated on historic knowledge rather than on prophetic insight, recalling how many times the party of Hamilton had been crushed at elections, remembering how the Whigs had never been able to carry the country on a cleancut Webster-Clay program, and counting upon the continued support of a huge array of farmers and mechanics marshaled behind the planters, imagined apparently that politics — viewed as the science of ballot enumeration — could resolve the problems of power raised by the maintenance of the Union.

And in this opinion they were confirmed by the outcome of the presidential campaign in 1852, when the Whigs, with General Winfield Scott, a hero of the Mexican war, at their head, were thoroughly routed by the Democratic candidate, General Franklin Pierce of New Hampshire. Indeed the verdict of the people was almost savage, for Pierce carried every state but four, receiving 254 out of 296 electoral votes. The Free-Soil party that branded slavery as a crime and called for its prohibition in the territories scarcely made a ripple, polling only 156,000 out of more than three million votes, a figure below the record set in the previous campaign.

With the Whigs beaten and the Free-Soilers evidently a dwindling handful of negligible critics, exultant Democrats took possession of the Executive offices and Congress, inspired by a firm belief that their tenure was secure. Having won an overwhelming victory on a definite tariff for revenue and pro-slavery program, they acted as if the party of Hamilton was for all practical purposes as powerless as the little band of abolitionist agitators. At the succeeding election in 1856 they again swept the country — this time with James Buchanan of Pennsylvania as their candidate. Though his triumph was not as magisterial as that of Pierce it was great enough to warrant a conviction that the supremacy of the Democratic party could not be broken at the polls.

During these eight years of tenure, a series of events occurred under Democratic auspices, which clinched the grasp of the planting interest upon the country and produced a correlative consolidation of the opposition. One line of development indicated an indefinite extension of the slave area; another the positive withdrawal of all government support from industrial and commercial enterprise. The first evidence of the new course came in the year immediately following the inauguration of Pierce. In 1854, Congress defiantly repealed the Missouri Compromise and threw open to slavery the vast section of the Louisiana Purchase which had been closed to it by the covenant adopted more than three decades before. On the instant came a rush of slavery champions from Missouri into Kansas determined to bring it into the southern sphere of influence. Not content with the conquest of the forbidden West, filibustering parties under pro-slavery leaders attempted to seize Cuba and Nicaragua and three American ministers abroad flung out to the world a flaming proclamation, known as the "Ostend Manifesto," which declared that the United States would be justified in wresting Cuba from Spain by force — acts of imperial aggression which even the Democratic administration in Washington felt constrained to repudiate.

Crowning the repeal of the Missouri Compromise came two decisions of the Supreme Court giving sanction to the expansion of slavery in America and assuring high protection for that peculiar institution even in the North. In the Dred Scott case decided in March, 1857, Chief Justice Taney declared in effect that the Missouri Compromise had been void from the beginning and that Congress had no power under the Constitution to prohibit slavery in the territories of the United States anywhere at any time. This legal triumph for the planting interest was followed in 1859 by another decision in which the Supreme Court upheld the fugitive slave law and all the drastic procedure provided for its enforcement. To the frightened abolitionists it seemed that only one more step was needed to make freedom unconstitutional throughout the country.

These extraordinary measures on behalf of slavery were accompanied by others that touched far more vitally economic interests in the North. In 1859, the last of the subsidies for trans-Atlantic steamship companies was ordered discontinued by Congress. In 1857, the tariff was again reduced, betraying an unmistakable drift of the nation toward free trade. In support of this action, the representatives of the South and Southwest were almost unanimous and they gathered into their fold a large number of New England congressmen on condition that no material reductions should be made in duties on cotton goods. On the other hand, the Middle States and the West offered a large majority against tariff reduction so that the division was symptomatic.

Immediately after the new revenue law went into effect an industrial panic burst upon the country, spreading distress among business men and free laborers. While that tempest was running high, the paper money anarchy let loose by the Democrats reached the acme of virulence as the notes of wildcat banks flooded the West and South and financial institutions crashed in every direction, fifty-one failing in Indiana alone within a period of five years. Since all hope of reviving Hamilton's system of finance had been buried, those who believed that a sound currency was essential to national prosperity were driven to the verge of desperation. On top of these economic calamities came Buchanan's veto of the Homestead Bill which the impatient agrarians had succeeded in getting through Congress in a compromise form — an act of presidential independence which angered the farmers and mechanics who regarded the national domain as their own inheritance. . . .

§

The amazing acts of mastery — legislative, executive, judicial — committed by the federal government in the decade between 1850 and 1860 changed the whole political climate of America. They betrayed a growing consolidation in the planting group, its increased dominance in the Democratic party, and an evident determination to realize its economic interests and protect its labor system at all hazards. In a kind of doom, they seemed to mark the final supremacy of the political army which had swept into office with Andrew Jackson. During the thirty-two years between that event and the inauguration of Lincoln, the Democrats controlled the Presidency and the Senate for twenty-four years, the Supreme Court for twenty-six years, and the House of Representatives for twenty-two years. By the end of the period, the old farmer-labor party organized by Jackson had passed under the dominion of the planting interest and the farming wing of the North was confronted with the alternative of surrender or secession.

In this shift of power the Whigs of the South, discovering the tendencies of the popular balloting, moved steadily over into the Democratic camp. Though unavoidable, the transfer was painful; the planting Whigs, being rich and influential, had little affection for the white farmers who rallied around the Jacksonian banner. According to the estimate of a southern newspaper in 1850, the Whigs owned at least three-fourths of all the slaves in the country and it was a matter of common knowledge that leaders among them disliked wildcat banking as much as they hated high duties on the manufactured goods they bought. Indeed to a southern gentleman of the old school the radical agrarianism of Andrew Johnson was probably more odious than the tariff schedules devised by Daniel Webster. It was said that one of them, when asked whether a gentleman could be a Democrat, snapped back the tart reply: "Well, he is not apt to be; but if he is, he is in damned bad company."

But the rich planters were relatively few in numbers and virtue was subject to the law of necessity; the populace had the votes, northern manufacturers were demanding protection, abolitionists were agitating, and in the end all but the most conservative remnant of the southern Whigs had to go over to the party that professed the dangerous doctrines of Jackson. The achievements of the years that lay between 1850 and 1860 seemed to justify the sacrifice.

Though the drift toward the irrepressible conflict was steady and strong, as events revealed, the politics of the decade had the outward semblances of dissolution. The abolitionists and free-soilers, while a mere minority as we have seen, were able to worry the politicians of both parties in the North. Largely deserted by their southern cohorts, the Whigs, whose organization had always been tenuous at best, could discover no way of mustering a majority of votes on the bare economic policies of Hamilton and Webster. Their two victories — in 1840 and 1848 — had been dubious and their only hope for a triumph at the polls lay in a combination with other factors.

To this confusion in party affairs, the intellectual and religious ferment of the age added troublesome factional disputes. A temperance element, strong enough to carry prohibition in a few states, was giving the politicians anxiety in national campaigns. A still more formidable cabal, the Know Nothing, or American Party, sprang up in the current opposition to foreigners, the papacy, infidelity, and socialism. Combining the functions of a party and a fraternal order, it nominated candidates for office and adopted secret rites, dark mysteries, grips, and passwords which gave it an atmosphere of uncertain vitality. Members were admitted by solemn ceremony into full fellowship with "The Supreme Order of the Star-spangled Banner," whose "daily horror and nightly specter was the pope." When asked about their principles, they replied mysteriously: "I know nothing." Appealing to deep-seated emotions, this movement showed strength in many localities and was only dissolved by the smashing energy of more momentous issues. . . .

§

Every shocking incident on the one side only consolidated the forces on the other. By 1860 leaders of the planting interest had worked out in great detail their economic and political scheme — their ultimatum to the serried opposition — and embodied it in many official documents. The economic elements were those made familiar to the country through twenty years of agitation: no high protective tariffs, no ship subsidies, no national banking and currency system; in short, none of the measures which business enterprise deemed essential to its progress. The remaining problem before the planting interest, namely, how to clinch its grip and prevent a return to the Hamilton-Webster policy as the industrial North rapidly advanced in wealth and population, was faced with the same penchant for definition.

Plans for accomplishing that purpose were mapped out by able spokesmen from the South in a set of Senate resolutions adopted on May 24–25, 1860: slavery is lawful in all the territories under the Constitution; neither Congress nor a local legislature can abolish it there; the federal government is in duty bound to protect slave owners as well as the holders of other forms of property in the territories; it is a violation of the Constitution for any state or any combination of citizens to intermeddle with the domestic institutions of any other state "on any pretext whatever, political, moral, or religious, with a view to their disturbance or subversion"; open or covert attacks on slavery are contrary to the solemn pledges given by the states on entering the Union to protect and defend one another; the inhabitants of a territory on their admission to the Union may decide whether or not they will sanction slavery thereafter; the strict enforcement of the fugitive slave law is required by good faith and the principles of the Constitution.

In brief, the federal government was to do nothing for business enterprise while the planting interest was to be assured the possession of enough political power to guarantee it against the reënactment of the Hamilton-Webster program. Incidentally the labor system of the planting interest was not to be criticized and all runaway property was to be returned. Anything short of this was, in the view of the planting statesmen, "subversive of the Constitution."

The meaning of the ultimatum was not to be mistaken. It was a demand upon the majority of the people to surrender unconditionally for all time to the minority stockholders under the Constitution. It offered nothing to capitalism but capitulation; to the old Whigs of the South nothing but submission. Finally — and this was its revolutionary phase — it called upon the farmers and mechanics who had formed the bulk of Jacksonian Democracy in the North to acknowledge the absolute sovereignty of the planting interest. Besides driving a wedge into the nation, the conditions laid down by the planters also split the Democratic party itself into two factions.

Soon after the Democratic convention assembled at Charleston in April, 1860, this fundamental division became manifest. The northern wing, while entirely willing to indorse the general economic program of the planters, absolutely refused to guarantee them sovereignty in the party and throughout the country. Rejecting the proposal of the southern members to make slavery obligatory in the territories, it would merely offer to "abide by the decisions of the Supreme Court on all questions of constitutional law." Since the Dred Scott case had opened all the territories to slavery, that tender seemed generous enough but the intransigent representatives of the plant-

ing interest would not accept it as adequate. Unable to overcome the majority
commanded in the convention by the
northern group, they withdrew from the
assembly, spurning the pleas of their
colleagues not to break up the union of
hearts on "a mere theory" and counter-
ing all arguments with a declaration of
finality: "Go your way and we will go
ours."

After balloting for a time on candidates without reaching a decision under
the two-thirds rule, the remaining
members of the Charleston conference
adjourned to meet again at Baltimore.
When they reassembled, they nominated
Stephen A. Douglas of Illinois, the apostle of "squatter sovereignty," who was
ready to open the territories to slavery
but not to guarantee the planting interest
unconditional supremacy in the Democratic party and the Union. Determined
to pursue their separate course to the bitter end, the Charleston seceders adopted
the platform rejected by the Douglas faction and chose as their candidate, John C.
Breckinridge of Kentucky, an unyielding
champion of planting aristocracy and its
labor system. The union of farmers and
slave owners was thus severed: the Republicans had carried off one large frag-
ment of the northern farmers in 1856;
Douglas was now carrying off another.

§

During the confusion in the Democratic ranks, the Republicans, in high
glee over the quarrels of the opposition,
held their convention in Chicago — a sectional gathering except for representatives from five slave states. Among its
delegates the spirit of opposition to slavery extension, which had inspired the
party assembly four years before, was
still evident but enthusiasm on that tick-
lish subject was neutralized by the pru-

dence of the practical politicans who,
sniffing victory in the air, had rushed to
the new tent. Whigs, whose affections
were centered on Hamilton's program
rather than on Garrison's scheme of salvation, were to be seen on the floor.
Advocates of a high protective tariff and
friends of free homesteads for mechanics
and farmers now mingled with the ardent opponents of slavery in the territories. With their minds fixed on the
substance of things sought for, the partisans of caution were almost able to prevent the convention from indorsing the
Declaration of Independence. Still they
were in favor of restricting the area of
slavery; they had no love for the institution and its spread helped to fasten the
grip of the planting interest on the government at Washington. So the Republican convention went on record in favor
of liberty for the territories, free homesteads for farmers, a protective tariff, and
a Pacific railway. As the platform was
read, the cheering became especially
loud and prolonged when the homestead
and tariff planks were reached. Such at
least is the testimony of the stenographic
report.

Since this declaration of principles
was well fitted to work a union of forces,
it was essential that the candidate
should not divide them. The protective
plank would doubtless line up the good
old Whigs of the East but tender consideration had to be shown to the Ohio
Valley, original home of Jacksonian
Democracy, where national banks, tariffs,
and other "abominations" still frightened
the wary. Without Ohio, Indiana, and
Illinois, the Republican managers could
not hope to win and they knew that the
lower counties of these states were filled
with settlers from the slave belt who had
no love for the "money power," abolition,
or anything that savored of them. In

such circumstances Seward, idol of the Whig wing, was no man to offer that section; he was too radical on the slavery issue and too closely associated with "high finance" in addition. "If you do not nominate Seward, where will you get your money?" was the blunt question put by Seward's loyal supporters at Chicago. The question was pertinent but not fatal.

Given this confluence of problems, a man close to the soil of the West was better suited to the requirements of the hour than a New York lawyer with somewhat fastidious tastes, obviously backed by fat purses. The available candidate was Abraham Lincoln of Illinois. Born in Kentucky, he was of southern origin. A son of poor frontier parents, self-educated, a pioneer who in his youth had labored in field and forest, he appealed to the voters of the backwoods. Still by an uncanny genius for practical affairs, he had forged his way to the front as a shrewd lawyer and politician. In his debates with Douglas he had shown himself able to cope with one of the foremost leaders in the Democratic party. On the tariff, bank, currency, and homestead issues he was sound. A local railway attorney, he was trusted among business men.

On the slavery question Lincoln's attitude was firm but conservative. He disliked slavery and frankly said so; yet he was not an abolitionist and he saw no way in which the institution could be uprooted. On the contrary, he favored enforcing the fugitive slave law and he was not prepared to urge even the abolition of slavery in the District of Columbia. His declaration that a house divided against itself could not stand had been counterbalanced by an assertion that the country will become all free or all slave — a creed which any southern planter could have indorsed. Seward's radical doctrine

that there was a "higher law" than the Constitution, dedicating the territories to freedom, received from the Illiois lawyer disapproval, not commendation.

Nevertheless Lincoln was definite and positive in his opinion that slavery should not be permitted in the territories. That was necessary to satisfy the minimum demands of the anti-slavery faction and incidentally it pleased those Whigs of the North who at last realized that no Hamiltonian program could be pushed through Congress if the planting interest secured a supremacy, or indeed held an equal share of power, in the Union. Evidently Lincoln was the man of the hour: his heritage was correct, his principles were sound, his sincerity was unquestioned, and his ability as a speaker commanded the minds and hearts of his auditors. He sent word to his friends at Chicago that, although he did not indorse Seward's higher-law doctrine, he agreed with him on the irrepressible conflict. The next day Lincoln was nominated amid huzzas from ten thousand lusty throats.

A large fraction of Whigs and some fragments of the Know Nothing, or American, party, foreseeing calamity in the existing array of interests, tried to save the day by an appeal to lofty sentiments without any definitions. Assuming the name of Constitutional Unionists and boasting that they represented the "intelligence and respectability of the South" as well as the lovers of the national idea everywhere, they held a convention at Baltimore and nominated John Bell of Tennessee and Edward Everett of Massachusetts for President and Vice-President. In the platform they invited their countrymen to forget all divisions and "support the Constitution of the country, the union of the states, and the enforcement of the laws." It was an overture of old men — men who had known and loved Webster and Clay and who shrank with horror from agitations that threatened to end in bloodshed and revolution — a plea for the maintenance of the status quo against the whims of a swiftly changing world.

§

A spirited campaign followed the nomination of these four candidates for the presidency on four different platforms. Huge campaign funds were raised and spent. Besides pursuing the usual strategy of education, the Republicans resorted to parades and the other spectacular features that had distinguished the log-cabin crusade of General Harrison's year. Emulating the discretion of the Hero of Tippecanoe, Lincoln maintained a judicious silence at Springfield while his champions waged his battles for him, naturally tempering their orations to the requirements of diverse interests. They were fully conscious, as a Republican paper in Philadelphia put it, that "Frémont had tried running on the slavery issue and lost." So while they laid stress on it in many sections, they widened their appeal.

In the West, a particular emphasis was placed on free homesteads and the Pacific railway. With a keen eye for competent strategy, Carl Schurz carried the campaign into Missouri where he protested with eloquence against the action of the slave power in denying "the laboring man the right to acquire property in the soil by his labor" and made a special plea for the German vote on the ground that the free land was to be opened to aliens who declared their intention of becoming American citizens. Discovering that the homestead question was "the greatest issue in the West," Horace Greeley used it to win votes in the East. Agrarians and labor reformers renewed the slogan: "Vote yourself a farm."

In Pennsylvania and New Jersey, protection for iron and steel was the great subject of discussion. Curtin, the Republican candidate for governor in the former state, said not a word about abolishing slavery in his ratification speech but spoke with feeling on "the vast heavings of the heart of Pennsylvania whose sons are pining for protection to their labor and their dearest interests." Warming to his theme, he exclaimed: "This is a contest involving protection and the rights of labor. . . . If you desire to become vast and great, protect the manufactures of Philadelphia. . . . All hail, liberty! All hail, freedom! freedom to the white man! All hail freedom general as the air we breathe!" In a fashion after Curtin's own heart, the editor of the Philadelphia American and Gazette, surveying the canvass at the finish, repudiated the idea that "any sectional aspect of the slavery question" was up for decision and declared that the great issues were protection for industry, "economy in the conduct of the government, homesteads for settlers on the public domain, retrenchment and accountability in the public expenditures, appropriation for rivers and harbors, a Pacific railroad, the admission of Kansas, and a radical reform in the government."

With a kindred appreciation of practical matters, Seward bore the standard through the North and West. Fully conversant with the Webster policy of commercial expansion in the Pacific and knowing well the political appeal of Manifest Destiny, he proclaimed the future of the American empire — assuring his auditors that in due time American outposts would be pushed along the northwest coast to the Arctic Ocean, that Canada would be gathered into our glorious Union, that the Latin-American republics reorganized under our benign influence would become parts of this magnificent confederation, that the ancient Aztec metropolis, Mexico City, would eventually become the capital of the United States, and that America and Russia, breaking their old friendship, would come to grips in the Far East — "in regions where civilization first began." All this was involved in the election of Lincoln and the triumph of the Republican party. Webster and Cushing and Perry had not wrought in vain.

The three candidates opposed to Lincoln scored points wherever they could. Douglas took the stump with his usual vigor and declaimed to throngs in nearly every state. Orators of the Breckinridge camp, believing that their extreme views were sound everywhere, invaded the North. Bell's champions spoke with dignity and warmth about the dangers inherent in all unwise departures from the past, about the perils of the sectional quarrel. When at length the ballots were cast and counted, it was found that the foes of slavery agitation had carried the country by an overwhelming majority. Their combined vote was a million ahead of Lincoln's total; the two Democratic factions alone, to say nothing of Bell's six hundred thousand followers, outnumbered the Republican army. But in the division and uproar of the campaign Lincoln, even so, had won the Presidency; he was the choice of a minority — a sectional minority at that — but under the terms of the Constitution, he was entitled to the scepter at Washington.

§

From what has just been said it must be apparent that the forces which produced the irrepressible conflict were very complex in nature and yet the momentous struggle has been so often reduced by historians to simple terms that a re-examination of the traditional thesis has become one of the tasks of the modern age. On the part of northern writers it was long the fashion to declare that slavery was the cause of the conflict between the states. Such for example was the position taken by James Ford Rhodes and made the starting point of his monumental work.

Assuming for the moment that this assertion is correct in a general sense, it will be easily observed even on a superficial investigation that "slavery" was no simple, isolated phenomenon. In itself it was intricate and it had filaments through the whole body economic. It was a labor system, the basis of planting, and the foundation of the southern aristocracy. That aristocracy, in turn, owing to the nature of its economic operations, resorted to public policies that were opposed to capitalism, sought to dominate the federal government, and, with the help of free farmers also engaged in agriculture, did at last dominate it. In the course of that political conquest, all the plans of commerce and industry for federal protection and subvention were overborne. It took more than a finite eye to discern where slavery as an ethical question left off and economics — the struggle over the distribution of wealth — began.

On the other hand, the early historians of the southern school, chagrined by defeat and compelled to face the adverse judgment of brutal fact, made the "rights of states" — something nobler than economics or the enslavement of Negroes — the issue for which the Confederacy fought and bled. That too like slavery seems simple until subjected to a little scrutiny. What is a state? At bottom it is a majority or perhaps a mere plurality of persons engaged in the quest of something supposed to be beneficial, or at all events not injurious, to the pursuers. And what are rights? Abstract, intangible moral values having neither substance nor form? The party debates over the economic issues of the middle period answer with an emphatic negative. If the southern planters had been content to grant tariffs, bounties, subsidies, and preferences to northern commerce and industry, it is not probable that they would have been molested in their most imperious proclamations of sovereignty.

But their theories and their acts involved interests more ponderable than political rhetoric. They threatened the country with secession first in defying the tariff of abominations and when they did secede thirty years later it was in response to the victory of a tariff and homestead party that proposed nothing more dangerous to slavery itself than the mere exclusion of the institution from the territories. It took more than a finite eye to discern where their opposition to the economic system of Hamilton left off and their affection for the rights of states began. The modern reader tossed about in a contrariety of opinions can only take his bearings by examining a few indubitable realities.

§

With reference to the popular northern view of the conflict, there stands the stubborn fact that at no time during the long gathering of the storm did Garrison's abolition creed rise to the dignity of a first rate political issue in the North. Nobody but agitators, beneath the contempt of the towering statesmen of the age, ever dared to advocate it. No great political organization even gave it the most casual indorsement.

When the abolitionists launched the Liberty party in the campaign of 1844 to work for emancipation, as we have noted, the voters answered their plea for "the restoration of equality of political rights among men" in a manner that demonstrated the invincible opposition of the American people. Out of more than two and a half million ballots cast in the election, only sixty-five thousand were recorded in favor of the Liberty candidate. That was America's answer to the call for abolition; and the advocates of that policy never again ventured to appeal to the electorate by presenting candidates on such a radical platform.

No other party organized between that time and the clash of arms attempted to do more than demand the exclusion of slavery from the territories and not until the Democrats by repealing the Missouri Compromise threatened to extend slavery throughout the West did any party poll more than a handful of votes on that issue. It is true that Van Buren on a free-soil platform received nearly three hundred thousand votes in 1848 but that was evidently due to personal influence, because his successor on a similar ticket four years afterward dropped into an insignificant place.

Even the Republican party, in the campaign of 1856, coming hard on the act of defiance which swept away the Missouri compact, won little more than one-third the active voters to the cause of restricting the slavery area. When transformed after four more years into a homestead and high tariff party pledged merely to liberty in the territories, the Republicans polled a million votes fewer than the number cast for the opposing factions and rode into power on account of the divided ranks of the enemy. Such was the nation's reply to the anti-slavery agitation from the beginning of the disturbance until the cannon shot at Sumter opened a revolution.

Moreover not a single responsible

statesman of the middle period committed himself to the doctrine of immediate and unconditional abolition to be achieved by independent political action. John Quincy Adams, ousted from the presidency by Jacksonian Democracy but returned to Washington as the Representative of a Massachusetts district in Congress, did declare that it was the duty of every free American to work directly for the abolition of slavery and with uncanny vision foresaw that the knot might be cut with the sword. But Adams was regarded by astute party managers as a foolish and embittered old man and his prophecy as a dangerous delusion.

Practical politicians who felt the iron hand of the planters at Washington -- politicians who saw how deeply intertwined with the whole economic order the institution of slavery really was — could discover nothing tangible in immediate and unconditional abolition that appealed to reason or came within the range of common sense. Lincoln was emphatic in assuring the slaveholders that no Republican had ever been detected in any attempt to disturb them. "We must not interfere with the institution of slavery in the states where it exists," he urged, "because the Constitution forbids it and the general welfare does not require us to do so."

Since, therefore, the abolition of slavery never appeared in the platform of any great political party, since the only appeal ever made to the electorate on that issue was scornfully repulsed, since the spokesman of the Republicans emphatically declared that his party never intended to interfere with slavery in the states in any shape or form, it seems reasonable to assume that the institution of slavery was not the fundamental issue during the epoch preceding the bombardment of Fort Sumter.

Nor can it be truthfully said, as southern writers were fond of having it, that a tender and consistent regard for the rights of states and for a strict construction of the Constitution was the prime element in the dispute that long divided the country. As a matter of record, from the foundation of the republic, all factions were for high nationalism or low provincialism upon occasion according to their desires at the moment, according to turns in the balance of power. New England nullified federal law when her commerce was affected by the War of 1812 and came out stanchly for liberty and union, one and inseparable, now and forever, in 1833 when South Carolina attempted to nullify a tariff act. Not long afterward, the legislature of Massachusetts, dreading the overweening strength of the Southwest, protested warmly against the annexation of Texas and resolved that "such an act of admission would have no binding force whatever on the people of Massachusetts."

Equally willing to bend theory to practical considerations, the party of the slavocracy argued that the Constitution was to be strictly and narrowly construed whenever tariff and bank measures were up for debate; but no such piddling concept of the grand document was to be held when a bill providing for the prompt and efficient return of fugitive slaves was on the carpet. Less than twenty years after South Carolina prepared to resist by arms federal officers engaged in collecting customs duties, the champions of slavery and states' rights greeted with applause a fugitive slave law which flouted the precious limitations prescribed in the first ten Amendments to the Constitution — a law which provided for the use of all the powers of the national government to assist masters in getting possession of their elusive property — which denied to the alleged slave, who might perchance be a freeman in spite of his color, the right to have a jury trial or even to testify in his own behalf. In other words, it was "constitutional" to employ the engines of the federal authority in catching slaves wherever they might be found in any northern community and to ignore utterly the elementary safeguards of liberty plainly and specifically imposed on Congress by language that admitted of no double interpretation.

On this very issue of personal liberty, historic positions on states' rights were again reversed. Following the example of South Carolina on the tariff, Wisconsin resisted the fugitive slave law as an invasion of her reserved rights — as a violation of the Constitution. Alarmed by this action, Chief Justice Taney answered the disobedient state in a ringing judicial decision announcing a high nationalism that would have delighted the heart of John Marshall, informing the recalcitrant Wisconsin that the Constitution and laws enacted under it were supreme; that the fugitive slave law was fully authorized by the Constitution; and that the Supreme Court was the final arbiter in all controversies over the respective powers of the states and the United States. "If such an arbiter had not been provided in our complicated system of government, internal tranquillity could not have been preserved and if such controversies were left to the arbitrament of physical force, our Government, State and National, would cease to be a government of laws, and revolution by force of arms would take the place of courts of justice and judicial decisions." No nullification here: no right of a state to judge for itself respecting infractions of the Constitution by the federal government; federal law is binding everywhere and the Supreme

Court, a branch of the national government, is the final judge.

And in what language did Wisconsin reply? The legislature of the state, in a solemn resolution, declared that the decision of the Supreme Court of the United States in the case in question was in direct conflict with the Constitution. It vowed that the essential principles of the Kentucky doctrine of nullification were sound. Then it closed with the rebel fling: "that the several states . . . being sovereign and independent, have the unquestionable right to judge of its [the Constitution's] infraction and that a positive defiance by those sovereignties of all unauthorized acts done or attempted to be done under color of that instrument is the rightful remedy."

That was in 1859. Within two years, men who had voted for that resolution and cheered its adoption were marching off in martial array to vindicate on southern battlefields the supremacy of the Union and the sovereignty of the nation. By that fateful hour the southern politicians who had applauded Taney's declaration that the Supreme Court was the final arbiter in controversies between the states and the national government had come to the solemn conclusion that the states themselves were the arbiters. Such words and events being facts, there can be but one judgment in the court of history; namely, that major premises respecting the nature of the Constitution and deductions made logically from them with masterly eloquence were minor factors in the grand dispute as compared with the interests, desires, and passions that lay deep in the hearts and minds of the contestants.

§

Indeed, honorable men who held diametrically opposite views found warrant for each in the Constitution. All parties and all individuals, save the extreme abolitionists, protested in an unbroken chant their devotion to the national covenant and to the principles and memory of the inspired men who framed it. As the Bible was sometimes taken as a guide for theologians traveling in opposite directions, so the Constitution was the beacon that lighted the way of statesmen who differed utterly on the issues of the middle period. Again and again Calhoun declared that his one supreme object was to sustain the Constitution in its pristine purity of principle: "to turn back the government," as he said, "to where it commenced its operation in 1789 . . . to take a fresh start, a new departure, on the States Rights Republican tack, as was intended by the framers of the Constitution."

This was the eternal refrain of Calhoun's school. The bank, subsidies to shipping, protection for industries, the encouragement of business enterprise by public assistance were all departures from the Constitution and the intentions of its framers, all contrary to the fundamental compact of the land. This refrain reverberated through Democratic speeches in Congress, the platform of the party, and the official utterances of its statesmen. "The liberal principles embodied by Jefferson in the Declaration of Independence and sanctioned by the Constitution . . . have ever been cardinal principles in the Democratic faith" — such was the characteristic declaration of the elect in every platform after 1840. The Constitution warrants the peaceful secession of states by legal process — such was the answer of Jefferson Davis to those who charged him with raising the flag of revolution. Everything done by the Democratic party while in power was constitutional and finally, as a crowning act of grace, the Constitution gave approval to its own destruction and the dissolution of the Union.

It followed from this line of reasoning as night the day that the measures advanced by the Whigs and later by the Republicans were unconstitutional. In fact, Calhoun devoted the burden of a great speech in 1839 to showing how everything done by Hamilton and his school was a violation of the Constitution. Party manifestoes reiterated the pronouncements of party statesmen on this point. In their platform of 1840, the Democrats highly resolved that "the Constitution does not confer upon the general government the power . . . to carry on a general system of internal improvement . . . the Constitution does not confer authority upon the federal government, directly or indirectly, to assume the debts of the several states . . . Congress has no power to charter a United States Bank . . . Congress has no power, under the Constitution, to interfere with or control the domestic institutions of the several states." This declaration was repeated every four years substantially in the same form. After the Supreme Court announced in the Dred Scott case that Congress could not prohibit slavery in the territories, the Democratic party added that the doctrine "should be respected by all good citizens and enforced with promptness and fidelity by every branch of the general government."

In the best of all possible worlds everything substantial desired by the Democrats was authorized by the Constitution while everything substantial opposed by them was beyond the boundaries set by the venerable instrument. Hamilton, who helped to draft the Constitution, therefore, did not understand or interpret it correctly; whereas Jefferson, who was in Paris during its formation was the infallible oracle on the intentions of its framers.

On the other hand, the Whigs and then the Republicans were equally prone to find protection under the ægis of the Constitution. Webster in his later years devoted long and eloquent speeches to showing that the Constitution contemplated a perpetual union and that nullification and secession were utterly proscribed by the principles of that instrument. He did not go as far as Calhoun. He did not declare free trade unconstitutional but he did find in the records of history evidence that "the main reason for the adoption of the Constitution" was to give "the general government the power to regulate commerce and trade." A protective tariff was therefore constitutional. Furthermore "it was no more the right than the duty" of Congress "by just discrimination to protect the labor of the American people." The provision of a uniform system of currency was also among "the chief objects" of the Fathers in framing the Constitution. A national bank was not imperatively commanded by the letter of the document but its spirit required Congress to stabilize and make sound the paper currency of the land. In fact Webster thought the Democrats themselves somewhat unconstitutional. "If by democracy," he said, "they mean a conscientious and stern adherence to the Constitution and the government, then I think they have very little claim to it."

In the endless and tangled debates on slavery, the orators of the age also paid the same sincere homage to the Constitution that they had paid when dealing with other economic matters. Southern statesmen on their side never wearied in pointing out the pro-slavery character of the covenant. That instrument, they said,

recognized the slave trade by providing that the traffic should not be prohibited for twenty years and by leaving the issue open after that period had elapsed. It made slavery the basis of taxation and representation, "thus preferring and fostering it above all other property, by making it alone, of all property, an element of political power in the union, as well as a source of revenue to the federal government." The Constitution laid a binding obligation upon all states to return fugitive slaves to their masters upon claims made in due course. It guaranteed the states against domestic violence, not overlooking the possibilities of a servile revolt. "Power to abolish, circumscribe, or restrain slavery is withheld but power is granted and the duty is imposed on the federal government to protect and preserve it." The English language could hardly be more explicit.

All this was no accident; it was the outcome of design. "The framers of the Constitution were slave owners or the representatives of slave owners"; the Constitution was the result of a compromise between the North and the South in which slavery was specifically and zealously guarded and secured. Such were the canons of authenticity on the southern side.

This view of the Constitution contained so much sound historical truth that the opposition was forced to strain the imagination in its search for an answer. In an attempt to find lawful warrant for their creed in 1844, the abolitionists made a platform that became one of the prime curiosities in the annals of logic. They announced that the principles of the Declaration of Independence were embraced in the Constitution, that those principles proclaimed freedom, and that the provision of the Constitution relative to the return of fugitive states was itself null and void because forsooth common law holds any contract contrary to natural right and morality invalid.

Although the Republicans did not go that far in their defensive romancing, they also asserted, in their platform of 1860, that the principles of the Declaration of Independence were embodied in the Constitution and they claimed that neither Congress nor a state legislature could give legal existence to slavery in any territory of the United States. But there was one slip in this reasoning: the Supreme Court of the United States, with reference to the Dred Scot case, had read in the same oracle that Congress could not deprive any slave owner of his property in the territories and that the abolition of slavery there by Congress was null and void.

Nevertheless, the Republicans neatly evaded this condemnation of their doctrine, by calling it "a dangerous political heresy, at variance with the explicit provisions of that instrument itself, with contemporaneous exposition, and with legislative and judicial precedent." In short, the Republicans entered a dissenting opinion themselves; while it was hardly authentic constitutional law it made an effective appeal to voters — especially those fond of legal proprieties.

Even in their violent disagreement as to the nature of the Union, the contestants with equal fervor invoked the authority of the Constitution to show that secession was lawful or that the perpetuation of the Union was commanded as the case might be. With respect to this problem each party to the conflict had a theory which was finely and logically drawn from pertinent data and given the appearance of soundness by a process of skillful elision and emphasis.

Those who to-day look upon that dispute without rancor must admit that the secessionists had somewhat the better of the rhetorical side of the battle. Their scheme of historicity was simple. The thirteen colonies declared their independence as separate sovereignties; they were recognized by Great Britain in the treaty of peace as thirteen individual states; when they formed the Articles of Confederation they were careful to declare that "each state retains its sovereignty, freedom, and independence and every power, jurisdiction, and right, which is not by this Confederation expressly delegated to the United States in Congress assembled." These were undeniable facts. Then came the formation of the Constitution. The states elected delegates to the federal convention; the delegates revised the Articles of Confederation; the revision known as the Constitution, was submitted for approval to the states and finally ratified by state conventions.

Q. E. D., ran the secessionist argument, the sovereign states that entered the compact can by lawful process withdraw from the Union just as sovereign nations may by their own act dissolve a treaty with other foreign powers.

There was, of course, some difficulty in discovering attributes of sovereignty in the new states carved out of the national domain by the surveyors' compass and chain and admitted to the Union under specific constitutional limitations — states that now outnumbered the original thirteen. But the slight hiatus in the argument, which arose from this incongruity, was bridged by the declaration that the subject territories when taken in under the roof were clothed with the sovereignty and independence of the original commonwealths.

The historical brief of those who maintained, on the other hand, that secession was illegal rested in part on an interpretation of the preamble of the Constitution, an interpretation advanced by Webster during his famous debate with Hayne. "It cannot be shown," he said, "that the Constitution is a compact between state governments. The Constitution itself, in its very front, refutes that idea; it declares that it is ordained and established by the people of the United States. . . . It even does not say that it is established by the people of the several states; but pronounces that it is established by the people of the United States in the aggregate." That is, the Constitution was not made by the states; it was made by a high collective sovereign towering above them — the people of the United States.

This fair argument, which seemed convincing on its face, was later demolished by reference to the journals of the Convention that drafted the Constitution. When the preamble was originally drawn, it ran: "We, the people of the states of New Hampshire, Massachusetts, &c., . . . do ordain and establish the following Constitution." But on second thought the framers realized that according to their own decree the new government was to be set up as soon as nine states had ratified the proposed instrument. It was obviously undesirable to enumerate the states of the Union in advance, for some of them might withhold their approval. Therefore the first draft was abandoned and the words "We the people of the United States" substituted. The facts of record accordingly exploded the whole thesis built on this sandy foundation.

This fallacy Lincoln was careful to avoid in his first inaugural address. Seeking a more secure historical basis for his faith, he pointed out that the Union was in fact older than the Constitution, older than the Declaration of Independence. It was formed, he said, by the Articles of Association framed in 1774 by the Continental Congress speaking in the name of revolutionary America. It was matured and continued in the Declaration of Independence which proclaimed "these United Colonies" to be free and independent states. It was sealed by the Articles of Confederation which pledged the thirteen commonwealths to a perpetual Union under that form of government; it was crowned by the Constitution designed to make the Union "more perfect."

Far more effective on the nationalist side was the argument derived through logical processes from the nature of the Constitution itself, by Webster, Lincoln, and the philosophers of their school. It ran in the following vein. The Constitution does not, by express provision or by implication, provide any method by which a state may withdraw from the Union; no such dissolution of the federation was contemplated by the men who drafted and ratified the covenant. The government established by it operates directly on the people, not on states; it is the government of the people, not of states. Moreover the Constitution proclaims to all the world that it and the laws and treaties made in pursuance of its terms, are the supreme law of the land and that the judges of the states are bound thereby, "anything in the constitution and laws of any state to the contrary notwithstanding." Finally, the Supreme Court of the United States is the ultimate arbiter in all controversies arising between the national government and the states. Chief Justice Marshall had proclaimed the doctrine in beating down the resistance of Virginia, Maryland, and Ohio to federal authority; Chief Justice Taney had proclaimed it in paralyzing the opposition of Wisconsin to the fugitive slave law. Such being the grand pledges and principles of the Constitution it followed, to use Lincoln's version, that no state could lawfully withdraw from the Union; secession was insurrectionary or revolutionary according to circumstances.

What now is the verdict of history on these verbal contests? Did the delegates at the Philadelphia convention of 1787 regard themselves as ambassadors of sovereign states entering into a mere treaty of alliance? Did they set down anywhere a pontifical judgment to the effect that any state might on its own motion withdraw from the Union after approving the Constitution? The answer to these questions is in the negative. Had they thought out a logical system of political theory such as Calhoun afterward announced with such precision? If so, they left no record of it to posterity.

What then was the Constitution? It was a plan of government designed to effect certain purposes, specific and general, framed by a small group of citizens, "informed by a conscious solidarity of interests," who, according to all available evidence, intended that government to be supreme over the states and enduring. They were not dominated by any logical scheme such as Calhoun evolved in defending his cause; they were engrossed in making, not breaking, a Union; they made no provision for, and if the testimony of their recorded debates be accepted as conclusive, did not contemplate the withdrawal of the states from the federation by any legal procedure. Surely it was not without significance that James Madison, the father of the Constitution, who lived to see secession threatened in South Carolina, denounced in unmistakable terms the smooth and well-articulated word-pattern of Calhoun, condemning secession as utterly without

support in the understandings of the men who made, ratified, and launched the Constitution.

But it may be said that the men of Philadelphia merely drafted the Constitution and that what counts in the premises is the opinions of the voters in the states, who through their delegates ratified the instrument. Did, then, the men who chose the delegates for the state ratifying conventions or the delegates themselves have clearly in mind a concept that made the great document in effect a mere treaty of alliance which could be legally denounced at will by any member? The records in the case give no affirmative answer. What most of them thought is a matter of pure conjecture. Were any of the states sovereign in fact at any time; that is, did any of them assume before the world the attributes and functions of a sovereign nation? Certainly not. Did the whole people in their collective capacity make the Constitution? To ask the question is to answer it; they did not.

When the modern student examines all the verbal disputes over the nature of the Union — the arguments employed by the parties which operated and opposed the federal government between the adoption of the Constitution and the opening of the Civil War— he can hardly do otherwise than conclude that the linguistic devices used first on one side and then on the other were not derived from inherently necessary concepts concerning the intimate essence of the federal system. The roots of the controversy lay elsewhere — in social groupings founded on differences in climate, soil, industries, and labor systems, in divergent social forces, rather than varying degrees of righteousness and wisdom, or what romantic historians call "the magnetism of great personalities."

In the spring of 1861 the full force of the irrepressible conflict burst upon the hesitant and bewildered nation and for four long years the clash of arms filled the land with its brazen clangor. For four long years the anguish, the calamities, and the shocks of the struggle absorbed the energies of the multitudes, blared in the headlines of the newspapers, and loomed impressively in the minds of the men and women who lived and suffered in that age.

Naturally, therefore, all who wrote of the conflict used the terms of war. In its records, the government of the United States officially referred to the contest as the War of the Rebellion, thus by implication setting the stigma of treason on those who served under the Stars and Bars. Repudiating this brand and taking for his shield the righteousness of legitimacy, one of the leading southern statesmen, Alexander H. Stephens, in his great history of the conflict, called it the War between the States. This, too, no less than the title chosen by the federal government, is open to objections; apart from the large assumptions involved, it is not strictly accurate for, in the border states, the armed struggle was a guerrilla war and in Virginia the domestic strife ended in the separation of several counties, under the ægis of a new state constitution, as West Virginia. More recently a distinguished historian, Edward Channing, entitled a volume dealing with the period The War for Southern Independence — a characterization which, though fairly precise, suffers a little perhaps from abstraction.

As a matter of fact all these symbols are misleading in that they overemphasize the element of military force in the grand denouement. War there was unquestionably, immense, wide-sweeping, indubitable, as Carlyle would say. For years the agony of it hung like a pall over the land. And yet with strange swiftness the cloud was lifted and blown away. Merciful grass spread its green mantle over the cruel scars and the gleaming red splotches sank into the hospitable earth.

It was then that the economist and lawyer, looking more calmly on the scene, discovered that the armed conflict had been only one phase of the cataclysm, a transitory phase; that at bottom the so-called Civil War, or the War between the States, in the light of Roman analogy, was a social war, ending in the unquestioned establishment of a new power in the government, making vast changes in the arrangement of classes, in the accumulation and distribution of wealth, in the course of industrial development, and in the Constitution inherited from the Fathers. Merely by the accidents of climate, soil, and geography was it a sectional struggle. If the planting interest had been scattered evenly throughout the industrial region, had there been a horizontal rather than a perpendicular cleavage, the irrepressible conflict would have been resolved by other methods and accompanied by other logical defense mechanisms.

In any event neither accident nor rhetoric should be allowed to obscure the intrinsic character of that struggle. If the operations by which the middle classes of England broke the power of the king and the aristocracy are to be known collectively as the Puritan Revolution, if the series of acts by which the bourgeois and peasants of France overthrew the king, nobility, and clergy is to be called the French Revolution, then accuracy compels us to characterize by the same term the social cataclysm in which the capitalists, laborers, and farmers of the North and West drove from power in the national government the planting aristocracy of the South. Viewed under the light of universal history, the fighting was a fleeting incident; the social revolution was the essential, portentous outcome.

To be sure the battles and campaigns of the epoch are significant to the military strategist; the tragedy and heroism of the contest furnish inspiration to patriots and romance to the makers of epics. But the core of the vortex lay elsewhere. It was in the flowing substance of things limned by statistical reports on finance, commerce, capital, industry, railways, and agriculture, by provisions of constitutional law, and by the pages of statute books — prosaic muniments which show that the so-called civil war was in reality a Second American Revolution and in a strict sense, the First. . . .

Frank Lawrence Owsley: THE SOUTHERN DEFENSE OF THE AGRARIAN IDEAL

Frank Lawrence Owsley, born in Alabama, studied history under William E. Dodd at the University of Chicago. In the South of the 1920's he associated himself with other young writers, like John Crowe Ransome, Stark Young, Allen Tate, and Robert Penn Warren, "to support a Southern way of life against what might be called the American or prevailing way." These Southern writers agreed that the best terms in which to represent the distinction are contained in the phrase "Agrarian vs. Industrial," and, in 1930, they issued a collective manifesto in the shape of a book of twelve essays entitled I'll Take My Stand. *Frank L. Owsley contributed an essay to that famous collection, and his interpretation of the causes of the Civil War is reprinted in its entirety.*

FROM 1830 to 1861 the North and South quarreled with a savage fury that was unknown in the history of any country whose sections had been bound together by voluntary agreement. Finally war came, and the war which came was a war such as history had never recorded until that date. Over three millions of men from first to last marched forth to deadly combat, and nearly a million went down. This, out of a population of little more than twenty-five millions of white men meant that nearly one man in every six went to war. Europe first smiled contemptuously at the armed mobs of civilian soldiers who ran from one another at first Manassas, but stood popeyed with wonder and awe when Anglo-Saxons stood within ten paces of one another at Chickamauga and fired point-blank, mowing down one-third of the combatants, or marched up Cemetery Ridge at Gettysburg as on dress parade, or charged twenty deep at Cold Harbor with their addresses pinned to their backs, so that their dead bodies might be identified after being torn by artillery at close range.

Seldom has there been such a peace as that which followed Appomattox.

While Sherman, Sheridan, and Grant had allowed their armies to harry and plunder the population of the invaded country all too much, using churches, universities, and state capitols with their archives as stables for horses and mean men, General Grant could pause long enough during the deadly Spotsylvania Courthouse campaign to remove his hat at the house where Stonewall Jackson had died the year before and say, "General Jackson was a gallant soldier and a Christian gentleman." And Grant and Sherman were generous enough to refuse to take the side-arms and horses from the Southern soldiers who surrendered. But after the military surrender at Appomattox there ensued a peace unique in history. There was no generosity. For ten years the South, already ruined by the loss of nearly $2,000,000,000 invested in slaves, with its lands worthless, its cattle and stock gone, its houses burned, was turned over to the three millions of former slaves, some of whom could still remember the taste of human flesh and the bulk of them hardly three generations removed from cannibalism. These half-savage blacks were armed. Their passions were roused against their former masters by savage political leaders like Thaddeus Stevens, who advocated the confiscation of all Southern lands for the benefit of the negroes, and the extermination, if need be, of the Southern white population; and like Charles Sumner, whose chief regret had been that his skin was not black. Not only were the blacks armed; they were upheld and incited by garrisons of Northern soldiers, by Freedman's Bureau officials, and by Northern ministers of the gospel, and at length they were given the ballot while their former masters were disarmed and, to a large extent, disfranchised. For ten years ex-slaves, led by carpetbaggers and scalawags, continued the pillages of war, combing the South for anything left by the invading armies, levying taxes, selling empires of plantations under the auction hammer, dragooning the Southern population, and visiting upon them the ultimate humiliations.

After the South had been conquered by war and humiliated and impoverished by peace, there appeared still to remain something which made the South different — something intangible, incomprehensible, in the realm of the spirit. That too must be invaded and destroyed; so there commenced a second war of conquest, the conquest of the Southern mind, calculated to remake every Southern opinion, to impose the Northern way of life and thought upon the South, write "error" across the pages of Southern history which were out of keeping with the Northern legend, and set the rising and unborn generations upon stools of everlasting repentance. Francis Wayland, former president of Brown University, regarded the South as "the new missionary ground for the national schoolteacher," and President Hill of Harvard looked forward to the task for the North "of spreading knowledge and culture over the regions that sat in darkness." The older generations, the hardened campaigners under Lee and Jackson, were too tough-minded to reëducate. They must be ignored. The North must "treat them as Western farmers do the stumps in their clearings, work around them and let them rot out," but the rising and future generations were to receive the proper education in Northern tradition.

The South, in the days after the so-called Reconstruction, was peculiarly defenseless against being educated by the North. Many leaders of the Civil War days were politically disfranchised or so saddened and depressed that they drew within themselves. From 1865 to 1880 the father of one of Alabama's later Governors refused to read a newspaper. His was only an extreme case of what was a general tendency, for the reading of the "news" was nothing but the annals of plunder, rape, murder, and endless injustices. Such old Spartans, living thus within themselves in order that they might live at all, built up around themselves a shell which cut them off spiritually from all that was going on about them. This, too, when many of them were still in their prime and fitted for many years of leadership. These were the men whom the Northern intellectual and spiritual plowmen were to plow around like stumps until they rotted out. Their older sons had been in the war. They adjusted themselves, if only to a degree. Their younger sons and daughters between 1865 and 1876 or later grew up wild and uncouth, either unable to attend school or too proud to attend school in company with their former slaves.

Hence, for thirty years after the Civil War the intellectual life of the South was as sterile as its own rocky uplands and sandy barrens. The rising generations read Northern literature, shot through with the New England tradition. Northern textbooks were used in Southern schools; Northern histories, despite the frantic protests of local patriotic organizations, were almost universally taught in Southern high schools and colleges, — books that were built around the Northern legend and either completely ignored the South or insisted upon the unrighteousness of most of its history and its philosophy of life. One would judge from the average history text and from the recitations conducted by the North-

ern schoolma'am that the Puritans and Pilgrim fathers were the ancestors of every self-respecting American. Southern children spoke of "our Puritan fathers." No child ever heard of the Southern Puritan fathers — the great horde of Scotch-Irish Presbyterians and German Lutherans and other strict and puritanical peoples who had pushed to the Mississippi River and far North of the Ohio before the New England population had got a hundred miles west of Boston.

In short, the South either had no history, or its history was tainted with slavery and rebellion and must be abjured. There was for the Southern child and youth until the end of the nineteenth century very little choice. They had to accept the Northern version of history with all its condemnations and carping criticisms of Southern institutions and life, with its chanting of "John Brown's Body," its hanging of Jeff Davis on a sour-apple tree, its hosannas to factories and mines and the growth of populations as the only criterion of progress, and the crying down and discrediting of anything agrarian as old-fashioned and backward. As time rolled on, the chorus of "John Brown's Body" swelled ever louder and louder until the lusty voices of grandchildren and great-grandchildren of rebels joined in the singing. Lee, largely through the perverse generosity of Charles Francis Adams, Jr., was permitted to be worshiped in the Southern edition of the Northern tradition because Lee made a good showing abroad as a representative of American military genius. However, Lincoln was the real Southern hero because Lincoln had saved the Union. So they were told!

Thus the North defeated the South in war, crushed and humiliated it in peace, and waged against it a war of intellec-

tual and spiritual conquest. In this conquest the North fixed upon the South the
stigma of war guilt, of slave guilt, of
treason, and thereby shook the faith of
its people in their way of living and in
their philosophy of life.

II

But a people cannot live under condemnation and upon the philosophy of
their conquerors. Either they must ultimately come to scorn the condemnation
and the philosophy of those who thrust
these things upon them, or their soul
should and will perish.

Not all the Southern minds, fortunately, were conquered by the Northern
conquest. Even a few Northern intellec-
tuals revolted against such an unnatural
and vicious procedure. The most out-
standing instance of this tough-minded-
ness is found in the Northerner, William
Archibald Dunning of Columbia University, and the group of Southern students
whom he gathered about him to study
the history of the Civil War and Reconstruction. It was among this group that
the Southern renascence began and the
holiness of the Northern legend was first
challenged. The history of the Civil War
and Reconstruction was written carefully
and ably and with detachment by this
group of Southern scholars, in such works
as Garner's *Reconstruction in Mississippi;*
Fleming's *Civil War and Reconstruction
in Alabama,* his *Documentary History of
Reconstruction,* and his *Sequel of Appomattox;* Hamilton's *Reconstruction of
North Carolina;* Ramsdall's *Reconstruction of Texas;* Staples' *Reconstruction of
Arkansas;* and Davis's *Reconstruction of
Florida.* The smugness of victory was
somewhat undermined. Later followed
other writers on this period of history
who have been less detached and more
outspoken: — such writers as Bowers,

Stryker, and Beale — Northerners; and
Eckenrode, Tate, Robert Penn Warren
and others — Southerners. These men
have scorned the injustice and hypocrisy
of the condemnation of the South. But
after all, mass opinion, prejudice, and
smugness have not been touched by the
efforts of such as these. The North still
sits in Pharisaical judgment upon the
South, beating its chest and thanking-
Thee-O-Lord-that-I-am-not-as-other-men
and imposing its philosophy of living and
life upon the South. The South, confused, ill informed because taught by an
alien doctrine so long, unconsciously
accepts portions of the Northern legend
and philosophy; sullenly and without
knowing why, it rejects other portions,
and withal knows not where to turn.

The South needs orientation and direction in its thinking, and all things must
begin at the point where it was thrown
from its balance. It must know that the
things for which it stood were reasonable and sound, that its condemnation
at the hands of the North has been contemptible, and that for it, at least, the
philosophy of the North is the religion
of an alien God. It is the hope of the
essayists in this book to aid the South in
its reorientation and in a return to its true
philosophy. It is the particular object of
this essay to point out the untruth of the
self-righteous Northern legend which
makes the South the war criminal.

III

What lay behind the bitter sectional
quarreling between 1830 and 1860?
What made the war which followed this
quarreling so deadly? Why the cruel
peace that followed war? Why the intellectual conquest of the South? The old
answer for these questions and the answer which is yet given by the average
Northerner is that the whole struggle

from beginning to end was a conflict between light and darkness, between truth and falsehood, between slavery and freedom, between liberty and despotism. This is the ready answer of the Babbitts, who, unfortunately, have obtained much of their information from historians such as James Ford Rhodes and John Bach MacMaster. The Southerner historians of the Dunning school, all the third-generation "rebel historians," and many of the recent Northern historians reject such an explanation as naïve if nothing else. They have become convinced that slavery as a moral issue is too simple an explanation, and that as one of the many contributing causes of war it needs an explanation which the North has never grasped — in fact, never can grasp until the negro race covers the North as thickly as it does the lower South. They are more inclined to take seriously the Southern championship of state rights in the face of centralization as a cause of the struggle; they see that the protective tariff was as fundamental in the controversy at times as the slavery question, and that the constant expansion of the United States by the annexation of territories and the constant admission of new states from these territories was a vital factor in producing the Civil War — in short, that the sectional controversies which finally resulted in the Civil War and its aftermath were deep rooted and complex in origin, and that slavery as a moral issue has too long been the red herring dragged across the trail.

Complex though the factors were which finally caused war, they all grew out of two fundamental differences which existed between the two sections: the North was commercial and industrial, and the South was agrarian. The fundamental and passionate ideal for which the South stood and fell was the ideal of an agrarian society. All else, good and bad, revolved around this ideal — the old and accepted manner of life for which Egypt, Greece, Rome, England, and France had stood. History and literature, profane and sacred, twined their tendrils about the cottage and the villa, not the factory.

When America was settled, the tradition of the soil found hospitable root-bed in the Southern colonies, where climate and land combined to multiply the rich-ness of an agrarian economy. All who came to Virginia, Maryland, the Carolinas and Georgia were not gentlemen; in fact, only a few were of the gentry. Most of them were of the yeomanry, and they were from rural England with centuries of country and farm lore and folk memory. Each word, name, sound, had grown from the soil and had behind it sweet memory, stirring adventure, and ofttimes stark tragedy. Thoughts, words, ideas, concepts, life itself, grew from the soil. The environment all pointed toward an endless enjoyment of the fruits of the soil. Jefferson, not visualizing the industrial revolution which whipped up the multiplication of populations and tore their roots from the soil, dreamed of America, free from England, as a boundless Utopia of farms taking a thousand generations to fill.

Men so loved their life upon the soil that they sought out in literature and history peoples who had lived a similar life, so that they might justify and further stimulate their own concepts of life and perhaps set a high goal for themselves among the great nations which had sprung from the land. The people whom they loved most in the ancient world were the Greeks and the Romans of the early republic. The Greeks did not appeal to them as did the Romans, for they were too inclined to neglect their farms and turn to the sea and to handicraft. But the even-poised and leisurely life of the Greeks, their oratory, their philosophy, their art — especially their architecture — appealed to the South. The Greek tradition became partly grafted upon the Anglo-Saxon and Scotch tradition of life. However, it was the Romans of the early republic, before land speculators and corn laws had driven men from the soil to the city slums, who appealed most powerfully to the South. These Romans were brave, sometimes crude, but open and without guile — unlike the Greeks. They reeked of the soil, of the plow and the spade; they had wrestled with virgin soil and forests; they could build log houses and were closer to many Southerners than even the English gentleman in his moss-covered stone house. It was Cincinnatus, whose hands were rough with guiding the plow, rather than Cato, who wrote about Roman agriculture and lived in a villa, whom Southerners admired the most, though they read and admired Cato as a fine gentleman with liberal ideas about tenants and slaves and a thorough knowledge and love of the soil. The Gracchi appealed to Southerners because the Gracchi were lovers of the soil and died in the attempt to restore the yeomanry to the land.

With the environment of the New World and the traditions of the Old, the South thus became the seat of an agrarian civilization which had strength and promise for a future greatness second to none. The life of the South was leisurely and unhurried for the planter, the yeoman, or the landless tenant. It was a way of life, not a routine of planting and reaping merely for gain. Washington, who rode daily over his farms and counted his horses, cattle, plows, and bushels of corn as carefully as a merchant takes stock of his supplies, inhaled the smell of ripe corn after a rain, nursed his bluegrass sod and shade trees with his own hands, and, when in the field as a soldier or in the city as President of the United States, was homesick at the smell of fresh-plowed earth. He kept vigil with his sick horses and dogs, not as a capitalist who guards his investments, but as one who watches over his friends.

The system of society which developed in the South, then, was close to the soil. It might be organized about the plantation with its wide fields and its slaves and self-sufficiency, or it might center around a small farm, ranging from a fifty-acre to a five-hundre-acre tract, tilled by the owner, undriven by competition, supplied with corn by his own toil and with meat from his own pen or from the fields and forests. The amusements might be the fine balls and house parties of the planter or the three-day break-down dances which David Crockett loved, or horse races, foot races, cock and dog fights, boxing, wrestling, shooting, fighting, log-rolling, house raising, or corn-shucking. It might be crude or genteel, but it everywhere was fundamentally alike and natural. The houses were homes, where families lived sufficient and complete within themselves, working together and fighting together. And when death came, they were buried in their own lonely peaceful graveyards, to await doomsday together.

IV

This agrarian society had its own interests, which in almost all respects diverged from the interests of the industrial system of the North. The two sections, North and South, had entered the revolution against the mother country with the full knowledge of the opposing interests of their societies; knowing this difference, they had combined in a loose union under the Articles of Confederation. Finally, they had joined together under the Constitution fully conscious that there were thus united two divergent economic and social systems, two civilizations, in fact. The two sections were evenly balanced in population and in the number of states, so that at the time there was no danger of either section's encroaching upon the interests of the other. This balance was clearly understood. Without it a union would not have been possible. Even with the understanding that the two sections would continue to hold this even balance, the sections were very careful to define and limit the powers of the federal government lest one section with its peculiar interests should get control of the national government and use the powers of that government to exploit the other section. Specific powers were granted the federal government, and all not specifically granted were retained by the states.

But equilibrium was impossible under expansion and growth. One section with its peculiar system of society would at one time or another become dominant and control the national government and either exploit the other section or else fail to exercise the functions of government for its positive benefit. Herein lies the irrepressible conflict, the eternal struggle between the agrarian South and the commercial and industrial North to control the government either in its own interest or, negatively, to prevent the other section from controlling it in its interests. Lincoln and Seward and the radical Republicans clothed the conflict later in robes of morality by making it appear that the "house divided against itself" and the irrepressible conflict which resulted from this division marked a division between slavery and freedom.

Slavery, as we shall see, was part of the agrarian system, but only one element and not an essential one. To say that the irrepressible conflict was between slavery and freedom is either to fail to grasp the nature and magnitude of the conflict, or else to make use of deliberate deception by employing a shibboleth to win the uninformed and unthinking to the support of a sinister undertaking. Rob Roy MacGregor, one of the chief corruptionists of the present-day power lobby, said that the way the power companies crush opposition and win popular support is to pin the word "bolshevik" upon the leaders of those who oppose the power-lobby program. The leaders of the Northern industrial system could win popular support by tagging their opponents as *"enemies of liberty"* and themselves as "champions of freedom." This they did. Lincoln was a politician and knew all the tricks of a politician. Seward was a politician and knew every *in* and *out*. This is true of other leaders of the "party of high ideals" which assumed the name of Republican party. Doubtless, Lincoln, Seward, and others were half sincere in their idea of an irrepressible conflict, but their fundamental purpose was to win elections and get their party into power — the party of the industrial North — with an industrial program for business and a sop of free lands for the Western farmer.

The irrepressible conflict, then, was not between slavery and freedom, but between the industrial and commercial civilization of the North and the agrarian civilization of the South. The industrial North demanded a high tariff so as to monopolize the domestic markets, especially the Southern market, for the South, being agrarian, must purchase all manufactured goods. It was an exploitative principle, originated at the expense of the South and for the benefit of the

North. After the South realized that it would have little industry of its own, it fought the protective tariff to the point of nullification in South Carolina and almost to the point of dissolving the Union. In this as in other cases Southerners saw that what was good for the North was fatal to the South.

The industrial section demanded a national subsidy for the shipping business and merchant marine, but, as the merchant marine was alien to the Southern agrarian system, the two sections clashed. It was once more an exploitation of one section for the benefit of the other.

The industrial North demanded internal improvements — roads, railroads, canals — at national expense to furnish transportation for its goods to Southern and Western markets which were already hedged around for the benefit of the North by the tariff wall. The South objected to internal improvements at national expense because it had less need of transportation than the North and because the burden would be heavier on the South and the benefits greater for the North — another exploitation of the Southern system. The North favored a government-controlled bank; but as corporate wealth and the quick turnover of money were confined to that section, such an institution would be for the sole benefit, the South believed, of the North. There were many other things of a positive nature which the system of society in the North demanded of the federal government, but those mentioned will illustrate the conflict of interest between North and South.

It is interesting to observe that all the favors thus asked by the North were of doubtful constitutional right, for nowhere in the Constitution were these matters specifically mentioned; it is further significant that all the powers and

favors thus far demanded by the North were merely negatived by the South; no substitute was offered. The North was demanding positive action on the part of the federal government, and the South was demanding that no action be taken at all. In fact, it may be stated as a general principle that the agrarian South asked practically nothing of the federal government in domestic legislation. It might be imperialistic in its foreign policy, but its domestic policy was almost entirely negative. Even in the matter of public lands the South favored turning over these lands to the state within which they lay, rather than have them controlled by the federal government.

Had these differences, inherent in agrarian and industrial civilizations, been the only ones, it is obvious that conflict would have been inevitable and that two different political philosophies would have been developed to justify and rationalize the conflict which was foreshadowed in the very nature of the demands of the sections: centralization in the North and state rights in the South. But there was another and deadlier difference. There was the slavery system in the South. Before examining the Southern doctrine of state rights, which was its defense mechanism for its entire system of society rather than, as has been claimed, for slavery alone, let us turn to the slavery problem as one of the elements of conflict between the two sections.

v

Slavery was no simple question of ethics; it cut across the categories of human thought like a giant question mark. It was a moral, an economic, a religious, a social, a philosophical, and above all a political question. It was no essential part of the agrarian civilization of the South — though the Southerners under attack assumed that it was. Without slavery the economic and social life of the South would not have been radically different. Perhaps the plantation life would not have been as pronounced without it, yet the South would long have remained agricultural — as it still is after sixty-five years of "freedom"! Certainly the South would have developed its political philosophy very much as it did. Yet the slavery question furnished more fuel to sectional conflict and created more bitterness than any or all the other elements of the two groups.

Slavery had been practically forced upon the country by England— over the protest of colonial assemblies. During the eighteenth century it had ceased to be profitable, and colonial moral indignation rose correspondingly. However, when the Revolution came and the Southern colonies gained their independence, they did not free the negroes. The eternal race question had reared itself. Negroes had come into the Southern Colonies in such numbers that people feared for the integrity of the white race. For the negroes were cannibals and barbarians, and therefore dangerous. No white man who had any contact with slavery was willing to free the slaves and allow them to dwell among the whites. Slaves were a peril, at least a risk, but free blacks were considered a menace too great to be hazarded. Even if no race wars occurred, there was dread of being submerged and absorbed by the black race. Accordingly, all slaveholders and non-slaveholders who objected to slavery, objected even more to the presence of the free negro. They argued that the slaves could never be freed unless they could be deported back to Africa or to the West Indies. This conviction became more fervent when the terrifying negro

insurrections in Santo Domingo and Hayti destroyed the white population and civilizations almost completely and submerged the remainder under barbarian control. All early abolitionists — which meant most of the Southern people up until around 1800 — were abolitionists only on condition of colonization. As a result there were organized many colonization societies, mostly in the South during this period.

But colonization was futile. It was soon realized by all practical slaveholders that the negroes could not be deported successfully. Deportation was cruel and expensive. Few of the black people wished to leave the South. The Southern whites shrugged their shoulders and deplored the necessity of continuing the negroes in bondage as the only alternative to chaos and destruction.

Then the invention of the cotton gin and the opening of the cotton lands in the Southwest, 1810–36, made the negro slave an economic instrument of great advantage. With the aid of the fresh cheap lands and the negro slave vast fortunes were made in a few years. Both North and South having now conceded that emancipation was impossible, the Southern planters made the most of their new cotton kingdom with a fairly easy conscience. They had considered emancipation honestly and fairly and had found it out of the question. Their skirts were clear. Let the blood of slavery rest upon the heads of those who had forced it upon the South.

But the opening of the "cotton kingdom" gave dynamic power to the agrarian section, and new lands were desired by the West and South. The now industrial East saw its interest threatened if the South should colonize the territories to the West, including those gained and to be gained. With the tremendous impetus given to the expansion of the Southern system by the growth of the cotton industry and culture, the North became uneasy and began to show opposition to the continued balance of power. This first became manifest in the struggle which resulted in the Missouri Compromise of 1822. Up to this point the objection to slavery was always tempered by the acknowledgment on the part of the North that the South was a victim of the system of slavery and ought to be sympathized with, rather than the instigator of the system, who ought to be condemned as a criminal.

But in 1831 a voice was raised which was drowned only in the roar of battle in 1861–5. It was the cry of William Lloyd Garrison that slavery was a crime and the slaveholders were criminals. He established the famous *Liberator,* which preached unremitting and ruthless war upon slavery and the slaveholder. He knew no moderation. He had no balance or sense of consequence. His was the typical "radical" mind which demands that things be done at once, which tries to force nature, which wants to tear up by the roots. Although he was completely ignorant of the South and of negro slavery, he dogmatically assumed an omniscient power of judgment over the section and the institution. In the *Liberator* or in the anti-slavery tracts fostered by the anti-slavery societies which he aided or instigated, he set no bounds of accusation and denunciation. The slave master, said Garrison, debauched his women slaves, had children by them, and in turn defiled his own children and sold them into the slave market; the slave plantation was primarily a gigantic harem for the master and his sons. The handsome octoroon coachmen shared the bed of the mistress when the master was away from home, and the daughters were frequently away in some secluded nook to rid themselves of undesirable negro offspring. Ministers of the gospel who owned or sanctioned slavery were included in his sweeping indictment of miscegenation and prostitution. In short, Garrison and the anti-slavery societies which he launched, followed soon by Northern churchmen, stigmatized the South as a black brothel. This was not all! The Southern slaveowners were not merely moral lepers; they were cruel and brooding tyrants, who drove their slaves till they dropped and died, who starved them to save food, let them go cold and almost naked to save clothing, let them dwell in filthy pole pens rather than build them comfortable cottages, beat them unmercifully with leather thongs filled with spikes, dragged cats over their bodies and faces, trailed them with bloodhounds which rent and chewed them, — then sprinkled their wounds with salt and red pepper. Infants were torn from their mothers' breasts and sold to Simon Legrees; families were separated and scattered to the four winds. This brutal treatment of the slaves reacted upon the masters and made them brutal and cruel in their dealings with their fellow whites. Such charges, printed in millions upon millions of pamphlets, were sent out all over the world. Sooner or later, much of it was accepted as true in the North.

In the South this abolition war begot Nat Turner's rebellion, in which negro slaves in Virginia under the leadership of Nat Turner, a freedman, massacred their masters, including women and children. The new situation, in turn, begot a revolution in Southern attitudes. Struck almost out of a clear sky by the Garrisonian blasts and the Nat Turner rebellion, Southern leaders were dazed. They discussed momentarily the expedient of freeing the slaves, then closed forever their minds upon the subject as too dangerous to undertake. Then came a counter-blast of fierce resentment, denying all accusations. The South threw up a defense mechanism. The ministers searched the Scriptures by day and night and found written, in language which could not be misunderstood, a biblical sanction of slavery. Abraham, Moses, the prophets, Jesus, and the disciples on many occasions had approved slavery. History from its dawn had seen slavery almost everywhere. A scriptural and historical justification was called in to meet the general indictment of the wrongfulness of slavery in the abstract. Partly as a result of this searching of the Scriptures there took place a religious revival in the South, which had tended heretofore to incline to Jeffersonian liberalism of the deistic type. The South became devoutly orthodox and literal in its theology. But the abolitionists were not willing to accept scriptural justification of slavery. There was an attempt to prove the wrongfulness of slavery by the same sacred book, but, finding this impossible, many abolitionists repudiated the Scriptures as of divine origin. Partly as a result, the North lost confidence in orthodoxy and tended to become deistic as the South had been. One could almost hear Puritan New England creaking upon its theological hinges as it swung away from its old position.

But there were philosophers and thinkers at work in the South who would meet the abolitionists upon their own grounds. Hammond, Fitzhugh, John C. Calhoun, Chancellor Harper, Thomas R. Dew, either because they felt that scriptural justification of slavery was inadequate or because they realized the necessity of getting away from the theological grounds in order that they might combat the abolitionists upon common ground, approached slavery from the social and economic standpoint. Their general conclusions were that two races of different culture and color cannot live together on terms of equality. One will dominate or destroy the other. There was no middle ground. It had ever been thus. They contended that the negro was of a backward, inferior race. Certainly his culture was inferior. He must either rule or be ruled. If he ruled, the white race would be destroyed or submerged and its civilization wiped out. For the Southern people there was no choice; the negro must be ruled, and the only way he could be controlled, they believed, was by some form of slavery. In other words, Calhoun, Fitzhugh, and the "philosophers of slavery" justified slavery upon the grounds of the "race question"—which U. B. Phillips has called the theme of Southern history, before and after the Civil War. Aside from the scriptural and social justification, these men defended slavery as an economic necessity. They contended that the culture of rice, tobacco, sugar cane, and especially cotton upon which the world depended could not be carried on without slaves. The South, including the up-country and the mountains, accepted the scriptural justification of slavery, to a great extent. The up-country did not accept the economics of slavery, but slavery, in its aspect as a race question, was universally approved in valleys, plains and mountains. It found, in fact, its strongest supporters among the poor whites and the non-slaveholding small landowners. Their race prejudice and fears were the stronger because they knew nothing of the better side of the negro and regarded him as a vicious and dangerous animal whose freedom meant war to the knife and knife to the death. It was the old fear which we have spoken of, common to all in the days of the Revolution and in the days when Jefferson and Washington were advocating emancipation only on condition that the freedman be sent from the country. Outside of the common agrarianism of the multitudinous sections of the South which acted as a common tie, the race question which underlay slavery, magnified and aggravated by the abolition crusade, was the hoop of steel which held men together in the South in the great final argument of arms.

This abolition crusade on the part of the North and justification of slavery by the South were principally outside of the realm of politics in the beginning. The abolitionists, in fact, had a tendency to abjure politics and demand "direct action," as some of our recent radicals do. But the leaven soon spread, and slavery became a burning political issue. The political leaders of the North, especially the Whigs, after the dynamic growth of the South in the first quarter of the nineteenth century, became fixed in their determination that the agrarian section should have its metes and bounds definitely limited. Industrialism, which had undergone an even greater development than had cotton-growing, declared that the balance of power between agrarian and industrial sections must go. Because slaveholding was the acid test as to whether a state would remain agrarian or become eventually industrial, the Northern leaders wished that no more slave states should be carved from the Western territories. Between 1836, when the annexation of slaveholding Texas was advocated by the South, and 1860, when Lincoln was elected upon a platform which declared that no more territory was open to slavery, the major issues in national politics were the struggles between North and South over the admission or exclusion of slavery from the national territories. That is, it was a question whether the territories would be equally open to both sections or whether the North should have an exclusive right in these territories to found its own states and system and thereby destroy the balance of power and control the federal government in the interest of its own economic and social system. Unfortunately for the South, the leaders of the North were able to borrow the language of the abolitionists and clothed the struggle in a moral garb. It was good politics, it was noble and convenient, to speak of it as a struggle for freedom when it was essentially a struggle for the balance of power.

So to the bitter war of the abolitionists and the bitter resentment of the South was added the fight over the balance of power in the form of the extension of slavery into the common territories.

VI

As it has been suggested, had there not been slavery as an added difference between the agrarian South and industrial North, the two sections would have developed each its own political philosophy to explain and justify its institutions and its demands upon the federal government. The North had interests which demanded positive legislation exploitative of the agrarian South; the South had interests which demanded that the federal government refrain entirely from legislation within its bounds — it demanded only to be let alone. While this conflict of interest was recognized as existing in the days of the Revolution when the first attempt at union was made, it was not until the first government under the Constitution was in power that it received a philosophical statement. In the beginning of Washington's administration two men defined the fundamental principles of the political philosophy of the two societies, Alexander Hamilton for the North and Jefferson for the South. The one was extreme centralization, the other was extreme decentralization; the one was nationalistic and the other provincial; the first was called Federalism, the other State Rights, but in truth the first should have been called Unitarianism and the second Federalism.

It has been often said that the doctrine of state rights was not sincere, but that it was a defense mechanism to protect slavery (implying that slavery was merely a moral question and the South entirely immoral). But Jefferson was an abolitionist, as nearly all the Southern people were at the time the doctrine was evolved and stated by Jefferson, and Calhoun's extreme doctrine of state sovereignty was fully evolved in South Carolina before the crusade had begun against slavery. However, there is no doubt that the bitter abolition crusade and the political controversies between the two sections between 1836 and 1861 over slavery in the territories gave added strength and exactness to the Southern doctrine. Another thrust has been made at the sincerity of the doctrine of state rights: the principle has been laid down that state rights is a cowardly defense used by the industrial interests to shield themselves against the unfriendly action of a more powerful government. Such examples are noted as the extreme sensitiveness of big business to state rights in the matter of federal child-labor laws, federal control of water power, and prohibition. It is not to be denied that it should be easier for the water-power companies to purchase a state than a national legislature — as the market price of a Congressman is supposed to be somewhat higher than a mere state legislator (though there are certain well-known purchases of Congressmen which seem to contradict this impression). But observe the other side of the question. Big business has more often taken refuge behind the national government than behind the state. I have only to call attention to the way in which corporations take refuge behind the Fourteenth Amendment to avoid state legislation, to the numberless cases brought before the Supreme Court of the United States by corporations whose charters have been vitiated or nullified by state action, to the refuge sought by the railroads in national protection against the state granger legislation, and to the eternal whine of big business for paternalistic and exploitative legislation such as the tariff, the ship and railroad subsidies. Historically, then, the vested interests of industrialism have not had any great use for state rights. They are the founders of the doctrine of centralization, of the Hamiltonian and Republican principles; they have controlled the Republican party; why should they be unfriendly to their own principles and their own political instrument? They have not been! It may be suggested as a principle that for positive exploitation big business has desired large and sweeping powers for the national government, and that for negative business of defense it will hide behind any cover convenient, whether it be a state or the Fourteenth Amendment. The assertion that state rights was a defense mechanism evolved by slaveowners, for corporations later to hide behind, is inadequate if nothing else.

But state rights was a defense mechanism, and its defensive ramparts were meant by its disciples to protect things far more fundamental and larger than slave property. It was the doctrine of an agrarian society meant in the first place to protect the South as a whole against the encroachments of the industrial and commercial North. By upholding the doctrine of a rigid division of powers between state and nation and the literal interpretation of the Constitution such legislation as protective tariffs, ship subsidies, national banks, internal improvements at federal expense, would be avoided. It would also protect one part of the South against another. While there were infinite diverging interests between the industrial North and agrarian South which made a doctrine of state rights the only safe bulwark against Northern exploitation and encroachment, there were great regional differences within the South itself which made legislation that was beneficial to one section, harmful to another. One section grew cotton and cane, another tobacco and rice, another produced naval stores and lumber; one had slaves, another had none. To throw all these interests into a hodge-podge under one government would be to sacrifice all the minority interests to the one which was represented by the largest population and body of voters. Even among themselves the agrarians felt their local interests safer in the hands of the state than in the hands of a national government. But this was not the end of the logic of local self-government and regional autonomy. The states in turn, because of diverging interests between the Tidewater and Piedmont areas, allowed a large sweep to county government, and built up a system of representation for both state and federal government which would tend to place legislative power in the hands of economic groups and regions rather than in the hands of the people according to their numbers.

The whole idea then was local self-government, decentralization, so that each region should be able to defend itself against the encroachment of the other regions. It was not a positive doctrine; it did not contemplate a program of exploitative legislation at the expense of other regions. An unmixed agrarian society such as Jefferson and Calhoun had in mind called for no positive program. Such a society, as Jefferson visualized it, called for only enough government to prevent men from injuring one another. It was, by its very nature, a *laissez faire* society, an individualistic society where land, water, and timber were practically free. It only asked to be let alone. State rights, local and regional autonomy, did not make for a uniform, standardized society and government. It took cognizance of the fundamental difference between the agrarian South and West on the one hand and the commercial and growing industrial system of the East on the other; and it still further took note, as we have said, of the regional and local differences within each of these systems. It might not make for a neat and orderly system of government, but this was the price of social and economic freedom, the price of bringing into one Union so many different groups and interests.

The interests pointed out have been largely economic and social. These were not the only interests which the state-rights doctrine was expected to protect from an overbearing and unsympathizing national government. Perhaps the greatest vested interest was "personal liberty," the old Anglo-Saxon principles expressed in the Magna Carta, bill of rights, habeas corpus act, supported in the American Revolution, and engrafted finally in every state constitution of the independent states, as "bills of rights." These bills of rights guaranteed freedom of religion, freedom of speech, of thought, of press, of assembly, right of petition, freedom from arbitrary arrest and imprisonment, right of trial by jury, and prohibited the taking of property without due process of law — guaranteed, in short, the fundamental rights which Jefferson had called the "inalienable rights of man" and Locke and Rousseau had called the "natural rights" — right of life, liberty, property, and the free pursuit of happiness as long as the free pursuit of this object did not encroach upon the pursuit of another's just rights. The famous Virginia and Kentucky Resolutions of 1798–9 had been directed at the violation of these liberties. The Alien and Sedition laws which had been pushed through Congress during the Adams administration had struck at many of these. Under the Sedition Act men had been prosecuted for criticizing the President or members of Congress or judges and had been sent to prison in violation of the Constitutional guarantee of freedom of speech. Opinion had been suppressed, meetings broken up, arbitrary arrests made, men held without trial; in fact, the whole body of personal liberties had been brushed aside by the Federalist or centralizing party eight years after the founding of the present federal system under the Constitution. Jefferson and Madison, supported by the state-rights apostle of Virginia, John Taylor of Caroline, and the irascible old democrat, John Randolph, proclaimed that the federal government had thus shown itself to be an unsafe protector of liberty. So Jefferson announced in his inaugural, which was made possible by the excesses of the centralizing party of the East, that the states were the safest guardians of human liberty and called on all to support "the state governments in all their rights, as the most competent administrations for our domestic concerns and the surest bulwark against anti-republican tendencies." The founder of the party of the agrarian South and West upheld state rights as the safest guardian of the liberties and the domestic interests of the people.

VII

Thus the two sections clashed at every point. Their economic systems and interests conflicted. Their social systems were hostile; their political philosophies growing out of their economic and social systems were as impossible to reconcile as it is to cause two particles of matter to occupy the same space at the same time; and their philosophies of life, growing out of the whole situation in each section, were as two elements in deadly combat. What was food for the one was poison for the other.

When the balance of power was destroyed by the rapid growth of the North, and the destruction of this balance was signalized in the election of Lincoln by a frankly sectional, hostile political party, the South, after a futile effort at obtaining a concession from Lincoln which would partly restore the balance of power, dissolved its partnership with the industrial North.

This struggle between an agrarian and an industrial civilization, then, was the irrepressible conflict, the house divided against itself, which must become according to the doctrine of the industrial section all the one or all the other. It was the doctrine of intolerance, crusading, standardizing alike in industry and in life. The South had to be crushed out; it was in the way; it impeded the progress of the machine. So Juggernaut drove his car across the South.

Rollin G. Osterweis: THE IDEA OF SOUTHERN NATIONALISM

Rollin G. Osterweis represents the modern generation of historians who are interested primarily in the history of ideas. Such historical writers have widened our range of understanding by examining the clusters of values and beliefs which hold social groups and whole societies together. Osterweis analyzes the idea of Southern nationalism as the "most ambitious impulse" in the powerful movement of Southern romanticism in the years before the Civil War. The selection is taken from Rollin G. Osterweis, Romanticism and Nationalism in the Old South.

THE idea of Southern nationalism, which developed chiefly in South Carolina during the decade before the Civil War, was the most ambitious romantic manifestation of the antebellum period. It is not unnatural that this energy-demanding and forward-looking trend should have been cradled in a hard-headed community. These were people anxious to lead — possessing political and intellectual talent, accumulated wealth, influential periodicals, and a past history of fiery, independent thinking. Around 1850 the Cotton Kingdom was looking for leadership; and the Palmetto State stood ready to fill that need. It was soon ahead of the times, waiting for the rest of the South to catch up with its daring plans.

The State of South Carolina, and the city of Charleston, were peculiarly well suited to lead the revolt toward separate Southern nationality. As Frederick Jackson Turner has pointed out, Charleston was the one important center of city life on the Atlantic seaboard below Baltimore. Every February planters from a radius of several hundred miles would gather for a month in their Charleston town houses; during the summer, the threat of malaria in the country would bring many of them back again. While in town, they mingled with informed people from other sections of the South, and from the North as well. Their wide range of experience in plantation management, mercantile activity, and political life gave them powerful advantages for leadership.

From the administration of Washington through that of Monroe, the tobacco planters of Virginia had ruled not only the South but, under the presidential dynasty, the nation itself. In the late 1820's, the center of power, below the Mason and Dixon line, was passing from the hands of Virginia to those of South Carolina. And, at the same time, the South as a unit was beginning to realize that it was becoming a minority section. The rapid growth of the cotton area was fixing slavery as a permanent and expanding institution and slavery was setting the section apart from the rest of the United States. When Northeast and Northwest tended to unite in fostering protective tariffs and internal improvement programs, which deprived the cotton states of their profits to enhance an industrial structure of no benefit to them, blood ran hot in Carolina.

The idea of Southern nationalism emerged about 1850 out of an experience mainly native and nonromantic. During

Reprinted by permission from Rollin G. Osterweis, *Romanticism and Nationalism in the Old South* (New Haven, Conn.: Yale University Press, 1949), pp. 132–154.

the ten years before the war, it took on a distinctive, romantic coloration. It lay rooted in the adventures of the American colonies themselves in 1776; in the Lockian philosophy of Thomas Cooper; in familiarity with the political devices suggested by the onetime American nationalist, John C. Calhoun; in the Tariff and Nullification episode between 1827 and 1833; in the problems produced by the territorial acquisitions of the Mexican war; in the various Southern economic conventions, down to and including the historic Nashville meeting of November, 1850. By the latter year, certainly, a group consciousness had developed, an *ethnocentrism*, an impulse for Southern nationalism. The impulse was so similar to the ideas of romantic nationalism, then prevalent in Europe, that it offered a natural affinity for those ideas.

The leadership for the translation of this impulse into action would come first from a group of South Carolinians, headed by Senator Barnwell A. P. Butler, and the elder Langdon Cheves. Later, others would take up the torch.

It is highly significant to note that, although he does not use the term "romantic Southern nationalism," Edward Channing calls the sixth volume of his history, *The War for Southern Independence, 1849–1865;* and opens that volume with excerpts from the speech of Langdon Cheves, Southern nationalist of South Carolina, at the Nashville convention, November 14, 1850. Channing interprets the crusade for separate Southern nationality as starting around 1849. In doing so he draws particular attention to Cheves of Carolina and to what he said at Nashville.

Launching his attack on Clay's compromise measures, known collectively as the Omnibus Bill, the aged Cheves had declared:

In nine months, in one session of Congress, by a great *coup d'état*, our Constitution has been completely and forever subverted. . . . What is the remedy? I answer: secession — united secession of the slave-holding States. . . . Nothing else will be wise — nothing else will be practicable. . . . Unite, and you shall form one of the most splendid empires on which the sun ever shone, of the most homogeneous population, all of the same blood and lineage, a soil the most fruitful, and a climate the most lovely. . . . O, Great God, unite us, and a tale of submission shall never be told.

Channing is at considerable pains to point out that this concept of a "homogeneous population, all of the same blood and lineage," was far removed from the actualities of the 1850 Southland. He notes that Charleston itself was a heterogeneous medley of English, French, Scotch-Irish, Germans, Portuguese, Jews, Irish Catholics, and Welsh. In another part of his speech, Cheves had asserted that the Southerners were "all of gentle descent," and Channing demolishes this exaggeration with breath-taking effectiveness.

There is a pertinent conclusion to be drawn from all this, namely, that Langdon Cheves, ardent Southern nationalist, was expressing the very essence of romantic nationalism at Nashville in November, 1850. Romantic nationalism, in the contemporary framework of reference, was cultural nationalism, and that is what Cheves was talking about — the longing of a "homogeneous population, all of the same blood and lineage," and possessing common institutions for national existence. The fact that this racial homogeneity was a myth, but passionately believed to be true, deepens the romantic coloring.

The Carolinian conviction that Southerners comprised a separate cultural unit

grew stronger from the concomitant belief that the rest of the country possessed
an inferior civilization. So obvious was
this attitude by 1860 that the correspondent of the London *Times* could grasp it
completely. In a letter dated "Charleston, April 30, 1861," William Howard
Russell declared:

Believe a Southern man as he believes himself and you must regard New England and
the kindred states as the birthplace of im-
purity of mind among men and of unchas-
tity in women — the home of Free Love, of
Fourierism, of Infidelity, of Abolitionism, of
false teachings in political economy and in
social life; a land saturated with the drip-
pings of rotten philosophy, with the poisonous infections of a fanatic press; without
honor or modesty; whose wisdom is paltry
cunning, whose valor and manhood have
been swallowed up in a corrupt, howling
demagogy, and in the marts of dishonest
commerce. . . . These [Carolinian] gentlemen are well-bred, courteous and hospitable.
A genuine aristocracy, they have time to cultivate their minds, to apply themselves to
politics and the guidance of public affairs.
They travel and read, love field sports,
racing, shooting, hunting, and fishing, are
bold horsemen, and good shots. But after
all, their state is a modern Sparta — an aristocracy resting on a helotry, and with nothing else to rest upon. . . . Their whole system
rests on slavery and as such they defend it.
They entertain very exaggerated ideas of the
military strength of their community. . . .

The terms "nationalism" and "'romantic nationalism" seem to cause endless
confusion. Much of the difficulty stems
from a tendency to merge the concepts
of totally different periods. The net result has been the scrambling of twentieth-
century phenomena like Italian fascism
and German nazism into a conglomera-
tion with nineteenth-century ideas, until
the picture has little in common with
historical truth.

The men of the romantic age rarely
used the word "nationalist" to describe
themselves; and if it is used about them,
care must be taken to place the modifier
"cultural" in front of it. The nationalism
of the romantic thinkers was a cultural
nationalism, with the emphasis on "peoples," who were the architects and trans-
mitters of distinct cultures. To these
thinkers, "the idea of imposing any nation's ways, speech, or art upon another
was repellent." After all, this had been
the great rationalist error of the French
Revolution on the march, which they
felt they were rebelling against. Herder,
Wordsworth, Victor Hugo, speaking in
the names of German, English, and
French romanticisms, all exemplify belief
in a nonaggressive, cultural nationalism.

The romantic view did imply longing,
striving, and, if necessary, struggling
to give expression to repressed cultural
nationalism. But this is a far cry from
Hitler's legions on the rampage through
Poland, or the bringing of the blessings
of Italian fascism to the barbarians of
Athens. There is a dichotomy between
Franz Liszt composing Hungarian rhap-
sodies, in exile from his enslaved fatherland, and the comrades of Horst Wessel
singing "Today we own Germany, To-
morrow the whole world."

The confusion in terms becomes all the
more understandable, however, in the
light of the fact that the land which most
conspicuously nurtured the ideas of romantic cultural nationalism was the same
land which, in the next century, would
pervert those ideas into the vicious tenets
of Nazi philosophy. A modern historian
has pointed out that nineteenth-century
nationalisms in France, England, and
Germany were all in the spirit of romantic thinking, but that the French trend
was revolutionary democratic, the English aristocratic, and the German a cul-

tural nationalism most closely related to the prevailing romantic concepts. He sees the German movement growing out of the *Sturm und Drang* school of the earlier day, with the concomitant increased interest in "folk language, folk literature, folk customs, and folk personality." These were the precursors of national language, national literature, national culture.

Another present-day scholar, in a brilliant discussion of romanticism, finds that the nationalism of the mid-nineteenth century belongs "in the bulk of its mature conformation primarily to German romanticism." He points to Carlyle and Coleridge as the chief importers and popularizers of these German ideas in England and the United States. It is worth noting that Coleridge, the more restrained of the two, had the greater influence in New England and the North. Carlyle was the favorite in South Carolina and Louisiana. The enlightened humanitarianism of Emerson, Thoreau, Bancroft, and Whitman emerged in the one section of the United States; the idea of Southern nationalism evolved in the other.

Not only Carlyle but Walter Scott, Herder, Michelet, and Lamartine may be identified as "carriers" of European ideas of romantic nationalism to South Carolina.

"Nationalism," according to Hans Kohn, "is first and foremost a state of mind, an act of consciousness, which since the French Revolution has become more and more common to mankind." He goes on to demonstrate that nationalities evolve from the living forces of history and are therefore always fluctuating. Even if a new nationality comes into being, it may perfectly well disappear again, absorbed into a larger or a different nationality. This will happen when the objective bonds that delimit the group are destroyed, for nationality is born of the decision to form a nationality. But the concept, in its developed stage, goes beyond the idea of the group animated by common consciousness. It comprehends also the striving by the group to find expression in the organized activity of a sovereign state. Thus, the nationalism of the nineteenth century was a fusion of an attitude of mind with a particular political form.

The application of these criteria to the history of the rise and fall of the Confederacy, and the subsequent reintegration of the South into the Union, is a documentary implementation of Kohn's definition.

The movement for Southern independence was a manifestation of romantic nationalism, as contrasted with the earlier nonromantic type best exemplified in the creation of the United States of America. This latter type may be conveniently labeled, "the nationalism of the American Revolution"; it had been fed by English national consciousness, evolving since Elizabethan days, transplanted to the new land — and by the natural-rights philosophies of the seventeenth century. American Revolutionary nationalism was a predominantly political occurrence, with the national state formed before, or at least at the same time as, the rising tide of national feeling. The emphasis was on universal standards and values — "inalienable Rights" and "Laws of Nature."

Southern nationalism, on the other hand, stressed the peculiarities of its particular traditions and institutions. In common with the romantic nationalisms of central Europe in the nineteenth century, the frontiers of the existing state and the rising nationality did not coincide. The movement expanded in protest against, and in conflict with, the de facto government. The objective was not to alter the existing political organization, as in the case of the thirteen colonies, but to redraw boundaries that would conform to mythical but credited ethnographic needs. That the realities behind the myth were the institution of Negro slavery and the plantation system do not affect the situation. They merely provide the identifying features.

The evolution of the idea of Southern nationalism, by 1860, was thus in the general stream of mid-nineteenth-century romantic thinking. "The Age of Nationalism," Professor Kohn suggests, "stressed national pasts and traditions against the rationalism of the eighteenth century with its emphasis on the common sense of civilization." The tendency in Europe was to weave the myths of the past and the dreams of the future into the picture of an ideal fatherland — an ideal to be striven for with deep emotional fervor.

This tendency was adapted to the Southern scene. From the past Virginia resurrected her George Washington, who had led an earlier crusade for independence; Maryland recalled her heroes in Randall's stirring stanzas; Carolina cherished the cult of Calhoun; Louisiana pointed to her proud Creole heritage.

All this hewed to the line of romantic nationalism in Europe, where "each new nation looked for its justification to its national heritage — often reinterpreted to suit the supposed needs of the situation — and strove for its glorification."

Romantic nationalism had its influence on the United States as a whole, apart from the specialized phase of the South, during the mid-nineteenth century. The chief manifestation was the "Mission of America" concept — the march toward a trusteeship of liberty and democracy, from which all the world would draw

benefit. The romantic historian, Bancroft of Massachusetts, was one of the prophets of this creed.

The maturing of the idea of Southern nationalism in Carolina followed a series of historical events and derived in part from the views of several local personalities. This background was essentially native and nonromantic but, by 1850, possessed a receptivity for the notions of European romantic nationalism. Carlyle, Scott, Herder, Hugo, Michelet, and Lamartine attracted South Carolina readers, who found their ideas congenial.

Carlyle evoked enthusiasm with his argument that the new forces released by the industrial revolution could only be stabilized by an "aristocracy of talent." Scott stimulated Southern nationalism with his mournful recollections of the past glories of a free Scotland. Herder, too, struck a responsive chord with his urging that Germans must cultivate their national genius and look back wistfully at the glamorous days of yore. Victor Hugo typified the climax of the romantic triumph in France; the South cared little for his humanitarian and socialistic ideas but found his patriotic notions appealing. Jules Michelet, romantic historian, emphasized his affection for the folk, in whom the old love of military honor survived, and his contempt for the unchivalrous, commerce-minded, French bourgeoisie. Carolinians could see in this contrast the reflection of themselves and the hated, materialistic Yankees.

Behind the years when Carolinians were discovering encouragement for Southern nationalism, in their favorite European writers, lay a sequence of events which served to put them in a mood receptive to such encouragement. The story properly begins in the late

1820's, when the leadership of the South was moving from the tobacco plantations of the Old Dominion to the intellectual capital of the expanding Cotton Kingdom, at Charleston. The first bow of the new leadership was made in connection with tariff troubles.

South Carolina had opposed the tariff from the earliest days of the republic. The very first Congress, in 1789, had included a group of Carolina representatives known as "anti-tariff men." When the Washington administration sponsored a mild import measure, Senator Pierce Butler of the Palmetto State brought the charge that Congress was oppressing South Carolina and threatened "a dissolution of the Union, with regard to that State, as sure as God was in his firmament." The tariff of 1816, passed in a wave of American national feeling after the War of 1812, found six out of ten Carolina members of the House voting against the bill. John C. Calhoun and the other three who supported the measure were severely censured at home.

Almost the entire South opposed the tariff of 1824. The spreading domain of King Cotton now had a well-defined grievance: the Northeast and the Northwest were uniting to levy taxes on goods exchanged for exported cotton; their protective tariff policy, and concomitant program for internal improvements, was benefiting their entire section at the expense of the South. The policy protected New England mills and furnished funds for linking the seaboard states of the North with the new Northwest by means of canals and turnpikes. The Southern planters paid the bills: they were forced to buy their manufactured supplies in a high market and their chief article of exchange, cotton, had fallen from thirty cents a pound in 1816 to fifteen cents in

1824. In addition, the internal improvements program offered them no compensation; the rivers took their cotton to the shipping points.

When the "Tariff of Abominations" was passed in 1828, all the Southeastern and Southwestern members of the House opposed it, except for three Virginians. In the Senate, only two Southerners supported "the legislative monstrosity."

The opposition to Northern tariff policy was most vociferous in the Palmetto State. From the milieu of this opposition, between 1828 and 1833, several important leaders emerged. They were Thomas Cooper, John C. Calhoun, and the elder Langdon Cheves. Others there were, of course, and the names of many spring to mind — Robert Hayne, A. P. Butler, Chancellor Harper, Francis Pickens, John Lyde Wilson, Joel Poinsett. But the three mentioned were to play especially significant roles in the events that led to the idea of Southern independence; and they began to play those roles in 1828.

Cooper was a gadfly, who buzzed about the ears of people until they listened to his startling suggestions. Calhoun was a vigorous leader, who gave the South group consciousness and his own State a sustained sense of trailblazing, which it carried right down to the December day in 1860, when it became the first to secede from the Union. Cheves was a cautious and conservative man, who declined to be stampeded but who, once convinced, would give his imagination full play. Cooper was a philosopher with a formula, Calhoun a lawyer with a case, and Cheves a strategist with a plan.

While discussing the attitude of South Carolina toward the hated tariff policy of the 1820's, Channing makes this observation: "Of all the fomenters of discord, Thomas Cooper, an Englishman by birth and then connected with the University of South Carolina, might well be regarded as first in ability and influence." His *Lectures on the Elements of Political Economy* (1826) and other writings of the period receive credit for doing much toward shaping opinion on the tariff. In 1827 he told Senator Martin Van Buren of New York that if the American system were pushed too far, the Carolina legislature would probably recall the State's representatives from Washington.

Cooper's biographer describes him as a disciple of Priestley and Locke, a humanitarian during his early life in England — a Jeffersonian, in the first phase of his American career, when he lived in Pennsylvania — and a man who "came to terms with his new social environment" after he settled in South Carolina in 1820. Seven years after arrival in the Palmetto State, he made the famous declaration that it was time for South Carolina "to calculate the value of the Union." This historic utterance of July 2, 1827, gave rise to shocked expressions of horror, even among some Carolina hotheads, but it had been indelibly burned into the thinking of a generation. It had a habit of cropping out down through the years. Webster and Hayne both alluded to it during their famous debate.

As the second president of South Carolina College, founded in 1805, Thomas Cooper was in a position to inculcate his philosophy and to prepare scores of young men for a dissolution of the Union, which he predicted but did not live to see. Dumas Malone quotes the younger Langdon Cheves, an exponent of Southern nationalism in 1860, as maintaining that the works of Dr. Cooper had done more to determine his political views than had Calhoun, Hayne, or even his illustrious father.

An English traveler, stopping at Columbia, South Carolina, in 1835, had the opportunity to hear Cooper expressing his opinions and to observe the attitude of those who surrounded the strong-minded college president. The visitor received an invitation to dine with Dr. Cooper, several of his professors, and some gentlemen of the Columbia area. After the occasion, he noted in his diary:

What particularly struck me at this dinner was the total want of caution and reserve in the ultra opinions they expressed about religion and politics; on these topics their conversation was not at all addressed to me but seemed to be the resumption of opinions they were accustomed to express whenever they met and upon all occasions. . . .

I could not help asking, in a good-natured way, if they called themselves Americans yet; the gentleman who had interrupted me before said, "If you ask *me* if I am an American, my answer is *No, Sir*, I am a South Carolinian."

If the children of these Nullifiers are brought up on the same opinions, which they are very likely to be, here are fine elements for future dissension; for imbibing from their infancy the notion that they are born to command, it will be intolerable to them to submit to be, in their own estimation, the drudges of the Northern manufacturers, whom they despise as an inferior race of men. Even now there is nothing a Southern man resents so much as to be called a Yankee. . . .

These significant comments, it should be emphasized, were made twenty-five years before the Civil War. He who made them was a scientist, a Fellow of the Royal Society, a trained observer.

Thomas Cooper's contribution to the idea of Southern independence has been summed up in these words:

Although he had little to do with the final events of the Nullification controversy, . . . [Cooper's] importance as a pioneer can scarcely be overemphasized. And no man more than he deserves to be termed the schoolmaster of state rights and the prophet of secession.

Cooper was no romantic Southern nationalist as one identifies that type after 1850. The people and the considerations which influenced his philosophy were not in the romantic tradition. Locke and Priestley, utilitarianism and skepticism, were the shaping molds for his thinking. He valued liberty more than union and calculated the worth of the latter purely in terms of its relationship to his adopted State. Yet this hardheaded utilitarian, like the equally hardheaded Calhoun, supplied the basic philosophy which fostered the later romantic concept of Southern nationalism.

John Caldwell Calhoun did more than contribute to the basic philosophy which led to the idea of Southern independence, although he did this with great effectiveness. He thought out the political devices which his section might use to defend itself against an encroaching majority in the councils of the Federal Government. In so doing he stimulated group-consciousness and hoisted the Palmetto flag of Carolina as the symbol of Southern leadership. "He forged in that busy smithy of his mind," Ralph Gabriel points out, "the intellectual weapons with which the champions of the Cotton Kingdom sought to defeat the democratic principles of majority rule."

In his early years, Calhoun had been an ardent American nationalist. A "War Hawk" who clamored for Britain's scalp in 1812, he had supported the American system in the period immediately following the Peace Treaty of Ghent. In de-

fiance of South Carolina tradition, Congressman Calhoun had voted for the tariff of 1816; he had also advocated internal improvements, especially military roads, and had actually sponsored the bill which chartered the second Bank of the United States.

It was the passage of the "Tariff of Abominations," in 1828, which brought him forward in a quite different role. The former American nationalist now became the exponent of the thesis that a state could refuse obedience to an act of Congress and at the same time not be involved in rebellion. Channing attributes the sudden turnabout principally to Calhoun's ambitions for the presidency and the need for the support of his own nullification-minded State. The motives behind his grasping the torch of sectional leadership, in 1828, are of less concern to present purposes than the fact that he did so.

In a letter written May 1, 1833, President Jackson expressed the conviction that the tariff had been only the pretext for crystallizing nullification sentiment in South Carolina. The real objective of the agitators, he insisted, was not tariff reform but the establishment of a Southern confederacy. "The next pretext," he suggested, "will be the negro, or slavery, questions." The other cotton states, however, had shown slight sympathy for Carolina's bold stand between 1828 and 1833 — and the tobacco states to the north were conspicuously indifferent. The nullification episode was a South Carolina, not a sectional incident; but it would have far reaching implications for the entire Southland as the years went on. It prepared the minds of men for disunion.

As for Calhoun's place in the march toward Southern nationalism, he was "the chosen leader of a predetermined course, in no sense a driver." South Carolina was intent on courses both in 1832, and again in 1850, which Calhoun did not originate but to which he gave his powerful support. With matchless clarity he propounded the point of view of his State, leading the rest of the Cotton Kingdom closer and closer to the time when it would adopt the Carolina course for its own. Yet all the while he preached a certain moderation, holding his associates back from too precipitate action, hoping always for solution within the framework of Union.

Speaking in Charleston in August, 1848, Calhoun still persisted in the belief that a Southern party would enable the South to achieve her ends in cooperation with sympathizers in the North. But he admitted that if this procedure failed to check the aggressive spirit of the abolitionists, then armed resistance by a united South would be indicated. "Though the union is dear to us, our honor and our liberty are dearer."

Ulrich Phillips felt that, "as long as Calhoun lived, his mighty championship exerted a subduing influence upon Southerners in private life." The Carolina statesman was ever reluctant to believe the impending conflict irrepressible. In his last years he seemed to waver between the hope of solution within the frame of the Union and the fear that Southern secession would become necessary. Many of his adherents wavered with him. Even after his death on the last day of March, 1850, Calhoun's project for a convention at Nashville triumphed over the call of the hotheads for an open break with the North, as proper answer to Clay's compromise measures.

Such was Calhoun in life. Death made him a symbol for Southern nationalism. During the decade between 1850 and the Civil War, he emerges from the pages of the *Southern Quarterly Review* as the romantic leader of the crusade for Southern independence.

As early as November, 1850, appeared the lengthy comment by "S. D. M. of Tuscaloosa, Alabama," occasioned by the obituary speeches honoring Calhoun in the United States Senate." That comment was characteristic of many others to follow.

One thing is certain, that, in this crisis of affairs, the bulwark of our strength is gone. We shall no more see the proud crest in the field of battle in defense of us and ours. . . . His mantle will yet fall upon worthy shoulders. We are still in possession of his chart and compass. . . . All over that chart you will see the beacon lights of liberty pointing out the way that leads to a people's glory and renown, and showing in what way only we may avoid that which leads to a people's shame.

Some months later, when the shadows of the impending struggle were growing even darker, the *Quarterly* seized the instance of the appearance in print of Hammond's "Oration on Calhoun" to glorify further the Carolinian statesman as a symbol of Southern nationalism. In this article, Calhoun's former "erroneous" support of the American system is attributed to "wide patriotism"; and his later leadership of the South, when he "very properly reversed his views," is treated as a normal development of greatness.

The cult of Calhoun as a symbol of Southern nationalism — which grew up after his death — was completely in the romantic tradition. It is reminiscent of the manner in which the Young France group, under the guidance of Hector Berlioz, had seized upon the recently deceased Beethoven and glorified him as the symbol of romantic music. Just as

Berlioz, Hugo, Lamartine, and the adherents of Saint-Simon imbued the figure of the composer with their own artistic and social ideals, so did the Southern nationalists of Carolina endow the figure of John C. Calhoun with the regalia of positive leadership in the movement for Southern independence. Calhoun, as a symbol after death, became almost as important in that movement as Calhoun, the defender of Southern rights within the framework of the Union, had been in his lifetime.

In addition to Calhoun and Cooper, Langdon Cheves made significant contributions to the growth of the idea of Southern nationalism. Cheves had formulated a plan for solving Carolina's problems as far back as the nullification controversy of 1828.

The wisdom of adopting a nullification program had divided South Carolina into two well-defined factions. Those who favored the program were led by Calhoun, Dr. Cooper, Robert Hayne, Francis Pickens, R. B. Rhett, and John Lyde Wilson. Opposed to nullification were the Union men — Senator William Smith, William Drayton, Joel R. Poinsett, James Louis Petigru, and other respected individuals.

The leaders of the Unionist faction did not underestimate the personal prestige or the long-pull ambitions of the Nullifiers. On the other hand, they seemed to feel that the rank and file of the people were averse to drastic action, in 1833. During April that year one Unionist wrote to another:

What have you been doing this great while? On the plantation, I suppose. Do you hear much from the Revolutioners lately? I believe they intend to open *for a Southern Confederacy* soon. . . . But they will not commit themselves just now. The people, I

fair think, are settling down to a more composed and moderate tone. They are not so much inflamed about politics, it seems to me, and more inclined to mind their own business. These are good symptoms, so far; they may be delusive, however. . . . We who have got the chivalry against us must carefully cultivate the good will of our neighbors. Adieu.

The reference in this letter to possible sentiment in favor of a Southern confederacy, among the Nullifiers, brings to mind the positive plan advocated by Langdon Cheves.

Cheves had remained aloof from both parties. He manifested little love for the Union but condemned nullification by a single state as an impractical procedure. To his mind, the problem of the tariff went far beyond the borders of South Carolina. The entire South would suffer from its blighting effects. Therefore, the entire South should act together. He proposed that representatives of all the Southern states should gather for a convention and that the convention should deliver an ultimatum to the Congress in Washington: either abandon the protecting policy or take the responsibility for the formation of a Southern confederacy.

Thus, three points of view appeared in the struggle over the tariff between 1828 and 1833 — cooperation with the Union at all costs, nullification of "unfair" Federal laws by South Carolina alone, and action by a united Southland. Clay's compromise tariff bill terminated the exciting episode and the antipathies of the three factions were temporarily forgotten.

But fourteen years later, when David Wilmot introduced in Congress his famous proviso prohibiting slavery in any territory that might be acquired incidental to the Mexican war, memories returned to the thoughts expressed by the Carolina leaders of 1832. Calhoun led the fight to beat the Wilmot Proviso in the Senate but the fat was in the fire and once again feelings ran high in the Palmetto State. This time the tension was not limited to South Carolina alone; the whole country was aroused. State legislatures "above the Line" passed resolutions extolling Congressman Wilmot. In the Southland, people looked toward Carolina, to watch for the formulation of a policy.

Between 1847 and 1852, three parties sprang to activity in the Palmetto State. Their programs recall the earlier alignments in the nullification incident. The three groups were known as: Immediate Secessionists, Unionists, Cooperationists. The Secessionists, led by R. B. Rhett, Governor Seabrook, Maxey Gregg, and Francis Pickens advocated immediate withdrawal by South Carolina from the United States. The Unionist party, headed by Joel Poinsett, James L. Petigru, William Grayson, and Benjamin Perry of Greenville stood for "Southern rights within the Union."

The party which merits particular attention, for it was the faction that eventually carried the day, bore the confusing label, "Cooperationists." This was the real Southern nationalist group. Its leaders included Langdon Cheves, the man with a plan back in 1832, Senators Barnwell and A. P. Butler, and Memminger, Hammond, Orr, and others. The Cooperationists were resolved that South Carolina should not find herself isolated again as she had in Nullification days. This time she must go forward with the support of the rest of the South. The aggressive North was not threatening the life of the Palmetto State alone. It was a whole "homogeneous section" that was under attack. If South Carolina is to lead the resistance, then it must only be with the *cooperation* of her Southern sisters.

If the latter are not yet ready to recognize the necessity of separate nationality, then Carolina must wait until they are ready — striving meanwhile to guide them down the road toward independence.

The Cooperationists made their views known during the election year 1848, when, operating out of Charleston, they attempted to get the Democratic party of the State to endorse an all-Southern presidential ticket of Taylor and A. P. Butler in opposition to Lewis Cass. They were beaten when the legislature voted for presidential electors, but their move stimulated the idea of an increasingly selfconscious Southern bloc.

The Unionist faction, during this period, was the weakest of the three, the struggle for power in the State quickly narrowing down to the Cooperationists and the Immediate Secessionists. The latter party drew its main support from the interior sections and revolved about the central figure of R. B. Rhett. A rather inflexible individual, Rhett "saw later issues always from the standpoint of 1832." On the other hand, the Cooperationists, drawing their strength from Charleston and its intellectual, social, and financial dependencies, boasted no single, dominating personality. Langdon Cheves, who had been the first of the leaders to espouse the idea of Southern nationalism, was important; but so also were Andrew Pickens Butler and R. W. Barnwell. Those three probably wielded the principal power in the group.

A head-on collision between the two chief factions in South Carolina political life was averted in 1850. Calhoun, adopting a course different from either but closer to the nationalists' than to Rhett's, strove to consolidate the South as a unit within the framework of the Union. To this end he gave his ebbing strength, in the early months of 1850. The result was the Nashville Convention, held in November of that year after the great statesman had already died. And at the Nashville Convention Langdon Cheves made his powerful bid for "united secession of the slave-holding states" and painted the picture of "one of the most splendid empires on which the sun ever shone."

Outside of Cheves's speech, the Nashville Convention was lifeless and dull. The passage of Clay's compromise measures had produced a temporary calm in the political arena. But when the Carolinian nationalist delegates returned to Charleston, they were imbued with implemented confidence in their cause. Early in 1851 they instituted a propaganda campaign against immediate secession of the Palmetto State — for which Rhett continued to agitate — and in behalf of eventual formation of a Southern confederacy. The Charleston *Mercury* was spokesman for the fire-eating Rhett, while the Cooperationists launched their attack in pamphlets, spread not only through South Carolina but all over the Cotton Kingdom.

In the election of delegates to a Southern convention during the fall of 1851, a test plebiscite between the two parties took place. The Rhett faction was soundly beaten, attributing its defeat to the "controlling interests of trade" centered at Charleston and dominated by Barnwell, Butler, and Cheves.

The South Carolinians split in 1851, not over the question of giving the Union another trial — which was the case in Georgia during this period — but over a much more subtle issue: the issue of secession by a single state versus the emerging recognition that the South had become a single community and must act as such. The idea which prevailed in South Carolina in 1851 was the idea which would prevail through the entire Southland ten years later. That idea was Southern nationalism — a product basically of independent native growth but with a coloring of European romantic notions.

Samuel Phillips Day, an English visitor who talked with many leaders of Southern thought in 1861, sensed the significance of that romantic nationalism. He wrote in his diary:

This is no civil strife: no struggle of Guelph and Ghibelline; no contest between York and Lancaster; but a war of alien races, distinct nationalities, and antagonistic governments. Cavalier and Roundhead no longer designate parties, but nations, whose separate foundations . . . were laid on Plymouth Rock and the banks of the James River. Whoever would rightly understand the causes of the present convulsion in America must find their explanation in the irreconcilable character of the Cavalier and Puritan, the antagonisms of agricultural and commercial communities, and the conflicts between free and slave labor, when the manufacturing and navigating interests attempt to wrest the sceptre from agriculture by unfriendly legislation.

The failure of Rhett and his Immediate Secessionist party left South Carolina, in 1852, within the Union but with an eye to a future break. For the next eight years her Southern nationalist leaders would be working toward the day when the rest of the Cotton Kingdom would be ready to act. The election of Lincoln in November, 1860, heralded the arrival of der Tag.

Between 1852 and 1860 the Southern nationalists controlled the politics of the Palmetto State. Powerful supporters gathered around the standard of Cheves and Butler and Robert Barnwell. When the first two of these veteran leaders died in 1857, capable successors stepped into their places. The new leadership included Congressman James Orr, C. G. Memminger, James Chesnut, Jr., and the influential writers, Simms and Timrod. Gravitating toward the Cooperationists, also, was D. F. Jamison, lawyer, planter, politician, and historian. Jamison had toyed with the idea of separate action by South Carolina, in 1851; but his growing enthusiasm for Southern nationalism brought him into the camp of the Cooperationists.

The agitators for a future confederacy did not limit themselves to the local politics of their own State. Having seized control of the propaganda machine, *The Southern Rights Association,* they proceeded to flood the Cotton Kingdom with pamphlets. This association had originally been founded by Maxey Gregg and R. B. Rhett, the secessionist firebrands, for their own purposes. The Cooperationists took the material, already prepared, which served their particular purposes, added more, and distributed the leaflets all over Dixie.

One such pamphlet, first published in 1850, was *The Rightful Remedy* by Edward B. Bryan. In it, "the slaveholders of the South particularly, and the citizens of the slaveholding states" are exhorted to unite in order to defend "the most time-honored institution extant," and to set up their own government.

A similar treatise, sponsored by the Carolinian Southern nationalists, declared that the establishment of a separate confederacy "with a homogeneous population and an united government" would relieve the South from her false and dangerous situation of being a nation within a nation.

Simms, in his *Southern Quarterly Review,* gave preferred position to such articles as "Is Southern Civilization Worth Preserving?" This lengthy appeal

for Southern nationalism, in 1851, set the tone for many others which followed during the next ten years.

Impartial observers had no trouble in recognizing the role of South Carolina in the crusade. The correspondent of the London *Times* described the Palmetto State, in May, 1861, as having been "the *fons et origo* of the secession doctrines and their development into the full life of the Confederate States."

The official historian of the State of South Carolina has characterized the period between 1852 and 1860, in the State's history, as "Waiting for the South." Discussing the dominant mood of that eight-year stretch, he asserted:

Here again we have that ideal of Southern nationalism voicing the feeling that the South was organically one, despite the constant insistence as a matter of legal theory on the sovereignty of the individual state. The latter was mainly defensive tactics against a hostile North.

The election of Lincoln liberated South Carolina from her self-imposed restraint. She knew now that the years of waiting were over — that where she would lead, others would follow. The ideal of Southern nationalism could become the actuality of a Southern nation. Judge J. S. Black of Pennsylvania, Buchanan's attorney general, put his finger on the true role of the Palmetto State. "Like Athens," he wrote of Carolina, "you control Greece — you have made and you will control, this revolution by your indomitable spirit."

As soon as it was clear that the United States had elected a president committed to an anti-slavery platform, the South Carolina legislature voted to call a State convention. The delegates met at Columbia on December 17, 1860, fully conscious that they were about to sign an ordinance of secession. Because of a case of smallpox in the town, they adjourned to Charleston on the eighteenth. Two days later, they voted unanimously to take their State out of the Union.

The proceedings of the convention are significant, for they indicate that the delegates were thinking in far bigger terms than the secession of South Carolina. A careful perusal of the *Journal of the Convention of the People of South Carolina* reveals exactly what they had in mind.

From such perusal one fact stands out immediately. The Southern nationalist faction was in complete control of the gathering. A. P. Butler and Langdon Cheves had died three years before but Langdon Cheves, Jr., was on hand to represent his father's point of view. Senator Robert Barnwell, last of the old triumvirate, was very much in evidence. D. F. Jamison was elected temporary chairman and, a few hours later, permanent president of the convention. He was elected on the fourth ballot, triumphing over two other Southern nationalists, Orr and Chesnut.

When Jamison was made temporary chairman at the beginning of the convention, in Columbia, he addressed the assemblage with these words:

Written Constitutions are worthless unless they are written at the same time in the hearts, and founded on the interests of a people; and there is no common bond of sympathy between the North and the South. All efforts to preserve this Union will not only be fruitless, but fatal to the less numerous section. . . .

At the moment of inaugurating a great movement like the present, I trust that we will go forward and not be diverted from our purpose by influences from without. In the outset of this movement, I can offer you

no better motto than Danton's, at the commencement of the French Revolution: "To dare! and again to dare! and without end to dare!"

These are clearly the ideas of a man thinking in larger terms than the secession of a single state. Furthermore, Jamison's allusion to Danton's romantic oratory arouses suspicion that this Southern nationalist may have had some knowledge of the notions of nationalism associated with the European romantic movements.

David Flavel Jamison, who had been a student at South Carolina College in the days of Thomas Cooper and Langdon Cheves, Jr., gave more credit for shaping his political views to Cooper than to his illustrious father. Jamison practiced law for two years, then turned planter. From 1836 to 1848 he represented his district of Orangeburg in the South Carolina legislature, where he sponsored the bill for establishing the South Carolina Military Academy. He attended the Nashville Convention with the elder Cheves, in 1850; and later played with the idea of separate action by South Carolina, during the excitement of 1851. In the years that followed he found his philosophies best expressed by the Southern nationalist group and became part of the circle surrounding William Gilmore Simms. At the secession convention, he represented Simms's district of Barnwell and was, in a sense, the mouthpiece of the romantic Southern nationalists associated with Simms and Timrod.

Jamison's chief interest in life was historical studies. His biographer says:

In the *Southern Quarterly Review* for January and July, 1843, January, April, and October, 1844, and October, 1849, there were reviews of Guizot, Mignet, Herder, Michelet, and Lamartine, which either by signature or internal evidence are to be ascribed to him. . . . To the Southern planter the lessons of modern European history seemed plain, and it was doubtless these studies as much as the long controversy over the Wilmot Proviso that matured his political philosophy.

The cat is out of the bag. This man Jamison, presiding officer at the South Carolina secession convention, was not only the product of the many native influences which promoted the idea of Southern nationalism in the Palmetto State. He was, also, steeped in the ideas of romantic nationalism coming out of the continent of Europe. His political philosophy, shaped by Cooper and the procession of local events, had been matured by Herder, Michelet, and Lamartine.

Jamison's commentary on Herder's *Outline of a Philosophy of the History of Man* was a lengthy, scholarly affair, which appeared as the first article in an 1844 issue of the *Southern Quarterly Review*. The analysis of Herder's masterpiece was clear and thorough. Jamison was anxious not only to understand the implications of cultural nationalism but to have others understand them also.

This digression from the South Carolina secession convention has revealed the sort of man who presided over its deliberations. That man seems the very symbol of the growth of the idea of Southern nationalism in his State — embodying an experience with the chief native influences behind the idea and a familiarity with the notions of romantic nationalism, coming out of the lands across the sea.

What of the secession convention itself? Did the delegates think that they were voting merely for dissolving the bonds of union between their State and the others?

The *Journal* of the convention makes it perfectly clear that the men present were confident that they were launching a movement for a Southern confederacy. When the first meeting took place, commissioners from Alabama and Mississippi, appointed by their respective governors, joined the group. Letters of encouragement arrived from the states of Florida and Arkansas. Georgia offered volunteers in case South Carolina's action should lead to armed reprisals.

The day after the convention had moved to Charleston, President Jamison announced that Commissioner Elmore of Alabama had handed him a telegram from Governor A. B. Moore of that State, which read, "Tell the Convention to listen to no propositions of compromise or delay." A few hours later the delegates voted to send representatives to all slaveholding states, inviting them to join South Carolina in a new confederacy. The next day, December 20, the convention passed the ordinance of secession. The sequence of events, the importance given to the communications sent by the other slaveholding states, the language of the delegates, all indicate that the idea of Southern nationalism was paramount.

If this is not enough, the formal action taken by the convention completes the evidence. The chief business on December 26 was the passage of an ordinance "Recommending and Providing for a Convention of the Slaveholding States of the United States, to form the Constitution of a Southern Confederacy." The meeting at Montgomery, Alabama, in February, 1861, was the direct result of this resolution.

One of the most interesting developments of the convention was the emergence of R. B. Rhett, the old leader of the Immediate Secessionist faction, as an exponent of Southern nationalism. When he moved for a committee to prepare an address to the people of the Southern states, he was made chairman of such a committee. His "Address to the Slaveholding States" portrayed the South as a distinct civilization, in the best romantic-nationalist manner. He went so far as to declare that the Federal Constitution had been an experiment from the first, an attempt to unite two peoples of different character and different institutions and that the experiment had failed. The interests of the two old hostile factions — the Immediate Secessionists and the Co-operationists — came together in the convention of December, 1860. Robert Rhett was now eager to preach the doctrines of the romantic nationalists.

The chips were down at the South Carolina secession convention. People recognized that most of the former talk about State rights had been window dressing. It was Southern rights that they were thinking about. An Alabama representative, present in official capacity, told the delegates:

Information obtained on diligent inquiry, in the last few days, justifies me in saying that the gallant sons of North Carolina and Virginia are now ready to rally around the standard of *Southern Rights and Honor,* which you have so gloriously raised. . . . To the bold, deliberate, and decisive action of your body are the people of the South indebted for the great movement which must end in the vindication of their rights.

That most astute of all Southern historians, Ulrich Phillips, maintained that State rights formed no object of devotion among the antebellum leaders for their own sake but only as a means of securing Southern rights. "State sovereignty," he pithily explained, "was used to give the insignia of legality to a stroke for national independence."

Regarding the fact that the framers of the Confederate Constitution gave official sanction to the State rights principle, Phillips concluded that this was, in large part, a mere saving of face. He said, "The movement was not so much a flying from the old center as a flying to the new; and it was not by chance that Timrod wrote in 1861, 'at last we are a nation among nations,' and entitled his poem of celebration 'Ethnogenesis.'"

Phillips' allusion to the poem "Ethnogenesis" is a happy one. He felt that "it was not by chance" that Timrod wrote in the vein that he did, with the emphasis on Southern nationalism. Nor was it by chance, either — it should be added — that he who wrote in this vein and who called his poem "Ethnogenesis" was a South Carolina romantic poet. In Henry Timrod's State, and among Henry Timrod's friends, the idea of Southern nationalism had matured. Who better could hail the meeting of the first Southern Congress, at Montgomery, with these lines?

Hath not the morning dawned with added light?
And shall not evening call another star
Out of the infinite regions of the night,
To mark this day in heaven? At last we are
A nation among nations; and the world
Shall soon behold in many a distant port
    Another flag unfurled!

V. THE REVISIONISTS AND THEIR CRITICS

Charles W. Ramsdell: THE NATURAL LIMITS OF SLAVERY EXPANSION

Charles W. Ramsdell was born in Texas, studied under William A. Dunning at Columbia University, and returned to a long teaching career at the University of Texas. Writing in 1937, Ramsdell located responsibility for the Civil War on the shoulders of Abraham Lincoln, charging that he had deliberately maneuvered the Confederates into firing the first shot at Fort Sumter, so that they and not he should take the blame for starting the war. In an earlier essay, Ramsdell examined the viability of slavery as an institution and concluded that agitation of the slavery issue by Northern leaders had been needless because slavery would have died out had it been left alone. In his thinking, the Civil War was not only a "needless war" but had created a whole host of new problems. The selection below is from the Mississippi Valley Historical Review.

IN the forefront of that group of issues which, for more than a decade before the secession of the cotton states, kept the northern and southern sections of the United States in irritating controversy and a growing sense of enmity, was the question whether the federal government should permit and protect the expansion of slavery into the western territories. If it be granted that this was not at all times the foremost cause of controversy between the sections, it must be acknowledged that no other question was the subject of such continuous and widespread interest nor of such acrimonious debate. While behind it lay the larger question whether slavery should be allowed to persist permanently where it already existed, it was this immediate problem of the extension of the institution that gave excitement to the political contests of 1843 to 1845, of 1847 to 1851, and of 1854 to 1860. It was upon this

particular issue that a new and powerful sectional party appeared in 1854, that the majority of the Secessionists of the cotton states predicated their action in 1860 and 1861, and it was upon this also that President-elect Lincoln forced the defeat of the compromise measures in the winter of 1860–61. It seems safe to say that had this question been eliminated or settled amicably, there would have been no secession and no Civil War.

The essential points in the controversy over slavery expansion are well known; but in order to focus attention upon the phase of the question here under discussion, it is desirable to cite them again. As stated by the supporters of the Wilmot Proviso and the opponents of the Kansas-Nebraska Bill, it was the question whether the plantation system of agriculture and negro slave labor should be allowed to take possession of the vast western plains, shut out the white home-owning small

Charles W. Ramsdell, "The Natural Limits of Slavery Expansion," *Mississippi Valley Historical Review*, XVI (1929), 151–171. Reprinted by permission from the *Mississippi Valley Historical Review*.

farmer and the white free laborer, and, by the creation of new slave states, so far increase the political strength of the "slave power" that it would be able to dominate the whole nation in its own interest. As stated by the pro-slavery men, it was the question whether an important and essential southern interest, guaranteed by the federal compact, should be stigmatized by the general government itself and excluded from the territories owned in common by all the states, with the inevitable consequence of so weakening the southern people politically that they would soon no longer be able to defend themselves against hostile and ruinous legislation. This brief explanation does not cover all the ground, but it may suffice for the present purpose. Each party to the controversy considered itself on the defensive and, therefore, to each the issue seemed of vital importance. Neither was willing to surrender anything.

Disregarding the stock arguments — constitutional, economic, social, and what not — advanced by either group, let us examine afresh the real problem involved. Would slavery, if legally permitted to do so, have taken possession of the territories or of any considerable portion of them? There is no question but that our own generation must, if the fears of the anti-expansionists were well founded, sympathize with the opposition to slavery extension. But were their apprehensions well founded? A number of eminent historians, while admitting that slavery could not have flourished on the high arid lands of New Mexico, have either ignored the question with respect to Kansas or have tacitly seemed to assume that the upper plains region would have become a slave section but for the uprising of the people of the free states. They have pointed to various projects for an-

nexations or protectorates to the south of the United States as further evidence of a dangerous program for the extension of the slave power. They have applauded the prophecy of Lincoln, in his "house-divided" speech, that slavery, if not arrested, would extend over the whole country, North as well as South. Despite a lingering disinclination to question Lincoln's infallibility, probably few students of that period today would fully subscribe to that belief. Indeed, many of them have already expressed their disbelief; but so far as I am aware the subject has never been examined comprehensively and the results set down. It is time that such an examination should be made; and, since those more competent have not attempted it, I shall endeavor in this paper to direct attention to the question, even if I throw little new light upon it.

The causes of the expansion of slavery westward from the South Atlantic Coast are now well understood. The industrial revolution and the opening of world markets had continually increased the consumption and demand for raw cotton, while the abundance of fertile and cheap cotton lands in the Gulf States had steadily lured cotton farmers and planters westward. Where large-scale production was possible, the enormous demand for a steady supply of labor had made the use of slaves inevitable, for a sufficient supply of free labor was unprocurable on the frontier. Within one generation, the cotton-growing slave belt had swept across the Gulf region from eastern Georgia to Texas. A parallel movement had carried slaves, though in smaller ratio to whites, into the tobacco and hemp fields of Kentucky, Tennessee, and Missouri. The most powerful factor in the westward movement of slavery was cotton, for the land available for other staples — sugar, hemp, tobacco — was limited, while slave labor was not usually profitable in growing grain. This expansion of the institution was in response to economic stimuli; it had been inspired by no political program nor by any ulterior political purpose. It requires but little acquaintance with the strongly individualistic and unregimented society of that day to see that it would have been extremely difficult, if not impossible, to carry out such an extensive program; nor is there any evidence that such a program existed. There was incentive enough in the desire of the individual slaveowner for the greater profits which he expected in the new lands. The movement would go on as far as suitable cotton lands were to be found or as long as there was a reasonable expectation of profit from slave labor, provided, of course, that no political barrier was encountered.

The astonishing rapidity of the advance of the southern frontier prior to 1840 had alarmed the opponents of slavery, who feared that the institution would extend indefinitely into the West. But by 1849–50, when the contest over the principle of the Wilmot Proviso was at its height, the western limits of the cotton-growing region were already approximated; and by the time the new Republican party was formed to check the further expansion of slavery, the westward march of the cotton plantation was evidently slowing down. The northern frontier of cotton production west of the Mississippi had already been established at about the northern line of Arkansas. Only a negligible amount of the staple was being grown in Missouri. West of Arkansas a little cotton was cultivated by the slaveholding, civilized Indians; but until the Indian territory should be opened generally to white settlement —

a development of which there was no immediate prospect — it could not become a slaveholding region of any importance. The only possibility of a further westward extension of the cotton belt was in Texas. In that state alone was the frontier line of cotton and slavery still advancing.

In considering the possibilities of the further extension of slavery, then, it is necessary to examine the situation in Texas in the eighteen-fifties. Though slaves had been introduced into Texas by some of Stephen F. Austin's colonists, they were not brought in large numbers until after annexation. Before the Texas Revolution, the attitude of the Mexican government and the difficulty of marketing the products of slave labor had checked their introduction; while during the period of the Republic, the uncertainty as to the future of the country, the heavy tariff laid upon Texas cotton by the United States, which in the absence of a direct trade with Europe was virtually the only market for Texas cotton, and the low price of cotton after 1839, had been sufficient in general to restrain the cotton planter from emigrating to the new country. Annexation to the United States and the successful termination of the war with Mexico removed most of these impediments. Thereafter there was no tariff to pay; slave property was safe; land agents offered an abundance of cheap rich lands near enough to the coast and to navigable rivers to permit ready exportation; and the price of cotton was again at a profitable figure. Planters with their slaves poured into the new state in increasing numbers. They settled along the northeastern border, where they had an outlet by way of the Red River, or in the east and southeast along the rivers which flowed into the Gulf. But these rivers were not navigable very far from the coast, and the planter who went far into the interior found difficulty in getting his cotton to market. He must either wait upon a rise in the river and depend upon occasional small steamers or the risky method of floating his crop down on rafts; or he must haul it during the wet winter season along nearly impassable pioneer roads and across unbridged streams to Houston or Shreveport, or some other far-off market. The larger his crop, the more time, difficulty, and expense of getting it to market.

Obviously, there was a geographic limit beyond which, under such conditions, the growth of large crops of cotton was unprofitable. Therefore, in the early fifties, the cotton plantations tended to cluster in the river counties in the eastern and southern parts of the state. While the small farmers and stockmen pushed steadily out into the central section of Texas, driving the Indians before them, the cotton plantations and the mass of the slaves lagged far behind. The up-country settlers grew their little crops of grain on some of the finest cotton lands of the world; and they sold their surplus to immigrants and to army posts. Few negroes were to be found on these upland farms, both because the prices demanded for slaves were too high for the farmers to buy them, and because the seasonal character of labor in grain growing rendered the use of slaves unprofitable. Though negro mechanics were in demand and were hired at high wages, the field hand had to be employed fairly steadily throughout the year if his labor was to show a profit. Negroes were even less useful in handling range stock than in farming and were rarely used for that purpose.

Therefore, the extension of the cotton plantation into the interior of Texas had

to wait upon the development of a cheaper and more efficient means of transportation. As all attempts to improve the navigation of the shallow, snag-filled rivers failed, it became more and more evident that the only solution of the problem of the interior planter lay in the building of railroads. Throughout the eighteen-fifties, and indeed for two decades after the war, there was a feverish demand for railroads in all parts of the state. The newspapers of the period were full of projects and promises, and scores of railroad companies were organized or promoted. But capital was lacking and the roads were slow in building. Not a single railroad had reached the fertile black-land belt of central Texas by 1860. There can hardly be any question that the cotton plantations with their working forces of slaves would have followed the railroads westward until they reached the black-land prairies of central Texas or the semi-arid plains which cover the western half of the state. But would they have followed on into the prairies and the plains?

It is important to recall that eastern Texas, like the older South Atlantic and Gulf cotton region, is a wooded country, where the essential problem of enclosing fields was easily solved by the rail fence. But in the black-land prairies there was no fencing material, except for a little wood along the creeks; and during the fifties the small fields of the farmers were along these streams. The prairies, generally, were not enclosed and put under the plow until after the introduction of barbed wire in the late seventies. Unless the planter had resorted to the expense of shipping rails from eastern Texas, there was no way in which he could have made more use of the prairie lands than the small farmers did. Here, then, in the central black-land prairies, was a temporary barrier to the westward movement of the slave plantation. Beyond it was another barrier that would have been permanently impassable.

Running north and south, just west of the black-land belt, and almost in the geographical center of the state, is a hilly, wooded strip of varying width known as the East and West Cross Timbers, which is prolonged to the south and southwest by the Edwards Plateau. West of the Cross Timbers begins the semi-arid plain which rises to the high, flat table-land of the Staked Plains, or Llano Estacado, in the extreme west and northwest. Except for a few small cattle ranches, there were almost no settlements in this plains country before 1860; and despite the heavy immigration into Texas after the Civil War, it was not until the eighties that farmers began to penetrate this section.

The history of the agricultural development of the Texas plains region since 1880 affords abundant evidence that it would never have become suitable for plantation slave labor. Let us turn, for a moment, to this later period. The Texas and Pacific Railroad, completed by 1882 and followed by the building of other roads into and across the plains, afforded transportation; and the introduction of barbed wire solved the fencing problem. State and railroad lands were offered the settlers at low prices. Farmers began moving into the eastern plains about 1880, but they were driven back again and again by droughts. It took more than twenty years of experimentation and adaptation with windmills, dry-farming, and new drought-resisting feed crops for the cotton farmer to conquer the plains. There is little reason to believe that the conquest could have been effected earlier; there is even less basis for belief that the region would ever have been filled with plantations and slaves. For

reasons which will be advanced later, it is likely that the institution of slavery would have declined toward extinction in the Old South before the cotton conquest of the plains could have been accomplished, even had there been no Civil War. But if the institution had remained in full vigor elsewhere, it would have been almost impossible to establish the plantation system in this semi-arid section where, in the experimental period, complete losses of crops were so frequent. With so much of his capital tied up in unremunerative laborers whom he must feed and clothe, it is hard to see how any planter could have stayed in that country. Moreover, in the later period the use of improved machinery, especially adapted to the plains, would have made slave labor unnecessary and unbearably expensive. The character of the soil and the infrequency of rainfall have enabled the western cotton farmer, since 1900, with the use of this improved machinery to cultivate a far larger acreage in cotton, and other crops as well, than was possible in the older South or in eastern Texas. The result has been the appearance of a high peak in the demand for labor in western Texas in the cotton-picking season. This has called for transient or seasonal labor as in the grain fields — a situation that could not be met by the plantation system of slave labor. During the last twenty-five years this section has become populous and prosperous; but the beginning of its success as a cotton-growing region came fifty years after the Republican party was organized to stop the westward advance of the "cotton barons" and their slaves. It may or may not have any significance that the negro has moved but little farther west in Texas than he was in 1860 — he is still a rarity in the plains country — although it may be presumed that his labor has been cheaper in freedom than under slavery.

But let us look for a moment at the southwestern border of Texas. In 1860 slavery had stopped more than one hundred and fifty miles short of the Rio Grande. One obvious explanation of this fact is that the slaveowner feared to get too close to the boundary lest his bondmen escape into Mexico. There is no doubt that this fear existed, and that slaves occasionally made their way into that country. But it is worth noting that very little cotton was grown then or is yet grown on that border of Texas, except in the lower valley around Brownsville and along the coast about Corpus Christi. Other crops have proved better adapted to the soil and climate and have paid better. More significant still is the fact that very few negroes are found there today, for Mexican labor is cheaper than negro labor now, as it was in the eighteen-fifties. During the decade before secession, Mexican labor was used exclusively south of the Nueces River. After emancipation there was still no movement of negroes into the region where Mexican labor was employed. The disturbances which began in Mexico in 1910 have sent floods of Mexicans across the Rio Grande to labor in the fruit and truck farms of the valley and the cotton fields of south Texas. An interesting result is that the Mexican has steadily pushed the negro out of south Texas and to a considerable degree out of south-central Texas. Wherever the two have come into competition either on the farms or as day laborers in the towns, the Mexican has won. This would seem to show that there was little chance for the institution of African slavery to make headway in the direction of Mexico.

There was another situation which checked the extension of slavery into southwestern Texas. A large area of the most fertile lands had been settled by German immigrants, who had begun coming into that district in the late eighteen-forties. Not only were the Germans opposed to slavery; they were too poor to purchase slaves. They needed labor, as all pioneers do; but their needs were met by the steady inflow of new German immigrants, whose habit it was to hire themselves out until they were able to buy small farms for themselves. The system of agriculture of these industrious and frugal people had no place for the African, whether slave or free. Even today one sees few negroes among the original and typical German settlements. In 1860, east and southeast of San Antonio, these Germans formed a barrier across the front of the slaveholders.

Before turning to the possibilities of slavery extension in other sections, let us consider another question that may be raised by those who still feel that possibly some political advantage was to be gained for the pro-slavery cause in Texas. It had been provided in the joint resolution for the annexation of Texas, in 1845, that as many as four additional states could be formed from the new state, with the consent of Texas, and that such states as should be formed from the territory "south of the line of thirty-six degrees and thirty minutes north latitude, commonly known as the Missouri Compromise line, shall be admitted into the Union with or without slavery, as the people of each state asking admission may desire." It is frequently said that this division, if made, would have had the effect, politically, of an extension of the slavery system through the addition of at least two and possibly eight pro-slavery votes for the South in the United States Senate. Though there was some suggestion of such a division from time to time in other parts of the South before 1860 — and sometimes in the North — the sentiment for it in Texas was negligible and it was never seriously contemplated by any considerable group. A strong state pride, always characteristic of the Texans, was against division. There was some sectional feeling between the east and the west, dating from the days of the Republic; and the only agitation of the subject before the war was in 1850 and 1851 when discontent was expressed in eastern Texas over the selection of Austin as the permanent location of the capital. The agitation was frowned upon by the proslavery leaders on the ground that separation would result in the creation of a free state in western Texas, which was then overwhelmingly non-slaveholding.

By the provisions of the Compromise of 1850, New Mexico, Utah, and the other territories acquired from Mexico were legally open to slavery. In view of well-known facts, it may hardly seem worth while to discuss the question whether slavery would ever have taken possession of that vast region; but perhaps some of those facts should be set down. The real western frontier of the cotton belt is still in Texas; for though cotton is grown in small quantities in New Mexico, Arizona, and California, in none of these states is the entire yield equal to that of certain single counties in Texas. In none is negro labor used to any appreciable extent, if at all. In New Mexico and Arizona, Mexican labor is cheaper than negro labor, as has been the case ever since the acquisition of the region from Mexico. It was well understood by sensible men, North and South, in 1850 that soil, climate, and native labor would form a perpetual bar to slavery in the vast territory then called New Mexico. Possibly southern California could have sustained slavery, but

California had already decided that question for itself, and there was no remote probability that the decision would ever be reversed. As to New Mexico, the census of 1860, ten years after the territory had been thrown open to slavery, showed not a single slave; and this was true, also, of both Colorado and Nevada. Utah, alone of all these territories, was credited with any slaves at all. Surely these results for the ten years when, it is alleged, the slave power was doing its utmost to extend its system into the West, ought to have confuted those who had called down frenzied curses upon the head of Daniel Webster for his Seventh-of-March speech.

At the very time when slavery was reaching its natural and impassable frontiers in Texas, there arose the fateful excitement over the Kansas-Nebraska Bill, or rather over the clause which abrogated the Missouri Compromise and left the determination of the status of slavery in the two territories to their own settlers. Every student of American history knows of the explosion produced in the North by the "Appeal of the Independent Democrats in Congress to the People of the United States," written and circulated by Senator Chase and other members of Congress. This fulmination predicted that the passage of the bill would result in debarring free home-seeking immigrants and laborers from a vast region larger, excluding California, than all the free states, and in converting it into a dreary waste filled with plantations and slaves. It was a remarkably skillful maneuver and it set the North, particularly the Northwest, on fire. But, in all candor, what of the truth of the prophecy? Can anyone who examines the matter objectively today say that there was any probability that slavery as an institution would ever have taken possession of either Kansas or Nebraska? Certainly Cotton could not have been grown in either, for it was not grown in the adjacent part of Missouri. Hemp, and possibly tobacco, might have been grown in a limited portion of eastern Kansas along the Missouri and the lower Kansas rivers; and if no obstacle had been present, undoubtedly a few negroes would have been taken into eastern Kansas. But the infiltration of slaves would have been a slow process.

Apparently there was no expectation, even on the part of the pro-slavery men, that slavery would go into Nebraska. Only a small fraction of the territory was suited to any crops that could be grown with profit by slave labor, and by far the greater portion of Kansas — even of the eastern half that was available for immediate settlement — would have been occupied in a short time, as it was in fact, by a predominantly non-slaveholding and free-soil population. To say that the individual slaveowner would disregard his own economic interest and carry valuable property where it would entail loss merely for the sake of a doubtful political advantage seems a palpable absurdity. Indeed, competent students who have examined this subject have shown that the chief interest of the pro-slavery Missourians in seeking to control the organization of the territorial government was not so much in taking slaves into Kansas as in making sure that no free-soil territory should be organized on their border to endanger their property in western Missouri. They lost in the end, as they were bound to lose. The census of 1860 showed two slaves in Kansas and fifteen in Nebraska. In short, there is good reason to believe that had Douglas' bill passed Congress without protest, and had it been sustained by the people of the free states, slavery could not have taken permanent root in Kansas if the decision were left to the people of the territory itself.

The fierce contest which accompanied and followed the passage of Douglas' Kansas-Nebraska Bill is one of the sad ironies of history. Northern and southern politicians and agitators, backed by excited constituents, threw fuel to the flames of sectional antagonism until the country blazed into a civil war that was the greatest tragedy of the nation. There is no need here to analyze the arguments, constitutional or otherwise, that were employed. Each party to the controversy seemed obsessed by the fear that its own preservation was at stake. The northern anti-slavery men held that a legal sanction of slavery in the territories would result in the extension of the institution and the domination of the free North by the slave power; prospective immigrants in particular feared that they would never be able to get homes in this new West. Their fears were groundless; but in their excited state of mind they could neither see the facts clearly nor consider them calmly. The slaveholding Southerners, along with other thousands of Southerners who never owned slaves, believed that a victory in Kansas for the anti-slavery forces would not only weaken southern defenses — for they well knew that the South was on the defensive — but would encourage further attacks until the economic life of the South and "white civilization" were destroyed. Though many of them doubted whether slavery would ever take permanent root in Kansas, they feared to yield a legal precedent which could later be used against them. And so they demanded a right which they could not actively use — the legal right to carry slaves where few would or could be taken. The one side fought rancorously for what it was bound to get without fighting; the other, with equal rancor, contended for what in the nature of things it could never use.

No survey of the possibilities for the expansion of slavery would be complete without giving some consideration to another aspect of the subject — the various proposals for the acquisition of Cuba and Nicaragua, for a protectorate over Mexico, and for the re-opening of the African slave trade. These matters can be dealt with briefly, for today the facts are fairly well understood.

The movement for the annexation of Cuba was one of mixed motives. There was the traditional American dislike of Spanish colonial rule, strengthened by a natural sympathy for the Cubans, who were believed to wish independence. There was wide-spread irritation over the difficulty of obtaining from the Spanish government any redress for indignities perpetrated upon American vessels in Cuban ports and the indifference of Spain to claims for losses sustained by American citizens. Many Americans believed that only the acquisition of the island would terminate our perennial diplomatic troubles with Spain. There was the ever-present desire for territorial expansion, which was by no means peculiar to any section of the country. This ambition was reinforced by an extraordinary confidence in the superiority of American political institutions and the blessings which they would confer upon the annexed peoples. There was also the fear on the part of southern men that British pressure upon Spain would result in the abolition of slavery in Cuba and in some way endanger the institution of slavery in the United States; and this fear was heightened by the knowledge that both Great Britain and France were hostile to American acquisition of the island. A powerful incentive in New Orleans,

the hotbed of the filibustering movements, and also in New York, was the hope for a lucrative trade with the island after annexation. There is evidence that some of the planters in the newer cotton belt hoped to get a supply of cheaper slaves from Cuba where the prices were about half what they were in the southern states. Finally, there was the desperate hope of the extreme southern-rights group that, by the admission of Cuba to the Union as a slave state, increased political strength would be added to the defenses of the South.

All these motives were so mixed that it is impossible to assign to each its relative weight. The southern demand for annexation, because of the frankness of the pro-slavery leaders who advocated it and because it was made the point of attack by the anti-slavery group, has been magnified out of its true proportion. Even in the South there was nothing like general approval, by responsible men, of the filibustering enterprises of Lopez and Quitman, for many of those pro-slavery leaders who admitted a desire for the island repudiated the suggestion of forcibly seizing it from Spain. Although both Presidents Pierce and Buchanan pressed offers of purchase upon Spain — or sought to do so — they were unwilling to go further when their offers were coldly rejected. In view of the action of the government in smothering Quitman's filibustering effort in 1854, the general political situation in the United States, and the attitude of Great Britain and France, it must be said that the prospect of acquiring Cuba was, at best, remote.

As to Nicaragua and the frequently asserted dictum that William Walker was but the agent of the slavery expansionists, it is now well enough known that Walker's enterprise was entirely his own, and that he had no intention whatever, if successful, of turning over his private conquest to the United States, though he endeavored to use the more fanatical pro-slavery men of the South to further his own designs. In fact, until he broke with Commodore Vanderbilt, he had much closer connection with powerful financial interests in New York than he had with the Southerners. Had Walker succeeded, those pro-slavery expansionists who had applauded him would most certainly have been sorely disappointed in him. There seems to have been little basis for the fear that Nicaragua would ever have become a field for slavery expansion, or that it could have strengthened in any way the institution of slavery in the southern states. Does the history of the subsequent advance of the United States into the southern islands and Central America induce ironical reflection upon the controversies of the eighteen-fifties?

The filibustering projects against Mexico in the decade of the fifties were of no importance. They were but the feeble continuation of those directed early in the century against the northern provinces of Spain. There is little evidence that any responsible southern leaders cherished the design of seizing additional territory from Mexico for the extension of slavery. They knew too well that it was futile to expect that slaves could be used in the high table-lands or even in the low country where cheaper native labor was already plentiful. It is true that in 1858 Senator Sam Houston of Texas introduced in the Senate a resolution for a protectorate over Mexico. But Houston never showed any interest in the expansion of slavery; and his avowed purpose was to restore peace in Mexico, then distracted by revolutions; to protect the border of the United States; and to enable the Mexican government to pay its debts and satisfy its foreign creditors. His proposal was rejected in the Senate. It was hardly a wise one, but it had nothing to do with slavery. Later in the same year, President Buchanan recommended to Congress the establishment of a temporary protectorate over the northern provinces of Mexico for the security of the American border; but it is difficult to read into this suggestion any purpose to expand slavery. Not even a permanent protectorate or annexation could have effected an appreciable expansion of the institution.

The agitation for the re-opening of the African slave trade is an interesting episode. Its proponents were a small group of extremists, mostly Secessionists, whose ostensible object was to cheapen the cost of labor for the small farmer who was too poor to pay the high prices for slaves that prevailed in the fifties. Another argument for re-opening the trade was that cheaper slave labor would enable the institution to extend its frontiers into regions where it was too expensive under existing conditions. Finally, the proponents of the movement insisted that unless the cost of slaves declined, the northern tier of slave states would be drained of their negroes until they themselves became free states, thus imperiling the security of the cotton states. There is some reason to suspect that their leaders designed to stir up the anti-slavery element in the North to greater hostility and to renewed attacks in the hope that the South would be driven into secession, which was the ultimate goal of this faction. These agitators were never able to commit a single state to the project, for not only did the border states condemn it but the majority of the people of the Gulf states also. Even Robert Barnwell Rhett, who was at first inclined to support the program, turned against it because he saw that it was dividing the state-rights faction and weakening the cause of southern unity. This in itself seems highly significant of the southern attitude.

If the conclusions that have been set forth are sound, by 1860 the institution of slavery had virtually reached its natural frontiers in the west. Beyond Texas and Missouri the way was closed. There was no reasonable ground for expectation that new lands could be acquired south of the United States into which slaves might be taken. There was, in brief, no further place for it to go. In the cold facts of the situation, there was no longer any basis for excited sectional controversy over slavery extension; but the public mind had so long been concerned with the debate that it could not see that the issue had ceased to have validity. In the existing state of the popular mind, therefore, there was still abundant opportunity for the politician to work to his own ends, to play upon prejudice and passion and fear. Blind leaders of the blind! Sowers of the wind, not seeing how near was the approaching harvest of the whirlwind!

Perhaps this paper should end at this point; but it may be useful to push the inquiry a little farther. If slavery could gain no more political territory, would it be able to hold what it had? Were there not clear indications that its area would soon begin to contract? Were there not even some evidences that a new set of conditions were arising within the South itself which would disintegrate the institution? Here, it must be confessed, one enters the field of speculation, which is always dangerous ground for the historian. But there were certain factors in the situation which can be clearly discerned, and it may serve some purpose to indicate them.

Reference has already been made to the increasingly high prices of slaves in the southwestern states throughout the eighteen-fifties. This price-boom was due in part to good prices for cotton; but though there had always previously been a fairly close correlation between cotton and slave prices, the peculiarity of this situation was that slave prices increased much faster than cotton prices from 1850 to the end of 1860. Probably the explanation lies in the abundance of cheap and fertile cotton lands that were available for planting in Louisiana, Arkansas, and Texas. Cheap lands enabled the planter to expand his plantation and to invest a relatively larger amount of his capital in slaves, and the continued good prices for cotton encouraged this expansion. These good prices for slaves were felt all the way back to the oldest slave states, where slave labor was less profitable, and had the effect of drawing away planters and slaves from Maryland, Virginia, North Carolina, Kentucky, and Missouri to the new Southwest. This movement, to be sure, had been going on for several decades, but now the migration from the old border states was causing alarm among the pro-slavery men. Delaware was only nominally a slave state; Maryland's slave population was diminishing steadily. The ratio of slaves to whites was declining year by year in Virginia, Kentucky, and even in Missouri. The industrial revolution was reaching into these three states, and promised within less than another generation to reduce the economic interest in planting and slaveholding, as already in Maryland, to very small proportions.

The pro-slavery leaders in Virginia and Maryland endeavored to arrest this change by improving the condition of the planter. They renewed their efforts for a direct trade with Europe, and further

stimulated interest in agricultural reforms. As already seen, the proponents
of the revival of the African slave trade
argued that cheaper slave labor in the
lower South was necessary to prevent the
border states from ultimately becoming
free-soil. Though agricultural reform
made headway, the other remedies failed
to materialize; and the slow but constant
transformation of the Atlantic border
region proceeded. The greatest impediments were in the reluctance of the families of the old states, where slavery was
strongly patriarchal, to part with their
family servants, and in the social prestige
which attached to the possesion of an
ample retinue of servants. It was evident,
however, that the exodus would go on
until the lure of the Southwest lost its
force.

As long as there was an abundance of
cheap and fertile cotton lands, as there
was in Texas, and the prices of cotton
remained good, there would be a heavy
demand for labor on the new plantations.
As far as fresh lands were concerned, this
condition would last for some time, for
the supply of lands in Texas alone was
enormous. But at the end of the decade,
there were unmistakable signs that a
sharp decline in cotton prices and planting profits was close at hand. The production of cotton had increased slowly,
with some fluctuations, from 1848 to
1857, and the price varied from about ten
cents to over thirteen cents a pound on
the New York market. But a rapid increase in production began in 1858 and
the price declined. The crop of 1860 was
twice that of 1850. Probably the increase
in production was due in part to the
rapid building of railroads throughout
the South toward the end of the decade,
which brought new lands within reach
of markets and increased the cotton acreage; but part of the increase was due to
the new fields in Texas. There was every
indication of increased production and
lower price levels for the future, even if
large allowance be made for poor-crop
years. There was small chance of reducing the acreage, for the cotton planter
could not easily change to another crop.
Had not the war intervened, there is
every reason to believe that there would
have been a continuous overproduction
and very low prices throughout the sixties
and seventies.

What would have happened then when
the new lands of the Southwest had come
into full production and the price of cotton had sunk to the point at which it
could not be grown with profit on the
millions of acres of poorer soils in the
older sections? The replenishment of the
soil would not have solved the problem
for it would only have resulted in the
production of more cotton. Even on the
better lands the margin of profit would
have declined. Prices of slaves must have
dropped then, even in the Southwest;
importation from the border states would
have fallen off; thousands of slaves would
have become not only unprofitable but a
heavy burden, the market for them gone.
Those who are familiar with the history
of cotton farming, cotton prices, and the
depletion of the cotton lands since the
Civil War will agree that this is no fanci-
ful picture.

What would have been the effect of
this upon the slaveowner's attitude
toward emancipation? No preachments
about the sacredness of the institution
and of constitutional guarantees would
have compensated him for the dwindling
values of his lands and slaves and the
increasing burden of his debts. It should
not be forgotten that the final formulation and acceptance of the so-called "pro-
slavery philosophy" belonged to a time
when slaveowners, in general, were pros-

perous. With prosperity gone and slaves an increasingly unprofitable burden, year after year, can there be any doubt that thousands of slaveowners would have sought for some means of relief? How they might have solved the problem of getting out from under the burden without entire loss of the capital invested in their working force, it is hard to say; but that they would have changed their attitude toward the institution seems inevitable.

There was one difficulty about the problem of emancipation that has been little understood in the North, one that the Abolitionist refused to admit. It was the question of what to do with the freed negro. Could he take care of himself without becoming a public charge and a social danger? Would it not be necessary to get rid of the slave and the negro at the same time? But to get rid of the negro was manifestly impossible. Should he not then remain under some form of control both in his own interest and in the interest of the larger social order? There is some evidence that this problem was actually being worked out in those older states which had a large population of free negroes. In Virginia and Maryland, where the number of slaves on the plantation had been reduced in the interest of economy as improved farming machinery came into use, free negroes were coming to be relied upon when extra or seasonable labor was required. Though it is impossible to say how far this practice would have gone in substituting free-negro labor for slave labor, it would inevitably have accustomed increasing numbers of employers to the use of free negroes and have weakened by so much the economic interest in slavery. The cost of rearing a slave to the working age was considerable, and it is well within the probabilities that, in an era of over-stocked plantations and low cotton prices, the planter would have found that he was rearing slaves, as well as growing cotton, at a loss. New codes for the control of the free negroes might easily, in the course of time, have removed the greatest objection on the part of the non-slaveowners to emancipation.

In summary and conclusion: it seems evident that slavery had about reached its zenith by 1860 and must shortly have begun to decline, for the economic forces which had carried it into the region west of the Mississippi had about reached their maximum effectiveness. It could not go forward in any direction and it was losing ground along its northern border. A cumbersome and expensive system, it could show profits only as long as it could find plenty of rich land to cultivate and the world would take the product of its crude labor at a good price. It had reached its limits in both profits and lands. The free farmers in the North who dreaded its further spread had nothing to fear. Even those who wished it destroyed had only to wait a little while — perhaps a generation, probably less. It was summarily destroyed at a frightful cost to the whole country and one third of the nation was impoverished for forty years. One is tempted at this point to reflections upon what has long passed for statesmanship on both sides of that long dead issue. But I have not the heart to indulge them.

James G. Randall: THE BLUNDERING GENERATION

James G. Randall was the foremost historical writer who developed a "revisionist" explanation of the causes of the Civil War. Trained at the University of Chicago, Randall taught and lived in Virginia for eight years before he returned to a long teaching career at the University of Illinois. Influenced in part by the disillusionment of Americans concerning our entrance into the first world war, Randall frequently expressed his disgust with war-making. He was convinced that there must be "at some point a psychopathic case" in the explanation of any war. And the explanation of the causes of the Civil War must also fail if one omits "bogus leadership," "manipulation," "false fronts," "made-up incidents," and "propaganda that is false in intent." These ideas are fully developed in the selection below from the Mississippi Valley Historical Review.

WHEN one visits a moving picture, or reads Hergesheimer's *Swords and Roses*, which is much the same thing, he may gather the impression that the Civil War, fought in the days before mechanized divisions, aerial bombs, and tanks, was a kind of *chanson de geste* in real life. "The Civil War in America," writes Hergesheimer, "was the last of all wars fought in the grand manner. It was the last romantic war, when army corps fought as individuals and lines of assault . . . charged the visible enemy." "The war created a heroism . . . that clad fact in the splendor of battle flags." Hergesheimer feeds his readers chunks of sombre beauty, winterless climate, air stirred with faint cool music, fine houses, Spanish moss and cypress, trumpet vine and bay blossom, live oaks and linden, bridal wreath, japonica, moonflower, and honeysuckle. In his foreword to "Dear Blanche" he writes: "Here is a book of swords . . . of old-fashioned dark roses . . . [of] the simpler loveliness of the past." His pages live up to the foreword. He gives dear Blanche "The Rose of Mississippi," "The Lonely Star," "Shadows on the Sea," and "Gold Spurs." Of "Jeb" Stuart he says:

Ladies in Maryland gave him the spurs and ladies wherever he chanced to be gave him the rosebuds. . . . Naturally he was in the cavalry. He was different. . . . [He] wore a brown felt hat . . . with . . . sweeping black plume; . . . his boots in action were heavy, . . . afterwards he changed them for immaculate boots of patent leather worked with gold thread; but he danced as well as fought in his spurs.

The picture is filled in with red-lined cape, French sabre, yellow sash and tassels, The Bugles Sang Truce, The Dew is on the Blossom, orders given when asleep, animal vitality dancing in brilliant eyes.

Escapists may put what they will between the covers of a book; unfortunately the historian must be a realist. Whatever may be the thrill, or the emotional spree, of treating the Civil War romantically, it may be assumed that this has not been neglected. This paper,

James G. Randall, "The Blundering Generation," *Mississippi Valley Historical Review* (1940), 3–28. Reprinted by permission from the *Mississippi Valley Historical Review*.

therefore, will attempt a very different task, that of weighing some Civil War realities, examining some of the irrational ideas of war "causation," and pondering some aspects of the Civil War mind.

Without stressing that Zeebrugge or Westerplatte or the Karelian Isthmus matched any Civil War exploit, or that aviation is as smart as cavalry, it is sufficient to note a few comparisons. If the World War produced more deaths, the Civil War produced more American deaths. If weapons have become more brutal, at least medicine and sanitation have advanced. One seldom reads of the Civil War in terms of sick and wounded. Medical officers of the sixties repeated the experience of a British medical officer in the Burmese War who advised his commander how to avoid scurvy and was told: "Medical opinions are very good when called for." A Union surgeon at Bull Run reported extreme difficulty in inducing field officers to listen to complaints of disease resulting from foul tents into which fresh air was "seldom if ever" admitted. Because ambulances were on the wrong side of the road, this also at Bull Run, twelve thousand troops had to pass before some of the wounded could be taken to the emergency hospital. Wounded men arriving from the field were thrust into freight cars where they lay on the bare floor without food for a day; numbers died on the road. One of the officers refused hospital admittance to wounded soldiers not of his regiment. Medical supplies were thrown away for want of transportation, injured men were exposed to heavy rain, gangrene resulted from minor wounds.

Romance and glory suggest at least the memory of a name. This implies an identified grave, but after making calculations based upon the official medical history issued by the surgeon general,

the student would have to inform dear Blanche, or perhaps Mr. Ripley, that if the surgeon general's figures are right the unknown dead for the Civil War exceeded the number killed in battle! In round numbers there were about 110,000 Union deaths from battle, but the surgeon general reported that in November, 1870, there were 315,555 soldier graves, of which only 172,109 had been identified by name, leaving over 143,000 unidentified graves. The number of soldiers known in the adjutant general's records to have died during the war is much greater than the number identified as to burial or reburial. It must be remembered that the soldier regularly carried no means of identification, that graves of men buried by comrades were marked by hasty devices, that Confederates appropriated Union arms and clothing, that teamsters, refugees, camp followers, or even fugitive slaves might have been buried with soldiers, and that the number reported as killed in action was inaccurate. Yet after making all these allowances, the vast number of the nameless leaves the inquiring mind unsatisfied. It is no more satisfactory to realize that about half the Union army became human waste in one form or another, as dead, disabled, deserted, or imprisoned.

"Jeb" Stuart may have worn gold spurs, but the common soldier was more familiar with fleas. Sashes may have adorned generals but privates were often in rags. It was reported that one of the army surgeons boarded for an entire winter on Sanitary Commission stores. Camps were dirty, sanitation was faulty, cooking was shiftless. Reporting on one of the hospitals, an inspector referred to a leaky roof, broken glass, dirty stairs, insufficient sanitary facilities, and unclean disgusting beds. The soldier who was brutally struck by a sentry of his own company or who contracted malaria would hardly think of his experience as a thing of romance. Without exposing all the euphemisms that obscure the truth of this subject, it may be noted that the great majority of Union deaths were from causes medically regarded as preventable, leaving aside the cynical assumption that war itself is not preventable. Pneumonia, typhus, cholera, miasmic fever, and the like hardly find their way into the pages of war romance, but they wrought more havoc than bayonets and guns. Where there was danger of infection the rule-of-thumb principle of the Civil War surgeon was to amputate, and from operating tables, such as they were, at Gettysburg, arms and legs were carried away in wagon loads. Marching was hatefully wearisome, desertion was rampant, corruption was rife. Individual injustices of the war were shocking. Some generals got credit that was undeserved, others were broken by false report or slandered by an investigating committee of Congress. The men who languished in prison were several times more numerous than those stopped by bullets. That there was heroism in the war is not doubted, but to thousands the war was as romantic as prison rats and as gallant as typhoid or syphilis.

One does not often speak or read of the war in reality, of its blood and filth, of mutilated flesh, and other revolting things. This restraint is necessary, but it ought to be recognized that the war is not presented when one writes of debates in Congress, of flanking movements, of retreats and advances, of cavalry and infantry, of divisions doing this and brigades doing that. In the sense of full realism war cannot be discussed. The human mind will not stand for it. For the very word "war" the realist would have to substitute some such term as "organized murder" or "human slaughterhouse." In drama as distinguished from melodrama murder often occurs offstage. In most historical accounts, especially military narratives, the war is offstage in that its stench and hideousness do not appear.

With all the recent revisionist studies it is difficult to achieve a full realization of how Lincoln's generation stumbled into a ghastly war, how it blundered during four years of indecisive slaughter, and how the triumph of the Union was spoiled by the manner in which the victory was used. In the hateful results of the war over long decades one finds partisanship at its worst. To see the period as it was is to witness uninspired spectacles of prejudice, error, intolerance, and selfish grasping. The Union army was inefficiently raised, poorly administered, and often badly commanded. In government there was deadlock, cross purpose, and extravagance. One can say that Lincoln was honest, but not that the country was free from corruption during the Lincoln administration. There was cotton plundering, army-contract graft, and speculative greed. Where Lincoln was at his best, where he was moderate, temperate, and far-seeing, he did not carry his party with him. Even those matters dissociated from the war, such as homesteading and railroad extension, came to be marred by exploitation and crooked finance. The period of the Civil War and the era of Jim Fisk and Jay Gould were one and the same generation.

If it was a "needless war," a "repressible conflict," as scholars now believe, then indeed was the generation misled in its unctuous fury. To suppose that the Union could not have been continued or slavery outmoded without the war and without the corrupt concomitants of the war, is hardly an enlightened assumption. If one questions the term "blundering generation," let him inquire how many measures of the time he would wish copied or repeated if the period were to be approached with a clean slate and to be lived again. Most of the measures are held up as things to be avoided. Of course it is not suggested that the generation of the sixties had any copyright on blundering. It is not that democracy was at fault. After all, civil war has not become chronic on these shores, as it has in some nations where politics of force is the rule. One can at least say that the Civil War was exceptional; that may be the best thing that can be said about it. A fuller measure of democracy would probably have prevented the war or at least have mitigated its abuses. To overlook many decades of American democracy and take the Civil War period as its test, would be to give an unfair appraisal. Nor does this probing of blunders involve lack of respect for the human beings of that generation. As individuals we love and admire them, these men and women who look at us from the tintypes and Brady photographs of the sixties, though we may have "malice toward some." The distortions and errors of the time were rather a matter of mass thinking, of social solidification, and of politics.

In the present vogue of psychiatry, individual mental processes and behavior have been elaborately studied. Psychiatry for a nation, however, is still in embryo, though it is much the fashion to have discussions of mass behaviorism, public opinion, pressure groups, thought patterns, and propaganda. Scholars in the field of history tend more and more to speak in terms of culture; this often is represented as a matter of cultural conflict, as of German against Slav, of Japanese against Chinese, and the like. Such concepts were given overemphasis at the meeting of the American Historical Association last December. Historians are doing their age a disservice if these factors of culture are carried over, as they often are, whether by historians or others, into justifications or "explanations" of war. The note of caution here should be a note of honest inquiry. It may be seriously doubted whether war rises from fundamental motives of culture or economics so much as from the lack of cultural restraint or economic inhibition upon militaristic megalomania. Modern wars do not relieve population pressure. Whether wars are needed for economic outlets or for obtaining raw materials is highly doubtful. International trade brings all that. Those who create war throttle the very flow of trade that would promote economic objectives. Where the economy of a nation hinges upon an export market, it may happen that plotters of war in that nation will stupidly kill that market by devices of economic autarchy and then claim that they have to go to war to have trade outlets. It is the same with incoming goods. Of such is the economic argument for war. War makers do not open up economic benefit so much as they stifle it. Their relation to culture is no better than their relation to economy.

There is the word astrology for bogus astronomy and alchemy for false chemistry. Ought there not to be some such word for the economic alchemists of this world? Perhaps it exists in the word autarchy. Is it not in the category of bogus economics, or *ersatz* economics, that one should put those who study war as a matter of trade, supply, resources, needs, and production? As for the Civil War the stretch and span of conscious economic motive was much smaller than the areas or classes of war involvement.

Economic diversity offered as much motive for union, in order to have a well rounded nation, as for the kind of economic conflict suggested by secession. One fault of writers who associate war-making with economic advantage is false or defective economics; another is the historical fault. It is surprising how seldom the economic explanation of war has made its case historically, *i.e.* in terms of adequate historical evidence bearing upon those points and those minds where actually the plunge into war occurred. One hears war treated as a matter of culture, but cultural and racial consciousness are as strong in Scandinavia or the Netherlands or Switzerland as in militarist-ridden countries. To make conquest a matter of culture is poor history. It may be the vanquished whose culture survives. Culture is not easily transplanted if force be the method. When war comes by the violence of a few in control and by the stifling of economic and cultural processes, it ill becomes the scholar to add his piping to the cacophonous blare of militaristic propaganda.

War causation tends to be "explained" in terms of great forces. Something elemental is supposed to be at work, be it nationalism, race conflict, or quest for economic advantage. With these forces predicated, the move toward war is alleged to be understandable, to be explained, and therefore to be in some sense reasonable. Thought runs in biological channels and nations are conceived as organisms. Such thought is not confined to philosophers; it is the commonest of mental patterns. A cartoonist habitually draws a nation as a person. In this manner of thinking Germany does so and so; John Bull takes this or that course, and so on. When thought takes so homely a form it is hardly called a philosophical concept; for that purpose the very same thing would appear under a Greek derivative or Freudian label. However labeled, it may be questioned whether the concept is any better than a poor figure of speech, a defective metaphor which is misleading because it has a degree of truth.

Ruritania — to be no more specific — does so and so in the sense that it has a government, the government acts for the nation, and for political purposes there is no other way in which the country can act. The doubtful part is to infer that there is one directing mind for Ruritania which is the distillation of all the millions of minds. Where government has a bogus quality such an inference is more doubtful than if government has a well grounded or established quality. Given certain conditions of forced leadership and suppressed thought, the oneness of executive action in a nation may in fact represent nothing at all in terms of consolidated will and intent distilled from the whole mass. What passes for mass thought these days is not so much distilled as it is translated from golden plates handed down on some ideological Hill of Cumorah and read through the magic of authoritarian Urim and Thummim. The terrifying fact is that such bogus thought can be manufactured; it can be produced wholesale and distributed at top speed; it can control a nation; it is the shabby mental *ersatz* of an abnormal period.

War-making is too much dignified if it is told in terms of broad national urges, of great German motives, or of compelling Russian ambitions. When nations stumble into war, or when peoples rub their eyes and find they have been dragged into war, there is at some point a psychopathic case. Omit the element of abnormality, or of bogus leadership, or inordinate ambition for conquest, and diagnosis fails. In the modern scene it fails also if one omits manipulation, dummies, bogeys, false fronts, provocative agents, made-up incidents, frustration of elemental impulses, negation of culture, propaganda that is false in intent, criminal usurpation, and terrorist violence. These are reflections on the present bedeviled age, but their pertinence to the subject at hand is seen in the fact that scholarly discussions in explanation of war on the economic or cultural basis frequently include the Civil War as a supposedly convincing example. The writer doubts seriously whether a consensus of scholars who have competently studied the Civil War would accept either the cultural motive or the economic basis as the effective cause.

If one were to explain how this or that group or individual got into the Civil War, he could rely on no one formula. He would have to make up a series of elements or situations of which the following are only a few that might be mentioned: the despairing plunge, the unmotivated drift, the intruding dilemma, the blasted hope, the self-fulfilling prediction, the push-over, the twisted argument, the frustrated leader, the advocate of rule or ruin, and the reform-your-neighbor prophet. Robert Toombs said he would resist Stephen A. Douglas though he could see "nothing but . . . defeat in the future"; there is your despairing plunge. Young Henry Watterson, a Tennessee antislavery Unionist who fought for the Confederacy, is an example of the unmotivated drift. To many an individual the problem was not to fight with the side whose policies he approved of, but to be associated with the right set. Such an individual motive could not be a process of multiplication become in any reasonable sense a large-group motive. Yet it would be understandable for the individual. Usually in war times individuals have no choice of side, though in the American Civil War they sometimes did, especially on the border. Even where such choice was possible, the going to war by the individual in the sixties was due less to any broad "cause" or motive than to the fact that war existed, so that fighting was the thing to do. The obtaining of soldiers is not a matter of genuine persuasion as to issues. War participation is not a proof of war attitude.

The intruding dilemma was found in the great border and the great upper South where one of two ugly courses had to be chosen, though neither choice made sense in terms of objectives and interests in those broad regions. The self-fulfilling prediction is recognized in the case of those who, having said that war must come, worked powerfully to make it come. The blasted hope, i.e. the wish for adjustment instead of butchery, was the experience of most of the people, especially in the border and upper South. The frustrated leader is seen in the Unionist who came to support secession, or in such northerners as Thurlow Weed and William H. Seward who sought compromise and then supported war. The plea that "better terms" could be had out of the Union, which implied a short secession gesture though uttered by determined secessionists, was the crafty argument for secession to be used in addressing Unionists. This might be dubbed the twisted argument. The push-over is seen in the whole strategy of secession leaders by which anti-secession states and Union-loving men were to be dragged in by the accelerated march of events.

These are things which belong as much to the "explanation" of the Civil War as any broad economic or cultural elemental factor. It should be remembered how few of the active promoters of secession became leaders of the Confederacy; their place in the drama was in the first act, in the starting of trouble. Nor should sectional preference cause one to forget how large a contribution to Union disaster, and how little to success, was given by northern radicals during the war. Clear thinking would require a distinction between causing the war and getting into the war. Discussion which overlooks this becomes foggy indeed. It was small minorities that caused the war; then the regions and sections got into it. No one seems to have thought of letting the minorities fight it out. Yet writers who descant upon the causation of the war write grandly of vast sections, as if the fact of a section being dragged into the slaughter was the same as the interests of that section being consciously operative in its causation. Here lies one of the chief fallacies of them all.

In writing of human nature in politics Graham Wallas has shown the potent effect of irrational attitudes. He might have found many a Civil War example. None of the "explanations" of the war make sense, if fully analyzed. The war has been "explained" by the choice of a Republican president, by grievances, by sectional economics, by the cultural wish for southern independence, by slavery, or by events at Sumter. But these explanations crack when carefully examined. The election of Lincoln fell so far short of swinging southern sentiment against the Union that secessionists were still unwilling to trust their case to an all-southern convention or to cooperation among southern states. In every election from 1840 to 1852 Lincoln voted for the same candidate for whom many thousands of southerners voted. Lincoln deplored the demise of the Whig party and would have been only too glad to have voted in 1856 for another Harrison, another Taylor, or another Fillmore. Alexander Stephens stated that secessionists did not desire redress of grievances and would obstruct such redress. Prophets of sectional economics left many a southerner unconvinced; it is doubtful how far their arguments extended beyond the sizzling pages of *DeBow's Review* and the agenda of southern commercial congresses. The tariff was a potential future annoyance rather than an acute grievance in 1860. What existed then was largely a southern tariff law. Practically all tariffs are one-sided. Sectional tariffs in other periods have existed without producing war. Southern independence on broad cultural lines is probably more of a modern thesis than a contemporary motive of sufficient force to have carried the South out of the Union on any cooperative, all-southern basis.

It was no part of the Republican program to smash slavery in the South, nor did the territorial aspect of slavery mean much politically beyond agitation. Southerners cared little about actually taking slaves into existing territories; Republicans cared so little in the opposite sense that they avoided the prohibition of slavery in those territorial laws that were passed with Republican votes in February and March, 1861. Things said of "the South" often failed to apply to southerners, or of "the North" to northerners. Thwarted "Southern rights" were more often a sublimation than a definite entity. "The North" in the militant pre-war sense was largely an abstraction. The Sumter affair was not a cause, but an incident resulting from pre-existing governmental deadlock; Sumter requires explanation, and that explanation carries one back into all the other alleged factors. In contemporary southern comments on Lincoln's course at Sumter one finds not harmony but a jangling of discordant voices. Virginia resented Lincoln's action at Sumter for a reason opposite to that of South Carolina; Virginia's resentment was in the anti-secessionist sense. By no means did all the North agree with Lincoln's course as to Sumter. Had Lincoln evacuated Sumter without an expedition, he would have been supported by five and a half of seven cabinet members, Chase taking a halfway stand and Blair alone taking a positive stand for an expedition. What Lincoln refused as to Sumter was what the United States government had permitted in general as to forts and arsenals in the South. Stronger action than at Sumter was taken by Lincoln at Pickens without southern fireworks. There is no North-versus-South pattern that covers the subject of the forts. Nor is the war itself to be glibly explained in rational North-versus-South terms.

Let one take all the factors — the Sumter maneuver, the election of Lincoln, abolitionism, slavery in Kansas, cultural and economic differences — and it will be seen that only by a kind of false display could any of these issues, or all of them together, be said to have caused the war if one omits the elements of emotional unreason and overbold leadership. If one word or phrase were selected to account for the war, that word would not be slavery, or state-rights, or diverse civilizations. It would have to be such a word as fanaticism (on both sides), or misunderstanding, or perhaps politics. To Graham Wallas misunderstanding and politics are the same thing.

The fundamental or the elemental is often no better than a philosophical will o' the wisp. Why do adventitious things, or glaringly abnormal things, have to be elementally or cosmically accounted for? If, without proving his point, the historian makes war a thing of "inevitable" economic conflict, or cultural expression, or *Lebensraum*, his generalizations are caught up by others, for it would seem that those historians who do the most generalizing, if they combine effective writing with it, are the ones who are most often quoted. The historian's pronouncements are taken as the statement of laws whether he means them so or not; he is quoted by sociologists, psychologists, behaviorists, misbehaviorists, propagandists, and what not; he becomes a contributor to those "dynamic" masses of ideas, or ideologies, which are among the sorriest plagues of the present age. As to wars, the ones that have not happened are perhaps best to study. Much could be said about such wars. As much could be said in favor of them as of actual wars. Cultural and economic difficulties in wars that have not occurred are highly significant. The notion that you must have war when you have cultural variation, or economic competition, or sectional difference is an unhistorical misconception which it is stupid in historians to promote. Yet some of the misinterpretations of the Civil War have tended to promote it.

Avery Craven: THE BREAKDOWN OF THE DEMOCRATIC PROCESS

Avery O. Craven, more than any of the revisionist historians, has given close attention in his writings to the way in which concrete issues were simplified into abstract principles and symbols. His writings help us to understand how the continued emphasis on absolutist positions of right and wrong can cause a breakdown of the normal political process in a democratic society. Craven believes that the political struggles of the 1840's had already gone a long way toward creating such patterns of political behavior. The following selection is an article entitled "The 1840's and the Democratic Process" from the Journal of Southern History.

THE most significant thing about the American Civil War is that it represents a complete breakdown of the democratic process. After years of strain, men ceased to discuss their problems, dropped the effort to compromise their differences, refused to abide by the results of a national election, and resorted to the use of force. After four years of bloody civil strife, one side was beaten into submission and the other had its way in national affairs. The emergence of modern America was largely the product of that outcome.

If the breakdown of the democratic process is the significant thing about the coming of the Civil War, then the important question is not *what* the North and South were quarreling about half so much as it is *how* their differences got into such shape that they could not be handled by the process of rational discussion, compromise, or the tolerant acceptance of majority decision. The question is not "What caused the Civil War?" but rather "How did it come about?" The two questions are quite different,

yet hopelessly tangled. The effort to distinguish between them, however, is important and needs to be stressed.

If one were to discuss the *causes* of the Civil War, he might begin with geography, move on to historical developments in time and place, trace the growth of economic and social rivalries, outline differences in moral values, and then show the way in which personalities and psychological factors operated. The part which slavery played would loom large. It might even become the symbol of all differences and of all conflicts. State rights, territorial expansion, tariffs, lands, internal improvements, and a host of other things, real and imagined, would enter the picture. There would be economic causes, constitutional causes, social causes, moral causes, political causes involving the breaking of old parties and the rise of sectional ones, and psychological causes which ultimately permitted emotion to take the place of reason. There would be remote or background causes, and immediate causes, and causes resting on other causes, until the most

Avery Craven, "The 1840's and the Democratic Process," *Journal of Southern History*, XVI (1950), 161–176, by permission of the Managing Editor.

eager pedagogue would be thoroughly satisfied.

The matter of how issues got beyond the abilities of the democratic process is, on the other hand, a bit less complex and extended. It has to do with the way in which concrete issues were reduced to abstract principles and the conflicts between interests simplified to basic levels where men feel more than they reason, and where compromise or yielding is impossible because issues appear in the form of right and wrong and involve the fundamental structure of society. This is not saying, as some have charged, that great moral issues were not involved. They certainly were, and it is a matter of choice with historians as to whether or not they take sides, praise or condemn, become partisans in this departed quarrel, or use past events for present-day purposes.

As an approach to this second more modest problem, a correspondence which took place between Abraham Lincoln and Alexander H. Stephens between November 30 and December 22, 1860, is highly revealing. On November 14, Stephens had delivered one of the great speeches of his life before the legislature of Georgia. It was a Union speech. He had begged his fellow Southerners not to give up the ship, to wait for some violation of the Constitution before they attempted secession. Equality might yet be possible inside the Union. At least, the will of the whole people should be obtained before any action was taken.

Abraham Lincoln, still unconvinced that there was real danger, wrote Stephens, as an old friend, for a revised copy of his speech. Stephens complied, and he ended his letter with a warning about the great peril which threatened the country and a reminder of the heavy responsibility now resting on the president-elect's shoulders. Lincoln answered with assurance that he would not "*directly,* or *indirectly,* interfere with the slaves" or with the southern people about their slaves, and then closed with this significant statement: "I suppose, however, this does not meet the case. You think slavery is right and ought to be extended, while we think it is *wrong* and ought to be restricted. That I suppose is the rub. It certainly is the only substantial difference between us."

The reduction of "the only substantial difference" between North and South to a simple question of *right and wrong* is the important thing about Lincoln's statement. It revealed the extent to which the sectional controversy had, by 1860, been simplified and reduced to a conflict of principles in the minds of the northern people.

Stephens' answer to Lincoln's letter is equally revealing. He expressed "an earnest desire to preserve and maintain the Union of the States, if it can be done upon the principles and in furtherance of the objects for which it was formed." He insisted, however, that private opinion on the question of "African Slavery" was not a matter over which "the Government under the Constitution" had any control. "But now," he said, "this subject, which is confessedly on all sides outside of the Constitutional action of the Government so far as the States are concerned, is made the 'central idea' in the Platform of principles announced by the triumphant Party." It was this total disregard of the Constitution and the rights guaranteed under it that lay back of southern fears. It was the introduction into party politics of issues which projected action by Congress outside its constitutional powers that had made all the trouble. Stephens used the word "Constitution" seven times in his letter.

The significant thing here is Stephens' reduction of sectional differences to the simple matter of southern rights under the Constitution. He too showed how completely the sectional controversy had been simplified into a conflict of principles. And he with Lincoln, speaking for North and South, emphasized the fact that after years of strife the complex issues between the sections had assumed the form of a conflict between *right* and *rights*.

To the scholar it must be perfectly clear that this drastic simplification of sectional differences did not mean that either Lincoln or Stephens thought that all the bitter economic, social, and political questions could be ignored. It simply meant that *right* and *rights* had become the symbols or carriers of all those interests and values. Yet it is equally clear that as symbols they carried an emotional force and moral power in themselves that was far greater than the sum total of all the material issues involved. They suggested things which cannot be compromised — things for which men willingly fight and die. Their use, in 1860, showed that an irrepressible conflict existed.

The question as to whether the Civil War was "a needless war" has, therefore, little to do with the bungling statesmanship of 1860–1861. It has much to do with the matter of how problems got beyond the ability of the democratic process. And as to that, we do know that the author of the Declaration of Independence, on which the Lincoln position rested, was a slaveholder. So was Madison and many other important leaders of the first great democratic drive in national life. The three men whom Arthur M. Schlesinger, Jr., names as the ones who carried the democratic torch on down to the age of Jackson — John Randolph, Nathaniel Macon, and John

Taylor of Caroline — were also slaveholders, as were Jackson himself and Thomas Hart Benton and Francis Preston Blair, his chief lieutenants. Even the father of Martin Van Buren held slaves. Evidently, in these years only a generation away from Civil War, the belief that slavery was morally wrong did not constitute "the only substantial difference" between those who sought to forward government "of the people, by the people, for the people" and their reactionary opponents.

Nor, by the same token, was everyone in the early South agreed on the value of slavery or its constitutional right to immunity from public criticism and political action. In the Virginia constitutional convention of 1829–1830 and in the legislature of 1832, men questioned the economic benefits of slavery, pointed out its social dangers, and shamed its violation both of Christian and democratic values. Bills were introduced and voted upon. True, it was a case of a state discussing and acting upon its own domestic affairs, but these men were talking about slavery as an institution, not as just a Virginia practice, and they were thoroughly conscious of the larger national implications of what was going on. Robert Stanard spoke of the impulse begun in Virginia passing "with the rapidity of lightning across the whole extent of this Union." James Monroe frankly admitted that he looked "to the Union to aid in effecting" emancipation; and James M'Dowell, Jr., bitterly denounced slavery because it created "a political interest in this Union" and produced conflicts in Congress and dissension in the nation. He saw the day when a national crusade against slavery would unite all rival interests against the South.

Slavery took its blows in other states as well, and there was anything but gen-

eral agreement on how to protect constitutional rights when South Carolina took
a try at nullification. However much
they might dislike the tariff, the other
southern states had not as yet returned
to the old anticonsolidation state-rights
position of their elder statesmen. The
issue outside of South Carolina was generally one of the merits of the tariff rather
than the constitutional rights of a state.
The younger Southwest, moreover, had
its own attitudes towards lands and internal improvements which kept these
issues on the level of interest rather than
on that of constitutionality.

The next few years, however, brought
important changes. The growing realization of failure to share equally in national
expansion, the new demand for slaves
with the spread of cotton, and the
increasing agitation against slavery all
contributed to a feeling of resentment
and insecurity on the part of the South.
Where the coming of the Industrial Revolution to the Northeast upset life to its
very roots and forced a reconsideration
of every old value and every relationship,
Southerners, who had experienced only
the extension of old agricultural patterns
into new agricultural areas, knew no
sharp break with their pasts and found
no reason to question the soundness of
old social and political institutions and
relationships. Conditions under the Constitution, as the fathers had made it, were
quite satisfactory.

Yet the matchless material growth that
had come to the nation in these years, the
deep ferment of ideas, and the rapid increase in the means of communication
denied the South the chance to live alone.
The nation was, in fact, in a state of
transition, politically, economically, and
socially. The attempt to apply old forms
to constantly changing conditions put
heavy strain on institutions and agencies

created in more simple times and tended
to thrust forward for decision the questions of just what kind of a government
we had set up in the United States, what
provisions it made for the protection of
minorities, and just what the relations
were between government and business.
Nor could southern institutions escape
the scrutiny that was being given to all
institutions and relationships in this age
of transition. The whole Northeast,
under the pressure of forces that would
ultimately produce modern America, was
rapidly becoming the center of social
unrest and of efforts at reform. The new
age was revealing too many contradictions between profession and practice.
Where before in a simple rural order the
true and the good were not beyond the
comprehension of every man through a
direct moral approach, and a good society was simply one composed of good
men, they now found environment a
force of major importance. The living of
the many was passing into the hands of
the few. Everywhere men were losing
their independence, and forces quite beyond individual control were shaping the
lives of the masses. Neither Christianity
nor democracy seemed to be working.
Something was wrong and it should be
righted. The Declaration of Independence with its emphasis on freedom and
equality ought again to become a force
in American life.

Out of the welter of reform movements
that resulted from such convictions came
the antislavery impulse and the resulting
struggle over antislavery petitions in
Congress. Joining hands with the great
religious revivals that were burning their
way through the lives of men and women
in a region spreading east and west from
upper New York, a group of earnest souls
had lighted fires of moral indignation
against the sin of slavery and were pour-

ing a flood of petitions into Congress demanding various steps against the evil. The South thus found itself faced by danger on a new front. It was thrown on the defensive. The Constitution and its clear statements of rights also needed to be brought back into American consciousness.

Already, in the tariff controversy, Robert J. Turnbull had argued that under changing conditions it was the interest of the North and West to make the government "more national," while the interest of the South was to continue it "Federal." In opposing Jackson's Force Bill, John C. Calhoun had insisted that the real issue was whether this was a federal union of states or a union of the American people in the aggregate. He made it perfectly clear that he thought it was the former, and that "To maintain the ascendency of the constitution over the law-making majority" was the great and essential thing for the preservation of the Union. When the petition struggle developed, he quickly picked up the charge that slavery was "sinful and odious, in the sight of God and man," and pronounced it "a general crusade against us and our institutions." "The most unquestionable right may be rendered doubtful," he insisted, if slavery were "once admitted to be a subject of controversy." The subject was beyond the jurisdiction of Congress — "they have no right to touch it in any shape or form," he said, "or to make it the subject of deliberation or discussion." And then, ignoring his own words, he bluntly pronounced "the relation now existing in the slaveholding States" between the two races to be "a positive good." Even though opposition to the very popular right of petition might weaken friends in Congress and strengthen the abolitionists, the enemy must be met "on the

frontier"; this was the southern "Thermopylae."

Later, on December 27, 1837, he introduced a series of resolutions which carefully defined the character, purposes, and powers of the government under the Constitution. It had been adopted by the "free, independent and sovereign States" as security against all dangers, "*domestic*, as well as foreign." The states retained the sole right over their domestic institutions, and any intermeddling with those institutions by other states or combinations of their citizens was unwarranted and "subversive of the objects for which the constitution was formed." And it was the duty of the government to resist all such meddling.

Negro slavery, he declared, was an important domestic institution in southern and western states and was such when the Constitution was formed. "No change of opinion or feeling, on the part of other States of the Union in relation to it, can justify them or their citizens in open and systematic attacks thereon." To do so was a "breach of faith, and a violation of the most solemn obligations, moral and religious." Furthermore, to attempt to abolish slavery in the District of Columbia, or in any of the territories, on grounds that it was immoral or sinful "would be a direct and dangerous attack on the institutions of all the slaveholding States"; and to refuse to increase the limits or population of these states by the annexation of new territory or states on the pretext that slavery was "immoral or sinful, or otherwise obnoxious" would destroy the equal "rights and advantages which the Constitution was intended to secure."

To resist the moral attacks of what was then a comparatively small group of Americans, who were none too popular in their own neighborhoods, Calhoun had asked Congress and the American people to accept his interpretation of the character of our government and his evaluation of the institution of slavery — accept them at a time when the whole course of developments in the Northeast, and to an increasing degree in the Northwest, were towards a more interdependent nationalism and a more humane and democratic social order. He had reduced the struggle to the level of abstract principles at the very moment when every principle for which he stood was being abandoned by the whole western world and invalidated by the onward rush of the incoming modern age.

It was a serious mistake. Or was it clear insight into realities which discerned the inevitable course of events and dictated a bold stroke at the very threshold in an effort to ward off consequences? Most leaders at the time thought it a serious blunder. Garret Dorset Wall of New Jersey thought the resolutions were just "political abstractions" of which the Senate ought not to take cognizance. John Jordan Crittenden of Kentucky declared, "More vague and general abstractions could hardly have been brought forward," and agreed with James Buchanan of Pennsylvania that they would serve only to stir more agitation. Robert Strange of North Carolina added, "Agitating this question in any shape was ruinous to the South." Thomas Hart Benton, at a later time commenting on results, said that it gave the antislavery forces "the point to stand upon from which they could reach every part of the Union. . . . Mr. Calhoun was a fortunate customer" for the abolitionists.

The roaring decade of the 1840's quickly demonstrated the soundness of Benton's opinion. They were spacious days. They brought the great developments going on in national life to a point where final patterns were quite discernible. The era of transition was coming to an end. Economic groups and geographic sections were becoming increasingly conscious of their unique interests, and the nation of its manifest destiny.

In these years the Cotton Kingdom rounded out its borders and demonstrated its right to speak for the section. The old Souths began to find their way through the difficulties that had beset them, some states to draw closer to the Cotton Kingdom, others to drift away into border-state position.

Meanwhile, the rapid expansion of New England and New York peoples along the Great Lakes and the rise of a Kingdom of Wheat where they and large bodies of foreign immigrants settled sharply altered the balance in the Old Northwest where, up until now, close alliance with the South had been taken for granted. A hungry home market for wheat and a Canadian demand for any surplus gave early prosperity, but produced a harsh depression when they failed. That turned attention to the English Corn Laws and produced a close alliance between the free-trade, antislavery elements in the two countries. That gave strange new support to the low Walker tariff, the passage of which, in turn, smoothed the way for Britain's acceptance of a compromise Oregon boundary. Thus while the antislavery men of the upper Northwest talked free trade and joined in the drive for a homestead law, they were, in spite of surface appearances, drawing closer to the older portion of the Northwest along the Ohio River, whose leaders were bitterly denouncing their fellow southern Democrats for betrayal of the Oregon-Texas bargain. The Old Northwest too was becoming self-conscious and independent in attitude. Henceforth it would seek its own interests and determine its own values.

In this same period industry entered a new phase in the northeastern corner of the nation. Hard times and bitter competition wrecked weaker concerns and left the field to the large, well-financed corporations. Work was speeded up and wages remained low. Strikes became frequent. Gradually the native girls gave way before the Irish and French-Canadians, and the factory and the factory town reached maturity. Industry sent its spokesmen into legislative halls, and the ardent complaint against local ills gave way steadily to the attack on southern slavery. A general acceptance of the new age of interdependent nationalism, already a business reality, marked the section. The questioning and criticism represented in Fruitlands, Brook Farm, and the Fourier associations gradually lost force. A new feeling of being in step with progress took its place. The development of a complex industrial order was a part of the nation's manifest destiny. Men, therefore, fell into line on domestic issues, but they did not yield their tough Puritan estimates of the ways of other Americans. Meanwhile the growth of internal commerce, now far more important than foreign trade, fostered the growing cities along the Atlantic coast, and the canal and the railroad, as the great new agents of transportation, more and more linked the interests of the Northwest to those of the commercial-industrial Northeast.

By these quick and drastic developments, the problems of lands, internal improvements, tariffs, and expansion were thrust forward in aggravated forms. They took on the character of sectional struggles. They became part of the right and the effort to achieve a manifest destiny. Sooner or later every one of them

became tangled with slavery and from it took new strength with which to wage their battles. Both Calhoun and the abolitionists connected slavery with the annexation of Texas. Benjamin Lundy declared the Texas revolution a scheme to wrest that territory from Mexico in order to establish a slave market, and John Quincy Adams and twelve associates denounced annexation as a pro-slavery scheme. Calhoun gave substance to their charge by insisting on annexation as necessary for the protection of southern slaveholders. Others connected it with the tariff and internal improvements. Joshua Giddings of Ohio in May, 1844, called attention to the balance and rivalry between North and South which produced a deadlock in legislation. " So equally balanced has been the political power," he said, "that for five years past our lake commerce has been utterly abandoned; and such are the defects of the tariff, that for years our revenues are unequal to the support of government." The annexation of Texas, secured "obviously to enhance the price of human flesh in our slave-breeding states," would now place "the policy and the destiny" of this nation in southern hands.

"Are the liberty-loving democrats of Pennsylvania ready to give up our tariff?" he asked. "Are the farmers of the West, of Ohio, Indiana, and Illinois, prepared to give up the sale of their beef, pork, and flour, in order to increase the profits of those who raise children for sale, and deal in the bodies of women? Are the free states prepared to suspend their harbor and river improvements for the purpose of establishing their slave-trade with Texas, and to perpetuate slavery therein?" "Our tariff," he added at a later time, "is as much an anti-slavery measure as the rejection of Texas. So is the subject of internal improvements and the distribution of the proceeds of the public lands. The advocates of perpetual slavery oppose all of them, they regard them as opposed to slavery."

Giddings represented an extreme position, but the proposed tax on tea and coffee brought from more moderate western men the charge that it was "a sectional tax." It was "wrong, unequal, and unjust," because while all free western laborers used these articles, the three million slave laborers scarcely touched them at all. President James K. Polk was asking for a war tax on tea and coffee "to make southern conquests, while northern territory [meaning Oregon] is given away by empires."

Slavery was also blamed for Polk's veto of a river and harbor bill intended largely to benefit shipping on the Great Lakes. "Is it not strange that enlightened men of the South cannot be persuaded that our lakes are something more than goose ponds?" asked the Chicago *Democrat*. "If we were blessed with the glorious institution of slavery this comprehension would not be so difficult." The Chicago *Daily Journal* was more blunt. It charged Southerners' opposition to western internal improvements to the fact that they were "slaveholders," but "not Americans." "If no measures for the protection and improvement of anything North or West are to be suffered by our Southern masters," it said, "if we are to be downtrodden, and all our cherished interests crushed by them, a signal revolution will eventually ensue."

By the close of the Mexican War, which brought proslavery charges to a climax, some men were frankly saying that the whole business had become a struggle for power. The extension or nonextension of slavery in the territories acquired from Mexico was a matter of increasing or decreasing the strength of

parties in Congress. Robert Barnwell Rhett of South Carolina was convinced that "Political power, the power of the different sections of the Union, seeking the mastery, is undoubtedly a strong element in the proposed exclusion of slavery from our territory." George Oscar Rathbun of New York was more explicit. He had figured out that by its three-fifths representation of slaves the South gained some twenty-three members in Congress. With this vote the section had "turned the scale upon every important question that had divided this country for the last forty years." The South had by this advantage elected presidents, filled the speakership, ruled the army and navy, and placed southern men in the office of Secretary of State during most of those years. Rathbun was, therefore, opposed to slavery in the territories because it gave "representation and political power." If the South would yield the three-fifths rule, he was willing for Southerners to go into any territory and freely to take their slaves with them. Southerners made it just as clear that the exclusion of slavery from the territories meant the reduction of their section to the position of a permanent minority and the ultimate destruction of their institutions. They were contending for equality in the nation.

The Wilmot Proviso was unquestionably, in part, a move to check southern strength in Congress and to end the restraints placed on northern and western development. It was, however, considerably more than that. It was an assertion of the fact that North and West had now definitely caught step with the modern world and had reached the point where they knew both their minds and their strength. They knew that the future belonged to urban industrial and financial capitalism, to democracy, and to a more social Christianity. They understood that slavery, as an impediment to each of these things, had no place in a nation whose manifest destiny was to round out its boundaries on this continent and, perhaps, to right the social and political balances in the whole western world.

That understanding gave a positiveness to northern opposition to the extension of slavery that knew no yielding. It easily took on the flavor of a moral crusade. Politicians and "sober, deliberate, and substantial men," who had "the good of the country at heart," as Charles Hudson of Massachusetts described them, let it be known that slavery could not advance a foot farther. Anyone who has read the debates in Congress on this issue knows that the question of whether slavery had reached its limits in the United States is a thoroughly academic one. And the answer has nothing to do with geography or profits. It could go no farther, for the simple reason that the North had made up its mind and had the strength to enforce its will.

And, regardless of how complex were the forces operating to produce this situation, the argument that carried the day was that slavery was a moral wrong and an impediment to progress. In the great debates on compromise which followed, Horace Mann and William H. Seward, not Daniel Webster, made the important northern statements. Mann insisted that to spread slavery was to "cast aside, with scorn, not only the teachings of Christianity, but the clearest principles of natural religion and of natural law." It was to sink back to the Dark Ages. To insist that men and women could rightly be called property was a trick for which any "juggler or mountebank" would be hissed off the stage in any respectable village. "I deliberately say, better disunion, better a civil or servile war — better anything that God in his providence shall send,

than an extension of the boundaries of slavery. Seward declared that we could be neither Christians nor real freemen if we imposed on another the chains we defied all human power to fasten on ourselves. He insisted that the Constitution had created a consolidated political state, in which the states had "submitted themselves to the sway of the numerical majority." The same Constitution had devoted the territories to freedom. And what was just as important, slavery itself in the long run would have to give way "to the salutary instructions of economy, and to the ripening influences of humanity." It was only a question of whether it be done peacefully or by force. And to those who offered the Constitution as an impediment to the forward sweep of material and moral progress, he offered the "higher law."

Some day the historian will understand that there is no break between Henry David Thoreau's "Civil Disobedience," William Lloyd Garrison's burning of the Constitution, and Seward's higher law. He will also understand the obligation which northern men felt to bring profession and practice into harmony in a nation whose manifest destiny was to uphold Christianity and democracy throughout the western world.

The South, on its part, met the Wilmot Proviso with an uncompromising insistence on the right to an equal share in the territories won by the common blood of the nation. Calhoun, as usual, brought forward a series of resolutions, declaring the territories to be the property of "the several States composing this Union" and denying the right of Congress to discriminate between the states or to deny to their citizens the full and equal opportunity to migrate to the territories with their property. Others took up the cry of "indefeasible right," and through their statements rang the word "Constitution" like the repeated call of the whippoorwill. "We invoke the spirit of the Constitution, and claim its guarantees," said the resolutions of the Nashville Convention. "I, for one, am for tearing asunder every bond that binds us together," said Alexander H. Stephens. "Any people capable of defending themselves, who would continue their allegiance to a Government which should deny to them a clear, unquestionable, constitutional right to the magnitude and importance of this to the people of the South, would deserve to be stigmatized as poltroons." Jefferson Davis summed up the situation as one in which the North was determined to deny to slavery its constitutional rights for "the sole purpose of gaining political power."

Some day the historian will also understand that there is no break between southern abhorrence of the strife and ferment in northern and European society and its deep reliance on the Scriptures and the Constitution for defense of a stable order. He may even come to understand that few peoples on this earth have ever extended freedom of speech to the point of permitting agitation that would destroy a goodly percentage of their material wealth and completely upset the existing structure of society. Southerners too felt an obligation to manifest destiny.

The struggles of the 1840's had thus gone a long way toward becoming a matter of *right* and *rights*. Issues had been caught up in the great fundamental developments of the age. "Right" had become a part of what men were calling progress, a part of a nation's manifest destiny — its obligation to the democratic dogma and experiment. "Rights" too had become a part of something fundamental in terms of a superior way of life, a sound form of government, and a sane treatment of property.

It seemed for a time that the final crisis had been reached, that the Union would go to pieces. Some expressed the hope that it would. That it did not do so was due largely to the strength of political party ties. Whigs and Democrats, North and South, still felt the tug of party loyalty and still retained confidence in the integrity of their fellows. By a supreme effort they forced the conflict back to the concrete issues involved in the immediate difficulty and were able to secure a compromise. It was a slender thread, but it held. It promised, however, little for the future, for third parties had already appeared and the rift in each of the dominant parties had perilously widened. They might not survive another crisis. And what was equally alarming was the growing tendency of issues, however material, to fall into the pattern of *right* and *rights* and to be linked to the matter of progress and national destiny. It might not be possible next time to throw aside this covering and to return to concrete issues.

The 1840's had certainly shown the weakness of the democratic process in dealing with issues cast as moral conflicts or having to do with the fundamental structure of society. It seemed to show, as Carl Becker has said, that "government by discussion works best when there is nothing of profound importance to discuss, and when there is plenty of time to discuss it. The party system works best when the rival programs involve the superficial aspects rather than the fundamental structure of the social system, and majority rule works best when the minority can meet defeat at the polls in good temper because they need not regard the decision as either a permanent or a fatal surrender of their vital interests."

That, however, was only half of the difficulty. The 1840's had also shown that a democratic society cannot stand still. The conservative urge to hold fast to that which has been established may prove as fatal as the fanatic's prod to constant change. Those who profess a belief in democracy must ever remember that alongside the Constitution of the United States stands that other troublesome document, the Declaration of Independence, with its promise of greater freedom and equality. If politicians and parties do not sometimes give it heed, they may learn to their sorrow that the great document was written to justify revolt. That too may be a fatal weakness in the democratic process.

Arthur M. Schlesinger, Jr.: A NOTE ON HISTORICAL SENTIMENTALISM

> *Arther M. Schlesinger, Jr., has made himself the leading historian of the American liberal tradition and, by and large, a stout defender of most of the ideological orientations of that tradition. In his* Age of Jackson, *he declared that the antislavery movement embraced the moral commitment of the Jacksonians to liberty and democracy. Hence, Schlesinger is moved not only to defend the moral position of the reformers who sought to eradicate the evil of slavery in American society, but also to assert that the moral issue of slavery was real and basic, indeed, "too profound to be solved by compromise." The selection is Schlesinger's article entitled "The Causes of the American Civil War: A Note on Historical Sentimentalism" from the* Partisan Review.

THE Civil War was our great national trauma. A savage fraternal conflict, it released deep sentiments of guilt and remorse — sentiments which have reverberated through our history and our literature ever since. Literature in the end came to terms with these sentiments by yielding to the South in fantasy the victory it had been denied in fact; this tendency culminated on the popular level in *Gone with the Wind* and on the highbrow level in the Nashville cult of agrarianism. But history, a less malleable medium, was constricted by the intractable fact that the war had taken place, and by the related assumption that it was, in William H. Seward's phrase, an "irrepressible conflict," and hence a justified one.

As short a time ago as 1937, for example, even Professor James G. Randall could describe himself as "unprepared to go to the point of denying that the great American tragedy could have been avoided." Yet in a few years the writing of history would succumb to the psychological imperatives which had produced *I'll Take My Stand* and *Gone with the*

Arthur M. Schlesinger, Jr., "The Causes of the American Civil War: A Note on Historical Sentimentalism," *Partisan Review*, XVI (1949), 968–81. Reprinted by permission.

Wind; and Professor Randall would emerge as the leader of a triumphant new school of self-styled "revisionists." The publication of two vigorous books by Professor Avery Craven — *The Repressible Conflict* (1939) and *The Coming of the Civil War* (1942) — and the appearance of Professor Randall's own notable volumes on Lincoln — *Lincoln the President: Springfield to Gettysburg* (1945), *Lincoln and the South* (1946), and *Lincoln the Liberal Statesman* (1947) — brought about a profound reversal of the professional historian's attitude toward the Civil War. Scholars now denied the traditional assumption of the inevitability of the war and boldly advanced the thesis that a "blundering generation" had transformed a "repressible conflict" into a "needless war."

The swift triumph of revisionism came about with very little resistance or even expressed reservations on the part of the profession. Indeed, the only adequate evaluation of the revisionist thesis that I know was made, not by an academic historian at all, but by that illustrious semi-pro, Mr. Bernard De Voto; and Mr. De Voto's two brilliant articles in *Harper's* in 1945 unfortunately had little influence within the guild. By 1947 Professor Allan Nevins, summing up the most recent scholarship in *Ordeal of the Union,* his able general history of the eighteen-fifties, could define the basic problem of the period in terms which indicated a measured but entire acceptance of revisionism. "The primary task of statesmanship in this era," Nevins wrote, "was to furnish a workable adjustment between the two sections, while offering strong inducements to the southern people to regard their labor system not as static but evolutionary, and equal persuasions to the northern people to

assume a helpful rather than scolding attitude."

This new interpretation surely deserves at least as meticulous an examination as Professor Randall is prepared to give, for example, to such a question as whether or not Lincoln was playing fives when he received the news of his nomination in 1860. The following notes are presented in the interests of stimulating such an examination.

The revisionist case, as expounded by Professors Randall and Craven, has three main premises. First:

1) that the Civil War was caused by the irresponsible emotionalization of politics far out of proportion to the real problems involved. The war, as Randall put it, was certainly not caused by cultural variations nor by economic rivalries nor by sectional differences; these all existed, but it was "stupid," as he declared, to think that they required war as a solution. "One of the most colossal of misconceptions" was the "theory" that "fundamental motives produce war. The glaring and obvious fact is the artificiality of war-making agitation." After all, Randall pointed out, agrarian and industrial interests had been in conflict under Coolidge and Hoover; yet no war resulted. "In Illinois," he added, "major controversies (not mere transient differences) between downstate and metropolis have stopped short of war."

Nor was the slavery the cause. The issues arising over slavery were in Randall's judgment "highly artificial, almost fabricated. . . . They produced quarrels out of things that would have settled themselves were it not for political agitation." Slavery, Craven observed, was in any case a much overrated problem. It is "perfectly clear," he wrote, "that slavery played a rather minor part in the life of the South and of the Negro."

What then was the cause of war? "If one word or phrase were selected to account for the war," wrote Randall, ". . . it would have to be such a word as fanaticism (on both sides), misunderstanding, misrepresentation, or perhaps politics." Phrases like "whipped-up crisis" and "psychopathic case" adorned Randall's explanation. Craven similarly described the growing sense of sectional differences as "an artificial creation of inflamed minds." The "molders of public opinion steadily created the fiction of two distinct peoples." As a result, "distortion led a people into bloody war."

If uncontrolled emotionalism and fanaticism caused the war, how did they get out of hand? Who whipped up the "whipped-up crisis"? Thus the second revisionist thesis:

2) that sectional friction was permitted to develop into needless war by the inexcusable failure of political leadership in the fifties. "It is difficult to achieve a full realization of how Lincoln's generation stumbled into a ghastly war," wrote Randall. ". . . If one questions the term 'blundering generation,' let him inquire how many measures of the time he would wish copied or repeated if the period were to be approached with a clean slate and to be lived again."

It was the politicians, charged Craven, who systematically sacrificed peace to their pursuit of power. Calhoun and Adams, "seeking political advantage," mixed up slavery and expansion; Wilmot introduced his "trouble-making Proviso as part of the political game;" the repeal clause in the Kansas-Nebraska Act was "the afterthought of a mere handful of politicians;" Chase's Appeal to the Independent Democrats was "false in its assertions and unfair in its purposes, but it was politically effective"; the "damaging" section in the Dred Scott decision was forced "by the political ambitions of dissenting judges." "These uncalled-for moves and this irresponsible leadership," concluded Craven, blew up a "crack-pot" crusade into a national conflict.

It is hard to tell which was under attack here — the performance of a particular generation or democratic politics in general. But, if the indictment "blundering generation" meant no more than a general complaint that democratic politics placed a premium on emotionalism, then the Civil War would have been no more nor less "needless" than any event in our blundering history. The phrase "blundering generation" must consequently imply that the generation in power in the fifties was *below* the human or historical or democratic average in its blundering. Hence the third revisionist thesis:

3) that the slavery problem could have been solved without war. For, even if slavery were as unimportant as the revisionists have insisted, they would presumably admit that it constituted the real sticking-point in the relations between the sections. They must show therefore that there were policies with which a non-blundering generation could have resolved the slavery crisis and averted war; and that these policies were so obvious that the failure to adopt them indicated blundering and stupidity of a peculiarly irresponsible nature. If no such policies could be produced even by hindsight, then it would seem excessive to condemn the politicians of the fifties for failing to discover them at the time.

The revisionists have shown only a most vague and sporadic awareness of this problem. "Any kind of sane policy in Washington in 1860 might have saved the day for nationalism," remarked Craven; but he did not vouchsafe the details of these sane policies; we would be satisfied to know about one. Similarly Randall declared that there were few policies of the fifties he would wish repeated if the period were to be lived over again; but he was not communicative about the policies he would wish pursued. Nevins likewise blamed the war on the "collapse of American statesmanship," but restrained himself from suggesting how a non-collapsible statesmanship would have solved the hard problems of the fifties.

In view of this reticence on a point so crucial to the revisionist argument, it is necessary to reconstruct the possibilities that might lie in the back of revisionism. Clearly there could be only two "solutions" to the slavery problem: the preservation of slavery, or its abolition.

Presumably the revisionists would not regard the preservation of slavery as a possible solution. Craven, it is true, has argued that "most of the incentives to honest and sustained effort, to a contented, well-rounded life, might be found under slavery. . . . What owning and being owned added to the normal relationship of employer and employee is very hard to say." In describing incidents in which slaves beat up masters, he has even noted that "happenings and reactions like these were the rule [sic], not the exception." But Craven would doubtless admit that, however jolly this system might have been, its perpetuation would have been, to say the least, impracticable.

If, then, revisionism has rested on the assumption that the nonviolent abolition of slavery was possible, such abolition could conceivably have come about through internal reform in the South;

through economic exhaustion of the slavery system in the South; or through some government project for gradual and compensated emancipation. Let us examine these possibilities.

1) *The internal reform argument.* The South, the revisionists have suggested, might have ended the slavery system if left to its own devices; only the abolitionists spoiled everything by letting loose a hysteria which caused the southern ranks to close in self-defense.

This revisionist argument would have been more convincing if the decades of alleged anti-slavery feeling in the South had produced any concrete results. As one judicious southern historian, Professor Charles S. Sydnor, recently put it, "Although the abolition movement was followed by a decline of antislavery sentiment in the South, it must be remembered that in all the long years before that movement began no part of the South had made substantial progress toward ending slavery. . . . Southern liberalism had not ended slavery in any state."

In any case, it is difficult for historians seriously to suppose that northerners could have denied themselves feelings of disapproval over slavery. To say that there "should" have been no abolitionists in America before the Civil War is about as sensible as to say that there "should" have been no anti-Nazis in the nineteen-thirties or that there "should" be no anti-Communists today. People who indulge in criticism of remote evils may not be so pure of heart as they imagine; but that fact does not affect their inevitability as part of the historic situation.

Any theory, in short, which expects people to repress such spontaneous aversions is profoundly unhistorical. If revisionism has based itself on the conviction that things would have been different if only there had been no abolitionists, it has forgotten that abolitionism was as definite and irrevocable a factor in the historic situation as was slavery itself. And, just as abolitionism was inevitable, so too was the southern reaction against it — a reaction which, as Professor Clement Eaton has ably shown, steadily drove the free discussion of slavery out of the South. The extinction of free discussion meant, of course, the absolute extinction of any hope of abolition through internal reform.

2) *The economic exhaustion argument.* Slavery, it has been pointed out, was on the skids economically. It was overcapitalized and inefficient; it immobilized both capital and labor; its one-crop system was draining the soil of fertility; it stood in the way of industrialization. As the South came to realize these facts, a revisionist might argue, it would have moved to abolish slavery for its own economic good. As Craven put it, slavery "may have been almost ready to break down of its own weight."

This argument assumed, of course, that southerners would have recognized the causes of their economic predicament and taken the appropriate measures. Yet such an assumption would be plainly contrary to history and to experience. From the beginning the South has always blamed its economic shortcomings, not on its own economic ruling class and its own inefficient use of resources, but on northern exploitation. Hard times in the eighteen-fifties produced in the South, not a reconsideration of the slavery system, but blasts against the North for the high prices of manufactured goods. The overcapitalization of slavery led, not to criticisms of the system, but to increasingly insistent demands for the reopening of the slave trade. Advanced southern writers like George Fitzhugh and

James D. B. DeBow were even arguing that slavery was adapted to industrialism. When Hinton R. Helper did advance before the Civil War an early version of Craven's argument, asserting that emancipation was necessary to save the southern economy, the South burned his book. Nothing in the historical record suggests that the southern ruling class was preparing to deviate from its traditional pattern of self-exculpation long enough to take such a drastic step as the abolition of slavery.

3. *Compensated emancipation.* Abraham Lincoln made repeated proposals of compensated emancipation. In his annual message to Congress of December 1, 1862, he set forth a detailed plan by which States, on an agreement to abolish slavery by 1900, would receive government bonds in proportion to the number of slaves emancipated. Yet, even though Lincoln's proposals represented a solution of the problem conceivably gratifying to the slaveholder's purse as well as to his pride, they got nowhere. Two-thirds of the border representatives rejected the scheme, even when personally presented to them by Lincoln himself. And, of course, only the pressure of war brought compensated emancipation its limited hearing of 1862.

Still, granted these difficulties, does it not remain true that other countries abolished slavery without internal convulsion? If emotionalism had not aggravated the situation beyond hope, Craven has written, then slavery "might have been faced as a national question and dealt with as successfully as the South American countries dealt with the same problem." If Brazil could free its slaves and Russia its serfs in the middle of the nineteenth century without civil war, why could not the United States have done as well?

The analogies are appealing but not, I think, really persuasive. There are essential differences between the slavery question in the United States and the problems in Brazil or in Russia. In the first place, Brazil and Russia were able to face servitude "as a national question" because it was, in fact, a national question. Neither country had the American problem of the identification of compact sectional interests with the survival of the slavery system. In the second place, there was no race problem at all in Russia; and, though there was a race problem in Brazil, the more civilized folkways of that country relieved racial differences of the extreme tension which they breed in the South of the United States. In the third place, neither in Russia nor in Brazil did the abolition of servitude involve constitutional issues; and the existence of these issues played a great part in determining the form of the American struggle.

It is hard to draw much comfort, therefore, from the fact that other nations abolished servitude peaceably. The problem in America was peculiarly recalcitrant. The schemes for gradual emancipation got nowhere. Neither internal reform nor economic exhaustion contained much promise for a peaceful solution. The hard fact, indeed, is that the revisionists have not tried seriously to describe the policies by which the slavery problem could have been peacefully resolved. They have resorted instead to broad affirmations of faith: if only the conflict could have been staved off long enough, then somehow, somewhere, we could have worked something out. It is legitimate, I think, to ask how? where? what? — at least, if these affirmations of faith are to be used as the premise for castigating the unhappy men who had the practical responsibility for finding solutions and failed.

Where have the revisionists gone astray? In part, the popularity of revisionism obviously parallels that of *Gone with the Wind* — the victors paying for victory by pretending literary defeat. But the essential problem is why history should be so vulnerable to this literary fashion; and this problem, I believe, raises basic questions about the whole modern view of history. It is perhaps stating the issue in too portentous terms. Yet I cannot escape the feeling that the vogue of revisionism is connected with the modern tendency to seek in optimistic sentimentalism an escape from the severe demands of moral decision; that it is the offspring of our modern sentimentality which at once evades the essential moral problems in the name of a superficial objectivity and asserts their unimportance in the name of an invincible progress.

The revisionists first glided over the implications of the fact that the slavery system was producing a closed society in the South. Yet that society increasingly had justified itself by a political and philosophical repudiation of free society; southern thinkers swiftly developed the anti-libertarian potentialities in a social system whose cornerstone, in Alexander H. Stephens's proud phrase, was human bondage. In theory and in practice, the South organized itself with mounting rigor against ideas of human dignity and freedom, because such ideas inevitably threatened the basis of their own system. Professor Frank L. Owsley, the southern agrarian, has described inadvertently but accurately the direction in which the slave South was moving. "The abolitionists and their political allies were threatening the existence of the South as seriously as the Nazis threaten the existence of England," wrote Owsley in 1940; ". . . Under such circumstances the surprising thing is that so little was done by the South to defend its existence."

There can be no question that many southerners in the fifties had similar sentiments; that they regarded their system of control as ridiculously inadequate; and that, with the book-burning, the censorship of the mails, the gradual illegalization of dissent, the South was in process of creating a real machinery of repression in order more effectively "to defend its existence." No society, I suppose, encourages criticism of its basic institutions. Yet, when a democratic society acts in self-defense, it does so at least in the name of human dignity and freedom. When a society based on bond slavery acts to eliminate criticism of its peculiar institution, it outlaws what a believer in democracy can only regard as the abiding values of man. When the basic institutions are evil, in other words, the effect of attempts to defend their existence can only be the moral and intellectual stultification of the society.

A society closed in the defense of evil institutions thus creates moral differences far too profound to be solved by compromise. Such a society forces upon every one, both those living at the time and those writing about it later, the necessity for a moral judgment; and the moral judgment in such cases becomes an indispensable factor in the historical understanding.

The revisionists were commendably anxious to avoid the vulgar errors of the post-Civil War historians who pronounced smug individual judgments on the persons involuntarily involved in the tragedy of the slave system. Consequently they tried hard to pronounce no moral judgments at all on slavery. Slavery became important, in Craven's phrase, "only as a very ancient labor system, probably at this time rather near the end

of its existence"; the attempt to charge this labor system with moral meanings was "a creation of inflamed imaginations." Randall, talking of the Kansas-Nebraska Act, could describe it as "a law intended to subordinate the slavery question and hold it in *proper* proportion" (my italics). I have quoted Randall's even more astonishing argument that, because major controversies between downstate and metropolis in Illinois stopped short of war, there was reason to believe that the Civil War could have been avoided. Are we to take it that the revisionists seriously believe that the downstate-metropolis fight in Illinois — or the agrarian-industrial fight in the Coolidge and Hoover administrations — were in any useful sense comparable to the difference between the North and South in 1861?

Because the revisionists felt no moral urgency themselves, they deplored as fanatics those who did feel it, or brushed aside their feelings as the artificial product of emotion and propaganda. The revisionist hero was Stephen A. Douglas, who always thought that the great moral problems could be solved by sleight-of-hand. The phrase "northern man of southern sentiments," Randall remarked, was "said opprobriously . . . as if it were a base thing for a northern man to work with his southern fellows."

By denying themselves insight into the moral dimension of the slavery crisis, in other words, the revisionists denied themselves a historical understanding of the intensities that caused the crisis. It was the moral issue of slavery, for example, that gave the struggles over slavery in the territories or over the enforcement of the fugitive slave laws their significance. These issues, as the revisionists have shown with cogency, were not in themselves basic. But they were the available issues; they were almost the only points within the existing constitutional framework where the moral conflict could be faced; as a consequence, they became charged with the moral and political dynamism of the central issue. To say that the Civil War was fought over the "unreal" issue of slavery in the territories is like saying that the Second World War was fought over the "unreal" issue of the invasion of Poland. The democracies could not challenge fascism inside Germany any more than opponents of slavery could challenge slavery inside the South; but the extension of slavery, like the extension of fascism, was an act of aggression which made a moral choice inescapable.

Let us be clear what the relationship of moral judgment to history is. Every historian, as we all know in an argument that surely does not have to be repeated in 1949, imports his own set of moral judgments into the writing of history by the very process of interpretation; and the phrase "every historian" includes the category "revisionist." Mr. De Voto in his paraphrases of the revisionist position has put admirably the contradictions on this point: as for "moral questions, God forbid. History will not put itself in the position of saying that any thesis may have been wrong, any cause evil. . . . History will not deal with moral values, though of course the Republican radicals were, well, culpable." The whole revisionist attitude toward abolitionists and radicals, repeatedly characterized by Randall as "unctuous" and "intolerant," overflows with the moral feeling which is so virtuously excluded from discussions of slavery.

An acceptance of the fact of moral responsibility does not license the historian to roam through the past ladling out individual praise and blame: such an attitude would ignore the fact that all individuals, including historians, are trapped in a web of circumstance which curtails their moral possibilities. But it does mean that there are certain essential issues on which it is necessary for the historian to have a position if he is to understand the great conflicts of history. These great conflicts are relatively few because there are few enough historical phenomena which we can confidently identify as evil. The essential issues appear, moreover, not in pure and absolute form, but incomplete and imperfect, compromised by the deep complexity of history. Their proponents may often be neurotics and fanatics, like the abolitionists. They may attain a social importance only when a configuration of non-moral factors — economic, political, social, military — permit them to do so.

Yet neither the nature of the context nor the pretensions of the proponents alter the character of the issue. And human slavery is certainly one of the few issues of whose evil we can be sure. It is not just "a very ancient labor system"; it is also a betrayal of the basic values of our Christian and democratic tradition. No historian can understand the circumstances which led to its abolition until he writes about it in its fundamental moral context. "History is supposed to understand the difference between a decaying economy and an expanding one," as Mr. De Voto well said, "between solvency and bankruptcy, between a dying social idea and one coming to world acceptance. . . . It is even supposed to understand implications of the difference between a man who is legally a slave and one who is legally free."

"Revisionism in general has no position," De Voto continues, "but only a vague sentiment." Professor Randall well suggested the uncritical optimism of that sentiment when he remarked, "To suppose that the Union could not have been continued or slavery outmoded without the war and without the corrupt concomitants of war is hardly an enlightened assumption." We have here a touching afterglow of the admirable nineteenth-century faith in the full rationality and perfectibility of man; the faith that the errors of the world would all in time be "outmoded" (Professor Randall's use of this word is suggestive) by progress. Yet the experience of the twentieth century has made it clear that we gravely overrated man's capacity to solve the problems of existence within the terms of history.

This conclusion about man may disturb our complacencies about human nature. Yet it is certainly more in accord with history than Professor Randall's "enlightened" assumption that man can solve peaceably all the problems which overwhelm him. The unhappy fact is that man occasionally works himself into a log-jam; and that the log-jam must be burst by violence. We know that well enough from the experience of the last decade. Are we to suppose that some future historian will echo Professor Nevins' version of the "failure" of the eighteen-fifties and write: "The primary task of statesmanship in the nineteen-thirties was to furnish a workable adjustment between the United States and Germany, while offering strong inducements to the German people to abandon the police state and equal persuasions to the Americans to help the Nazis rather than scold them"? Will some future historian adapt Professor Randall's formula and write that the word "appeaser" was used "opprobriously" as if it were a "base" thing for an American to work with his Nazi fellow? Obviously this revisionism of the future (already foreshadowed in the

work of Charles A. Beard) would represent, as we now see it, a fantastic evasion of the hard and unpleasant problems of the thirties. I doubt whether our present revisionism would make much more sense to the men of the eighteen-fifties.

The problem of the inevitability of the Civil War, of course, is in its essence a problem devoid of meaning. The revisionist attempt to argue that the war could have been avoided by "any kind of sane policy" is of interest less in its own right than as an expression of a characteristically sentimental conception of man and of history. And the great vogue of revisionism in the historical profession suggests, in my judgment, ominous weaknesses in the contemporary attitude toward history.

We delude ourselves when we think that history teaches us that evil will be "outmoded" by progress and that politics consequently does not impose on us the necessity for decision and for struggle. If historians are to understand the fullness of the social dilemma they seek to reconstruct, they must understand that sometimes there is no escape from the implacabilities of moral decision. When social conflicts embody great moral issues, these conflicts cannot be assigned for solution to the invincible march of progress; nor can they be bypassed with "objective" neutrality. Not many problems perhaps force this decision upon the historian. But, if any problem does in our history, it is the Civil War.

To reject the moral actuality of the Civil War is to foreclose the possibility of an adequate account of its causes. More than that, it is to misconceive and grotesquely to sentimentalize the nature of history. For history is not a redeemer, promising to solve all human problems in time; nor is man capable of transcending the limitations of his being. Man generally is entangled in insoluble problems; history is consequently a tragedy in which we are all involved, whose keynote is anxiety and frustration, not progress and fulfillment. Nothing exists in history to assure us that the great moral dilemmas can be resolved without pain; we cannot therefore be relieved from the duty of moral judgment on issues so appalling and inescapable as those involved in human slavery; nor can we be consoled by sentimental theories about the needlessness of the Civil War into regarding our own struggles against evil as equally needless.

One must emphasize, however, that this duty of judgment applies to issues. Because we are all implicated in the same tragedy, we must judge the men of the past with the same forbearance and charity which we hope the future will apply toward us.

Pieter Geyl: THE AMERICAN CIVIL WAR AND THE PROBLEM OF INEVITABILITY

Pieter Geyl, the Dutch historian, has a well-established interest in key problems of historical explanation that have arisen in the historiographical traditions of Europe and America. His well-known work on the problem of Napoleon demonstrates that the history of historical writing contains some of the more fascinating intellectual problems in the Western intellectual tradition. This essay is from the New England Quarterly.

"THE quarrel which broke up the Union in 1860–1861 was about slavery. It had been gathering strength for a long time and at last erupted with elemental violence. The North and the South, divided by a moral issue of the first magnitude, the one detesting slavery, the other glorifying it as the basis of its social system, were unable to understand each other and the Civil War came as an inevitable result."

This is a fair summary of what was once the view taken by most American historians of the origins of the great crisis of the sixties. The picture was presented in different colorings: all sorts of admissions or reservations were made and complications introduced. Nevertheless, this is in the main the impression that one will gather from Rhodes and Woodrow Wilson, from Channing and Morison, from Lord Charnwood, from James Truslow Adams, and from countless others.

For some time now this interpretation has been subjected to attack. First, the proposition that the quarrel was about slavery came under fire. Charles and Mary Beard, true to their system of economic interpretation, transposed the whole matter from the moral sphere to the sphere of the struggle of interests, and placed in opposition, instead of slavery and liberty, agrarian economy and capitalism, free trade and protection.

Pieter Geyl, "The American Civil War and the Problem of Inevitability," *New England Quarterly,* XXIV (1951), pp. 147–68. Reprinted by permission from the *New England Quarterly.* This is also to be reprinted in *Debates with Historians,* by Pieter Geyl © 1958 by Meridian Books, Inc.

Their view has had a profound influence, and rightly so, for they emphasized phenomena which had not, indeed, been completely overlooked, but which had not received the attention which they deserve. It is only when they attempt to substitute the economic factor for the moral issue that one feels bound to part company with them. One notices, on looking critically at their argument, that they glide over the awkward fact that at the moment of decision the most powerful capitalistic interests in the North were all for compromise. One reflects that the hysterical excitement and self-glorification of the South can hardly be understood as a reaction to a merely economic menace, especially not as the country happened to be doing so well in a material sense. This mood cannot be explained except as the reply to a moral indictment. The accusation of the Abolitionists was such a painful hit because in it there spoke the spirit of the times. Behind that little group of fanatics there stood the silent condemnation of the free North, of Europe, of the world. By clinging to its "peculiar institution" the South cut itself adrift from the modern development of Western civilization, isolated itself in an obstinate and wilful self-righteousness, and fell under the spell of its wildest, blindest, and most reactionary elements.

A good deal more could be said about the economic thesis of the Beards, but the point that I propose to deal with in this essay is the other one on which for some time now the critics of the traditional interpretation of the origins of the Civil War have concentrated their energies, that of the inevitability of the conflict. Here the Beards did not depart from the tradition. To them the economic forces seemed to be as ineluctable as had the moral issue to their predeces-

sors. Yet I think that their view, and the despiritualization of the whole episode which resulted from it, contributed to bring about the state of mind in which others soon proceeded to question the traditional presentation of an "irrepressible conflict."

I shall not try to trace the emergence of the rival view that the Civil War was a mistake, which could have been, and ought to have been, avoided. I came across this new interpretation years ago in a little book that I picked up in the shilling box of a shop in the Charing Cross Road in London, a somewhat irresponsible little book, but one which I found very illuminating, and which is indeed not only amusing but written with ability. It is *The Secession of the Southern States* (1933) by Gerald W. Johnson. I have never found it mentioned in any bibliography, but it has played a part in my education. "The fatalistic theory," Mr. Johnson writes, "grows more and more unsatisfactory to modern writers." And he goes on to quote from the well-known book by Dwight L. Dumond, *The Secession Movement* (1931): "That idea implies that the American people were incapable of solving a difficult problem except by bloodletting, and confuses the designs of party politicians with the art of statesmanship."

Many books have appeared since in which the period preceding the outbreak of war is studied, and in several this line of argument has been pursued. Prominent among them is, of course, the work of Avery Craven; but for the sake of clearness I shall concentrate on the writings of J. G. Randall, in which the thesis of the avoidability of the conflict forms a central theme. I shall deal mainly with the first two volumes of his *Lincoln the President* (1945), but shall also glance occasionally at his earlier work, *Civil*

War and Reconstruction (1937), and at his volume of essays, *Lincoln the Liberal Statesman* (1947).

I admire the work of Professor Randall, and I am conscious of my own status as an amateur in the field where he is an acknowledged master. If I venture upon a discussion of his view, it is because I feel that his argument springs from a philosophy of history — or of life, for it comes to the same thing — against which I am tempted to pitch my own; and the more so as I have to do with a man who not only places a wealth of historical documentation fairly before his reader, but who presents his case with a vigorous and practised historical dialectic.

Randall detests the thesis of the irrepressible conflict and his work is a sustained attempt to refute it. He argues that we cannot do justice to the pre-war years if we will see them only in the light of the war *we* know was coming. There were expressions of antagonism no doubt, but if we compose our account of the period preceding 1860–1861 by simply combining those, we subject the past to a mere literary device. One should not read back from the fact of war to the supposition that war-making tendencies were the nation's chief preoccupation in the fifties. "In those years shipowners were interested in the merchant marine, writers in literature, captains of industry in economic enterprise; if any class was concerned chiefly with factors of sectional antagonism it would seem to have been certain groups of politicians and agitators."

The warning that a period can be torn out of focus by interpreting it too resolutely with the help of the familiar outcome is one after my own heart, but that does not mean that criticism will have to disarm when looking at the actual practice.

No, Randall says elsewhere, there was no irreconcilable contrast between North and South. The very concept of two sections was an oversimplification. A further trick was played: the politicians and the agitators, in their pamphlets, their speeches, and their newspaper articles, pictured the two sections as hopelessly antagonistic. Yet there were influences making for peace; only, they attracted insufficient attention. Alarms tending toward war, on the other hand, whose appeal was not to reason, were loud and vociferous. Their menace was in a kind of emotional unbalance. Their language was that of name-calling, shibboleths, tirades. In that way normal life could be upset, and a conflict precipitated, that no majority in any section would have deliberately willed. "One of the most colossal of misconceptions is the theory that fundamental motives produce war. The glaring and obvious fact is the artificiality of war-making agitation."

There we have the thesis, and to establish it Randall marshals his evidence with inexhaustible energy and ingenuity. His material consists largely of incontrovertible facts. It is the great advantage of a mental attitude like his that it is perceptive of the rich diversity of life. Randall discerns an infinity of shadings where most historians had been content with clear-cut contrasts. He is himself very much aware of this. He refers repeatedly to his historical revisionism, although he prefers the terms "realism" or "historical restoration." This latter word strikingly reveals his faith in the attainability of objectivity. He does not seem to realize that it is not *the* Civil War that emerges as a result of his revisions, but that, in spite of the undoubted finality of some of his fact-finding, it is still *his* Civil War and *his* Lincoln. His judgments of persons and of actions — and he works with judgments as well as with facts — are governed by a definite attitude of mind, the same in fact as that from which springs his thesis itself. Even incontrovertible facts can be used for arguments which are not equally acceptable to all of us.

It can readily be conceded that in no part of the country did there exist at any moment before the actual crisis a majority for extreme solutions. Lincoln's two-fifths share of the poll of 1860 no doubt comprised a majority of the votes cast in the North, but Lincoln, for all that the South pictured him as the secret ally of the Abolitionists, consistently did what he could to reduce the conflict to the smallest proportions. Of the Northern electors who cast their votes for him, the large majority therefore never meant a pronouncement in favor of war, either to liberate the slaves or to establish an economic domination.

As regards the South, Breckinridge, the candidate of the extreme state-rights party, remained in a minority there compared with the aggregate of votes cast for his rivals. But Breckinridge himself was comparatively moderate: he never mentioned secession as did Yancey and Rhett. No more than the North, therefore, did the South pronounce in favor of secession in November, 1860. And when now suddenly, starting from South Carolina, the secession snowball was set rolling, it was because people saw in Lincoln's election a victory of the spirit of John Brown and because they attributed to the new President the most evil designs against the South — because, in other words, people labored under grievous misconceptions. At the same time, moreover, the opinion was propagated that the North would stand by inactively when the slaveholding states seceded. As a matter of fact, some Abolitionists had

on occasion shouted for a separation from the immoral South, and there were moderates, too, who were prepared to say, with the old commander of the Union army, Winfield Scott: "Wayward sisters, depart in peace!" Yet it was an idea completely divorced from reality to think that the North would allow the Union to be broken up without resistance. The prospect had the immediate effect of causing the Northwest to feel itself one with the Northeast. It was an intolerable thought for those new regions that the lower course of the Mississippi, their main outlet to the outside world while the overland connections with the East were still defective, would come to be situated in foreign territory. But in the entire North, Union sentiment, quite apart from the feelings about slavery, was strong.

So it was fear, and at the same time it was illusion, that dominated men's minds in the South. But even so the secession had to be forced through in a manner which was denounced as dictatorial by its opponents. The convention of South Carolina refused to have its decision subjected to a referendum. Yet, once proclaimed, the secession immediately created ambitions and a loyalty of its own. Jefferson Davis, who had lately had leanings towards unionism and who had tried to put on the brakes at the last moment, nevertheless accepted the dignity of the presidency of the Confederation. Alexander Stephens, who had grumbled bitterly at the excitability of the crowd when in state after state the conventions were passing the secession resolutions (several against considerable minorities), let himself be elected Vice-President as soon as the issue was determined. In the slave states on the border, which were still sitting on the fence, feverishly discussing schemes of compromise and negotiating with Lincoln, it was only the shots fired on Fort Sumter which brought about the decision.

How different a picture can be constructed out of all these complications and divisions from that of the inevitable war arising out of a clear-cut contrast. One seems to discern all sorts of side-paths and ways out to a very different future from that of these four terrible years of war, followed by that miserable episode of Reconstruction. And the impression is strengthened when one looks more closely at the North after the rupture and observes how weak were the foundations of Lincoln's position, in his own section, now that as War President he admitted no other aim than that of the restoration of the Union, that is to say of a continuation of the struggle down to the complete subjugation of the states in revolt. It is true that not all the criticism, not all the opposition which he had to endure, came from the moderates or the doubters. There were, too, the violent, the impatient. The Abolitionists now felt themselves carried along by the tide of events and urged and pushed Lincoln on. But the moderates and the doubters were a powerful party for all that. The accusation of the South, describing Lincoln as the despot trying by brute force of arms to do violence to free American states, found echoes in the Northern press and in the Congress at Washington. "Negotiate!" — was a loud clamour, not merely an underground murmur. After the early death in 1861 of Douglas, who had supported Lincoln's view, the entire Democratic party in the North adopted that cry, and in 1864, when the presidential election came along, it looked for some time as if its candidate would win. In that case the fate of a country would have been entrusted to the man whose tenderness for the interests of the slave-holders had been a difficulty when Lincoln in 1862 contemplated his Emancipation Decree, the commander who had been suspected of not really wanting to beat Lee.

But why go on piling up instances and particulars? I am quite ready to concede the point. The American people had suddenly found themselves in the Civil War and the majority in none of the sections had deliberately willed it. But what does this prove? Does it prove that the war might therefore have been avoided? Is it not rather one more proof of the general truth that the course of history is not governed by the conscious will of the majority? Jefferson Davis was a believer in this truth. In 1864 two Northerners came across the lines under a white flag and laid a proposal before the President of the Confederation — which had not, however, Lincoln's sanction. They suggested that a truce should be concluded in order to hold a referendum, and that both North and South should promise to abide by the result. But Jefferson Davis was not interested. "Neither current events nor history," he said, "show that the majority rules, or ever did rule. The contrary I think is true."

And is not this indeed what we can read on every page of the book of history? Did the majority of the Netherlands people will the complete rupture with Philip II and with the Roman Church, the independence and the change of religion? Did they will these things in 1566, in 1572, in 1579, in 1581? There can be only one reply — even though we cannot for the sixteenth century as for the nineteenth rely on election statistics — : no. Did the majority of the English people will the overthrow of the monarchy and the execution of Charles I, in 1642, in 1649? — no. Did the French people will the Republic and the execution of Louis XVI? In 1789, in 1790, even in 1791, those who had ever thought of these developments as within the sphere of possibility must have been a tiny minority; but in 1792 and 1793 as well: no. Did the majority of the Belgian people in 1830 will the break-up of the union with Holland? Till the very last moment the leaders themselves spoke only of an administrative separation, but even when it happened — did they will it? — no. Did the majority of the German people in 1933 want Hitler, did they will war? — no. When the English people in 1939 took up the challenge of the Third Reich they already found themselves in a position of compulsion. Or if one wants to look at it from a different angle, one can say that the bulk of them had no notion yet of what they were letting themselves in for, and at any rate in 1940, when their eyes were opened, the position of compulsion was there beyond a doubt. But who does not remember the storm of cheers that greeted Neville Chamberlain and Munich in 1938, and not only in England, but in Germany, in France, in a country like Holland? The large majority wanted peace. "The ship-owner thought of his ships, the writer of his books, the manufacturer of his machines." Here, there and everywhere peace was what men wanted, "and the war came." The instinctive aversion of the mass of people is no evidence that it might have been avoided. It is possible to believe — note that I am not saying, one can prove — that there were forces at work, stronger than individual desires or fears, or than their sum as resulting from the ballot box, which made it inevitable. How striking in this connection is the example of recent American history. I need hardly recall the way in which the United States entered both the First and the Second World Wars. This

is a controversial subject, but to me it seems that in the light of his own country's experiences, Randall's postulate of a strict majority democracy as a fixed standard of historical judgment comes to wear a somewhat ghostly look of unreality.

"Forces? indeed!" Randall will say: "Name calling, shibboleths, epithets, tirades." An appeal, not to reason or to true interest, but to the emotions. And who will deny that sentiment, passion, extra-rational conviction, supply a fertile soil to the monster growth of misunderstanding and exaggeration, misrepresentation, hatred and recklessness! The question remains whether one is justified in labelling these extra-rational factors with contemptuous terms and deny to them, as Randall does, a rightful rôle in the drama of history, relegating them without further ado to the category of "artificial agitation," which can on no condition be reckoned among "fundamental causes."

Two histories might be written — so says the Count de la Gorce in his striking little book on Louis XVIII — about the Restoration. One would be the sober and serious history of the good services rendered by that régime to France from day to day and in an unsensational manner. The other one is the history of violent incidents, the execution of Ney, the expulsion of Manuel, et cetera, which, pictured in colorful prints, struck the popular imagination. And it is this second history which culminates in the revolution of 1830. You will notice here, in the writing of the French royalist, the same idea — merely indicated in passing however —, that the historian's rational criticism, working after the events, can detach from the total of what happened the emotions which brought about the catastrophe and that in the other sequence he will retain the real, the proper history. The suggestion is at least that this ought to have been the real history.

Now this idea is the basic idea of Randall's work. He constantly comes back to it. The Americans of the fifties both surprise and irritate him. An essay in which he recapitulates his grievances against them bears the title *A Blundering Generation*. How was it possible for these people to work up such excitement over trifles! All problems are distorted by them. Look how they made mountains out of molehills and exaggerated matters which seen in their true size would never have stood in the way of a peaceful settlement.

Take the Kansas-Nebraska Bill, with which Douglas in 1854 set going so fateful a controversy. Randall is much concerned to exculpate Douglas. Douglas is a man after his heart: a practical man, a man who wanted to do business, and with Northerners and Southerners alike. Can one wonder if Douglas was astonished at the hubbub? Was it such a crime that by his principle of popular sovereignty he created the possibility of slavery in those territories situated so far North? The very fact of the situation of Kansas and Nebraska made it most improbable that slavery would ever take root there. The raving in the North about a mere theoretical possibility was therefore, according to Randall, lacking in all sense of reality; it was an example of the hollowness of all that vehement quarreling.

But now let us try to picture to ourselves the state of affairs. Shortly before, in 1850, the new Compromise had been reached, intended to put an end to the dangerous tension that had been growing up over the disposal of the newly acquired Western lands. The Compromise was worthless if it did not confine the extension of slavery within limits accepted by both sides. But here in effect the demarcation line of 1820, which had been looked upon as fixed, was wiped out, among loud cheers from the South. Moreover, what dominated the situation was Southern fears of the rapid increase in power of the North, and Northern suspicions that the South, to ward off that danger, was trying by all means to fasten its grip on the Federal Government. Must one not wilfully blindfold one's historical imagination in order to avoid seeing that the excitement was natural?

Besides, what happened? Had it been possible to apply the principle of popular sovereignty honestly, as doubtless Douglas had intended, then indeed neither Kansas nor Nebraska would have thought of introducing slavery. But the slaveholders from the neighboring slave states sent settlers with slaves to Kansas. A race developed between supporters of the two systems: a civil war in miniature. At last an unrepresentative, tumultuous, armed assembly passed a constitution with slavery and sent it to Washington. Douglas shrank from an approval which must have definitely alienated the North. In fact, the proceedings in Kansas were a mockery of his proudly proclaimed principle. His opposition to recognition roused much ill-feeling against him among the Democrats in the South, with whom he had all along wanted to strengthen the ties. Meanwhile "Bleeding Kansas" had become a new slogan to arouse the North. But, Randall reflects, why is it that "squatter sovereignty" came to be a source of confusion? "Not so much because of genuine conflict of local interests, but because a minority of trouble makers, aided by outside agitators, made turbulence rather than reasonable pacification their busi-

ness." And that is probably a fair statement of the case. But it does not in the
least affect the fact that, in the circumstances, and with the public temper prevailing in the United States at that moment, the principle introduced by Douglas could not but be a new occasion for
quarrel over the old point at issue, and
that his policy was therefore a capital
mistake. Douglas had wanted to do business, but he had underestimated the inflammable state of public opinion concerning that great point which he had
thought he could safely use for a bargain. "Morally blind" is the way Morison
describes him.

In 1858, on the occasion of a senatorial
election, the famous debates between
Lincoln and Douglas were held up and
down Illinois. Lincoln kept on, indefat-
igably, directing his attacks to the questions of Kansas, popular sovereignty,
slavery in the Western territories. To
Randall's mind it is but a foolish business. There might have been sense in it
if the speakers had at least discussed
slavery in general, but Lincoln, as everybody knows, was as little prepared to
interfere in the internal affairs of the
Southern States as was his opponent. So
the debates ran on slaves in those regions
where there were hardly any and where
there were not likely ever to be many
slaves. Was this really the only subject
on which to claim the attention, for
weeks at a stretch, of the electors of Illinois and of the newspaper readers of the
United States? Would not the time of
the speakers have been better employed
if they had dealt with problems like
immigration, tariff, international policy,
promotion of education?

This is indeed a striking instance of
Randall's somewhat masterful attitude
towards his personages. In effect, he tells
the speakers of 1858 what subjects they

ought to have treated. Is it not the historian's more obvious line simply to conclude from their choice, and from the
enormous impression they made, that the
country's mood was strained to the utmost by the Kansas-Nebraska compli-
cation?

And this was indeed a great question.
It did bring along, in spite of what Randall says, a discussion of the slavery question itself. Some of Lincoln's gravest,
most profoundly moving utterances
about the Negro's fate were made in
those speeches. Douglas attacked him
over his phrase, "A house divided cannot
stand," in which he professed to read an
incitement to civil war. Lincoln replied
that he had only drawn attention to an
undeniable danger. The generation of
the Founding Fathers had believed that
slavery was dying a natural death, so it
had not been hard then to practice
mutual forbearance and to compromise.
Now, on the contrary, the slave power
was full of self-confidence, or even of
imperialistic ardor. Was not the recent
verdict of the Supreme Court in the case
of Dred Scott startling evidence of this?
The Supreme Court, under its judicial
mask, had always been a political body
and it was now, after nominations by a
succession of Southern Presidents, dominated by the Southerners. The split of
the churches, too, was touched upon. It
is as if Lincoln is polemicising with Randall when he says that here at least it is
impossible to suspect the hand of "the
politicians" or "the agitators." Furthermore he commented on the restraints on
freedom of speech in the South, and on
the Southern desire that the North should
keep silent on slavery. But even silence
was not enough. What they really
wanted was express approval and admiration. The survival of democracy itself
seemed concerned with the resistance to

Southern arrogance; that is a point to which Lincoln frequently recurs. Does Randall in earnest want us to believe that the attention of Lincoln's audiences was thrown away on questions like these?

Even the Fugitive Slave Law is, according to Randall, all things considered, but a small matter. And, indeed, one can say: were a few hundred fugitive slaves worth the risk of getting enmeshed in a destructive civil war? Answer: neither for the slave-holders, nor for the Northerners, who had to look on, on very rare occasions and in very few localities, when one was seized and forcibly carried back. Lincoln himself said that we must not act upon all our moral or theoretical preferences. "Ungodly," he exclaimed sadly, when once he came into contact with a case; "but it is the law of the land!" One can accept a personality in which were united deep moral feeling with caution, a sense of responsibility, and a capacity for weighing for and against in the scales of reason. But is it not just as understandable that a crowd assembled when a captured fugitive in Boston was taken to the harbor and that a battalion of soldiers and a war vessel had to be commandeered to see that the law was executed? The Southerners clung to the law because they desired to have from the North an acknowledgment of their right rather than because of the material advantage. A moral revulsion in the North soon made the execution impracticable, and this in its turn created bad blood in the South. Seen in this way — and it seems a truer way than the merely statistical one —, this was a considerable matter. It carried grist to the mills of the Abolitionists.

But Randall thinks himself entitled to brush aside the whole of that group as fundamentally insignificant — and here the Beards had set the example. Like the Beards he always points to their small numbers and to the fact that their extreme position excludes them from practical politics. Their only significance, and a baleful one, he sees in the exaggerated importance attached in the South to their periodicals and speeches. Misunderstanding once again. Later, when the war results in making them more influential and they finally help to decide the course taken by the North, he lays all stress on the disastrous effects of their intervention. Here again Randall is representative of a current in modern thought on these questions. The narrowness and cultivation of hatred of the puritan idealists during the Reconstruction period have given them a bad press with contemporary American historians. Nothing is more readily understandable. But should that lead us to overlook the dynamic strength which their ideas, in spite of their isolated position, showed in the prewar years? . . .

The two main points on which the conventional conceptions of the origins of the war have of recent times been criticized, as I said at the outset, are that of slavery as the central issue, and that of the inevitability of the conflict. As regards the first, I have clearly enough expressed my opinion that neither with the one-sided attention to economic aspects of the Beards nor with Randall's determination to reduce everything to exclusively practical and reasonable terms can the importance of the moral problem be done justice.

As regards the second, I want to guard myself against a possible misunderstanding. I have not been arguing that the war was inevitable, not even — for that is what the discussion is mostly about — in the ten years preceding the outbreak. I have been arguing that Randall's argument in favor of the opposite contention is unconvincing. The question of evitable or inevitable is one on which, it seems to me, the historian can never form any but an ambivalent opinion. He will now stress other possibilities, then again speak in terms of a coherent sequence of causes and effects. But if he is wise, he will in both cases remain conscious that he has not been able to establish a definite equilibrium between the factors, dissimilar and recalcitrant to exact valuation as they are, by which every crisis situation is dominated.

And here I return to a point on which I find it possible to speak more positively. Randall's way of distinguishing between fundamental and artificial causes seems to me inadmissible. With his impressive scholarship and keen intelligence, schooled in historical dialectic, he counts among artificial causes everything that does not agree with the wishes of the majority or with its true interests, defined by himself in accordance with the best rational standards. But in the sequence of cause and effect, of which the human mind will never have complete command, the category of the *imponderabilia,* passion and emotion, conviction, prejudice, misunderstanding, have their organic function. No doubt it is this very fact which makes that command unattainable for us, but we are not therefore entitled to ignore those non-rational factors or to argue them away with the help of wisdom after the event.

VI. THE PROBLEM OF SYNTHESIS

Allan Nevins: THE ORDEAL OF THE UNION

Allan Nevins is the author of the latest large-scale history of the American Civil War. His history begins with the mid-1840's and is designed to cover the entire Civil War era. Nevins' multi-volumed study is the first major effort to write a detailed history of the Civil War era since the days of James Ford Rhodes. In a sense, therefore, Nevins' volumes represent an attempt at a grand historical synthesis of the new data and insights which have appeared in the staggering number of books and articles written largely since the time of James Ford Rhodes' History. Consequently, he must create an historical explanation which will be accepted as reasonable by a generation of historians whose critical attitudes have been sharpened by recent writings concerning the history of the Civil War. This selection by Nevins is from The Ordeal of the Union *and* The Emergence of Lincoln.

[THE FAILURE OF LEADERSHIP]

From the long study he has given to the years preceding the Civil War, the author has concluded that this period can best be understood if a number of dominant themes or clues are kept in mind. It seems clear, in the first place, that the conflict of North and South, of slave area and free, was part of a broader movement for the unification of the nation, and for the merging of elements both varied and conflicting into a homogeneous whole. The country felt a strong tendency to organize its energies, knit closer its economic structure, and standardize its moral and social values. Most of the forces created by science, invention, and business technology thrust toward unification. This tendency had to contend against centrifugal impulses born of the wide spaces of the land, the varied national origins of the people, and the existence of two utterly different labor systems. The slavery quarrel and the social differences of North and South were simply the most important of certain disruptive tendencies; but all were gradually being forced to yield to the powerful impulses that were making the United States homogeneous in economic life, political ideals, and social outlook. By 1860 men who gave their patriotism to region, not country, saw the handwriting on the wall. Irresistible factors were making unity triumph over sectionalism, homogeneity over heterogeneity.

Another consideration to be kept in mind is that the sectional issue is not only oversimplified but essentially misstated when it is discussed in terms of North and South alone. The Upper Mississippi and Lower Missouri valleys held one main key to the history of the era. The Southern attempt to gain Kansas, and the Southern hope that St. Louis might continue to drain most of the wealth of the Northwest toward the Gulf, represented a desperate effort to maintain a precari-

Allan Nevins, *The Ordeal of the Union*, Vol. I, pp. viii–x, 532–35; Vol. II, pp. 537–44, 553–54. Reprinted with the permission of Charles Scribner's Sons from *Ordeal of the Union*, Volumes I and II, by Allan Nevins, copyright, 1947, Charles Scribner's Sons.

ous sectional balance. The rise of Chicago and other lake ports, the Northwestern surge of agriculture, and the riveting of railroad chains between the upper Mississippi and North Atlantic, wrote economic laws far more powerful than any statute of Congress. Still another cardinal fact to be remembered is that the slavery question can also be readily oversimplified. The problem offered by the millions of Negroes far transcended slavery. Dominant elements North and South saw all too dimly that the one really difficult problem was that of permanent race-adjustment, that the abolition of slavery would only present it in starker form, and that the united efforts of all sections would be needed to cope with it. Had this truth been clearly grasped, the country might have struggled out of its blind drift toward disaster.

Certain other considerations are perhaps more obvious and familiar. As the sectional struggle developed, nearly all groups involved in it steadily substituted emotion for reason. They used stereotypes for facts, and epithets in lieu of cool arguments; they forgot the emollient grace of humor and the wisdom of the long view. The angry issue of slavery in the Territories, settled by the great compromise of 1850 but wantonly reopened in 1854, was practically settled again by the end of 1858. But by 1858 passions had been so deeply aroused that large sections of the population could not view the situation calmly or discuss it realistically; fear fed hatred, and hatred fed fear. The unrealities of passion dominated the hour. Had some great leader appeared, he might have broken through this emotional fabric. But the sectional tension distorted the party mechanism (none too well adjusted at best); and in three successive elections, 1848, 1852, and 1856, a nation which needed a President of penetrating vision, moral courage, and practical grasp was given three singularly incompetent chieftains. Zachary Taylor was stubbornly wrong-headed; Franklin Pierce impulsively erratic; James Buchanan timidly fumbling. It has never been sufficiently emphasized that in their weakness, these men leaned to an extraordinary degree upon groups of aides. Zachary Taylor turned to Seward, Weed, and a few others; in the days of Pierce, Jefferson Davis and Caleb Cushing swayed the sceptre; and when Buchanan occupied the White House, he was guided first by a Southern circle including Howell Cobb, Jacob Thompson, and John B. Floyd, and later, when his course had to be sharply altered, by a Northern group headed by Jeremiah Black, Edwin M. Stanton, and John A. Dix. Particularly under Pierce and Buchanan, the country was governed by a Directory rather than by a President. . . .

[SLAVERY, RACE ADJUSTMENT, AND THE FUTURE]

With the emancipationist impulse of the fathers dead, with colonization impracticable, with the position of the free Negro tragic in the North and almost intolerable in parts of the South, what was the solution of the great problem? A rising Southern chorus chanted its answer: slavery must be accepted as beneficent, immutable, and eternal. Northerners for the most part held that slavery was a temporary system to be maintained until it could safely yield to gradual emancipation. The abolitionists of course demanded immediate and unconditional liberation. But as they remained a relatively small and uninfluential group, the substantial choice lay between slavery as an immutable discipline, and slavery as an institution evolving toward freedom.

It is a law of history that whenever peaceful evolution fails to effect a needed set of changes, some revolutionary agency steps in and does so. Change and growth are so indispensable in human affairs that whenever an effort is made to erect an immovable dam, the force of the piling waters finally becomes absolutely irresistible. The calamitous error of Southern leadership lay in its refusal to treat slavery as a dynamic institution. By statesmanlike effort reforms could have been introduced (as Robert Toombs advocated in his famous lecture on slavery) to safeguard marriage and the family life of the bondsmen; to give all Negroes fitted for it some education, and to allow those who displayed exceptional enterprise, intelligence, and industry to escape from servitude — in short, to make slavery an educative and transitional labor-system, thus laying the groundwork for a rational permanent adjustment between the races. To be sure, all this would have demanded sacrifice and would have imposed risks. But neither would have been comparable with those incurred when the waters finally broke through with destructive roar.

The great concurrent error of the North was that it did nothing of a practical nature to assist in racial adjustment on a new basis. Merely to rail at the Southerners for holding slaves and to demand instant emancipation was a deplorably barren policy. Why did none of these Northern abolitionists who could easily raise considerable sums of money send agents southward, buy up slaves, and bring them North for settlement? Those who fled from their masters were welcomed, but practically nothing was done to purchase any from their owners. Doubtless one reason was that such a course would have raised slave-prices,

encouraged slave-breeding, and done little to solve the problem. But another and larger reason was that Northern workers would not have permitted this solution, even had it been valid, for they disliked colored neighbors and colored rivalry. Abolitionists wished to liberate the slaves to compete with the small farmers and workmen of the South; they did not wish to bring them North to compete with farmers, mechanics, and laborers of the free areas. Wealthy Gerrit Smith did distribute an inhospitable tract of land in northern New York among free and escaped Negroes, but that inadequate effort stood alone, cost little in money or care, and demanded no Northern effort at social readjustment. Why did Northern leaders not rally about Webster's proposal that the proceeds of the public lands be used for gradual compensated emancipation, perhaps with some systematic Northern resettlement? Tough-minded men asked these questions. Said the New York *Journal of Commerce* in 1850 of the slaves:

The North first made property of them, and owe much of their gains to them. How many *hundreds* did they ever liberate? On the contrary, when a single individual at the South first liberated sixty, worth as property then at least $30,000, it was found difficult, nay impossible, to raise at the North $3,000 to send them to Africa; and a large proportion of that insignificant sum was contributed from the South. Where is the Northern man, old or young, living or dying, that leaves any bequest of any kind to liberate and restore these people, whom their fathers or themselves have plundered and robbed from Africa, to their homes?

The consequence of these two refusals — the refusal of Southerners to treat slavery as a progressive and evolutionary system, leading by regular gradations to freedom, and the refusal of Northerners to acknowledge that in equity they must share the heavy burdens of racial readjustment — was to place slavery in a position where it became more and more perilous to the body politic. It had to be moved toward a new position, but neither side was willing to move it by gradual plan. Year by year a violent solution of the problem became more probable. The North was quite as much at fault as the South.

Each side could easily rationalize its attitude. Northerners could assert that as the South had for two centuries profited from the unrequited labor of the slave, so now it should meet all the difficulties of assimilating them to its own society. They could also declare that no important problem existed, for the Negro possessed such high intellectual and moral characteristics that he could rapidly and painlessly be lifted to equality with the whites. This sentimental exaggeration of the Negro's immediate potentialities (something very different from his ultimate capacities) was particularly common among abolitionists who knew little of the slave at first hand, and who by an easy process of generalization fancied nearly every field hand a Robert Purvis or Frederick Douglass. Southerners meanwhile rationalized their attitude by so exaggerating the dangers and difficulties of change as to pronounce it utterly impossible. More importantly, as we have seen, they could contrast the worst side of industrialism with the best side of slavery. And most fortifying of all to the Southern spirit, they could consciously or unconsciously take the view that the Negro had never been fit for any position but that of bondsman, and never would be. This became a traditional conviction bulwarked by habit, indolence, timidity, and the desire for security.

The assertion that the Negro was an inferior creation, a being of natural incapacity, lent itself to a thought-pattern which opposed all change in slavery. Cultural, democratic, and humanitarian assumptions applied only to man, not brutes, and the Negro was nearer brute than man — so the implicit syllogism ran. The Negro was a creature of great physical strength, of limited intellectual power (scientifically explained by contracted cranial capacity, early closing of the frontal skull-sutures, and special characteristics of the brain-cells), of natural indolence, conquerable only by stern driving, of powerful sexual impulses, dangerous unless rigidly restrained, of innate superstition, and of constant readiness to revert to savagery.

"We recognize the fact of the inferiority stamped upon the race of men by the Creator," said Jefferson Davis in the Senate, "and from the cradle to the grave, our government as a civil institution, marks that inferiority."

This supposed biological inferiority, stated by science and the Bible, condemned the Negro to permanent servility. Convenient instances were selected from the mass of evidence at hand to support the defensive generalization. As Cuffy was stupid, and Meg unchaste, so all Negroes were stupid and unchaste; it being forgotten that Joe was very bright and Sally a model of wifely constancy. Beliefs in the mendacity, thievishness, emotional instability, and laziness of Negroes were thus systematically cultivated in order to build up a defensive pattern supporting the slavery relationship — and behind it a fixed caste relationship.

Such rationalizations, with clashing economic interests and general divergences of culture, created a greater and greater gulf of misunderstanding. As the two sections faced each other across the chasm, with rising excitement and growing antipathy, each side gave way more and more to irrational emotion; each seemed to catch the far-off note of throbbing drums and sounding bugles. . . .

[THE CONTRAST OF CULTURES]

They were sectional because two distinct cultures, Northern and Southern, each shading off toward the West in newer and not dissimilar forms, but nevertheless on the whole sharply differentiated, had come into existence. In two areas the sectional characteristics were intensified. Van Wyck Brooks has spoken of the "peculiar flavor of that old New England culture, so dry, so crisp, so dogmatic, so irritating," and though the word stimulating should be added, the qualifications are accurate. At the opposite pole was the culture of the Lower South, genial, elegant, so old-fashioned that it was sometimes antique, and though alert enough in political directions, otherwise largely sterile. Boston and Charleston were now preoccupied with sectional stereotypes and antipathies, and as Garrisonian abolitionism colored all the thought of one city, so Calhounian nullification tinged all the ideas of the other. As Whittier's "Expostulation" was an arraignment of Southern society and its cultural ideals, so Grayson's "The Hireling and the Slave" was an indictment of the Northern economic and social order. New England and the Lower South had become almost incapable of understanding each other, and the Potomac and Ohio separated areas of wide mutual incomprehension.

No one dominant fact explains the special characteristics of Southern culture, which was a complex result of intricate causes. The idea of white domination,

which has been called the "central theme" of the section's life, was certainly of fundamental importance. The race question set a ritual for the Southern people which was followed long after slavery was dead. Other students have varied the formula. They have said that Southern culture was stamped above all by a conservatism based upon class stratification and the absence of competitive struggle, engendering an aristocratic, leisurely ideal of life, with much pride of family, scope for learning, and attachment to outdoor pursuits. It is certainly true that agrarian traits marked the South. In contrast with the more and more urbanized, industrialized North, its life was rural — so rural that Augustus Baldwin Longstreet hesitated to accept the presidency of the College of South Carolina because he thought it unwise to subject students to the temptations of a metropolis like Columbia, with its six thousand people. Southerners themselves liked to explain their special culture in terms of ideals. Instead of being restless, unstable, and ruthlessly progressive, they said, they put their surplus energy into the life of the mind, and cultivated the greatest of all arts, the art of living.

In this art of living the tournaments, dinners, and balls of Virginia, the fox-hunting of the Shenandoah, the race-week of Charleston, the theatres and carnivals of New Orleans, were less important than the peaceful pursuits of plantations where the owner (like Jefferson Davis) divided his time among business, politics, and study. The Southern ideal, according to this view, approximated closely to the ideals of eighteenth-century English life. It is easy to romanticize the old South, and a myth-making process which unduly minimizes the importance of middle-class elements and ignores the squalor of the disinherited has gained much too wide an acceptance. Nevertheless, the elements emphasized by Basil L. Gildersleeve — pride of State and lineage, love of classical erudition, courtesy, reverence for the traditions of a static order, ambition to cultivate the graces of existence — did throw a charm over rather limited groups.

A distinctive economic and social pattern, which was basic, became intermeshed with a specialized body of ideas and customs. The South, completely committed to agriculture, and in great degree to the plantation system; to a labor force which had to be kept ignorant and unenterprising; to a patriarchal ideal of social organization; to such limited production of wealth that great bodies of illiterate, shambling, badly-nourished whites became accepted as natural; to a soil-and-labor exploitation which gave one or two classes the means of elegance, learning, and leadership; to the mental conservatism which is bred by isolation — this land had peculiar defects and special virtues. In the Revolutionary period the South had produced more citizens of the world and thinkers of international repute than any other section. Mount Vernon, Monticello, Gunston Hall, Montpelier, had thrown a long shadow across the map. By 1846 the South was more largely withdrawn from the general movement of Western civilization than any other sizable area peopled by an English-speaking stock. Even its code of ethics, its conscience, had been immobilized; by Jefferson's standards, had been moved backward.

The South liked to think of itself as having a warmly human civilization while that of the North was bookish and mechanical. In Yankeeland the long, dreary winters, the business appurtenances of society, the hard drive of the towns, and (said Southerners) the ab-

sence of social sympathies, led to the incessant production of technological devices and books. Below the Potomac the open air, bland climate, and agreeable society tempted men to blither pursuits. Southerners read for personal enjoyment and cultivation; Northerners read to invent or write. "The best thing which could happen for the New England literary mind," wrote one observer, "would be the banishment of all books from the studies of her foremost men." The South, according to her sons, fostered conversational talent, while her platform oratory stimulated political thought more forcibly than the newspaper articles of the North. Where was better talk to be heard than at the table of well-educated Virginia planters, or in Natchez drawing-rooms, or at Russell's bookshop on busy King Street in Charleston, where seats were placed for the literary men of the town — William Gilmore Simms, Paul H. Hayne, J. L. Petigru, William J. Grayson, Alfred Huger, Mitchell King, and others? The rural Southerner, going to church, lounging at the crossroads store, and attending muster, barbecues, and co't day, equally loved talk. Visiting Northerners, it was agreed in Richmond and Mobile, never equalled the clear, bold, graceful expression of their hosts. And the topics of which Yankees conversed were inferior; however well-informed and earnest on business subjects, they were at a loss whenever abstract ideas came up.

It was another staple belief of Southerners that their conservatism was wise and healthy. The North was swept by the Kossuth craze, but the South stood by the old principle of non-intervention in foreign quarrels. The North was full of Millerism, Shakerism, Spiritualism, Mormonism, and what not; the South clung to its pure and ancient religion. Northern politics was flawed by fads, theories, and unpredictable innovations, but Southern voters held the principles of their fathers. While the Southerner was heartily philanthropic and generous, the Yankees strangely compounded charity with cant, and mercy with malevolence. So ran the generalizations, all open to endless unprofitable argument, but all advanced with a force which went far toward proving that the South *was* different.

* * *

It is necessary to pierce behind these rather meaningless generalizations to discrete matters of fact. Asked just where, in detail, the differences of the South lay, we can answer under numerous headings.

The white population of the South was far more largely Anglo-Saxon than that of the North, for despite its numerous Germans, its hundred thousand Irish folk by 1860, its French Huguenots, and others, it was one of the purest British stocks in the world. Its dominant attitudes, particularly as to the color line, were Anglo-Saxon. Its life was not merely rural, but rural after a special pattern; for the section was dotted over with large holdings representing great capital values and employing large bodies of slaves. It was a land of simple dogmatism in religion; of Protestant solidarity, of people who believed every word of the Bible, and of faith frequently refreshed by emotional revivalism. Its churches provided an emphasis on broadly social values contrasting with the intellectualization of morals to be found in the North. In the South the yoke of law and government rested more lightly upon the individual than in other sections. Counties, often sprawling in extent, were the chief units of local administration; the States followed the rule that the best government was the least

government; and the nation was held at arm's length.

The South drew from its economic position a special set of tenets, naturally accepting Francis Wayland's condemnation of protection as a violation of morality and common sense. With equal inevitability, it drew from its minority position in the political fabric another special set of doctrines. It was a country in which romantic and hedonistic impulses, born of the opulence of nature, had freer rein than in the North. The phrases "the merry South," "the sunny South," connoted a great deal. Genuine gusto went into William Elliot's *Carolina Sports by Land and Water*, describing thrilling adventures with devil-fishes in Port Royal Sound, and with wildcats and bears in upland Carolina woods; real delight colored the portrayal of plantation festivities in Caroline H. Gilman's *Recollections of a Southern Matron*, a bit of reality thinly garbed in fiction. The remote quality attaching to much Southern life, which made some travellers feel they had dropped into another world, and the sharp contrast of races, added to the atmosphere of romance.

To a far greater degree than the North, the South was a land of class stratification and vestigial feudalism. Various explanations were given for this fact. One was later repeated by N. S. Shaler when he remarked that Southerners were descendants of that portion of the English who were least modernized, and who "still retained a large element of the feudal notion." It is now known that no such distinction existed between Northern and Southern colonists, for honest middle-class folk, not feudal-minded cavaliers, made up the bulk of Virginia as of Massachusetts settlers. Slavery, the large plantation, and the agrarian cast of life, with some traditional inheritances from colonial days, accounted for the class structure. "Slavery helped feudalism," correctly remarked a Southern writer, "and feudalism helped slavery, and the Southern people were largely the outcome of the interaction of these two formative principles."

The great colonial plantations, established along the South Atlantic seaboard and in Louisiana in days when tobacco, rice, and sugar reigned without thought of a new monarch named cotton, had possessed much the atmosphere and influence of the English manors. Even North Carolina had its first families, the Winstons, Taylors, and Byrds of the Tidewater. The planters enjoyed the social dignities and political leadership of the English squires. They revered the old order, dispensed hospitality, and benignly guided their inferiors in Sir Roger de Coverley style. As a rigorous code of personal honor was enforced by the duel rather than by law, and gentlefolk deemed themselves highly sensitive to slights, they developed a punctilious courtesy. Yet the ideal Southern gentleman seldom appeared in perfection; politeness, gallantry, and dignity had often to be reconciled with the sudden passion of a Preston Brooks, and, as James Branch Cabell has mentioned, a weakness for miscegenation. A planter who entertained much, thought much of the good old times, and handed down his home acres to his oldest son even when primogeniture was no more, naturally made much of family ties. Kinship was counted to remote cousinhood, the penniless spinster who bore the family name had a welcome place in the household, and summer visitings from State to State, across many hundreds of miles, were common. Family did much to knit the South together.

Yet class lines can easily be over-emphasized, for they were subject to powerful solvents. The fact that many a poor farmer and rich planter looked back to a common ancestor was one; wealth in such instances usually bowed before relationship. The fact that all white men had a sense of solidarity as against the Negro, and as against the encroaching North, also tended to reduce class stratification. As sectional tensions increased, the political elite of the South were more and more drawn from non-aristocratic levels. It cannot too often be emphasized that such men as Yancey, Wigfall, Reagan, Jefferson Davis, and A. H. Stephens in no wise represented the old aristocracy. Among the wealthy planters a large place was always taken by the *nouveaux riches*, and in the South no less than the North the transition from poverty to opulence and back to poverty, three generations from shirtsleeves to shirtsleeves, was not uncommon. It should be said, too, that the egalitarian theories of Thomas Jefferson (despite all the uneasy effort by various leaders to prove them outworn) made a real impression on thoughtful Southerners.

As in the North the advancing frontier was an unquestionable force for democracy, in the South it at least modified the features of aristocracy. The opening of the old Southwest had furnished a field in which the ambitious, energetic, and able pushed rapidly to the front. Combining cheap land and labor, they built up rich estates. It was not the old Tidewater aristocracy which took possession of the wealth of the western reaches, but younger and more aggressive elements. Of course the new aristocracy modelled its social order broadly after the coastal pattern. But comparatively few of the patrician names of Virginia, Carolina, and Louisiana — not more than five hundred all told — figured in the new bead-roll of gentility. Many a rich planter, like the Hairstons, was conscious of his humble origin, felt best at home in associating with the commonalty, and was ready himself to work in the fields. Across the Mississippi in Texas and Arkansas the atmosphere grew more democratic still.

But taken as a section, stretching from the Atlantic to the Father of Waters and from the Ohio to the Gulf, the South had a life of far more aristocratic tone than the North. Both the central weakness of the South, and the main flaw in American social homogeneity, lay in the want of a great predominant body of intelligent, independent, thoughtful, and educated farmers in the slave States to match the similar body at the North. The nation had always drawn most of its sturdy common sense and integrity of character from its farmers. A really strong Southern yeomanry could have clasped hands with Northern tillers of the soil. But the plantation system was inimical to any such body. Whether developing or declining, it wasted soil and toil, reduced the mass of blacks and whites to poverty, kept them in ignorance, and destroyed their hopes. It was not a preparation for the appearance of an independent, industrious farmer class, but a "preface to peasantry." It gave the South the "forgotten man" that Walter Hines Page described in his memorable address at Greensboro a generation later; men too poor, ignorant, and politician-beguiled to be discontented with their poverty, ignorance, and docility.

With all its natural gaiety, simplicity, and love of olden ways the South combined a trait common in countries with unhappy institutions, like Spain, and in lands left behind by modern progress,

like Ireland: the trait of uneasy defensiveness. At the beginning of the century most Southerners had believed that Virginia would keep her primacy among the States in wealth, population, and influence, that their whole section would grow faster than the chilly North, and that their grasp on the national tiller would be unshaken. That belief had withered before the Mexican War. Clear-eyed men realized that in nearly all material elements of civilization the North had far outstripped them; and they knew that slavery stood indicted not merely as a moral wrong, but as responsible for this painful lag in progress. In the Southern mind a defensive mechanism clicked into operation. Slavery? It was a blessing. The Negro? They best understood him. "Whatever defects may belong to our system, it certainly has the merit of preserving the Negro and improving his situation. Look at the moderating influences. Look at their own advance in health, comfort, virtue, and numbers." Progress? No sane man wanted the "calculating avarice" that, as Calhoun said, marked the factory owner driving his wage slaves.

Hand in hand with this defensive attitude, as all observers noted, went a passionate Southern pride. The Charlestonian loved to descant on St. Michael's, the Society Library, the Broad Street Theatre, the statue of Pitt. If you hinted that his college was but an academy, he spoke of the hospital, the St. Cecilia Society, and the three newspapers. If a visitor suggested that the city needed a good market, men described the ample shipments that came down to every gentleman from his plantation. An aristocratic society is always proud, and we might trace far back into colonial times the Southern conviction of superiority to

Northern and British shilling-grabbers. Many slaveholders liked to talk, at first confidentially but later in speeches frankly addressed to Northern ears, of the defects of shirtsleeves democracy, Yankee industrialism, and the vomit of European slums. More and more, this pride was related to that inferiority complex which is so often a mark of superior peoples set amid unfavorable environments. The pride of the ruling class was bulwarked by an intellectual factor, the influence of the old writers — Hobbes in government, Dryden in poetry, Clarendon in history — who regarded aristocracy as the best form of social control.

In none of its varied manifestations was sectional pride more dangerous than in its constant assertions of superior fighting power. "If it comes to blows between the North and the South," a Yankee heard William Gilmore Simms exclaim, "we shall crush you as I would crush an egg." John B. Gordon heard a judge remark that in the event of war, the South could "whip the Yankees with children's pop-guns." The well-born Southerner was convinced that he was a man of far more spirit and resource than the Northern counter-jumper. Nothing struck William H. Russell more forcibly, in his travels over the South just before the Civil War, than the widespread conviction that the free States would never fight, or if they did would be quickly put in their places. A later writer on "the fighting South" has ascribed its militancy to the old habit of living dangerously, and to a depth of conviction, a "totality of purehearted affirmation" natural in a simple society. Perhaps more important were the conditions of Southern life, with much hunting, general use of horses, and frequent marksmanship contests; the existence of two fine schools

of war, the Virginia Military Institute at Lexington, and the South Carolina Military Academy or "Citadel" at Charleston; and the memory of Southern prowess in the Mexican War. The leading officers, Scott, Taylor, Quitman, Twiggs, and Davis, were all Southrons — if one forgot Kearny or Worth. Indeed, in what war had not Southern commanders stood foremost?

*   *   *

Altogether, South and North by 1857 were rapidly becoming separate peoples. The major Protestant denominations had broken in twain; one major party, the Whigs, had first split in half and then disappeared; press, pulpit, and education all showed a deepening cleavage. With every passing year, the fundamental assumptions, tastes, and cultural aims of the two sections became more divergent. As tension grew, militant elements on both sides resented the presence of "outsiders"; Southerners were exposed to insult at Northern resorts, while Yankees in the South were compelled to explain their business to a more and more suspicious population.

The Southerners loved the Union, for their forefathers had helped build it, and the gravestones of their patriot soldiers strewed the land. But they wanted a Union in which they could preserve their peculiar institutions, ancient customs, and well-loved ways of life and thought. They knew that all the main forces of modern society were pressing to create a more closely unified nation, and to make institutions homogeneous even if not absolutely uniform. Against this they recoiled; they wanted a hegemony, a loose confederacy, not a unified nation and a standardized civilization. They regarded the Union as an association of sovereign States and an alliance of regions that possessed national attributes. The North wishes to dictate to us on the slavery question, wrote Simms in 1852. "But we are a people, *a nation,* with arms in our hands, and in sufficient numbers to compel the respect of *other nations;* and we shall never submit the case to the judgment of *another people,* until they show themselves of superior virtue and intellect."

This schism in culture struck into the very substance of national life. Differences of thought, taste, and ideals gravely accentuated the misunderstandings caused by the basic economic and social differences; the differences between a free labor system and a slave labor system, between a semi-industrialized economy of high productiveness and an agrarian economy of low productiveness. An atmosphere was created in which emotions grew feverish; in which every episode became a crisis, every jar a shock.

The sands were running out. A few years more remained in which the national fabric might be reknit stronger than ever — if statesmanship were adequate to the task. But Congress had become an arena of constant sectional strife. Pierce had let the Presidency be drawn into the vortex of passion. And in the first weeks of 1857 brief warning items about the case of one Dred Scott began to appear in the press; a case on which the Supreme Court was soon to make a momentous pronouncement. Through the clash and clangor of the times men seemed to hear an ominous note of the future:

"So fierce you whirr and pound you drums — so shrill you bugles blow."

*   *   *

[GREAT AND COMPLEX EVENTS HAVE
GREAT AND COMPLEX CAUSES]*

Great and complex events have great and complex causes. Burke, in his *Reflections on the Revolution in France,* wrote that "a state without the means of some change is without the means of its conservation," and that a constant reconciliation of "the two principles of conservation and correction" is indispensable to healthy national growth. It is safe to say that every such revolutionary era as that on which the United States entered in 1860 finds its genesis in an inadequate adjustment of these two forces. It is also safe to say that when a tragic national failure occurs, it is largely a failure of leadership. "Brains are of three orders," wrote Machiavelli, "those that understand of themselves, those that understand when another shows them, and those that understand neither by themselves nor by the showing of others." Ferment and change must steadily be controlled; the real must, as Bryce said, be kept resting on the ideal; and if disaster is to be avoided, wise leaders must help thoughtless men to understand, and direct the action of invincibly ignorant men. Necessary reforms may be obstructed in various ways; by sheer inertia, by tyranny and class selfishness, or by the application of compromise to basic principles — this last being in Lowell's view the main cause of the Civil War. Ordinarily the obstruction arises from a com-

*The remainder of this selection is from Allan Nevins, *The Emergence of Lincoln,* Vol. II, pp. 462–71 (New York: Charles Scribner's Sons, 1947, 1950). Reprinted with the permission of Charles Scribner's Sons from *The Emergence of Lincoln,* Volume II, by Allan Nevins, copyright, 1950, Charles Scribner's Sons.

bination of all these elements. To explain the failure of American leadership in 1846–1861, and the revolution that ensued, is a bafflingly complicated problem.

Looking backward from the verge of war in March, 1861, Americans could survey a series of ill-fated decisions by their chosen agents. One unfortunate decision was embodied in Douglas's Kansas-Nebraska Act of 1854. Had an overwhelming majority of Americans been ready to accept the squatter sovereignty principle, this law might have proved a statesmanlike stroke; but it was so certain that powerful elements North and South would resist it to the last that it accentuated the strife and confusion. Another disastrous decision was made by Taney and his associates in the Dred Scott pronouncement of 1857. Still another was made by Buchanan when he weakly accepted the Lecompton Constitution and tried to force that fraudulent document through Congress. The Northern legislatures which passed Personal Liberty Acts made an unhappy decision. Most irresponsible, wanton, and disastrous of all was the decision of those Southern leaders who in 1858–60 turned to the provocative demand for Congressional protection of slavery in all the Territories of the republic. Still other errors might be named. Obviously, however, it is the forces behind these decisions which demand our study; the waters pouring down the gorge, not the rocks which threw their spray into the air.

At this point we meet a confused clamor of voices as various students attempt an explanation of the tragic denouement of 1861. Some writers are as content with a simple explanation as Lord Clarendon was when he attributed the English Civil War to the desire of Parliament for an egregious domination of the government. The bloody conflict, declared James Ford Rhodes, had "a single cause, slavery." He was but echoing what Henry Wilson and other early historians had written, that the aggressions of the Slave Power offered the central explanation. That opinion had been challenged as early as 1861 by the London *Saturday Review,* which remarked that "slavery is but a surface question in American politics," and by such Southern propagandists as Yancey, who tried to popularize a commercial theory of the war, emphasizing a supposed Southern revolt against the tariff and other Yankee exactions. A later school of writers was to find the key to the tragedy in an inexorable conflict between the business-minded North and the agrarian-minded South, a thrusting industrialism colliding with a rather static agricultural society. Still another group of writers has accepted the theory that the war resulted from psychological causes. They declare that agitators, propagandists, and alarmists on both sides, exaggerating the real differences of interest, created a state of mind, a hysterical excitement, which made armed conflict inevitable.

At the very outset of the war Senator Mason of Virginia, writing to his daughter, asserted that two systems of society were in conflict; systems, he implied, as different as those of Carthage and Rome, Protestant Holland and Catholic Spain. That view, too, was later to be elaborated by a considerable school of writers. Two separate nations, they declared, had arisen within the United States in 1861, much as two separate nations had emerged within the first British Empire by 1776. Contrasting ways of life, rival group consciousness, divergent hopes and fears made a movement for separation logical; and the minority people, believing its peculiar civilization in danger of suppression, began a war for independence. We are told, indeed, that two types of nationalism came into conflict: a Northern nationalism which wished to preserve the unity of the whole republic, and a Southern nationalism intent on creating an entirely new republic.

It is evident that some of these explanations deal with merely superficial phenomena, and that others, when taken separately, represent but subsidiary elements in the play of forces. Slavery was a great fact; the demands of Northern industrialism constituted a great fact; sectional hysteria was a great fact. But do they not perhaps relate themselves to some profounder underlying cause? This question has inspired one student to suggest that "the confusion of a growing state" may offer the fundamental explanation of the drift to war; an unsatisfactory hypothesis, for westward growth, railroad growth, business growth, and cultural growth, however much attended with "confusion," were unifying factors, and it was not the new-made West but old-settled South Carolina which led in the schism.

One fact needs emphatic statement: of all the monistic explanations for the drift to war, that posited upon supposed economic causes is the flimsiest. This theory was sharply rejected at the time by so astute an observer as Alexander H. Stephens. South Carolina, he wrote his brother on New Year's Day, 1861, was seceding from a tariff "which is just what her own Senators and members in Congress made it." As for the charges of consolidation and despotism made by some Carolinians, he thought they arose from peevishness, rather than a calm analysis of facts. "The truth is, the South, almost in mass, has voted, I think,

for every measure of general legislation that has passed both houses and become law for the last ten years." The South, far from groaning under tyranny, had controlled the government almost from its beginning, and Stephens believed that its only real grievance lay in the Northern refusal to return fugitive slaves and to stop the antislavery agitation. "All other complaints are founded on threatened dangers which may never come, and which I feel very sure would be averted if the South would pursue a judicious and wise course." Stephens was right. It was true that the whole tendency of Federal legislation 1842–1860 was toward free trade; true that the tariff in force when secession began was largely Southern-made; true that it was the lowest tariff the country had known since 1816; true that it cost a nation of thirty million people but sixty million dollars in indirect revenue; true that without secession no new tariff law, obnoxious to the Democratic Party, could have passed before 1863 — if then.

In the official explanations which one Southern State after another published for its secession, economic grievances are either omitted entirely or given minor position. There were few such supposed grievances which the agricultural States of Illinois, Iowa, Indiana, Wisconsin, and Minnesota did not share with the South — and they never threatened to secede. Charles A. Beard finds the tap-root of the war in the resistance of the planter interest to Northern demands enlarging the old Hamilton-Webster policy. The South was adamant in standing for "no high protective tariffs, no ship subsidies, no national banking and currency system; in short, none of the measures which business enterprise deemed essential to its progress." But the Republican platform in 1856 was silent on the tariff; in

1860 it carried a milk-and-water statement on the subject which Western Republicans took, mild as it was, with a wry face; the incoming President was little interested in the tariff; and any harsh legislation was impossible. Ship subsidies were not an issue in the campaign of 1860. Neither were a national banking system and a national currency system. They were not mentioned in the Republican platform nor discussed by party debaters. The Pacific Railroad was advocated both by the Douglas Democrats and the Republicans; and it is noteworthy that Seward and Douglas were for building both a Northern and a Southern line. In short, the divisive economic issues are easily exaggerated. At the same time, the unifying economic factors were both numerous and powerful. North and South had economies which were largely complementary. It was no misfortune to the South that Massachusetts cotton mills wanted its staple, and that New York ironmasters like Hewitt were eager to sell rails dirt-cheap to Southern railway builders; and sober businessmen on both sides, merchants, bankers, and manufacturers, were the men most anxious to keep the peace and hold the Union together.

We must seek further for an explanation; and in so doing, we must give special weight to the observations of penetrating leaders of the time, who knew at first hand the spirit of the people. Henry J. Raymond, moderate editor of the New York *Times*, a sagacious man who disliked Northern abolitionists and Southern radicals, wrote in January, 1860, an analysis of the impending conflict which attributed it to a competition for power:

In every country there must be a just and equal balance of powers in the government, an equal distribution of the national forces. Each section and each interest must exercise its due share of influence and control. It is always more or less difficult to preserve their just equipoise, and the larger the country, and the more varied its great interests, the more difficult does the task become, and the greater the shock and disturbance caused by an attempt to adjust it when once disturbed. I believe I state only what is generally conceded to be a fact, when I say that the growth of the Northern States in population, in wealth, in all the elements of political influence and control, has been out of proportion to their political influence in the Federal Councils. While the Southern States have less than a third of the aggregate population of the Union, their interests have influenced the policy of the government far more than the interests of the Northern States. . . . Now the North has made rapid advances within the last five years, and it naturally claims a proportionate share of influence and power in the affairs of the Confederacy.

It is inevitable that this claim should be put forward, and it is also inevitable that it should be conceded. No party can long resist it; it overrides all parties, and makes them the mere instruments of its will. It is quite as strong today in the heart of the Democratic party of the North as in the Republican ranks; and any party which ignores it will lose its hold on the public mind.

Why does the South resist this claim? Not because it is unjust in itself, but because it has become involved with the question of slavery, and has drawn so much of its vigor and vitality from that quarter, that it is almost merged in that issue. The North bases its demand for increased power, in a very great degree, on the action of the government in regard to slavery — and the just and rightful ascendency of the North in the Federal councils comes thus to be regarded as an element of danger to the institutions of the Southern States.

In brief, Raymond, who held that slavery was a moral wrong, that its economic and social tendencies were vicious, and that the time had come to halt its growth with a view to its final eradication, believed that the contest was primarily one for power, and for the application of that power to the slave system. With this opinion Alexander H. Stephens agreed. The Georgian said he believed slavery both morally and politically right. In his letter to Lincoln on December 30, 1860, he declared that the South did not fear that the new Republican Administration would interfere directly and immediately with slavery in the States. What Southerners did fear was the ultimate result of the shift of power which had just occurred — in its application to slavery:

Now this subject, which is confessedly on all sides outside of the constitutional action of the Government, so far as the States are concerned, is made the "central idea" in the platform of principles announced by the triumphant party. The leading object seems to be simply, and wantonly, if you please, to put the institutions of nearly half the States under the band of public opinion and national condemnation. This, upon general principles, is quite enough of itself to arouse a spirit not only of general indignation, but of revolt on the part of the proscribed. Let me illustrate. It is generally conceded by the Republicans even, that Congress cannot interfere with slavery in the States. It is equally conceded that Congress cannot establish any form of religious worship. Now suppose that any one of the present Christian churches or sects prevailed in all the Southern States, but had no existence in any one of the Northern States, — under such circumstances suppose the people of the Northern States should organize a political party, not upon a foreign or domestic policy, but with one leading idea of condemnation of the doctrines and tenets of that particular church, and with an avowed object of preventing its extension into the common Territories, even after the highest judicial tribunal of the land had decided they had no such constitutional power. And suppose that

a party so organized should carry a Presidential election. Is it not apparent that a general feeling of resistance to the success, aims, and objects of such a party would necessarily and rightfully ensue?

Raymond and Stephens agreed that the two sections were competing for power; that a momentous transfer of power had just occurred; and that it held fateful consequences because it was involved with the issue of slavery, taking authority from a section which believed slavery moral and healthy, and giving it to a section which held slavery immoral and pernicious. To Stephens this transfer was ground for resuming the ultimate sovereignty of the States. Here we find a somewhat more complex statement of James Ford Rhodes's thesis that the central cause of the Civil War lay in slavery. Here, too, we revert to the assertions of Yancey and Lincoln that the vital conflict was between those who thought slavery right and those who thought it wrong. But this definition we can accept only if we probe a little deeper for a concept which both modifies and enlarges the basic source of perplexity and quarrel.

The main root of the conflict (and there were minor roots) was the problem of slavery *with its complementary problem of race-adjustment;* the main source of the tragedy was the refusal of either section to face these conjoined problems squarely and pay the heavy costs of a peaceful settlement. Had it not been for the difference in race, the slavery issue would have presented no great difficulties. But as the racial gulf existed, the South inarticulately but clearly perceived that elimination of this issue would still leave it the terrible problem of the Negro. Those historians who write that if slavery had simply been left alone it would soon have withered overlook this heavy impediment. The South as a whole in 1846–61 was not moving toward emancipation, but away from it. It was not relaxing the laws which guarded the system, but reinforcing them. It was not ameliorating slavery, but making it harsher and more implacable. The South was further from a just solution of the slavery problem in 1830 than it had been in 1789. It was further from a tenable solution in 1860 than it had been in 1830. Why was it going from bad to worse? Because Southern leaders refused to nerve their people to pay the heavy price of race-adjustment. These leaders never made up their mind to deal with the problem as the progressive temper of civilization demanded. They would not adopt the new outlook which the upward march of mankind required because they saw that the gradual abolition of slavery would bring a measure of political privilege; that political privilege would usher in a measure of economic equality; that on the heels of economic equality would come a rising social status for the Negro. Southern leadership dared not ask the people to pay this price.

A heavy responsibility for the failure of America in this period rests with this Southern leadership, which lacked imagination, ability, and courage. But the North was by no means without its full share, for the North equally refused to give a constructive examination to the central question of slavery as linked with race adjustment. This was because of two principal reasons. Most abolitionists and many other sentimental-minded Northerners simply denied that the problem existed. Regarding all Negroes as white men with dark skins, whom a few years of schooling would bring abreast of the dominant race, they thought that no difficult adjustment was required. A much more numerous body of Northern-

ers would have granted that a great and terrible task of race adjustment existed — but they were reluctant to help shoulder any part of it. Take a million or two million Negroes into the Northern States? Indiana, Illinois, and even Kansas were unwilling to take a single additional person of color. Pay tens of millions to help educate and elevate the colored population? Take even a first step by offering to pay the Southern slaveholders some recompense for a gradual liberation of their human property? No Northern politician dared ask his constituents to make so unpopular a sacrifice. The North, like the South, found it easier to drift blindly toward disaster.

The hope of solving the slavery problem without a civil war rested upon several interrelated factors, of which one merits special emphasis. We have said that the South as a whole was laboring to bolster and stiffen slavery — which was much to its discredit. But it is nevertheless true that slavery was dying all around the edges of its domain; it was steadily decaying in Delaware, Maryland, western Virginia, parts of Kentucky, and Missouri. Much of the harshness of Southern legislation in the period sprang from a sense that slavery was in danger from *internal* weaknesses. In no great time Delaware, Maryland, and Missouri were likely to enter the column of free States; and if they did, reducing the roster to twelve, the doom of the institution would be clearly written. Allied with this factor was the rapid comparative increase of Northern strength, and the steady knitting of economic, social, and moral ties between the North and West, leaving the South in a position of manifest inferiority. A Southern Confederacy had a fair fighting chance in 1861; by 1880 it would have had very little. If secession could have been postponed by two decades, natural forces might well have placed a solution full in sight. Then, too, the growing pressure of world sentiment must in time have produced its effect. But to point out these considerations is not to suggest that in 1861 a policy of procrastination and appeasement would have done anything but harm. All hope of bringing Southern majority sentiment to a better attitude would have been lost if Lincoln and his party had flinched on the basic issue of the restriction of slavery; for by the seventh decade of nineteenth century history, the time had come when that demand had to be maintained.

While in indicting leadership we obviously indict the public behind the leaders, we must also lay some blame upon a political environment which gave leadership a poor chance. American parties, under the pressure of sectional feeling, worked badly. The government suffered greatly, moreover, from the lack of any adequate planning agency. Congress was not a truly deliberative body, and its committees had not yet learned to do long-range planning. The President might have formulated plans, but he never did. For one reason, no President between Polk and Lincoln had either the ability or the prestige required; for another reason, Fillmore, Pierce, and Buchanan all held that their duty was merely to execute the laws, not to initiate legislation. Had the country possessed a ministerial form of government, the Cabinet in leading the legislature would have been compelled to lay down a program of real scope concerning slavery. As it was, leadership in Washington was supplied only spasmodically by men like Clay, Douglas, and Crittenden.

And as we have noted, the rigidity of the American system was at this time a grave handicap. Twice, in the fall of 1854 and of 1858, the elections gave a stunning rebuke to the Administration. Under a ministerial system, the old government would probably have gone out and a new one have come in. In 1854, however, Pierce continued to carry on the old policies, and in 1858 Buchanan remained the drearily inept helmsman of the republic. Never in our history were bold, quick planning and a flexible administration of policy more needed; never was the failure to supply them more complete.

Still another element in the tragic chronicle of the time must be mentioned. Much that happens in human affairs is accidental. When a country is guided by true statesmen the role of accident is minimized; when it is not, unforeseen occurrences are numerous and dangerous. In the summer and fall of 1858, as we have seen, the revival of a conservative opposition party in the upper South, devoted to the Union, furnished a real gleam of hope. If this opposition had been given unity and determined leadership, if moderate Southerners had stood firm against the plot of Yancey and others to disrupt the Democratic Party, if Floyd had been vigilant enough to read the warning letter about John Brown and act on it, the situation might even then have been saved. Instead, John Brown's mad raid fell on public opinion like a thunderstroke, exasperating men everywhere and dividing North and South more tragically than ever. The last chance of persuading the South to submit to an essential step, the containment of slavery, was gone.

The war, when it came, was not primarily a conflict over State Rights, although that issue had become involved in it. It was not primarily a war born of economic grievances, although many Southerners had been led to think that they were suffering, or would soon suffer, economic wrongs. It was not a war created by politicians and publicists who fomented hysteric excitement; for while hysteria was important, we have always to ask what basic reasons made possible the propaganda which aroused it. It was not primarily a war about slavery alone, although that institution seemed to many the grand cause. It was a war over slavery *and* the future position of the Negro race in North America. Was the Negro to be allowed, as a result of the shift of power signalized by Lincoln's election, to take the first step toward an ultimate position of general economic, political, and social equality with the white man? Or was he to be held immobile in a de-graded, servile position, unchanging for the next hundred years as it had remained essentially unchanged for the hundred years past? These questions were implicit in Lincoln's demand that slavery be placed in a position where the public mind could rest assured of its ultimate extinction.

Evasion by the South, evasion by the North, were no longer possible. The alternatives faced were an unpopular but curative adjustment of the situation by the opposed parties, or a war that would force an adjustment upon the loser. For Americans in 1861, as for many other peoples throughout history, war was easier than wisdom and courage.

Thomas J. Pressly: THE CONFUSION OF VOICES

Thomas J. Pressly belongs to the most recent generation of historians concerned with the problem of the American Civil War. Trained at Harvard University, he was strongly influenced by Professor Paul H. Buck, who has written a classic work on the reconciliation of the North and South after the Civil War. Pressly reveals a strong sympathy for the "nationalist tradition" in the historical writing concerning the Civil War and apparently would like to see a reconciliation of clashing historical viewpoints concerning the Civil War. In any case, Thomas Pressly, together with Lee Benson, sought to demonstrate to the American Historical Association in 1956 a way in which "differences in interpretations of the causes of the American Civil War can be resolved objectively." Pressly's careful study of the interpretations of the Civil War since the 1860's reveals very clearly the problems of historical interpretation which have developed in recent decades. The selection is from Thomas J. Pressly, Americans Interpret Their Civil War.

ALLAN NEVINS, the author of the latest large-scale history of the Civil War, was born in Illinois in 1890 and received his undergraduate and graduate training at the University of Illinois. His history, *Ordeal of the Union*, began with the end of the 1840's and, in the four volumes published by 1950, spanned the years through the inauguration of Lincoln; it was the first major detailed study

Reprinted by permission from Thomas J. Pressly, *Americans Interpret Their Civil War* (Princeton, N. J.: Princeton University Press, 1954), pp. 310–323.

of this era since the volumes of Rhodes (Channing and Cole had each covered the period from approximately 1850 to 1865 in one volume), and was, so far, on a larger scale than Rhodes' *History* (the first three volumes of which were devoted to the years from 1850 to 1862). Historians reviewing Nevins' volumes noted the wide research displayed in them as well as the felicitous style of writing; there were many predictions that these volumes would rank as a major work in American historiography. Rhodes' *History* had reflected many of the viewpoints on the Civil War dominant in the era in which it was published, and it had also helped to shape those viewpoints. The question arose: Would this also be the role of Nevins' *Ordeal of the Union?*

If Nevins' interpretation of the causes of the Civil War be described in terms of the attitudes so far discussed in this study, it was clearly not an economic interpretation, Marxian or Beardian (although economic forces were discussed at some length), nor was it similar to the Owsley type of vindication of the South. Instead, it seemed to represent a combination of some "revisionist" attitudes with some of the elements of the "new nationalist tradition" — a "combination" rather than a "synthesis," for those two sets of ideas were so different that it seemed impossible to assimilate them into one consistent and coherent pattern, and as a result several historians reviewing *Ordeal of the Union* suggested that there was a persistent dualism in Nevins' explanation of the coming of war.

Like the "revisionists," Nevins seemed at times to center his interpretation of the war's causes primarily upon the outbreak of hostilities in 1861 (rather than upon sectional conflict); war in 1861, he asserted, was easier than wisdom and courage, and he seemed to insist that war should have been averted and could have been averted. Like the Second World War, he wrote, the Civil War

should have been avoidable. Because the people and leaders of the United States did not act with determination and sagacity in solving the problems of slavery, sectional irritation, and a right adjustment of races, part of the country was half ruined for generations, and all of it set back by decades.

The primary task of statesmanship in this era, in Nevins' opinion, was to provide a workable adjustment between North and South, and at the same time to persuade Southerners to modify and gradually abolish the institution of slavery while persuading Northerners to be helpful rather than critical during the process. He seemed at times to imply that these objects could have been accomplished and war averted had it not been for the "errors" of political leaders, for the defects of the American political machinery, and for the baneful influences of emotionalism.

Writing of the "failure of American leadership" in the 1850's, Nevins singled out the Presidents for blame: "Zachary Taylor was stubbornly wrongheaded; Franklin Pierce was impulsively erratic; James Buchanan timidly fumbling." In addition to the weaknesses of these individuals, the government which they headed, declared Nevins, did not have adequate planning agencies; the American political system was handicapped by its rigidity (in 1854 and 1858 the administration remained in office after being rebuffed at the polls) and political parties in the United States worked badly in the face of sectionalism. In the atmosphere of such sectionalism in the 1850's, there were misunderstandings between

North and South, and Nevins stated that the "unrealities of passion" were frequently dominant. At times he seemed to approach the slavery question from this standpoint of emotional unrealities, criticizing the abolitionists and implying that if men had just been "reasonable" about slavery, there would have been no cause for dispute:

Had both North and South sat down quietly, appraised the number and value of the fugitive slaves, got at the truth about all the reports of the kidnapping of free Negroes, and refrained from emotion and exaggeration, agreement might have been possible. Both sides were equally guilty of hysteria.

If judged only from the passages so far cited, it might well be concluded that Nevins' interpretation of the causes of the Civil War, while not precisely the same as that of the "revisionists," was nevertheless quite close to their position. Yet, throughout Nevins' volumes there was, in the opinion of the present author, stronger emphasis upon attitudes which were more similar to the "new nationalist tradition" than to the "revisionist" viewpoint. For Nevins constantly placed stress upon the existence of a deep and fundamental cleavage between North and South — differences in ideas, ideals, aims, and outlook — which all added up to two divergent cultures by the 1850's. He specifically stated (in contrast to the possible implication of some of the remarks noted above) that the historian must keep his eye focused upon that cleavage and the fundamental forces which produced it in order to explain the causes of the Civil War. That struggle, he declared,

was not a war created by politicians and publicists who fomented hysteric excitement; for while hysteria was important, we have always to ask what basic reasons made possible the propaganda which aroused it.

Similarly, while Nevins noted the ill-fated decisions by American political leaders, he explicitly declared that there should be examination of more basic influences:

Obviously . . . it is the forces behind these decisions [by political leaders] which demand our study; the waters pouring down the gorge, not the rocks which threw their spray into the air.

As a matter of fact, Nevins' viewpoint, in many important respects, seemed most of all to represent the basic ideas of Rhodes brought up to date in terms of some of the findings of historical scholarship in the United States since the 1890's. Rhodes had more or less ignored the role of economic forces in his description of an irrepressible conflict; Nevins, while he discussed economic trends and factors at length, minimized their importance in producing a breach between North and South. Between the plantation-agriculture South and the Northeast with its developing manufactures there were economic differences, he stated, but the effect of economic forces worked more toward holding the sections together than in splitting them apart. He repeatedly emphasized his contention that the war was not one born primarily of economic grievances or of divisive economic forces:

One fact needs emphatic statement: of all the monistic explanations for the drift to war, that posited upon supposed economic causes is the flimsiest. . . . The war was caused primarily by social, moral, and political, not economic forces.

The basic forces which, in the opinion

of Nevins, were responsible for sectional conflict and war were not economic in nature but were concerned with the related questions of slavery and racial adjustment (like Ulrich B. Phillips, Nevins constantly emphasized the factor of race). When Nevins described these questions, he sounded much more like Rhodes than like the "revisionists":

The main root of the conflict (and there were minor roots) was the problem of slavery *with its complementary problem of race-adjustment;* the main source of the tragedy was the refusal of either section to face these conjoined problems squarely and pay the heavy costs of a peaceful settlement. . . . It was a war over slavery *and* the future position of the Negro race in North America. Was the Negro to be allowed, as a result of the shift of power signalized by Lincoln's election, to take the first step toward an ultimate position of general economic, political, and social equality with the white man? Or was he to be held immobile in a degraded, servile position, unchanging for the next hundred years as it had remained essentially unchanged for the hundred years past?

The basic differences between the sections centering around the related problems of slavery and racial adjustment seemed in the pages of Nevins, just as they had in the pages of Rhodes, to be irreconcilable. The slavery question, Nevins stated, was "in fact irrepressible" — "it could not be compromised; one section must yield its fundamental position." (Nevins, like Phillips, placed much more stress than had Rhodes upon difference of race as the fundamental factor which made a solution of the slavery problem difficult; but, as we have seen, Rhodes, especially in his discussion of Reconstruction, had voiced his opinion of the importance of the "race question" and the "Negro question.")

Nevins did not shield the unsavory aspects of the institution of slavery from sight, and, unlike most of the "revisionists," he was forthright in his criticism of the institution — "the greatest wrong, the greatest misery, the greatest curse to white and black alike that America has ever known." Yet, in a fashion similar to Rhodes, he took pains to point out his conviction that the evils of slavery belonged to the institution itself rather than to any special wickedness of the Southern people, and that both Northerners and Southerners were to "blame" for the perilous deadlock on the slavery question (Northerners, wrote Nevins, refused to "acknowledge that in equity they must share the heavy burdens of racial readjustment," while white Southerners refused to "treat slavery as a progressive and evolutionary system, leading by regular gradations to freedom"). Southerners, Rhodes had declared in 1893, deserved sympathy rather than censure on the question of slavery; the South, Nevins asserted in 1947, needed compassion and help rather than condemnation.

Nevins insisted that some positive action toward solving the slavery question was necessary in the 1850's, and this aspect of his thought served once more to point up differences between his (and Rhodes') point of view, on the one hand, and that of the "revisionists" on the other. The "revisionists" seemed to say and to imply that if the abolitionists had not attacked slavery, then the Southerners would not have defended it as a positive good, and it would eventually have withered away; similarly, they seemed to say and to imply that if the United States had just followed the lead of Stephen A. Douglas, and if the Republicans in 1860–1861 had just been willing to compromise on the issue of slavery in the territories, war could have been averted and all would have been well.

Nevins, by contrast, declared that drift was not enough to solve the problem of slavery and that this problem could not be shelved; he specifically disagreed with the supposition that slavery would have disappeared of its own accord had it been left alone, asserting that the *ante-bellum* South had been moving progressively further, not nearer, to emancipation and a "just solution" to the slavery problem. While not as severe in his criticism of Stephen A. Douglas as Rhodes had been, Nevins was quite unsympathetic to Douglas in his sponsorship of the Kansas-Nebraska Act of 1854. Douglas, Nevins asserted, never understood the opposition of Lincoln on moral grounds to the Kansas-Nebraska Act, for he was a man of "dim moral perceptions" whose mind was "closed to the highest moral considerations as some ears are deaf to the finest harmonies of music"; Douglas through the Kansas-Nebraska Act, in the opinion of Nevins, converted more men to the free soil doctrine in two months than the militant abolitionists had converted to their position in twenty years. Finally (and this was quite unlike most of the discussions of the subject by "revisionist" historians) Nevins upheld Lincoln's policy of refusal to compromise on the issue of slavery in the territories in the crisis of 1860–1861. A compromise course of "procrastination and appeasement" at that time, Nevins declared, would have brought only harm:

All hope of bringing Southern majority sentiment to a better attitude would have been lost if Lincoln and his party had flinched on the basic issue of the restriction of slavery.

Perhaps the most accurate index of Nevins' interpretation of the causes of the Civil War was contained in his statement that the war "should have been avoidable." That this phrase was ambiguous in the sense that it was liable to different interpretations by competent historians was demonstrated, as will be indicated shortly, in the reviews of Nevins' volumes. To the present writer, however, these words of Nevins, when examined in the light of the first four volumes of his history, signify an explanation of the coming of the Civil War which was more in accord with the general pattern of the "new nationalist tradition" than with the "revisionist" position. The "revisionist" viewpoint could be expressed in the declaration that the Civil War "was avoidable" — and was avoidable because, in the opinion of the "revisionists," if the men of the 1850's and 1860's had only been unemotional and realistic, they would have realized that their differences were not great enough to warrant combat. By contrast, Nevins' position that the Civil War "should have been avoidable" implied that armed hostilities might have been evaded only if steps had been taken to end the irreconcilable differences between North and South; since, in the view of Nevins, the most important irreconcilable difference was that over slavery and racial adjustment, it followed that enduring peace between North and South depended upon some step which would have marked the beginning of the end of the institution of slavery.

The reaction to Rhodes' *History* among historians of that day (in the fifteen years after the publication of its first two volumes in 1893) had indicated at least two things: that there was a considerable measure of agreement in attitudes toward the causes and nature of the Civil War, and that many historians could write of the Civil War, only thirty years after it ended, dispassionately and without rancor. By contrast, the published reaction among historians to Nevins' *Ordeal of the Union* (in the four years after the publication of its first two volumes in 1947) demonstrated that almost the reverse was now true on both counts: the reviews of the volumes of Nevins revealed not only a sharp disagreement in interpretations of the causes of the Civil War but also that some historians in the 1940's and 1950's wrote of the Civil War with a greater emotional intensity than had their predecessors a half-century earlier.

Several historians (including Edward C. Kirkland, Oscar Handlin, and Arthur M. Schlesinger, Jr.) noted the above-mentioned dualism in Nevins' interpretation of the causes of the war and expressed the opinion that he had not made his viewpoint on this subject clear. This alleged dualism might have been expected to elicit a certain diversity of opinions from reviewers, but by itself it could not have produced the widely different responses which greeted *Ordeal of the Union.*

Nevins' point of view was condemned by two Southern historians, Fletcher M. Green of the University of North Carolina and Robert H. Woody of Duke University — both of whom were born in the South, had received their undergraduate and graduate training at Southern universities, and had lived in the South all their lives. Green and Woody censured Nevins on the ground that he was biased in favor of the North, and they charged that this partiality was due to his opposition to slavery on moral grounds. "Like the abolitionists of the period of which he writes," Green asserted, "Nevins seems to be blinded by his sense of moral values." Woody also compared Nevins to the antislavery crusaders of the Civil

War era, and declared that it "may all be very well to take one's stand with freedom as against slavery; it is worth suggesting, however, that it makes difficult an impartial account."

But in a contrast about as pronounced as can be imagined, Nevins was criticized for almost precisely the opposite reasons by two other historians, Arthur M. Schlesinger, Jr., and Oscar Handlin — both of whom were born outside the South and had never lived there, both of whom had received their graduate training at Harvard and had remained there as members of the faculty. Whereas Nevins, in the opinion of Green and Woody, was too sympathetic to the abolitionists, he was, in the opinion of Handlin, too severe in his strictures against the abolitionists, making charges against them which Handlin stated were "not true." Handlin and Schlesinger, Jr., were dissatisfied not because Nevins' moral judgments against slavery were too much in evidence in his interpretation of the causes of the Civil War but because such judgments were not enough in evidence. Nevins, Handlin asserted, classed together the extremists of North and South without making an ethical distinction between the two: "There is surely a difference between being a fanatic for freedom and being a fanatic for slavery." In a similar vein, Schlesinger, Jr., charged that Nevins "never gives the moral factor full weight," and that he wrote "as if those who believed in human freedom and those who believed in human slavery were equally at fault" in the conflict between North and South.

In between the positions represented by Green and Woody, on the one hand, and Handlin and Schlesinger, Jr., on the other, some historians expressed praise for the viewpoint of Nevins — but for quite different reasons. James G. Randall, the "revisionist," reviewed the four volumes with approval, singling out for special commendation their "appreciative treatment of things Southern" and hazarding the speculation that the South had "captured" Nevins; Randall's reviews left the reader with the impression that Nevins' outlook was quite similar to that of the "revisionists," although it was noted Stephen A. Douglas was "given a surprisingly unfavorable treatment." By contrast, John D. Hicks praised the *Ordeal of the Union* on grounds just the opposite from those cited by Randall; Hicks noted with approval that the institution of slavery got "no whitewash whatever" in the volumes, and voiced the suspicion that Nevins was "weary of appeasing the tender susceptibilities of over zealous defenders of the Old South."

If the reviews of the volumes of Nevins accurately reflected the attitudes prevailing among historians, they seemed to indicate that in the 1940's — unlike the 1890's — it would be impossible to formulate a synthesis which could reconcile all the current widely divergent interpretations of the causes of the Civil War. Perhaps the reviews themselves furnished one clue as to why this was so — for in the reviews of *Ordeal of the Union* there was a recurrent theme which had not been present in the reviews of Rhodes' *History:* historians (including Ralph H. Gabriel, Richard W. Leopold, Oscar Handlin, Arthur M. Schlesinger, Jr., and James G. Randall) now drew a parallel between the Civil War era and their own day, with its wars and threats of wars. The experience of the United States in the 1850's, these historians declared, carried a message for the 1940's and 1950's, but they were not agreed as to the nature of that message.

The lack of agreement can be seen most clearly by comparing the statements of James G. Randall with those of Arthur M. Schlesinger, Jr. Randall, writing in 1947, made a direct comparison between the 1850's and his own day, the similarity resting in their "false agitation, proceeding downward in the direction of a needless war." He seemed to imply that just as, in his opinion, war could have been averted in the 1860's had men remained reasonable, unemotional, and realistic in their outlook, so also by the same methods could present-day (i.e., 1947) problems be satisfactorily solved short of war.

Schlesinger, Jr., also writing in 1947, drew a parallel between the Civil War era and the present, and like Randall implied that that era held lessons valuable for his own day in its effort to avoid war. But quite unlike Randall, Schlesinger, Jr., defined the question of war or peace in terms of alternative policies of "appeasement or resistance." He seemed to equate the "revisionist" position with that of "appeasement" and to argue that, just as the policy of "appeasement" did not avert war in the 1930's, so it had not offered the best hope of preventing war in the 1850's and did not offer the best hope in 1947:

A future ["revisionist"] historian might say . . . that the primary task of statesmanship in the 1930's was to furnish a workable adjustment between the U.S.A. and Germany, while offering strong inducements to the German people to abandon the police state, and equal persuasion to the Americans to help the Nazis rather than scold them. In essence, this is Mr. Wallace's current thesis about the Russians. Comparisons with the issues of the Civil War may perhaps be extreme; yet one must face the hard fact that closed and authoritarian social systems tend to create a compulsive intransigence in their own ruling groups — and that these groups may respond much more to a firmness which wakens them to some sense of actuality than to a forbearance which is never great enough and always to be discounted.

(In this analogy, presumably, the position of Stephen A. Douglas before he split with the pro-Southern wing of the Democratic Party in the late 1850's was comparable to that of Henry A. Wallace before he split with the Progressive Party in 1950.)

Disagreement in interpretations of the causes of the Civil War was intertwined, in the case of Randall and Schlesinger, Jr., with disagreement in analyses of the crisis of their own day. The fundamental question of how to secure peaceful settlement of intersectional and international disputes gave the Civil War experience, in the opinion of some historians, pertinence for the 1940's and 1950's; it also gave rise to differences of opinion held with intense emotions. Urgent feelings about the crisis of their own day reinforced the urgent feelings of historians about the crisis of the 1860's.

Thus, by the 1950's an anomalous situation prevailed: the further the Civil War receded into the past, the greater the disagreement among twentieth century historians over its causes, and the greater the strength of the emotions with which these divergent viewpoints were upheld. One could almost fancy himself back in the 1860's once again. Charges and countercharges of "abolitionist" and "defender of slavery" filled the air. Comparisons between contemporary figures and those of the Civil War era suggested themselves: Herbert Aptheker, writing of the South's "bloodstained, militaristic oligarchy," could be compared to the most extreme abolitionist; at the opposite pole, in a position analogous to the Southern "fire-eaters," was Frank L.

Owsley writing of Yankee "crusades" against the South, and Yankee "egocentric sectionalism"; more moderate defenders of the South could be represented by Fletcher M. Green and Robert H. Woody, and more moderate supporters of the Union by Bernard De Voto and Arthur M. Schlesinger, Jr.; and, to make the parallel to the 1860's complete, Avery Craven and James G. Randall could occupy a place comparable to Vallandigham, Foote, and the other "discontented peace advocates." Here was material from which some twentieth century Swift could pen a new "Battle of the Books," not between the Ancients and the Moderns, but between the successors to the embattled Confederates, Unionists, and peace men of the nineteenth century.

The reason why this parallel could be drawn, be it repeated, was because historians in the middle of the twentieth century still found vital the issues involved in the struggle of the 1860's: the role of the Negro in American life; the interrelationship between majority will, as expressed through the national government, and the "minority rights" of geographical sections; and the question of how to secure peaceful settlement of intersectional and international disputes.

Historical interpretation seemed to have completed almost a full cycle. Some prominent twentieth century historians, like the men of the 1860's, were sharply disagreed over the causes and character of the Civil War. Once again, clashing viewpoints were upheld with ardor, and some historians now sought to assign personal and sectional "guilt" for the war. The words Oliver Wendell Holmes, Jr., had spoken back in the 1880's now seemed prophetic, now seemed to apply to a generation other than his own: Civil War issues, it appeared, could still draw fire from the hearts and minds of Americans.

They were drawing fire, too, in a fashion which suggested a comparison with the French and their most divisive national experience. The American Revolution, insofar as it was a movement which secured national independence and replaced a monarchical system of government with a constitutional republic, represented a settlement of certain fundamental questions; Americans, by and large, have been agreed that this settlement was wise and desirable. This area of agreement on issues of basic importance has spared the nation disruptive quarrels and has provided a framework within which solutions to problems could be sought by democratic and constitutional methods. One could have predicted, in the first decade of the twentieth century, that a similar pattern of interpretation would be characteristic of the Civil War. By the 1950's, however, a different parallel seemed perhaps more appropriate — the attitudes of the French toward their Revolution of 1789. The disagreement of the French people in evaluating their Revolution has been reflected in divisions of major proportions in many areas of their national life. The cleavages in the United States over Civil War questions by the 1950's was clearly not so deep nor so wide as that in France over the Revolution. But it was nevertheless true that the disagreement among historians over the meaning of the Civil War experience was matched, in the middle of the twentieth century, by sharp controversy in the arena of politics over issues related to those of Civil War days.

Edwin C. Rozwenc: THE PRESENT CRISIS IN THE HISTORICAL EXPLANATION OF THE CAUSES OF THE AMERICAN CIVIL WAR

ONE hundred years after the sectional crisis which led to civil war, American historians are beset by a crisis of historical interpretation concerning the causes of "the American tragedy." Disagreements among contemporary historians are expressed with a sharpness of tone and a strength of emotion which makes the academic controversy over the causes and character of the American Civil War seem as irreconcilable as the divergent viewpoints in the sectional controversy of the 1850's.

The present crisis of historical explanation concerning the causes of the Civil War is all the more serious because it has a double aspect. The more obvious side of this "battle of the books" is the repetition of the older attitudes and loyalties of embattled abolitionists, compromisers, Confederates and Unionists — all refurbished by imaginative identifications with present political issues. A less obvious though equally fundamental side of this crisis of historical interpretation is the uncertainty among historians about the meaning and the usefulness of the idea of causation. Let us look more closely at both aspects of this problem.

We might begin with the commonplace statement that the historian is inescapably caught in a trap of personal values, tastes, and preconceptions. History, therefore, cannot be as objective as the physical sciences because, as Allan Nevins writes in *The Gateway to History,*

"history is violently personal — stars and molecules have no loves and hates, while men do."[1]

The wisdom of this commonplace assertion seems to be demonstrated with particular force by the behavior of American historians who write about the Civil War. Indeed, philosophers writing about the nature of historical explanation almost invariably use the American Civil War as a stock example of this predicament. And we might add that the problem of American historians who write about the Civil War is especially difficult because the Civil War is America's great national trauma — creating deep feelings of love and hate, of guilt and remorse, which have found expression in our history and literature ever since. The staggering number of historical and fictional books dealing with the Civil War which have poured from the presses over the past hundred years reveals the compulsive need of Americans to read and talk about their bloody moment of fratricide.

Henry Seidel Canby, in his introduction to Stephen Vincent Benét's *John Brown's Body*, suggests the powerful appeal of the Civil War in these terms:

Our Civil War is dramatic with a sharp and simple theme — karma: destiny as determined by irrevocable acts, a conflict of two civilizations bound together like twin enemies in a trap of their own making, the heavy payment of innocent men for the will of their ancestors, the fierce struggle of moral codes unlike though resemblant, the cruel consequences of an impersonal economics pouring like a rock slide over happy valleys.[2]

Yet we must remember that the Civil War is more than a dramatic theme to Americans who read of it. The Civil War is *our* civil conflict, and the shock of recognition that comes to most Americans is the realization that we must still make heavy payment for the will of our ancestors as we face contemporary issues of race adjustment, of majority will and minority rights, and of coping with impersonal economic forces. Most literate Americans recognize that the conflict of the 1860's marks a bloody dividing line across American history, coinciding with a crucial stage in the transition from an agrarian to an industrial America, from a rural to an urban America, from a white, Protestant and Anglo-Saxon America to a melting pot of race, nationality and religion.

Little wonder, then, that the voices of historians who try to explain the meaning of this great event seem to recapitulate its partisan emotions. Indeed, the author of a recent study of the historiography of the Civil War concludes that "the further the Civil War receded into the past, the greater the disagreement among twentieth century historians over its causes and the greater the strength of the emotions with which these divergent viewpoints were upheld."[3]

In support of such a conclusion, we may be tempted to say, as Mr. Pressly does in his *Americans Interpret Their Civil War*, that historians writing about the Civil War tend to be apologists for "geographical, social and other influences" in their personal backgrounds. Thus, for example, Frank L. Owsley becomes a frank apologist for the Southern agrarian tradition; James G. Randall's interpretation may be said to display an overly strong sympathy for moderates like Stephen A. Douglas and

[1] Allan Nevins, *The Gateway to History* (New York, 1938), p. 29.
[2] Stephen Vincent Benét, *John Brown's Body* (New York, 1941), p. viii.
[3] Thomas J. Pressly, *Americans Interpret Their Civil War* (Princeton, 1954), p. 321.

James Buchanan; or Arthur M. Schlesinger, Jr., may be characterized as being closely linked in historical thinking to the spirit of Seward's "irrepressible conflict" ideas as well as to the moral urgency of the abolitionist tradition.

Yet, having said all of this, would anyone wish to extend Mr. Pressly's conclusion about the relation between the increase of present disagreements among historians and the lengthening of time since the Civil War into a general behavioristic law concerning Civil War historians? Are we prepared to announce to the world that the possibility of attraction by agreement among Civil War historians varies inversely with the square of the distance in time since the Civil War?

We realize, therefore, that we have not gone very far in our understanding of problems of historical explanation if we refer, with a knowing wink, to all the evidence of a relationship between each historian's interpretation and the geographical, social, and other influences in his personal background. It is also true that historians, whatever their regional and social loyalties, are compelled by the growth of historical knowledge to identify and to characterize more fully the causal variables which they must take account of in their explanations of the causes of the American Civil War.

A demonstration of this truth can be found in our textbooks which offer a crude measure of what is taken seriously by present historians despite their differences of interpretation. Can any historian after Beard fail to reckon with the economic basis of sectional politics before 1860? Can any historian after Beard and Owsley fail to recognize that a clash between business and agriculture was more than a contention between two economic interest groups — that it also ex-

cited two sets of emotional attitudes and values? Can any historian after the writings of Ulrich B. Phillips fail to take account of deep-seated racial attitudes and the problem of race adjustments in the South? Can anyone, after reading W. J. Cash's *The Mind of the South,* or Charles S. Sydnor's *The Development of Southern Sectionalism* and Avery Craven's *The Growth of Southern Nationalism* fail to come to terms with the ideas and symbols of Southern self-consciousness? Can anyone read Roy Nichols' *The Disruption of American Democracy,* or the works of Craven and Randall without making some effort to explain the techniques and styles of political leadership and the disruption of major political parties in the 1850's? Can anyone who reads the voluminous historical writing of the twentieth century about the antislavery movement fail to reckon with its varied appeal to particular social groups and classes as well as with its moral impact and its fanatical zeal?

Such questions serve to remind us that there is widespread agreement among twentieth century historians as to what is relevant to a serious inquiry into the causes of the Civil War. By and large, the concerns taken seriously by the historians are a measure of the fruitful relationship which has developed between history and the social sciences since James Harvey Robinson and Charles A. Beard raised the banner of a "new history."

But we have not fully escaped from the jaws of the absurd trap which lies in the apparent propensity of disagreement among historians to grow greater the further the Civil War recedes into the past. Every practicing historian knows that the more the historian learns from the social sciences, the greater are the number of variables which he is forced to take into account. And if the historian is committed to making a causal explanation of so complex an event as the Civil War, how is he to "weigh" the many causal variables? Are all causal variables equal no matter how widespread or limited their incidence may be in the particular historical situation, or is there any valid way of determining "chief," "main," "primary," or "most important" causal factors? Any teacher of history will recognize the great and alarming mischief in this question.

Ernest Nagel, one of our leading logicians, assures us that the "weighting" of causal factors by historians cannot be dismissed as an essentially arbitrary and meaningless activity. He demonstrates that there is a verifiable sense which can be attached to the historians' habit of ascribing relative importance to the various determinants of human events. Logic and common sense both tell us that if we are trying to explain the necessary and sufficient conditions for an historical occurrence, we need to measure the frequency and the magnitude of such causal factors.[4]

We must realize, immediately, that what we are saying here may be comforting to the historian in one sense, but devilishly discomforting in another. It is very reassuring to have a competent logician tell us that when a historian is citing "main," "primary," or "chief" causal factors he is not making statements that have only a rhetorical purpose; rather, he is making an explanation sketch which points to measurements of empirical data that tell us something about the frequency of particular human

beliefs and actions in a given historical situation. Such statements have definite meaning which any other historian can analyze by testing for himself the relative frequency of the occurrences which are assumed to be determinants of the historical event being explained. Thus, for example, he may analyze the relative frequency of changes in industrial production in the North, the profits of slave production, the publicly expressed attitudes toward slavery and the expansion of slavery, and the social types of political leaders being elected to office in the period before the Civil War.

While it is comforting to discover that a competent historian does intend to convey a verifiable content when he makes his causal explanations, the basic trouble in the area of historical inquiry is that we do not have any explicitly formulated schema for weighing the evidence for any given historical hypothesis, nor have we learned to use any elaborate and precise statistical methods to measure the relative frequency of phenomena which are of special concern in our investigations of human affairs. Historians, therefore, are compelled to rely upon crude estimates and vague impressions in assigning weights to causal factors.

It has often been said that these defects in current historical research are not likely to be remedied because the probable cost in improvement in terms of labor and money would be staggering. To the historian of moderate means reflecting on this matter in his book-lined college study, this seems to be a conventional wisdom which should be cheerfully accepted by all concerned. But, we must remember that this is the day of the electronic computing machine and of the lavish research grant. These colossi of our modern intellectual world offer to historians tremendous possibilities of ac-

[4] Ernest Nagel, "Some Issues in the Logic of Historical Analysis," in Patrick Gardiner, ed., *Theories of History* (Glencoe, Illinois, 1959), pp. 373–385.

quiring the statistical material that they have had to do without, simply because no humanistic historian in his right mind was ever willing to deaden his poetic and speculative interests with the drudgery of comprehensive statistical research.

If the moment has arrived for historians to enrich the body of statistical material in their researches, the further investigation of the American Civil War deserves to be the first large effort of that kind. A comprehensive attack, with abundant tables and measurements, upon the causal variables in the explanation of the American Civil War would be a supreme test of the possibilities and the limits of measurement methods in historical explanation. Of course, the gains of such a project could be successfully realized only if it were accompanied with a published journal which would record every statistical measurement, no matter how small the sample, in the same way in which scientific papers are published.

To be sure, the mere thought of such an enormous structure of statistical data terrifies many historians. Some are fearful that historical writing will lose the literary value which it has held for so long in Western civilization and become smothered in statistical tables and statistical jargon. This is a needless imaginary horror, if we remember that some of our most successful literary historians have been able to use statistical measures without destroying the literary value of their histories. Henry Adams demonstrated this seventy years ago by the skillful way in which he used census data and other official statistics to write his classic chapters describing America in 1800.

The reflective historian, however, recognizes that the basic problem is not the threat of more precise measures to the literary value of history. The more serious question is whether the idea of causality can have any usefulness even with better statistical materials. Historians have long been aware of David Hume's critical analysis of causality made in his famous *Treatise of Human Nature* (1739–40), although very few historians were influenced by such radical skepticism concerning causal explanations in history until twentieth century developments in quantum physics and in the study of symbolic logic seemed to undermine all the older notions of cause and effect and to replace them with theories of probability and indeterminism. We realize that it is becoming fashionable to say, as does the English philosopher, Bertrand Russell, that "causality . . . is a relic of a bygone age, surviving like the monarchy, only because it is erroneously supposed to do no harm."[5]

This uncertainty about the usefulness of the idea of causation adds a deeper dimension to the crisis of historical thought about the causes of the American Civil War.[6] Indeed, some historians are ready to assert that we are tilting at windmills when we seek to explain the "causes" of the Civil War and that the time may have arrived to exclude the word "cause" from the vocabulary of historians even as physicists and philosophers are doing in their respective disciplines.

Most historians, however, would be reluctant to surrender without a fight a

[5] Bertrand Russell, "On the Notion of Cause with Some Applications to the Free Will Problem" in Herbert Feigl and May Broderick, *Readings in the Philosophy of Science* (New York, 1953), p. 387.

[6] For an explicit avowal of this uncertainty, see Thomas N. Bonner, "Civil War Historians and the Needless War Doctrine," *Journal of the History of Ideas* (1956), Vol. 17, p. 193.

most cherished word in their vocabulary. And they would have important
allies in such a fight because there are
reputable philosophers and physicists
who are not willing to abandon the principle of causality completely. Karl Popper, indeed, has proposed the following
methodological rule for all inquiry into
natural and social phenomena: "that we
are not to abandon the search for universal laws and for a coherent theoretical
system, nor ever give up our attempts
to explain causally any kind of event we
can describe."[7]

If we, as historians, continue our
search for causal explanations, can we
ever hope to reconcile the present confusion of voices in the interpretation of the
American Civil War? The answer of
course must be negative if the aim is to
attain some kind of universal agreement
which will have all of the certainty that
Newton's laws of motion were once assumed to have. No human inquiry which
operates on an empirical basis can attain
a position of real impregnability. Every
scientist knows that his favorite laws and
theories may be overturned by new investigations, and the scientist is supposed
to discipline himself to accept such possibilities cheerfully and generously.

But the acceptance of the inevitability
of controversy and change in the world
of knowledge does not require the historian to resign himself to a chaos of historical discourse which is completely
subjective and partisan. The historian
dealing with the causes of the Civil War
or with any other problem of historical

[7] Karl Popper, *The Logic of Scientific Discovery*
(London, 1959), p. 61.

explanation can live by the same rule as
the scientist to bring some order into his
world of explanation. When he deals
with a causal explanation of the Civil
War he should try to assess what tests,
what trials it has withstood. He should
try to assess how far it has been able to
prove its fitness to survive by standing
up to tests of the authenticity of evidence, the adequacy of statistical measurements, and the rigor of logical structure. With these tests, there is legitimate
reason to hope for the reduction of some
of the noise and tumult in the present
crisis of historical explanation of the
causes of the American Civil War by
exposing and controlling current confu-
sions in historical method.

Of course we can never hope to attain
even the same degree of universal ac-
ceptability which is so often the case for
laws of physics or chemistry, or even for
the laws and principles of economics.
The historian by the very nature of the
questions he asks must deal with more
variables than the physicist or the economist. Consequently, historical explanations will always tend to be tenuous and
speculative. But this only adds more
excitement to the enterprise of history.
Uncertain as that enterprise is, man has
an insatiable curiosity to know himself
and his society. This search for self-
knowledge in his history has made historical writing one of the oldest and most
enduring forms of literature in Western
civilization. This, too, is what makes the
history of the American Civil War worth-
while. In the history of this national
trauma we can discover ourselves in a
multitude of ways.

Suggestions for Additional Reading

An indispensable introduction to the many historical writings about the Civil War is Thomas J. Pressly's excellent book, *Americans Interpret Their Civil War* (Princeton, 1954). Also useful is Howard K. Beale's essay, "What Historians Have Said about the Causes of the Civil War" in *Theory and Practice in Historical Study: A Report of the Committee on Historiography* (Social Science Research Council, 1946), pp. 55–102.

The various works from which the selections in this volume have been taken deserve to be read in their entirety, and the necessary bibliographic information appears in the editor's notes preceding each selection. Anyone seriously interested in the background of the Civil War should read the five volumes of Allan Nevins' work with great care: *The Ordeal of the Union*, 2 vols. (New York, 1947); *The Emergence of Lincoln*, 2 vols. (New York, 1950); *The War for the Union*, Vol. I (New York, 1959). Also useful for background reading is James G. Randall's standard survey, *Civil War and Reconstruction* (Boston, 1953), especially the earlier chapters.

The importance of slavery in bringing on the conflict is emphasized in such classic works as James F. Rhodes, *History of the United States from the Compromise of 1850* (New York, 1900–1919), especially volumes 1–5; James Schouler, *History of the United States under the Constitution* (Washington, 1882–1894), especially volumes 4–6; and Hermann E. von Holst, *The Constitutional and Political History of the United States* (Chicago, 1877–1892, 8 vols.). The same emphasis is found in such shorter works as

Albert Bushnell Hart, *Slavery and Abolition* (New York, 1906); Theodore C. Smith, *Parties and Slavery* (New York, 1906); and Jesse Macy, *The Anti-Slavery Crusade* (New Haven, 1919). Recent works which shed more light on the anti-slavery movement are Gilbert Barnes, *The Anti-Slavery Impulse* (New York, 1933); Dwight Dumond, *Anti-Slavery Origins of the Civil War in the United States* (Ann Arbor, 1939), and Russel B. Nye, *Fettered Freedom: Civil Liberties and the Slavery Controversy* (East Lansing, Michigan, 1949).

The Southern constitutional position is best presented in Alexander H. Stephens' work already noted in this volume. A similar point of view is to be found in Jefferson Davis, *The Rise and Fall of the Confederate Government* (Richmond, 1881, 2 vols.). The "nationalist" attack on this states'-rights position can be found in John W. Burgess, *The Civil War and the Constitution* (New York, 1901, 2 vols.). The relative importance of the states'-rights issue is analyzed in Arthur M. Schlesinger, *New Viewpoints in American History* (New York, 1922), 220–243.

There are many excellent works on the growth of Southern self-consciousness which deserve to be read. A good starting point is Ulrich B. Phillips' classic essay on "The Central Theme of Southern History" in the *American Historical Review*, 34 (October, 1928), 30–43. This and other provocative essays make up a useful collection of Phillips' ideas in *The Course of the South to Secession* (New York, 1939), edited by E. M. Coulter. Other valuable works on Southern sectional consciousness are: Charles S. Sydnor, *The Development of Southern Sectionalism, 1819–1848* (Baton Rouge, 1949); Avery Craven, *Growth of Southern Nationalism, 1848–1861* (Baton Rouge, 1953); Jesse T. Carpenter, *The South as a Conscious Minority, 1789–1861* (New York, 1930). A good survey of the ante-bellum South is Clement Eaton's *History of the Old South* (New York, 1949).

The institution of Negro slavery in the South also deserves careful study. Ulrich B. Philips' earlier works are a useful starting point: *American Negro Slavery* (New York, 1933) and *Life and Labor in the Old South* (Boston, 1929). A more recent work, using modern sociological knowledge and expressing attitudes different from those of Phillips toward the Negro and the slaveowner, is Kenneth Stampp's *The Peculiar Institution* (New York, 1956). Even more daring in its methodology is Stanley M. Elkins, *Slavery: A Problem in American Institutional and Intellectual Life* (Chicago, 1959). On the profitableness of slavery, several provocative articles have appeared in recent years: Robert R. Russel, "The General Effects of Slavery upon Southern Economic Progress," *Journal of Southern History*, 4 (February, 1938), 35–54; Thomas P. Govan, "Was Plantation Slavery Profitable?", *Journal of Southern History*, 7 (November, 1942), 512–535; A. A. Conrad and J. K. Meyer, "The Economics of Slavery in the Ante-Bellum South," *Journal of Political Economy*, 46 (April, 1958), 95–130. An important work by a Negro scholar is John Hope Franklin's *From Slavery to Freedom* (New York, 1947).

Southern attitudes toward slavery may be discovered by a reading of William S. Jenkins' *Pro-Slavery Thought in the Old South* (Chapel Hill, 1935). George

Fitzhugh's effort to develop a sociology for the South in the 1850's may be sampled in the recently reissued *Cannibals All! or Slaves Without Masters* (Cambridge, 1960), edited by C. Vann Woodward. The first part of W. J. Cash, *The Mind of the South* (New York, 1941), also contains many suggestive ideas on this and other aspects of Southern attitudes.

An early economic interpretation of the causes of the American Civil War was developed by Algie Simons in his *Social Forces in American History* (New York, 1911), although Charles A. Beard is probably the best-known exponent of such an interpretation. In the same tradition is Louis M. Hacker, *The Triumph of American Capitalism* (New York, 1940), especially Part III. Philip S. Foner's *Business and Slavery* (Chapel Hill, 1941) offers important modifications for Beard's thesis. On the Southern side, the ablest effort to develop an economic interpretation is Robert R. Russel, *Economic Aspects of Southern Sectionalism, 1840–1861* (Urbana, Illinois, 1922).

The revisionist group of Civil War historians have contributed works worthy of our attention. The first volume of James G. Randall's *Lincoln the President* (New York, 1945) should be read for his final views about Lincoln and the coming of the war. Avery O. Craven's earlier works, *The Repressible Conflict* (Baton Rouge, 1939) and *The Coming of the Civil War* (New York, 1942) are also important in this connection.

A valuable study of the political breakdown in American democracy in the four years before the Civil War is Roy Nichols' *The Disruption of American Democracy*. Two indispensable books on the events of the secessionist crisis immediately preceding the outbreak of the war are David M. Potter, *Lincoln and His*

Party in the Secession Crisis (New Haven, 1942), and Kenneth Stampp, *And the War Came* (Baton Rouge, 1950).

Contemporary sources offer an invaluable aid to the critical testing of causal explanations. The opening sections of Henry Steele Commager's collection of documents entitled *The Blue and the Gray* (Indianapolis, 1950) gives us a sampling of views as the secessionist crisis moved toward war. Particularly useful are Dwight L. Dumond, ed., *Southern Editorials on Secession* (New York, 1931), and Howard Cecil Perkins, *Northern Editorials on Secession* (New York, 1942, 2 vols.). A marvelous collection of speeches, proclamations, songs, poetry, etc., before and during the Civil War is Frank Moore's work known as *Putnam's Record of the Rebellion* (New York, 1861–1869, 12 vols.).